THE COMPLETE GUIDE TO SPREAD TRADING

OTHER BOOKS IN THE MCGRAW-HILL TRADER'S EDGE SERIES

Pattern Recognition and Trading Decisions by Chris Satchwell

Mastering Futures Trading by Bo Yoder

One Shot, One Kill Trading by John Netto

Techniques of Tape Reading by Vadym Graifer and Chris Schumacher

Quantitative Trading Strategies by Lars Kestner

Understanding Hedged Scale Trading by Thomas McCafferty

Traders Systems That Work by Thomas Stridsman

Trading Systems and Money Management by Thomas Stridsman

The Encyclopedia of Trading Strategies by Jeffrey Owen Katz and Donna L. McCormick

Technical Analysis for the Trading Professional by Constance Brown

Agricultural Futures and Options by Richard Duncan

The Options Edge by William Gallacher

The Art of the Trade by R.E. McMaster

THE COMPLETE GUIDE TO SPREAD TRADING

KEITH SCHAP

McGraw-Hill

New York Chicago San Francisco Lisbon London Madrid
Mexico City Milan New Delhi San Juan Seoul
Singapore Sydney Toronto

The McGraw-Hill Companies

1 2 3 4 5 6 7 8 9 0 DOC/DOC 0 9 8 7 6 5

ISBN 0-07-144844-6

Library of Congress Cataloging-in-Publication Data

Schap, Keith.
The complete guide to spread trading / by Keith Schap.
p. cm.
Includes index.
ISBN 0-07-144844-6 (hardcover : alk. paper)
1. Futures. 2. Speculation. 3. Investment analysis. I. Title.
HG6024.A3S343 2005
332.64'52—dc22

2005004083

For Anthony John Schap,
Staff Sergeant, Indiana Army National Guard

CONTENTS

ABOUT THE AUTHOR

Keith Schap was a writer in the market and product development department of the Chicago Board of Trade. All of the articles and educational material on the CBOT's website on spreading were written by him. Previously, he was a senior editor with Futures magazine, where he developed market outlooks for numerous markets. He has contributed hundreds of articles to magazines and journals, including Treasury and Risk Management and Derivative Strategies.

CHAPTER 1

Introduction—A Motive for Trading Spreads

Spread trading dates back to the earliest days of the futures markets. The reason for the early adoption of this trading approach isn't hard to find. A 1989 *Futures* magazine article quotes a veteran trader on the subject: "The guy who spreads and makes a little every day is the one who walks away with the big money."

The key phrase in that remark is "makes a little every day." Seldom will a spread trader make the spectacular gains that speculators in outright futures or options can, occasionally, make. Seldom, too, will a spread trader make the spectacular losses that can befall a trader in outrights because a spread represents a compromise. Spread traders forgo the spectacular for the slow and steady. Spreads also create more ways to be right, and they capture real economic forces.

One of the most successful Treasury bond futures traders of the 1980s and early 1990s told an interviewer that while the object of trading is to make money, if the money is what a trader focuses on, the results are unlikely to be good. Rather, the trader must concentrate on the economic factors that are likely to move the market and on making disciplined and well-motivated trades.

Spreads help traders do that.

THE PLIGHT OF THE ACTIVE TRADER

An interesting development during the last several years has been the rise of stock market day traders or, as the futures market people say, active traders. Extremely low trading fees and more or less direct access to the markets through electronic trading have made it possible for people to trade more actively than they could only a few years ago.

For a time, the financial media delighted in stories about people from various walks of life who made stunning amounts of money in relatively short periods of time and in just a small number of smashingly successful trades. Some of these people became so enamored of their trading successes that they actually gave up their day jobs to devote more time to trading.

The follow-up stories have been less in evidence. The interesting question is whether these people continued to make successful trades or whether they ultimately gave the big gains back to the market. You may remember a story that appeared in one of the business papers several years ago about a trader who quit her job to trade full time and in 10 or 11 months managed to work a fortune of between $2 million and $3 million, all made in trading, down to a less than $200,000 shoestring.

Sadly, futures market lore abounds with stories about traders who make large fortunes in one or two trades, only to give most or all of the gains back to the market in just as short a time. This happens because outright futures or stock traders face a number of challenges. By "outright" it is meant that these traders trade only S&P (Standard & Poors) 500 stock index futures, 10-year Treasury note futures, or XYZ Corp. stock. They may trade 500 contracts or 500 shares of whichever it is, but they trade only the one thing.

If these traders buy in expectation of a rallying market and the market makes a large downward move, these traders can suffer big losses before they can move to rescue their positions. Outright traders can also experience dead markets. At certain times, the economic news is such that it motivates no directional move. The market will bob around in a range so narrow that successful trading becomes difficult. Any gains will be small and will be gobbled up in transaction costs.

Imagine a trader who sells 10-year Treasury note futures at a price of 109-22 in anticipation of a large yield increase. The dollar equivalent value of one contract is $109,687.50. This trader is so convinced that this yield spike will happen that this trade is made in size—say, 1,000 contracts.

Suppose that a day or two after this trade is put on, market disappointment with a fed move causes the 10-year Treasury note yield to shoot up 40 basis points and that this drives the dollar equivalent value of one futures contract from $109,687.50 to $106,827. This is a $2,860.50 difference, which constitutes a gain for a futures seller. Indeed, for a seller of 1,000 contracts, this is a $2.86 million gain if the trader unwinds at

106-26+ (which is the conventional price notation that translates into $106,827).

Next, suppose this trader decides this 40 basis point (bp) yield move marks the limit and believes yields have to drop. Falling yields mean a rallying futures market. So convincing is the argument for falling yields that this trader buys 1,000 contracts at this 106-26+ price.

The next morning, an economic report suggests that higher inflation is on the way. In response to this report, the 10-year yield shoots up another 35 bps, and this move drops the dollar equivalent value of one contract another $2,528.75 to $104,298.25 (104-09+). The trouble is that this trader is on the wrong side of this move. The 1,000 contract trade size will multiply this into a $2,528,750 loss. This takes away all but $331,250 of the original gain. At this point, if this trader were to get on the wrong side of a yield move as small as 5 bps at this 1,000 contract size, the three-trade net would slip into negative territory. This trader would have made a bundle and then managed to give it all back and then some.

This is a hypothetical story, but actual stories like this are all too common in the stock and futures markets. Clearly, this is no way to get ahead. That $2.86 million gain on one trade will cause big talk around the markets, but this trader will be no wealthier for the celebrity this one blockbuster trade brings if the next trades give it all back.

GIVE UP A LITTLE, GET A LOT MORE

Contrast this hypothetical outright trader with a hypothetical spread trader. Suppose this spread trader had decided that the same fed action that would probably cause the 10-year Treasury note yield to rise would also cause the 5-year Treasury note yield to fall slightly. Because of this belief about the market reaction, this spread trader might have bought 5-year Treasury note futures and sold 10-year Treasury note futures in an appropriately structured yield curve spread trade.

Given the 40 bp increase in the 10-year yield and a 5 bp drop in the 5-year yield, suppose this trade netted a $1.9 million gain in round terms. This is almost a million less than the outright 10-year Treasury note futures trade gained. This is not a bad result, but this is not a trade that will cause much talk—certainly not as much as the outright trade.

Next, suppose this spread trader had reversed course, selling fives and buying tens, again in the appropriate spread structure. Now suppose the 10-year yield shot up another 35 bps, as before, and the 5-year yield rose 10 bps. This would cause the 5-year leg of the spread to earn a little over $400,000, but the 10-year leg would lose well over a million. The net loss might be in the neighborhood of $1.065 million.

The net of the two spread trades might be in the neighborhood of $830,000 where the net of the two outright trades was half a million dollars less. Who's better off?

To repeat, stories of the same general character abound in all the futures markets.

A baseball analogy may help. The biggest buzz around the major league ballparks results from the towering home runs a few of the sluggers can hit from time to time. Even after the home team loses, the fans will walk out of the park talking about the three home runs the local hero blasted. Singles hitters seldom make the headlines until the end of the year when it's time to notice who the batting champion is. A few singles hitters tend to be in the running. Fans love these majestic home run shots and so do a lot of managers and general managers.

Yet it isn't obvious that the legendary slugger is as valuable to his team as a good singles hitter. Years ago, there was a player whose home runs were such that he's still spoken of in fond terms in the various cities where he played. Playing at the same time was a player who averaged five home runs a year but who might have helped his team more. Consider the numbers for each from one season. This isn't about personalities but rather about approaches to a game or trading that can have long-term beneficial effects, so call one player the slugger and the other the singles hitter. Incidentally, these are actual numbers from the same season.

EXHIBIT 1.1

Which Is the Better Way?

	Slugger	Singles Hitter
At bats	474	605
Hits	113	200
Home runs	37	9
Runs	70	97
Runs batted in	86	90
Walks	28	67
Strikeouts	135	52
Batting average	.238	.331

The question that matters concerns which player helped his team more that year. Sure, the home runs were awesome, but these statistics should speak for themselves. The singles hitter got on base, by hit or by walk, almost twice as many times as the slugger. Further, the singles hitter put the ball in play all but 52 of 605 times. When the ball is in play, good things can happen. When the batter strikes out, they cannot.

In the world of trading, spread traders are analogous to singles hitters. Their trades are unlikely to be the stuff of legend, but at the end of the year, the spread traders are likely to have the higher batting averages in terms of percentage of trades that made solid gains. They will have scored more runs in terms of numbers of trades showing positive results. This is why so many professionals trade spreads. Spreads, long term and in the aggregate, produce better results than outright trades in futures or stocks.

WHO THIS BOOK CAN HELP

So the first group for whom this book has been written is the active traders in stocks or futures, who are tired of the alternation of spectacular gains and spectacular losses. For any of these people who are serious about making successful trades over the long haul and who are looking for ideas about how to do that, this book can help. These people, and any others who are new to spread trading, will find the basic nuts and bolts of spread trading that they need to get started. They will also find, in the examples used to illustrate the various trades, ideas about what kinds of markets offer opportunities and when in the trading year these opportunities are most likely to be available

Traders familiar with one market sector who want to diversify—say, from grains to interest rates—will find discussions that will help them locate these new opportunities. Perhaps some of the examples will even suggest kinds of trading opportunities that these people have overlooked.

More advanced traders will find this a handy reference guide when they need a refresher on a kind of trade they haven't used recently.

Further, brokerage and money management firms (including hedge funds) can use this book for training new employees in the kinds of relative value trades that are the financial lifeblood of proprietary trading desks and many hedge fund operations.

THE STRUCTURE OF THE BOOK

This book has two basic parts—one presenting a variety of futures spreads, the other a variety of option spreads. However, Chapter 2 discusses the general idea of spread trading and some general principles that should inform all spread trades. Similarly, Chapter 18 presents background for option spread trading—basically, a review of some of the fundamental factors that shape option trades.

The futures section then presents a representative sample of futures spreads in a series of 15 short chapters. The first several of these chapters focus on such physical commodities markets as corn, wheat, cotton, heating oil, unleaded gasoline, and crude oil and cover old crop–new crop spreads, seasonal spreads, and calendar spreads. However, some of these ideas apply to the financial markets, as a chapter on the 10-year Treasury note futures calendar spread illustrates.

Some of the most interesting spreads involve contracts traded on different exchanges. One such intermarket spread is the Kansas City wheat–Chicago corn spread, which turns on the economics of supplying protein to livestock. Another that seems especially interesting is the gold-platinum spread, which seems to react mainly to whether the market is optimistic about prospects for economic growth or concerned about the status of the U.S. dollar and the growth of inflation.

Another slightly more complex kind of intermarket trade involves a value-added process. The soybean crush spread and the petroleum crack spread model these value-added processes and isolate the gross profit margin of these businesses.

For some reason, stock index futures traders seem to have done less with spreads than have specialists in other markets. This is too bad because interesting spread opportunities are available in these markets. One that is fairly actively traded is a spread between a large cap index (such as the S&P 500) and a small cap index (such as the NASDAQ 100). These indexes tend to react differently to economic news and to various stages of the market cycle. Another way to capture similar divergences is to structure spread trades between indexes and small groups of single stock futures. The possibilities are endless and endlessly intriguing—to spread traders.

Finally, the futures section includes a series of chapters that deal with yield curve spreads. The first of these chapters covers yield curve spread background, especially what changes in these spreads can tell you about the economy. The next three chapters discuss specific yield curve spreads that provide overlapping but slightly different kinds of trading opportunities.

OVERLOOKED OPTIONS

For some reason, large numbers of traders seem to have overlooked the option markets. Traders who are serious about generating a steady stream of positive results can find in options a rich source of spread trading opportunity. Better yet, option spreads make it possible to benefit from markets that simply will not do much for futures traders.

Perhaps much of the reluctance to take advantage of these trading tools results from unfamiliarity and from what seems at first glance a daunting body of technical jargon and knowledge. To help you overcome that, Chapter 18 reviews options basics. It doesn't contain all there is to know about options, but it should be enough to help you get started on solid footing.

Option spreads allow you to trade on the basis of a variety of factors. You can trade bullish or bearish opinions, as with futures, but option spreads make it possible for you to express degrees of confidence in your opinions. The chapters on bull call, bear put, and butterfly spreads suggest useful ways to do this. The returns on these spreads are modest, but they can greatly reduce the downside risk of being in whatever market you choose to trade.

Also, using option spreads, you can isolate certain other market phenomena such as implied volatility shifts. The straddle and strangle chapter discusses the basic spreads that can help you do this and provides a basis for thinking about which kind of spread to use. Further, you can use option spreads to focus on relative differences between the way the volatility in two markets will react to harvest news (in the case of corn and soybeans), or to a fed move (in the case of the Treasury note markets).

Finally, option spreads exist that can generate at least modest gains in seemingly dead markets. The chapters that deal with selling straddles and strangles and with trading call calendar and diagonal spreads illustrate trading approaches that can gain in relatively static markets.

Every spread strategy chapter follows a basic pattern. Each one presents an informal discussion of the market background that makes the trade being discussed seem appropriate and of the economic factors that drive it. It moves on to show how market data can be expected to respond to these economic factors. It defines the spread and the logic of this spread in the cases where there is no established usage and shows how to structure the spread trade. Finally, it reviews how such trades can be expected to perform under a given set of assumptions about the current market situation and your forecast of what will happen during the term of the trade.

A SUGGESTION ABOUT HOW TO USE THIS BOOK

This is not a book that must be read through from cover to cover. It can be read that way, but it need not be. You should feel free to go directly to the kind of spread that interests you.

If you are new to this kind of trading, you will find the introductory material of Chapter 2 helpful. Having considered that, you should feel free to sample whatever ideas intrigue you. As you gain confidence with one or two kinds of spread trades, you can go on to build a spread trading repertoire by studying other kinds of spreads or by applying what you know to additional markets. After all, once you understand the basic ideas and structures and potential danger points, these principles can apply to trading in any market that interests you.

If you are a veteran spread trader, the introductory material may have less interest for you. Feel free to skip anything that goes over old ground. This book can still serve you in that it may provide a helpful review of a kind of spread you haven't used for a while or of a spread that lies outside your experience so far.

Whatever your level of trading experience, you will find a certain amount of repetition from chapter to chapter. This results from the attempt to make each chapter more or less self-contained. Again, feel free to skip to the parts of each discussion that add value for you.

In a few cases, a chapter section, or even a whole chapter, is called an advanced idea. The sections that are flagged in this way can help you achieve a deeper understanding of the market forces that drive these spreads, of why these spreads work the way that they do. However, you can probably trade the spread very well without studying this section of the chapter. Suit yourself. If this information intrigues you, dig in. If it doesn't, don't. You can always come back to these topics if you change your mind.

As you become more familiar with spread trading, you will realize more and more that this book gives you a good start. Once you master the spread logic of the various markets and the structuring of the various kinds of trades, you can apply this knowledge to any other futures market or any other option market.

Also, as you become more familiar with spread trading, you may want to delve more deeply into the mechanics and economics of a particular market. A sample of helpful resources is listed in the appendix, but don't overlook how helpful the Internet can be and, especially, how helpful your broker can be. Many brokerage firms produce resources that will help. Your broker can help you find them.

CHAPTER 2

Spread Trading Background

A spread trade involves buying one futures contract and selling another. You might buy July soybeans and sell November soybeans. You might sell 2-year Treasury note futures and buy 10-year Treasury note futures. In either case, you do so because you think one contract will gain or lose relative to the other. That is, all soybean prices may seem likely to rise, but your market analysis suggests that July soybeans will gain more than November soybeans. If the market does what you expect, the July soybean futures position will gain more than the November soybean futures position will lose. The net result will be a gain. Similarly, you may believe that all Treasury yields will rise and push Treasury futures prices lower, but the 2-year yield will rise more than the 10-year yield will rise. In this case, the expectation is that the 2-year position will gain more than the 10-year position will lose.

People who adopt this style of trading are often called *relative value traders*. They make these trades because they have an idea about how one market will perform relative to another.

A WORD WITH MULTIPLE USES

The word *spread* has a variety of uses. The bid-ask spread is the largest transaction cost for any trade. Futures price displays are called *spreads*. And the word refers to an extended family of trades. What all these uses of the word have in common is that they refer to a difference between two prices, or among sets of prices.

EXHIBIT 2.1

Kansas City Wheat Price Spreads

Contract Month	Open	High	Low	Settlement
Jul 04	376.50	377.50	374.25	375.50
Sep	383.00	384.00	381.00	382.25
Dec	393.00	394.00	390.50	391.50
Mar 05	398.00	398.00	396.75	398.00
May	395.00	395.00	395.00	395.00

Take the bid-ask spread. When you see, for example, CBOT (Chicago Board of Trade) Treasury note futures quoted at 109-29 bid and 109-30 asked (or 29 at 30, as the traders say, assuming that you know that the market is at the 109 "handle"), you know that, if you are selling, you will receive 109-29. If you are buying, you will pay 109-30. This 1/32 difference is the cost of doing business in this market—along with brokerage and exchange fees.

When you pull up a quote page or look at the futures quotes in a newspaper, you will see a display more or less like the one in Exhibit 2.1.

Focus on the settlement column and notice this sequence of prices: the September price is 6.75 cents per bushel higher than the July price; the December price is 9.25 cents higher than the September price; the March 2005 price is 6.50 cents higher than the December 2004 price; and it's a fair guess that the May contract didn't trade on the day these spreads were reported. The point is that these price differences are spreads, and they can tell an interesting story, as you shall see shortly.

Finally, you can trade spreads. A simple spread trade might involve buying or selling July wheat at the settlement price shown in Exhibit 2.1 and selling or buying September wheat at the settlement price. To illustrate, suppose you believe that the September–July spread will widen from the current 6.75 cents per bushel to 10 cents per bushel. Exhibit 2.2 shows one of the many ways that could happen and also shows that such a spread trade could earn 3.25 cents per bushel.

Go back to the description of a spread trader's expectations going into a trade. You expect that if both prices rise, the price of the September contract will rise more and that the September contract that you bought will gain more than the July contract that you sold will lose. The net will be a gain, as the exhibit shows.

EXHIBIT 2.2

Trading a Widening Spread

Initial Position	Ending Position	Result
Sell Jul @ 375.50	Buy Jul @ 378.25	–2.75
Buy Sep @ 382.25	Sell Sep @ 388.25	+6.00
Spread result		+3.25

EXHIBIT 2.3

Trading an Inverting Spread

Initial Position	Ending Position	Result
Buy Jul @ 375.50	Sell Jul @ 379.00	+3.50
Sell Sep @ 382.25	Buy Sep @ 374.00	+8.25
Spread result		+11.75

Conversely, suppose you believe that the September–July spread will invert—that is, it will go from a positive 6.75 cents to a negative 5 cents per bushel. Exhibit 2.3 shows one way that could happen and also shows the spread to have earned 11.75 cents on this set of assumptions.

A more complex spread trade might involve buying or selling crude oil futures for one month while simultaneously selling or buying unleaded gasoline and heating oil futures for the next month out. Yet another kind of spread trade might balance a 5-year Treasury note futures position against a 10-year Treasury note futures position or an e-mini S&P position against an e-mini NASDAQ position. The result in every case is the relative difference between the price changes of two contracts.

Of course, it isn't quite this simple.

These other uses of the term spread matter, but the focus of this book is on a series of these relative value trades. In fact, every futures trade discussed in this book is a relative value trade of some kind regardless of whatever colorful name it goes by in the marketplace.

WHY THE PROFESSIONALS TRADE SPREADS

Spread trading is the bread-and-butter business of most professionals. The attractions of this trading style include the facts that it is easier to predict spreads than outright prices, spreads give traders more ways to be right, and exchanges typically give margin breaks on spread trades.

Spreads Are More Predictable

Grain traders often say that price has no history. Only spreads have history. Technical analysts will beg to differ.

What is assuredly true is that prices can be rallying or falling. Prices can be higher than average or lower than average. Whatever the case with futures prices, certain spreads behave in predictable ways.

Take heating oil futures as one example. Prices can be quite high or very low. In either case, the month-to-month spreads exhibit seasonal patterns that are remarkably regular. In early summer, these spreads most often show higher prices the farther out you look. The August price will be higher than the July. The September price will be higher than the August, and so on out to about the January price. In short, the heating oil price spreads at this time of year will be analogous to the wheat spreads in Exhibit 2.1. Furthermore, during the summer and much of the fall, these differences are likely to become somewhat greater. Then in December or January this pattern will reverse. Each subsequent price will be lower. Again, the differences can start small and expand as winter goes on.

This spread configuration is more predictable, year in, year out, than the actual price level.

Similarly, if the Fed is raising its fed funds target rate, you can almost always count on seeing the 2-year Treasury note yield rise more than the 10-year Treasury note yield. Never mind where prices are before the Fed moves. This will be the normal reaction of these yields, and the price changes will follow.

All the agricultural futures contracts exhibit remarkably regular seasonal patterns. That is, the spreads tend to follow these patterns even when the outright prices seem not to be doing what you might normally expect at a particular time of year. Indeed, when a spread does not do what the market expects, this is the big news, not whatever the nearby price is doing. Yet this can happen, and the signals are often in the market well in advance—for those who pay attention to the spreads.

From this, it should be clear that one reason so many market professionals trade spreads is that they are more predictable than any futures price in isolation.

More Ways to Be Right

Another key fact about spreads is that they give you more ways to be right. Because a spread trade, by any name and in any market, is a relative value trade, a spread trader is expressing a market opinion not that the price will rise or fall but that the spread will widen or narrow. Never mind the price, the shape of the spread is the focus of a spread trader.

Suppose that July soybeans are trading at $8.40 per bushel in early April and November soybeans are trading at $6.95 per bushel. To define the relevant spread, subtract the July price from the November price. The spread in this case is –$1.45 per bushel ($6.95 – $8.40). As the end of the current crop year approaches, the market will express a willingness to pay a premium for July delivery of current stocks as opposed to November delivery of them.

An outright futures trader might take this to mean that the July price will rally and so buy July futures. If the July contract rallies from $8.40 up to $8.50 or even $8.85, this trader will make money. But if it trades to $8.25, this trader will make a loss. When you trade an outright futures position, or stock position, you have one chance to be right. For a buyer, the market must rally for the trade to earn a positive result.

A spread trader might prefer to trade the July–November spread in the expectation that the spread will become even more negative. Among the possible outcomes, Exhibit 2.4 identifies three.

Ending I shows a situation in which both prices rose, but the July price rose more. The ending spread in this case is –$1.75 per bushel, so the spread earns $0.30 per bushel. Ending II shows a situation in which both prices fell, but the November price fell more. Again, the ending spread is –$1.75 and the net gain is $0.30 per bushel. Ending III shows a case in which the July price rose, the November price fell, and, by the magic of hypothetical example construction, the net result is the same as in the first two cases. You can find actual examples of all three kinds of outcome in every market—grains, energy, fixed income, stock indexes, or the softs.

The plain fact is that a spread trade gives you more ways to be right. This is a strong motivation for the professional traders to trade spreads. Any trading style can lead to losses, but a spread trade gives you more chances to have something good happen.

EXHIBIT 2.4

Three Ways an Inversion Can Deepen

Futures Contract	Initial Futures Price	Ending Futures Price I	Ending Futures Price II	Ending Futures Price III
July	8.40	8.85	8.25	8.50
November	6.95	7.10	6.50	6.75
Spread	–1.45	–1.75	–1.75	–1.75

Margin Breaks

Obviously, the lower your transaction costs, the more of the gains you keep. The futures exchanges recognize that spreads are typically lower-risk trades than outright futures trades. For example, if you trade two CBOT corn contracts, as of the fall of 2004, the initial margin was $338 per contract or $676 for two. However, the initial margin for a new crop–old crop spread was $135. Similarly, any of the CBOT Treasury note contracts had $1215 per contract initial margins. Trade five contracts outright, and the total initial margin would have been $6075. However, trade a yield curve spread with, say, a three-to-two ratio, and the exchange will grant an 85 percent spread credit. That is, the initial margin will be $911.25 (15 percent of $6075). The most extreme spread margin break is the one for Treasury note calendar spreads. Currently, these require no margin. The margin for the position you buy nets to zero against the margin for the position you sell.

All the futures exchanges offer similar spread margin discounts. And each exchange Web site shows a list of these. However, not all exchanges express things the same way. Also, a few well-known, and fairly often traded, spreads seem not to be listed.

Where the Chicago exchanges list margin credits, the New York Mercantile Exchange lists the percent of initial margin you must pay. For example, you can put on a 3-2-1 crack spread for 75 percent of the sum of the six initial margins. If these six margins sum to $28,350 (as they did in the fall of 2004), the spread margin would be $21,262.50 for a nonmember customer.

The New York Board of Trade seems not to list spread credits. And, although you can easily find the spread credit for a Kansas City–Chicago wheat spread, the Kansas City wheat–Chicago corn spread seems not to be listed.

Remember, too, that margins change as market conditions change. Every clearinghouse and exchange has periodic meetings to assess the risk inherent in each of its markets. At these meetings, the clearinghouse and exchange officials adjust margins up or down as conditions mandate. Because this is true, because not all spreads seem to be listed, and because the listings can seem confusing, you should check margin rates with your broker early in your spread planning process.

What this summary of the margin situation should make clear is that margin breaks are a significant motive for trading spreads.

FACT AND FICTION ABOUT SPREAD TRADES

Probably no one should be surprised that some potentially dangerous misconceptions have grown up around spread trading. Usually, all it takes for such ideas to take root is an activity that has gone on for a long time.

For example, you may hear people say that successful spread trading depends on locating two contracts, one of which is undervalued or overvalued relative to the other. This defines an arbitrage opportunity, not a spread. When one futures contract is rich or cheap compared to another, arbitragers step in and trade away the mismatch—usually in a very short time. These arbitrage opportunities are fleeting at best and should be left to the specialists who have the advantages of superior capitalization and superior market information and analysis.

Real spreads derive from well-established market economics and are relatively stable. To cite only one, the new crop–old crop spreads in any of the agricultural markets are highly likely to follow predictable patterns year after year no matter what the outright prices are doing.

Another wrong idea that you may hear is that spreads are safe.

Spreads are speculative trades. A spread trader focuses on some kind of price relationship rather than on simple price direction. Nevertheless, spreads are view-driven trades. They are not hedges. And any forecast can be proven wrong. When spread traders make wrong market calls, their trades suffer losses.

What is true of spreads is that they are safer than outright trades, and they give you more ways to be right. Still, *safer* is not the same as *safe*.

Finally, on the subject of mistaken ideas about spreads, probably every broker in the history of futures markets has had customers ask to spread out of losing trades. The broker will have called to request that the customer either cash out or meet a margin call. Yet the customer wants to trade another contract.

The idea that you can make a bad trade good by adding another trade to it has no logical support. If the July–December cotton spread is a good trade, its value derives from the fact that the market wants cotton put into storage or drawn out of storage. This trade has a solid basis in the current supply-demand situation of the cotton market. Because of that, the trader should have put on the spread from the start.

Selling December futures against an already failing July position will not rescue the situation. The only correct action, facing a bad trade, is to get out of it. Take the loss and be done.

ACCENTUATE THE POSITIVE

If the confusion with arbitrage and the mistaken notions that spreads are safe and that traders can spread out of losing trades are well known but mistaken ideas, there are other ideas about spreads that are less well known, or at least not commonly discussed. This is unfortunate because these ideas are key to solid thinking about spreads in any market.

Spreads Carry Economic Information

At its most basic, a spread trade consists of two futures or options positions—referred to as *legs*. In a two-legged spread—for example, a July–December corn spread—traders buy one leg and sell the other. They will simultaneously buy July corn and sell December corn futures perhaps. However, that doesn't make any pair of long and short positions a spread.

Imagine a trader who goes long coffee futures and short copper futures. These markets have no relationship to each other. No one can learn anything about the economy, or any segment of it, from watching the price movement of copper relative to that of coffee. This is two outright futures positions and no spread worthy of the name.

Any legitimate spread carries information that has economic significance. The simplest spreads are implicit in the month-to-month price arrays that appear on quote screens or on the commodities pages of newspapers. Chicago Board of Trade (CBOT) corn trades a December, March, May, July, September cycle. New York Mercantile Exchange (NYMEX) unleaded gasoline offers monthly contracts—January, February, March, and so on through the year. Most of the financial futures trade on a quarterly cycle—March, June, September, December.

In early May 2004, soybean and unleaded gasoline futures settled at the prices shown in Exhibit 2.5. Both contracts quote in cents, so the May soybean price is 1018½ cents per bushel, or $10.18½ per bushel. The unleaded price is 131²⁰⁄₁₀₀ cents per gallon, or $1.312 per gallon. The

EXHIBIT 2.5

Soybean and Unleaded Gasoline Prices and Spreads

	Soybean Futures Price	Spread		Unleaded Gasoline Futures Price	Spread
May	1,018½		Jun	131.20	
Jul	1,000½	–18	Jul	126.67	–4.53
Aug	941	–59½	Aug	121.87	–4.80
Sep	825	–116	Sep	116.22	–5.65
Nov	767½	–57½	Oct	109.39	–6.83

soybean contract calls for delivery of 5000 bushels. The unleaded contract calls for delivery of 42,000 gallons. Notice that in both markets the nearby price (May for soybeans and June for unleaded) is the highest and that successive prices are lower, in some instances a lot lower.

These spreads deliver similar messages. The grain trade calls a market where the spreads go lower and lower in this fashion an *inverted market.* The New York and London markets tend to prefer the term *backwardation.* This unleaded market is a market in backwardation. An inverted or backwardated market indicates a supply shortage, an anticipated supply shortage, or the fear of one. These spreads indicate that the market wants the commodity delivered now, not stored for future delivery.

This makes sense given the situation in the two markets. The 2003 soybean crop was a poor one. Yields fell well short of predictions. As a result, the market was paying a hefty premium for present rather than future delivery.

The message of the unleaded gasoline spreads is the same. In early May, the market was anticipating the summer driving season. What with the unsettled situation in the Middle East and constraints on refining capacity, the fear was that summer demand could well outstrip supplies. These spreads indicate that the market wants gasoline now, not later. To emphasize, the message of both the soybean and unleaded gasoline spreads on this day was, "Don't store these commodities. Deliver now."

At other times, the spreads tell the markets that commodities should go into storage. Consider the corn, cocoa, and cotton markets just after the middle of October 2004. Exhibit 2.6 displays the price arrays you would have seen on a quote screen or on a newspaper commodities page on October 21, 2004. It also shows the spreads for each market, which the quote sources typically do not display.

EXHIBIT 2.6

Spreads That Signal a Need for Storage*

10/21/04	Corn Price	Spread	Cocoa Price	Spread	Cotton Price	Spread
Dec	2.0425		1,434		45.81	
Mar	2.1500	0.1075	1,451	17	45.59	–0.22
May	2.2200	0.0700	1,463	12	46.71	1.12
Jul	2.2850	0.0650	1,475	12	47.93	1.22
					50.65	2.72

*Corn prices = dollars per bushel,; cocoa prices = dollars per ton; cotton prices = cents per pound.

Notice that in the corn and cocoa cases, the nearby December price is the lowest one and subsequent prices are successively higher. This makes for positive spreads, in contrast to the negative spreads of Exhibit 2.5. The December–March cotton spread is an exception, but from March forward, those spreads are also positive. The grain trade calls this price configuration a *carry market.* In the New York and London markets, this configuration is called a *contango,* or a market *in contango.* Call it what you will, the message is the same. The market wants these crops to go into storage. Present supplies are sufficient to meet current demand, these spreads say, and the new crop should go into storage.

Small wonder, especially in the case of corn and cotton. U.S. producers of these crops had ideal weather for planting, for each phase of crop development, and for harvest. Granted, the early fall hurricanes damaged southeastern cotton, but Mississippi delta and Texas cotton crops more than made up for the loss. As this story developed, the spreads would have told you what was going on daily. Often, the spreads are a slightly leading indicator, in fact.

Exhibit 2.7 displays the cotton prices and spreads at roughly one-week intervals from the end of September 2004 until slightly after the middle of October 2004.

These are all carry spreads, with the one October 21 exception, and two aspects of this display seem important to notice. First, the prices trended steadily lower. Even the October 21 nearby price is 2.20 cents per pound lower than the September 28 price for that contract. The October 21 March price is 4.09 cents per pound lower than the September 28 price for that contract. Second, despite these lower prices, the spreads widened, with the one exception. Lower prices are only to be expected after big harvests, but these widening spreads suggest that the economic message system oper-

EXHIBIT 2.7

The Market Revises the Signal

	9/28/04		10/5/04		10/12/04		10/21/04	
	Price	Spread	Price	Spread	Price	Spread	Price	Spread
Dec	48.01		47.23		44.79		45.81	
Mar	49.68	1.67	49.15	1.92	46.70	1.91	45.59	−0.22
May	50.65	0.97	50.35	1.20	47.90	1.20	46.71	1.12
Jul	51.60	0.96	51.40	1.05	48.90	1.00	47.93	1.22
Dec	53.77	2.17	53.40	2.00	51.10	2.20	50.65	2.72

ates independently of price trends—at least for the most part. It is possible to find instances of narrowing spreads during periods of falling prices and of widening spreads during periods of rising prices. The point is that the spread and not the prices should be the focus for spread traders and also for anyone who wants a reading on the economic situation of this market.

Interest Rates—Different Markets, Similar Messages

While it hardly seems germane to speak in terms of storage signals when speaking of the interest rate markets, it is germane in a way. Yield curve spreads tell a rich story about the economy in general and credit supply and demand in particular. Further, yield spreads provide this information in advance. Because of this, yield spreads are an official leading indicator—one of the indexes of leading indicators considered by the Conference Board, the Fed, and anyone else trying to predict U.S. economic growth.

Conventional wisdom holds that a normal yield curve, one in which each longer-dated yield is higher than the last, signals a growing, healthy economy. The flip side of this picture is that an inverted yield curve, one where the shortest maturity yield is the highest and each successive yield is lower, signals an approaching recession—or at least slower economic growth. Not only is this conventional view an oversimplification, but it misses an important part of the story. What really matters is not this or that yield curve state—whether it is normal or inverted—but how the yield curve spread is changing—whether it is widening or narrowing.

The message of a yield curve spread derives from an interesting interplay among economic forces. The shifting relationships between the demand for credit and the creation of credit that a yield curve spread depicts may provide a useful gauge of the potential for economic growth.

The long end of the curve, anchored by the benchmark 10-year Treasury note, responds to the demand for credit in the economy. When the demand for credit rises, yields on longer-maturity securities should also rise. When more people want something, the cost tends to rise. Conversely, a diminished demand for credit should lower yields. After all, when fewer people want something, sellers cannot exact a premium for it. An increasing demand for credit typically goes hand in hand with rising gross domestic product (GDP) growth. People and businesses borrow, in the ordinary case, to buy more goods and services.

At the short end of the yield curve, the Fed targets the fed funds rate as a means of regulating the flow of credit into the economy. Within the context of the U.S. economy, the Fed uniquely has the power to create credit.

It follows that, when the longer maturity leg of a yield curve spread is rising relative to the fed funds rate—that is, when the yield curve spread is widening—this suggests that an increasing demand for credit is being accommodated by the supply of credit created by the Fed. Conversely, when the longer maturity leg of a yield curve spread is falling relative to the fed funds rate—that is, when the yield curve spread is narrowing—this suggests that the Fed is cutting back on the amount of credit it is creating relative to the demand for credit. Thus a widening yield curve spread typically signals that faster real economic growth will occur about two quarters forward. A narrowing yield curve spread signals slower real economic growth about two quarters forward.

The stock index markets convey similar information. When you see shifts in the relationship between indexes that represent small cap stocks and those that represent large cap stocks, this gives you means to define where the economy is in a recovery, how mature the current bull market is, and so on.

Similarly, when certain stock market sectors seem poised to outperform the market in general, these developments convey information about the state of the economy. One concern during the most recent recovery, if recovery it is, is that companies have not been making many investments in new technology. It follows that if the technology sector seems to be outperforming the general market, you would think you could expect to see an upturn in economic growth in the near future. When corporations are cutting back on these purchases and the technology stocks are underperforming, this is a sign that the economy could be faltering.

The Process Spreads

The soybean crush spread and the petroleum crack spread configure multiple futures contracts to capture the economics of crushing soybeans or refining crude oil. During much of 2004, the price of crude oil was been big news. Because of the threat of supply interruptions caused by war, political unrest, and weather catastrophes, the price of crude oil soared.

What really matters, it seems, is whether the activity of refining is profitable or not. If it is, refiners will do more of it. If it is profitable enough, oil companies will find motivation to look for new sources of supply. Plug enough profit into the equation, and the oil companies may even decide it is worthwhile to build new refining facilities or expand existing ones.

Along with a clear message about the profitability of refining, the crack spread carries a complex message about the supply-demand balance.

The soybean crush spread offers a parallel case. If crushing soybeans is profitable enough, this can set off a long chain reaction. When there is heavy demand for soybean meal and soybean oil, prices of those commodities will rise. When crushing is profitable, crushers will want to do more of it, and they will be willing to pay more for soybeans. When the price of soybeans gets high enough, farmers will want to grow more. When the crop is especially large, the prices cannot trade especially high, and crushing will be profitable. And so the supply–demand merry-go-round continues.

SPREADS HAVE STRUCTURE

The process spreads are obvious examples of spreads in which the configuration of the trade is crucial to capturing the economics of the process.

Consider the petroleum refining spread. Refiners buy crude oil at one end of the process and sell refined products at the other end. Traditionally, the 3-2-1 spread (three crude oil contracts, two unleaded gasoline contracts, and one heating oil contract) approximates the barrel yield of those two products. When the heavier Arabian crudes became more commonplace, some refiners claimed that a 5-3-2 spread made more sense. The point is that it takes more than a stringing together of one contract of each to capture the economic reality of the refining process.

So, too, the soybean crush. Soybean crushers buy soybeans and crush them to produce soybean meal and soybean oil. Again, if the goal is to capture the economics of this process, you cannot simply string together single contracts of each spread component.

To start with, one 60-pound bushel of soybeans yields 44 pounds of soy meal, 11 pounds of soy oil, and 5 pounds of waste. In percentage terms, the bushel yield is 73.33 percent meal, 18.33 percent oil, and 8.33 percent waste. If you translate everything into pounds, you will discover that it takes a ratio of 11 soy meal contracts and 9 soy oil contracts to 10 soybean contracts to capture soybean crushing economics with suitable accuracy.

Yet even apparently simple two-legged spread trades exhibit discernible structure. For, just as you cannot trade any two contracts and have a spread mean anything useful in terms of economic content, so you cannot trade just any two contracts of related markets. Suppose you want to trade a corn spread to capture old crop–new crop dynamics. In this regard, the September and March contracts seem to have little relationship—or at least little relationship to the old crop–new crop issue. Rather, a valid spread must have a structure that ties it to the economic reality you are trying to capture. The end of the old crop year is July. The first futures contract in the new crop year is the December contract. Thus a July–December corn spread has a valid structure while a September–March spread may not have enduring interest.

Similarly, if you want to trade the seasonality of heating oil or unleaded gasoline, it would seem to make no sense to try to spread, say, a May contract against a November contract. Either market is most likely to be trying to accomplish opposite things. In May, the unleaded gasoline market will most probably be trying to draw supplies out of storage, whereas it will be trying to drive them into storage in November. In May, the heating oil market will probably be trying to encourage storage, whereas it may well be starting to pull supplies out of storage in November. These spreads may generate gains in the odd case, but they will have no economic connection. Their structure does not tie either one to the realities of the storage signals.

Structure is even more important in the case of yield curve spread trades. Here, the object is to isolate the effect of a change in the width of the yield curve spread. The trade should respond to that and nothing else. Suppose that CBOT 5-year Treasury note futures and 10-year Treasury note futures are trading at 109-04+ and 109-10+, respectively. Now suppose that the yields of the underlying Treasury issues both rise 10 basis points. This will drive the futures prices lower—to 108-23 and 108-15+, respectively. This amounts to a $430 per contract change in the price of the 5-year Treasury note futures and a $486 per contract change in the price of the 10-year Treasury note futures contract. When there is no change in the shape of the yield curve, a yield curve spread should show equal price changes, and a 1-to-1 spread does not do that.

To highlight the difference in these results, consider a trade in which you sell 1000 contracts of 5-year Treasury note futures and buy 1000 contracts of 10-year Treasury note futures. Exhibit 2.8 shows the relevant details.

Both futures prices dropped in response to rising yields, and the minus signs in the second column indicate that. The minus sign in the Number of Contracts column indicates contracts sold, and this results in a positive

EXHIBIT 2.8

How Equal Numbers of Contracts React to a Parallel Yield Shift

	One-Contract $ Price Change	Number of Contracts	Total $ Result
5-year Treasury note futures	–430	–1,000	430,000
10-year Treasury note futures	–846	1,000	–846,000
Net			–416,000

EXHIBIT 2.9

How Ratioed Numbers of Contracts Respond to a Parallel Yield Shift

	One-Contract $ Price Change	Number of Contracts	Total $ Result
5-year Treasury note futures	–430	–1,000	430,000
10-year Treasury note futures	–846	508	–429,768
Net			232

result. The downward price movement of the 10-year Treasury note position results in a loss that overwhelms the gain by the $416,000 net.

These price changes are what they are because the price of a 5-year Treasury note will respond less to a given yield change than the price of a 10-year Treasury note. To compensate for that, yield curve spreads must use a ratioed structure. Suppose that you had sold 1000 5-year Treasury note futures as before but bought only 508 10-year Treasury note futures. Exhibit 2.9 shows how this trade would have performed given these same 10 bp yield shifts.

The $232 net of this trade is vastly different from the –$416,000 of the other.

Never mind for the moment how you know that you should trade in this 1000 to 508 contract ratio in this situation. This is covered in Chapter 15. The point here is that the spread structure of Exhibit 2.9 causes the two legs of this yield curve spread to respond essentially equally to equal yield shifts. Further, when this yield structure does produce a result, it will mean something. This spread structure is tied to the economics of the yield curve and will convey the message that a yield curve shift is meant to convey.

The Relative Safety of Spreads Has a Statistical Basis

Market practitioners and clearinghouse officials believe that spread trades are safer than outright trades. This belief finds expression in the margin breaks granted spread trades. It also finds expression in the frequency with which professional traders resort to spread positions. Further, economists and market professionals find that spreads are more predictable than outright prices. As a result, spreads have proved useful in any number of forecasting applications.

Neither feature of spreads is accidental. The statistical phenomenon of cointegration accounts for the relative safety and predictability of spreads. The basic idea is simple even if the math looks complicated. When you have two related but nonstationary variables, the difference will be stationary. Put another way, when two time series trend together (which in this case will be two series of futures prices), the difference between the trends will be relatively stationary. There will be a common trend, a relationship between these two series.

"Trend together" in this use of the phrase does not mean go the same direction at the same rate, although this can happen. Both time series can be trending in the same direction but at different rates, or one can be trending in one direction while the other trends in the other direction. What matters is that both trends will be responding to the same set of economic drivers.

This cointegration property accounts for the mean reverting property of all true spreads. Spreads trade around long-term means. They can work higher or lower than this mean, but, in the normal course of events, they will work back to the mean. A true spread will never just shoot off into space as a single price can. The economic forces that create the spread will kick in to drive it back toward the long-term mean. This is what makes spreads safer and more predictable than outright futures markets.

IN SUM

This discussion should make it clear that the preference of professional traders for approaching the markets through the medium of spread trades is no accident. These trades have a basis in the economics of the market or markets involved. They exhibit a structure that responds to the economic drivers. And they are therefore more predictable, safer, and more cost-effective to trade than outright futures contracts.

The next 15 chapters focus on particular futures spread trades to show how each kind of trade responds to these economic and structural factors and how each exhibits the other properties of spread trades. The hope is that these discussions can serve you as exemplars or templates for trades in other markets.

CHAPTER 3

New Crop–Old Crop Corn Spreads

Futures markets emerged in the first place to trade the grain contracts. Spread trading took hold almost at once, and the new crop–old crop spreads were among the first to be traded, if not the first. Despite the long history of spread trading in the grain markets, market users have arrived at precious little agreement on spread logic and terminology. This seems an important place to start any discussion of spread trading.

SPREAD LOGIC AND TERMINOLOGY

In a given year, the July corn contract typically represents the old crop, while the December contract represents the new crop—e.g., a typical new crop–old crop spread will balance the July 2003 contract against the December 2003 contract, or the July 2004 contract against the December 2004 contract. (The parallel trade in soybean futures will balance the July and November contracts.) Another version of a new crop–old crop trade balances the December contract of one year against the December contract of the next year. Most frequently, though, a reference to a new crop–old crop corn spread assumes the July–December trade. That much is a given and is fairly universal.

This next situation is where you may find confusing talk. Typically, as is implicit in the language of the prior paragraph, you will see screen references to, or hear talk about, the July–December corn spread, but the most sensible way to calculate the spread is to subtract the nearby price from the deferred price—the new crop minus the old crop. Suppose July corn is trading at $2.3825 per bushel and December corn is trading at $2.3950 per bushel. (Note that the contract specifications indicate that these contract prices are in terms of cents per bushel, and many quote sources give these prices as 238¼ or 239½. This discussion converts these prices into dollars per bushel to make it easier to see the arithmetic.) This spread is $0.0125 (2.395 – 2.3825). This isn't always how it's done, but this ultimately makes more sense.

The logic of calculating the spread this way should become apparent if you consider the typical market situation in the early part of the calendar year. In January, the grain bins are normally full, so the market impulse should be to push future corn into storage. One tool the market can use to accomplish this rationing goal is the new crop–old crop spread. Participants can bid up the price of the new crop contract relative to the price of the old crop contract. A positive spread encourages storage. The closer the spread gets to the full cost of carry (*carry* is the sum of the storage, financing, insurance, and shrinkage costs), the stronger the encouragement. That is, the wider the spread, the stronger the storage imperative.

As the U.S. Department of Agriculture (USDA) and various market observers issue reports and adjust their estimates of the supply-demand situation, the new crop–old crop spreads will shift to reflect new information, perceptions, and concerns.

Widening and Narrowing

When the consensus is that supplies are plentiful relative to demand, the impulse to store will be strong and the new crop–old crop spreads will widen. When the consensus is that supplies are insufficient or that they may become insufficient, the market will reverse course and motivate movement out of storage. In this case, the spreads will narrow.

Widening and *narrowing* are terms that require thought because during much of the crop year, you can find negative, or inverted, grain spreads. Consider six dates in March, April, and May of 2003. Exhibit 3.1 shows the July corn (C N3) and December corn (C Z3) prices for each day shown and the spread (December minus July).

Between March 10 and March 28, the spread moved from 0.0125 to 0.0325, so it widened 2 cents per bushel. From March 28 to April 3, the spread moved from 0.0325 to 0.0050, so it narrowed 2.75 cents per bushel. This should be obvious enough to seem trivial.

This terminology becomes less than obvious when the spreads invert. It seems fairly clear that the April 3 to April 14 move represents a further 2.25 cents per bushel narrowing of the spread. Let's agree, then, that the

EXHIBIT 3.1

Spread Widening and Narrowing

	C N3	C Z3	Spread
3/10/03	2.3825	2.3950	0.0125
3/28/03	2.2800	2.3125	0.0325
4/3/04	2.3925	2.3975	0.0050
4/14/03	2.3975	2.3800	–0.0175
5/16/03	2.5425	2.4975	–0.0450
5/19/03	2.4675	2.4450	–0.0225

move from –0.0175 to –0.0450 is also a narrowing of the spread. Even though there is more numerical space between zero and –0.0450 than between zero and –0.0175, it seems more logical in terms of trading spreads to call this a narrowing. Later, if the spread were to move to –0.0225, this would be a widening—even though –0.0225 is a lot narrower still than the 0.0325 of March 28.

In sum, in the interest of spread logic, it seems useful to think of widening and narrowing in this way:

- When a positive spread becomes more positive, it is widening (March 3 to March 28 in Exhibit 3.1).
- When a positive spread becomes less positive, it is narrowing (March 28 to April 3).
- When a negative spread becomes less negative, it is widening (May 16 to May 19).
- When a negative spread becomes more negative, it is narrowing (April 14 to May 16).

The last two bulleted items may take some getting used to, but they can help you keep track of spread trade structure in a sensible way.

BUYING AND SELLING A NEW CROP–OLD CROP CORN SPREAD

This use of the terms *widening* and *narrowing* begins to make more sense when you consider the logic of buying or selling the new crop–old crop spreads.

In any kind of trading, you want to buy a thing when you anticipate that it will increase in value. You want to sell a thing when you anticipate that it will decrease in value. That is obvious in the buying or selling of stocks or outright futures positions. When you think the market will go up, you buy. When you think the market will go down, you sell.

A widening spread is a spread that is gaining value. A narrowing spread is a spread that is losing value. Logically enough, you will want to buy a spread that you expect to widen and sell a spread that you expect to narrow.

It seems fairly standard usage in grain trading circles that you buy or sell the new crop–old crop spread in terms of what you do with the new crop, or deferred, contract. That is, to buy the spread, you will buy December corn and sell July corn. To see how the mechanics of this trade might work, suppose that you had decided to buy the spread on March 10, 2003, and had unwound the trade on March 28. Exhibit 3.2 presents the relevant details of this trade.

You can actually keep track of spread results by simply calculating the spread difference in terms of subtracting the initial spread from the ending spread (0.0325 ending spread minus 0.0125 initial spread equals 0.0200 spread net) and multiplying by 5000 bushels. At 2 cents per bushel, this trade would have grossed $100 for each one-lot spread you bought.

You can understand the dynamics of a spread better if you use a matrix such as the one in Exhibit 3.2. To begin, if you subtract the *buy* price from the *sell* price for each leg of the spread, you will always get the gains and losses right in the Result row. The Spread net in the C Z3 column is the sum of the two results. Calculating both this and the spread difference in the Spread column provides a useful check. The two numbers in the Spread net row should be the same, although the signs can differ. Finally, the Spread net times 5,000 bushels is the Spread $ net. You want this to be positive, but it may not always be.

Suppose that you had put on this trade on March 10, as in Exhibit 3.2, but had waited until April 3 to unwind it. Exhibit 3.3 shows that buying the spread will result in a loss if the spread narrows.

EXHIBIT 3.2

Buying the New Crop–Old Crop Corn Spread

	Action	C N3	Action	C Z3	Spread
3/10/03	Sell	2.3825	Buy	2.3950	0.0125
3/28/03	Buy	2.2800	Sell	2.3125	0.0325
Result		0.1025		–0.0825	
Spread net				0.0200	0.0200
Spread $ net				100.00	

EXHIBIT 3.3

When You Expected a Zig but Got a Zag

Date	Action	C N3	Action	C Z3	Spread
3/10/03	Sell	2.3825	Buy	2.3950	0.0125
4/3/03	Buy	2.2925	Sell	2.3975	0.0050
Result		–0.0100		0.0025	
Spread net				–0.0075	–0.0075
Spread $ net				–37.50	

EXHIBIT 3.4a

Selling the Spread in Anticipation of Spread Narrowing

Date	Action	C N3	Action	C Z3	Spread
4/3/03	Buy	2.3925	Sell	2.3975	0.0050
4/14/03	Sell	2.3975	Buy	2.3800	–0.0175
Result		0.0050		0.0174	
Spread net				0.0225	–0.0225
Spread $ net				112.50	

This is not a large loss, but this example does show that losses are possible when your market call proves erroneous.

However, suppose you had sold the spread on April 3 and unwound it at the April 14 prices shown in Exhibit 3.1. Alternatively, suppose you had sold it on April 14 and unwound it at the May 16 prices shown in that exhibit. Exhibits 3.4a and 3.4b show how these trades would have performed, given these assumptions.

Notice the minus sign in the fourth cell of the Spread column. When you calculate the spread change by subtracting the initial spread value from the ending spread value (–0.0450 minus –0.0175), a positive result will indicate a widening spread, while a negative result will indicate a narrowing spread.

These four trade examples, fortuitously, allow for the making of an important point about spread trading. It is often tempting to look at the results of a trade, such as the one illustrated in Exhibit 3.4b, to notice the $0.1450 July result and to wonder why you should give back $0.1175 of that by doing the December leg.

EXHIBIT 3.4b

Selling the New Crop–Old Crop Corn Spread

Date	Action	C N3	Action	C Z3	Spread
4/14/03	Buy	2.3975	Sell	2.3800	–0.0175
5/16/03	Sell	2.5425	Buy	2.4975	–0.0450
Result		0.1450		–0.1175	
Spread net				0.0275	–0.0275
Spread $ net				137.50	

EXHIBIT 3.5

Another Way for the Spread to Narrow

	Action	C N3	Action	C Z3	Spread
Initial date	Buy	2.4000	Sell	2.3800	–0.0200
Ending date	Sell	2.3600	Buy	2.3100	–0.0500
Result		–0.0400		0.0700	
Spread net				0.0300	–0.0300
Spread $ net				150.00	

One reason to trade these spreads is that spreads are typically more predictable than outright futures trades. You may be reasonably confident that this spread will narrow at this time of year, but you can't be sure how that narrowing will take place. In this case, both prices rose, but the July price rose more. It can also happen that both prices will fall but the December price will fall more, as shown in Exhibit 3.5.

A third alternative is that one price may rise while the other falls, as shown in Exhibit 3.4a. When this happens, both legs make gains.

Finally, while it is true that the December loss reduces the Spread net in Exhibit 3.4b, it is also true that the December gain in Exhibit 3.3 slightly mitigates the July loss of that trade. You trade spreads because you believe that you have a better chance of knowing what the spread will do in a given situation than you have of knowing what either single price will do. Because of this, it is a good idea to focus on the spread as a whole, not on the individual legs of the spread. Either one can come through for you or, sometimes, both can.

THIS YEAR MAY NOT BE LAST YEAR

Even though a spread may typically behave in a certain way in certain seasons, you can't blindly rely on that. In a normal year, the market should build at least some carry in the weeks and months after harvest. That is, the July–December spread should be close to or slightly positive during this part of the year. By April, or thereabouts, the carry should start to melt away and, eventually, the July–December spread is likely to invert as the market bids up the old crop (July) prices to pull grain out of storage. The thing is that a study of charts of this spread for the first 28 weeks of each of the last 20 or so years shows that new crop–old crop spread behavior varies greatly from year to year.

Old timers in the grain trade often say something to the effect that you'd better know something when you trade these spreads. What they mean is that you'd better have at least some idea of what kind of crop has just come in, how much has been carried over from the previous year, and what kinds of things are going on with regard to demand. Part of demand is livestock feeding requirements. Another part is the export market. Recently, ethanol requirements have become a bigger part of the picture. Most brokerage houses have analysts who generate useful summaries of all this. A variety of other advisory services can help out, too.

Exhibit 3.6 provides an overview of how the July–December spread behaved from the beginning of January to almost the middle of July in 2003 and 2004.

You can see that the 2003 spread approximates normalcy in the sense that the spread was slightly positive for much of the early part of 2003. Further, it inverted sharply about the middle of June 2003 as the market moved to draw corn out of storage.

The graphic of Exhibit 3.6 embodies an important general fact about commodity market spreads. Notice that there is twice as much space below the zero axis as above. Positive spreads in these markets are strictly limited by the cost of full carry. They never go above that level. No such economic boundary limits inverted spreads. They can, and often do, invert much farther even than this chart shows. In thinking about these spreads, it is important to be aware of this.

In contrast to the 2003 spread, the 2004 July–December spread started the year at –0.05 and immediately worked down to the –0.10 area. This spread traded in a fairly narrow range around –0.10 until the beginning of April. After bouncing around for several weeks, this 2004 spread widened sharply in late May. By June 4, the spread was 2.5 cents per bushel positive, and it widened steadily. Finally, this spread spent all but two days of the

EXHIBIT 3.6

New Crop–Old Crop Corn Spreads

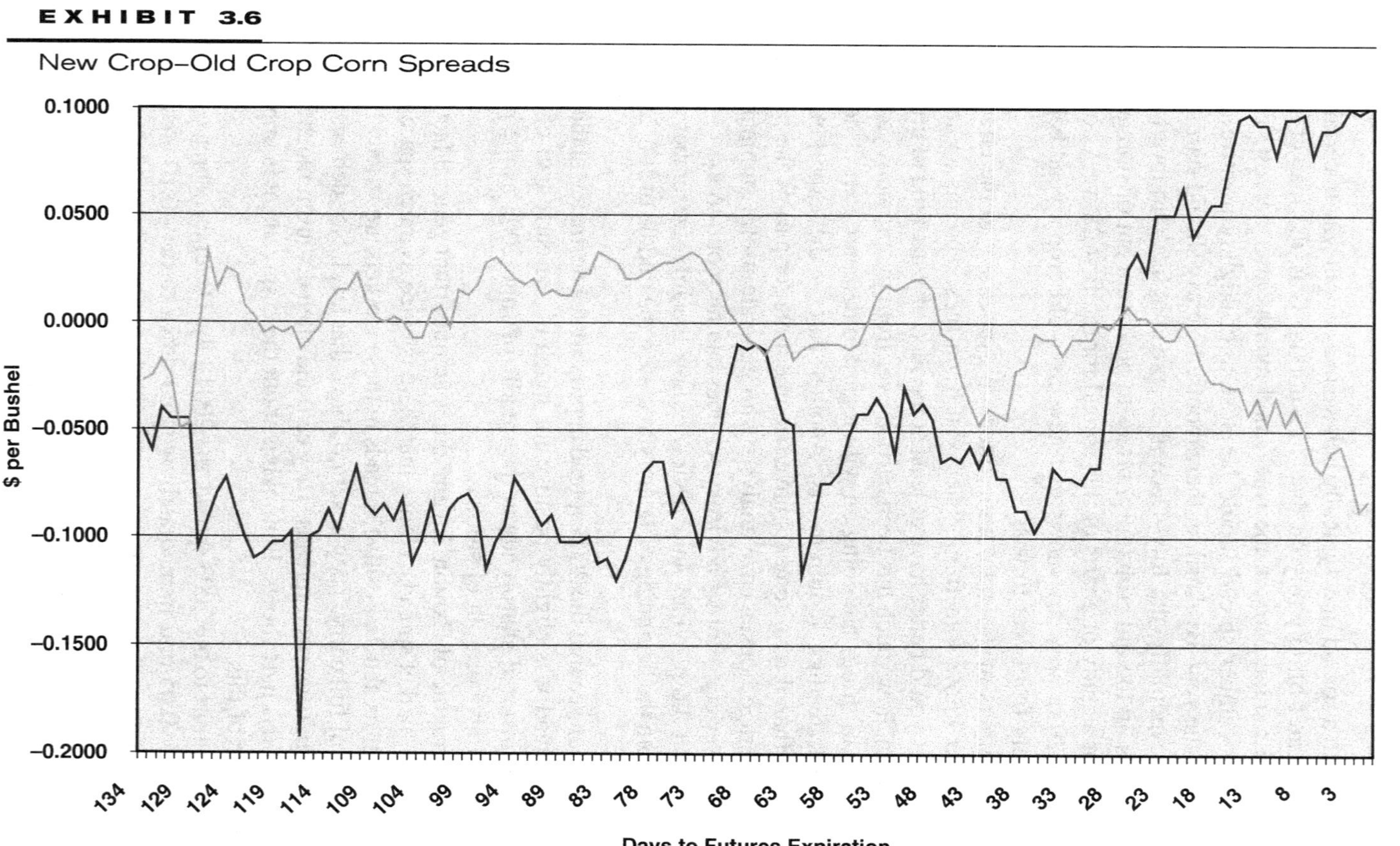

period from June 22 to July 13, the end of this data series, above 9 cents and finished at 10 cents per bushel.

This chart of the 2004 July–December spread depicts a truly unusual situation in the corn market. Keep in mind that the United States is the main supplier of corn to the world. In very approximate terms, the United States has grown about 40 percent of the world crop for the last several years. The next largest corn producing country has been China with roughly 20 percent of the world crop. In contrast, since 2000, the South American soybean crop (the Brazilian and Argentine crops taken together) has surpassed the U.S. crop, and Brazil has been turning more and more land into soybean acreage. And wheat has always been a world crop. When something happens to the U.S. soybean or wheat crops, then, the sense of alarm is much less than it would be for corn because there are major alternative sources. However, when the U.S. corn crop proves to be less than expected, this is a matter for universal concern because the world still looks to the United States for the bulk of its corn. And January 2004 brought the corn market an ugly surprise.

On January 12, 2004, the U.S. Department of Agriculture (USDA) issued a report that revised the corn stock on hand downward by 400 million bushels. For the first time in memory, the market feared that it could run out of corn in 2005.

Estimates such as this are based on trendline projections. The estimators take several years' worth of crop production and demand growth data and determine the trends of the changes in growth. These trendlines can then be projected forward. As long as supply slightly exceeds demand, no one worries. This is normally the case, and the market checks the situation and relaxes. In early 2004, though, the large downward revision to the supply of corn and a greater-than-expected rate of demand growth, mostly fueled by the needs of ethanol producers, seemed omens of a dire situation in the near future. This had never happened.

The demand growth rate, based on what the market knew as of January 12, 2004, exceeded the average rate of increase in crop production. Enough additional corn was being processed into ethanol so that it was shifting the supply-demand balance. These concerns account for the fact that the July–December 2004 corn spread was trading back and forth across the –$0.10 per bushel level from mid-January to early April 2004.

But then spring weather in the corn belt was close to ideal, and farmers were able to get the bulk of the corn crop planted by the end of the first week of May 2004, about two weeks earlier than usual. This early planting along with a continuation of the nearly ideal weather conditions suggested that yields would be excellent. By late May 2004, this awareness made itself felt in the market in the form of wider spreads. The July–December 2004 spread was still negative in late May, but the spread was now trading at around –$0.05 per bushel rather than at around –$0.10 per bushel as had been the case in February and March.

Further, the late June USDA crop report revealed what at least much of the market seemed to have sensed already. Not only was the crop planted under almost perfect conditions, but farmers had switched over 3 million acres from soybeans to corn. This drove an already widening spread even wider.

TRADING THE NEW CROP NEWS

Having gotten wind of all this, you might well have seen in the –0.0675 July–December spread of May 28, 2004, a good opportunity to buy the spread. Ideal planting conditions and more acres planted suggest the possibility of a huge crop and a strong storage impulse in the form of widening spreads. Suppose you had bought the spread on May 28 and unwound it on June 30, just before the start of the July delivery month. Exhibit 3.7 shows that this trade could have earned $812.50 for each spread traded on the 16.25 cents per bushel spread widening, based on these assumptions.

Obviously, this July–December spread stops trading when the July contract goes off the board, but it may be a good precaution to stop trading it before the start of the July delivery month. Certainly, if you were selling the spread, so that you had bought July futures, you wouldn't want to risk getting tangled up in the delivery process. In this case, you were selling the July contract because you bought the spread. Because the seller chooses whether to deliver, you would not be in danger from that aspect. Still, toward

EXHIBIT 3.7

Buying the July–December Spread in Anticipation of a Widening Spread

	Action	C N3	Action	C Z3	Spread
5/28/04	Sell	3.0400	Buy	2.9725	–0.0675
6/30/04	Buy	2.5750	Sell	2.6700	0.0950
Result		0.4650		–0.3025	
Spread net				0.1625	0.1625
Spread $ net				812.50	

the end of trading, the market might get a little one-sided or otherwise become distorted enough to affect your trading results. Because of this, it seems good policy to avoid delivery months.

A NEW CROP–OLD CROP SPREAD FOR LATER IN THE YEAR

Of course, news about the new crop wouldn't stop just because that one contract stopped trading. In fact, as the summer of 2004 wore on, the crop that was in the ground began to look better and better. From midsummer on, the December 2004 corn futures price trended steadily lower. By early September, word was out that this crop could easily produce 1.2 billion bushels of corn. As the October 12 crop report approached, the early September estimate began to seem low. This is the kind of crop situation that can widen spreads and widen them by huge amounts. It matters also that the news was fairly widely anticipated. You could have known well in advance of the September harvest and the early October USDA crop report what was likely to happen.

Because all this is true, another fairly commonly used new crop–old crop spread is the December–December spread. On June 30, 2004, when the July–December spread was a relatively wide 0.0950, the December 2004–December 2005 spread was –0.0275. Exhibit 3.8 shows how this December '04–December '05 spread developed from the beginning of June 2004 to the end of October 2004.

Exhibit 3.9 shows snapshots taken at roughly 15-day intervals starting on June 30 and continuing through the summer to show how the market was absorbing the news about the current corn crop.

You can almost follow the ebb and flow of the crop news and, perhaps more to the point, market participants' concerns about the 2004 crop as the summer wore on. What matters to a spread trader is that this was a solid widening trend—a strong signal to buy the December '04–December '05 spread.

Suppose you had bought this spread when you unwound the July–December spread. On June 30, the December 2004 futures contract was trading at \$2.6700 per bushel, and the December 2005 futures contract was trading at \$2.6425 per bushel. To buy the spread, you would have bought the December 2005 contract and sold the December 2004. Assume that you unwound it at the September 30 prices shown in Exhibit 3.9. Relative to the other spread trades used as examples in this chapter, this would have been a blockbuster trade, earning \$2,137.50, as Exhibit 3.10 shows.

EXHIBIT 3.8

New Crop–Old Crop Corn Spread (Dec 05–Dec 04)

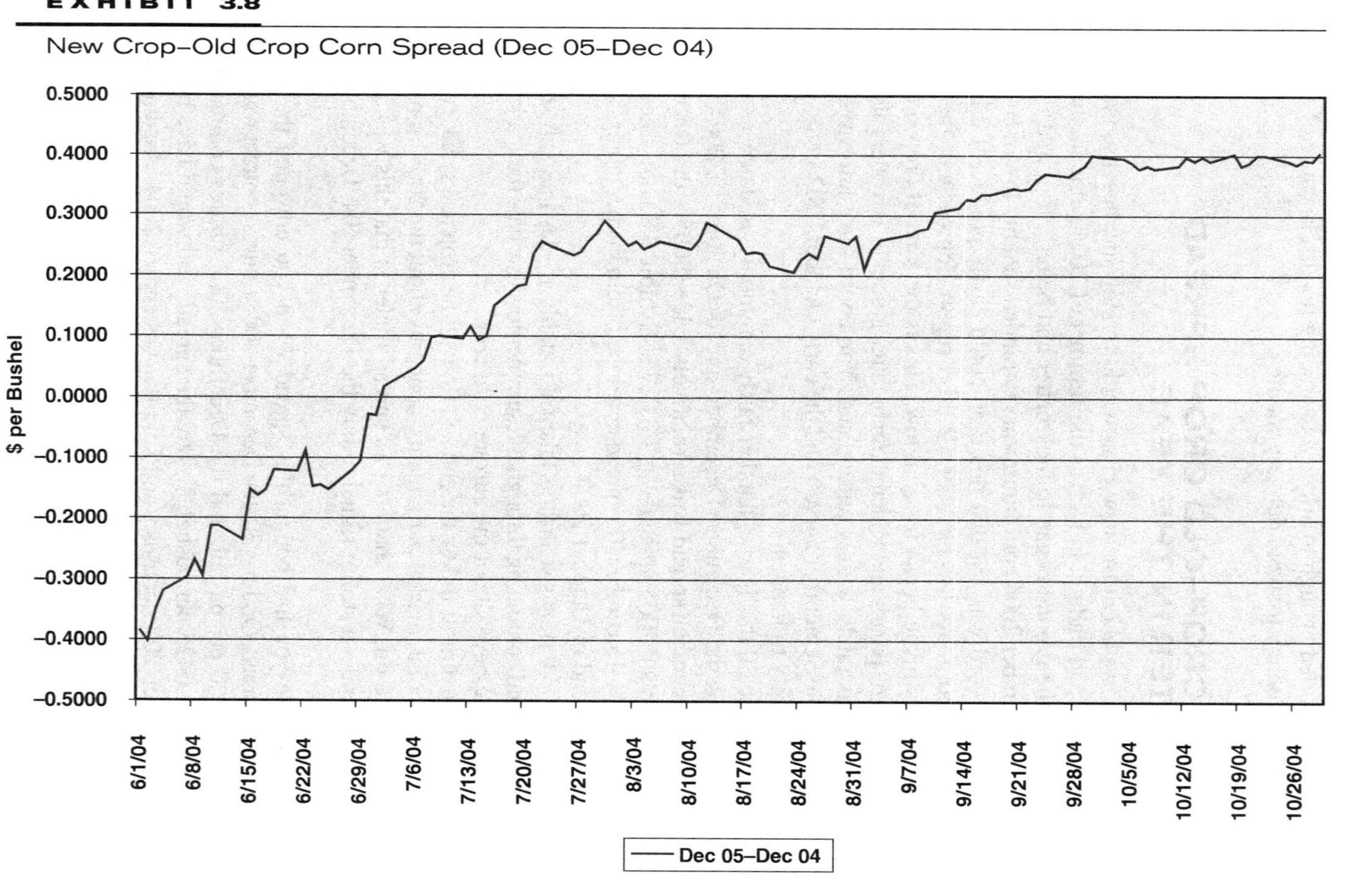

EXHIBIT 3.9

Following the December 04–December 05 Corn Spread, Summer 2004

	C Z4	C Z5	Spread
6/30/04	2.6700	2.6425	–0.0275
7/15/04	2.5025	2.6025	0.1000
7/30/04	2.2550	2.5450	0.2900
8/16/04	2.3300	2.5875	0.2575
8/31/04	2.3775	2.6425	0.2650
9/15/04	2.1850	2.5100	0.3250
9/30/04	2.0550	2.4550	0.4000

EXHIBIT 3.10

Buying the December–December Spread

	Action	C Z4	Action	C Z5	Spread
6/30/04	Sell	2.6700	Buy	2.6425	–0.0275
9/30/04	Buy	2.0550	Sell	2.4550	0.4000
Result		0.6150		–0.1875	
Spread net				0.4275	0.4275
Spread $ net				2,137.50	

A spread situation such as the one illustrated in Exhibit 3.9 gives you numerous chances. Suppose, for whatever reason, you had not acted on June 30. You could still have made the trade on July 15. Actually, the spread touched the 0.10 mark on July 9 and bounced around between 0.09 and 0.10 for several days. Further, after the spread widened to 0.40 on September 30, it bounced around in a narrow range for the next month. The lowest October spread level was 0.3775. You could have unwound at any time in October and done well. Just to demonstrate that all would not have been lost, assume that you had put on the trade on July 15 and unwound it on October 12 (USDA crop report day) with the spread at 0.3975. This 0.2975 spread widening would have earned $1,487.50 for each one-lot spread that you bought on July 15.

A WORD OF CAUTION

One advantage of trading spreads is that they tend to be more predictable than outright prices. Another advantage is that spreads give you more ways to be right—as Exhibits 3.4a, 3.4b, and 3.5 illustrate.

Still, it is important always to remember that spreads are speculative trades, and a wrong market call will result in a loss, as Exhibit 3.3 illustrates.

Another important point is that you must not trade spreads mechanically. Just because a spread has behaved in a certain way the last several times doesn't mean that it will this time. To reduce the possibility of losing spread trades, you need to pay attention to fundamental news. Seven or eight years ago, ethanol production was a negligible factor in the corn supply-demand picture. Currently, it is a large and growing part of the picture. Luckily, most brokerages have analysts who stay on top of all this and who can provide help in understanding how the spreads may perform given current information.

That said, these new crop–old crop spreads can provide a steady stream of modest but still satisfying trading results.

CHAPTER 4

New Crop–Old Crop Cotton Spreads

During the early 1990s, when disparaging remarks about derivatives in general and structured notes in particular were the fashion, a speaker at a risk management symposium showed a slide of a bond certificate that had been issued in the early 1860s by the Confederate States of America. What was remarkable about this bond was that it paid coupon interest that derived from the London delivered price of cotton. The speaker wanted to demonstrate that derivatives weren't new. His example also demonstrates that cotton has been an important part of the U.S. economic picture for a long time and that the export market has always figured large in cotton economics.

Like wheat, cotton is an international crop. The United States produces the second largest crop, after China, but major amounts of cotton are produced on every continent and subcontinent of the world. This means that traders must take a panoramic view in assessing the supply-demand situation in the cotton market. New crop–old crop spreads using the cotton futures contracts traded on the New York Board of Trade (NYBOT) incorporate this panoramic view and provide solid trading opportunities as the cotton crop year develops.

DEFINING THE SPREAD

The NYBOT contracts trade on a March, May, July, October, and December cycle. For new crop–old crop spread purposes the May and July contracts represent the old crop in a given year, and the December contract represents the new crop. As with the grains, it makes sense to define the spread as the new crop–old crop difference—the new crop price minus the old crop price. That is, on January 30, 2004, July cotton (CTN4) traded at 73.56 cents per pound while December cotton (CTZ4) traded at 68.10 cents per pound. This makes the July–December spread for that day –5.46 cents per pound (68.10 – 73.56).

Also like the grains, the cotton market has a seasonal rhythm, and prices vary to some extent according to seasonal causes for concern. During spring, the concerns focus on how much farmers intend to plant and on whether planting weather is favorable. Weather becomes an issue at each crop development stage, and finally there is the matter of how the harvest has gone—whether yields were as anticipated, greater, or less. During all these times, if weather conditions and crop mechanics seem favorable, the market can worry about the export questions such as whether the Chinese textile makers will import as much this year as they did last year and whether other growing countries will capture market share that they didn't get in prior years—in effect, wrest market share away from the U.S. producers.

The new crop–old crop spreads smooth away the noisier elements of these developments and concerns to provide a fairly accurate picture of the supply-demand situation as the market sees it at the moment. This spread responds to the same kind of storage impulse that drives the grain spreads. When the market foresees a supply-demand imbalance weighted to the supply side, the spread will widen to encourage storage. When demand outruns supply, the spread will narrow to pull supplies out of storage.

Exhibit 4.1 plots both the May–December and July–December spreads from the beginning of 2004 until early May, for the May–December spread, and early July, for the July–December spread.

THE MESSAGE OF THE NEW CROP–OLD CROP SPREADS

When the consensus is that supplies are plentiful relative to demand, the impulse to store will be strong, and the new crop–old crop spreads will widen. When the consensus is that supplies are insufficient or the market fears that they may become insufficient, the market will reverse course, and the spreads will narrow to motivate movement out of storage.

Widening and *narrowing* are terms that require thought, because during much of the crop year, you can find negative, or inverted, cotton spreads. Exhibit 4.2 isolates several moments in the run of the July–December spread that will orient the ideas of *narrowing* and *widening*. These data can also help you begin to see what these spreads can tell you about the cotton market during the first half of 2004.

EXHIBIT 4.1

New Crop–Old Crop Cotton Spreads

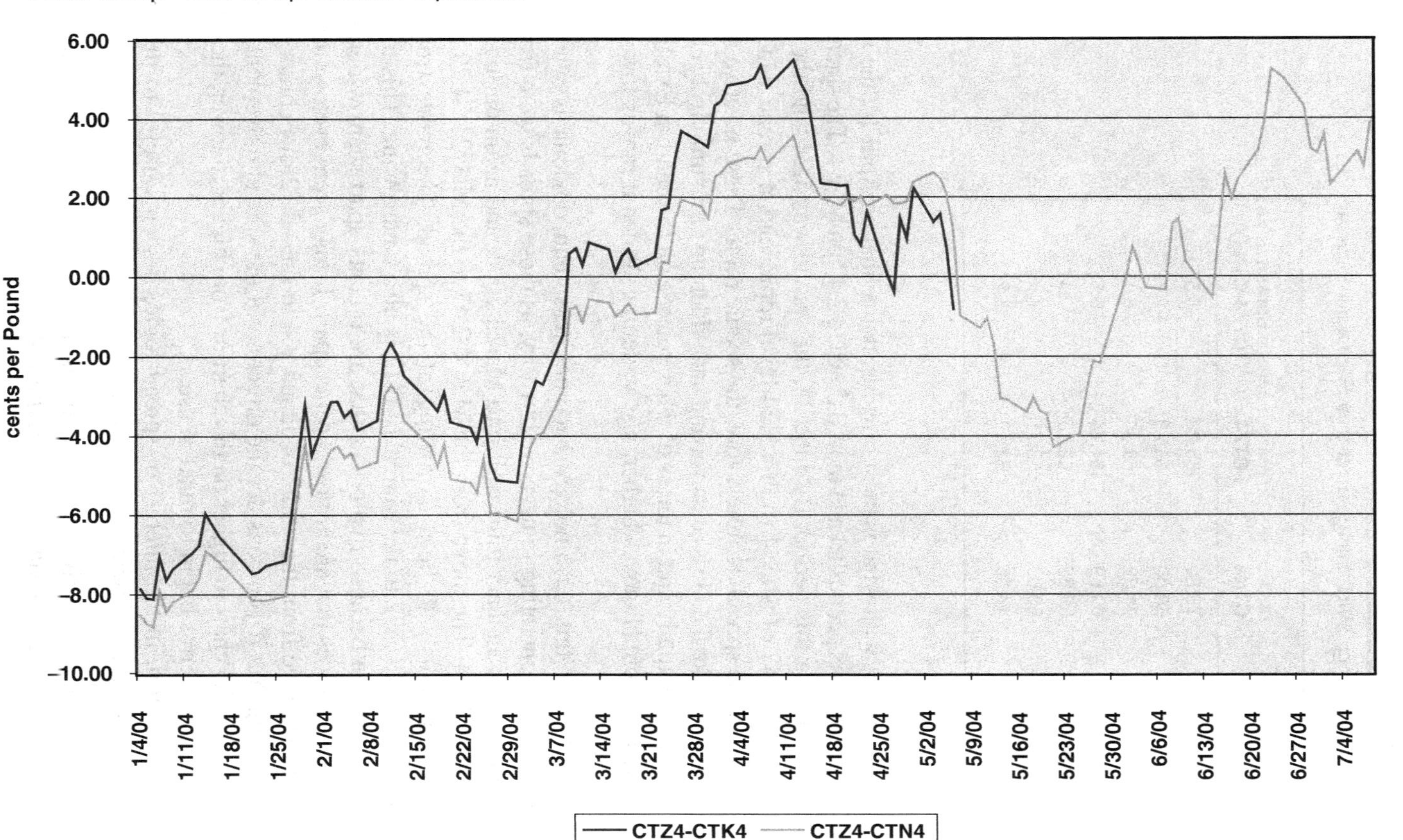

EXHIBIT 4.2

Narrowing, Widening, and the Storage Signal

	CTN4	CTZ4	Spread (CTZ4-CTN4)
1/4/04	76.80	68.28	–8.52
2/11/04	68.00	65.28	–2.72
3/1/04	74.52	68.35	–6.17
4/12/04	60.69	64.24	3.55
5/4/04	59.68	62.15	2.47
5/21/04	63.00	58.71	–4.29
6/23/04	47.95	53.19	5.24

To start with what is most obvious, notice that on April 12, the spread was 3.55 cents per bushel and moved down to 2.47 on May 4. The spread narrowed during this period. By June 23, the spread was 5.24, and the move from the 2.47 of May 4 to this 5.24 level represents a spread widening, although the spread definitely took the scenic route. These positive spread numbers make the ideas of narrowing and widening seem intuitively correct, both conceptually and in terms of what you see on the chart in Exhibit 4.1. When the spread moves higher, it is widening. When it moves lower, it is narrowing.

Where this terminology becomes less than obvious is when the spreads are operating in negative territory, as these spreads were from the beginning of January until well into March 2004, and again during much of May 2004. The move from the May 4 2.47 to the May 21 –4.29 seems fairly obviously to be a narrowing of the spread. The move from the February 11 –2.72 to the March 1 –6.17 is also a narrowing. This may be harder to see because two prices that are 6 cents apart seem wider apart than two prices that are almost 3 cents apart. It may seem even weirder to call the move from the –8.52 of January 4 to the –2.72 of February 11 a widening. Yet if you consider the direction of the spread movement, from lower on the chart to higher on the chart or from higher to lower, then perhaps these terms begin to make sense.

In sum, in the interest of spread logic, it seems useful to think of widening and narrowing in this way:

- When a positive spread becomes more positive, it is widening (March 3 to March 28 in Exhibit 4.1).

- When a positive spread becomes less positive, it is narrowing (March 28 to April 3).
- When a negative spread becomes less negative, it is widening (May 16 to May 19).
- When a negative spread becomes more negative, it is narrowing (April 14 to May 16).

The last two bulleteted items may take some getting used to, but they can help you keep track of spread trade structure in a sensible way.

BUYING AND SELLING A NEW CROP–OLD CROP COTTON SPREAD

This use of the terms widening and narrowing begins to make more sense when you consider the logic of buying or selling the new crop–old crop spreads.

In any kind of trading, you want to buy a thing when you anticipate that it will increase in value. You want to sell a thing when you anticipate that it will decrease in value. That is obvious in the buying or selling of stocks or outright futures positions. When you think the market will go up, you buy. When you think the market will go down, you sell.

A widening spread is a spread that is gaining value. A narrowing spread is a spread that is losing value. Logically enough, you will want to buy a spread that you expect to widen and sell a spread that you expect to narrow.

It seems fairly standard usage that you buy or sell the new crop–old crop cotton spread in terms of what you do with the new crop, or deferred, contract. That is, to buy the spread, you will buy December cotton and sell July cotton (or May if that is the spread you want to trade). To see how the mechanics of this trade might work, suppose that you had decided to buy the spread on January 4 and had unwound the trade on February 11. Exhibit 4.3 presents the relevant details of this trade.

One simple way to keep track of spread results is to subtract the initial spread from the ending spread (–2.72 minus –8.52 equals 5.80 cents per pound). A spread that is widening will result in a positive number, as in this case. The NYBOT cotton futures contract contains 50,000 pounds, so 5.80 cents per pound is 290,000 cents, or $2,900.00.

You can understand the dynamics of the spread better if you use a matrix such as the one shown in Exhibit 4.3 and figure out what happened to each leg of the spread. To begin, if you subtract the Buy price from the Sell price for each leg of the spread, you will always get the gains and losses

EXHIBIT 4.3

Buying the New Crop–Old Crop Cotton Spread

	Action	CTN4	Action	CTZ4	Spread
1/4/04	Sell	76.80	Buy	68.28	–8.52
2/11/04	Buy	68.00	Sell	65.28	–2.72
Result		8.80		–3.00	
Spread net				5.80	5.80
Spread $ net				2,900.00	

EXHIBIT 4.4

Selling the New Crop–Old Crop Cotton Spread

	Action	CTN4	Action	CTZ4	Spread
2/11/04	Buy	68.00	Sell	65.28	–2.72
3/1/04	Sell	74.52	Buy	68.35	–6.17
Result		6.52		–3.06	
Spread net				3.45	–3.45
Spread $ net				1,725.00	

right in the Result row. The Spread net in the CTZ4 column is the sum of the two results. Calculating both this and the spread difference in the Spread column provides a useful check. The two numbers in the Spread net row should be the same, although the signs can differ. Finally, the Spread net times 50,000 pounds and divided by 100 is the Spread $ net. You want this to be positive, but it may not always be—if you buy the spread and it narrows, for example.

When you expect the spread to narrow, you want to sell it by selling the December contract and buying the July. A trade based on the February 11 and March 1 prices of Exhibit 4.2 provides an example of spread selling and also reinforces the logic of spread narrowing in an environment of negative numbers.

Notice that in this case the Spread net in the Spread column is a negative number to show that the spread narrowed during this time interval. Also, the buy and sell indications are the opposite of the trade shown in Exhibit 4.3, but otherwise the analysis of this trade operates in the same fashion.

EXHIBIT 4.5

Selling the New Crop–Old Crop Cotton Spread

	Action	CTK4	Action	CTZ4	Spread
2/11/04	Buy	66.94	Sell	65.28	−1.66
3/1/04	Sell	73.51	Buy	68.35	−5.18
Result		6.59		−3.07	
Spread net				3.52	−3.52
Spread $ net				1,760.00	

DEVELOPING AN OUTLOOK TO SHAPE YOUR SPREAD TRADES

An outlook for the new crop–old crop cotton spread requires a slightly different orientation from a price outlook. The factors that shape your forecast are the same. The difference lies in what you make of them.

During the early part of 2004, all indications were that demand for U.S. cotton was strong and that supplies were slightly lower than they had been a year earlier. To a flat price trader, this probably suggested support for prices. Prices were likely to at least stay in the mid to upper 60s and might even rise. To a new crop–old crop spread trader, this set of circumstances probably suggested that the spread would narrow as buyers competed for supplies from the 2003–2004 crop. Toward the middle of February 2004, that is, you might have seen in this information a good opportunity to sell the spread.

Assume that you sold the May–December spread on February 11 and unwound this trade on March 1 at the prices and spread levels shown in Exhibit 4.5. To sell the May–December spread, remember, you sell December futures and buy May futures.

Notice that this is almost the same trade as the one illustrated in Exhibit 4.4. The difference is that this trade uses the May contract rather than the July and the May–December spread narrowed slightly more than the July–December spread. That extra seven hundredths of a cent per pound translates into $35 more on the bottom line of a one-lot spread.

A SHIFTING SITUATION MOTIVATES A STRATEGY SHIFT

As the 2004 planting season drew near, early reports were that U.S. cotton farmers planned to increase acreage devoted to cotton by about 7 percent over the acreage devoted to this crop the year before. Not all commentators believed that all these acres would actually be put to cotton, but that estimate of increasing acreage was rather widely in the market.

Outright futures traders might see this as a signal that prices would begin to fall. New crop–old crop spread traders might not particularly care whether prices were about to rise or fall. If the new crop were to be a big one, this would create a strong impulse to push the new crop into storage. That is, the May–December and July–December spreads might be on the brink of a fairly drastic widening.

Based on this opinion, you might have bought either of these spreads in early March. Assume that you bought one or the other on March 1, 2004, and unwound it on April 7 or April 12. Exhibits 4.6a–d show how the May–December spread would have performed based on the dates and prices shown in the exhibits. Exhibit 4.6a assumes that between March 1 and April 7 the May–December spread widened by 10.52 cents per pound based on the prices shown. This spread widening would have caused this trade to earn $5,260 for a one-lot spread.

Exhibit 4.6b assumes that the May–December spread ran from March 1 to April 12. This version of the trade would have earned $5,330 on the 10.66 cents per pound widening shown.

Exhibit 4.6c assumes that between March 1 and April 7 the July–December spread widened by 9.43 cents per pound to earn $4,715.

Exhibit 4.6d assumes the March 1 to April 12 time span, during which the July–December spread widened by 9.72 cents per pound given the prices shown, to earn $4,860.

It is worth noting that all three prices fell during the period of this trade—the May, the July, and the December. This makes no difference. The spread widening was what mattered.

EXHIBIT 4.6a

Buying the New Crop–Old Crop Cotton Spread On Reports of Increased Cotton Acres

	Action	CTK4	Action	CTZ4	Spread
3/1/04	Sell	73.53	Buy	68.35	–5.18
4/7/04	Buy	61.68	Sell	67.02	5.34
Result		11.85		–1.33	
Spread net				10.52	10.52
Spread $ net				5,260.00	

EXHIBIT 4.6b

Buying the New Crop–Old Crop Cotton Spread On Reports of Increased Cotton Acres

	Action	CTK4	Action	CTZ4	Spread
3/1/04	Sell	73.53	Buy	68.35	–5.18
4/12/04	Buy	58.76	Sell	64.24	5.48
Result		14.77		–4.11	
Spread net				10.66	10.66
Spread $ net				5,330.00	

EXHIBIT 4.6c

Buying the New Crop–Old Crop Cotton Spread On Reports of Increased Cotton Acres

	Action	CTN4	Action	CTZ4	Spread
3/1/04	Sell	74.52	Buy	68.35	–6.17
4/7/04	Buy	63.76	Sell	67.02	3.26
Result		10.76		–3.07	
Spread net				9.43	9.43
Spread $ net				4,715.00	

EXHIBIT 4.6d

Buying the New Crop–Old Crop Cotton Spread On Reports of Increased Cotton Acres

	Action	CTN4	Action	CTZ4	Spread
3/1/04	Sell	74.52	Buy	68.35	–6.17
4/12/04	Buy	60.69	Sell	64.24	3.55
Result		13.83		–4.11	
Spread net				9.72	9.72
Spread $ net				4,860.00	

EXHIBIT 4.7

Buying the New Crop–Old Crop Cotton Spread But Missing the Optimal Days

	Action	CTN4	Action	CTZ4	Spread
3/2/04	Sell	71.94	Buy	66.80	–5.14
4/8/04	Buy	60.69	Sell	64.24	3.55
Result		11.25		–2.56	
Spread net				8.69	8.69
Spread $ net				4,345.00	

As a spread trader, you won't always catch the market turns exactly. This makes a difference in trade results, but it is hardly a fatal one. Exhibit 4.7 assumes that you bought the July–December cotton spread on March 2.

Notice that the spread had already widened by 1.03 cents. The exhibit also assumes that this trade was unwound at the April 8 prices, which results in a 3.55 spread. On the chart in Exhibit 4.1, you can see that this one-day difference is a little bit costly, too. Still, this version of the trade would have earned $4,345. Granted, this is less than the trades shown in Exhibits 4.6c and 4.6d, but it is nevertheless a solid gain.

FALLING PRICES DON'T NECESSARILY LEAD TO A NARROWING SPREAD

By early May, the U.S. Department of Agriculture was forecasting record world cotton production and increasing cotton consumption. Unfortunately, from the viewpoint of those with physical cotton to sell, consumption wasn't increasing as fast as production. This kind of news sends cotton prices tobogganing down a fairly steep slope. From the point of view of new crop–old crop spread traders, this kind of news creates a strong impulse to store more cotton, and the new crop–old crop spread is likely to widen to motivate storage.

Suppose that on May 21, 2004, you had decided that the July–December cotton spread was poised to widen dramatically as the market began pushing cotton into warehouses. Based on this market opinion, you might have bought the July–December spread at the prices shown in Exhibit 4.8. Assume, further, that you unwound the trade just over a month later at the June 23 prices shown in the exhibit.

EXHIBIT 4.8

The Spread Widens as Prices Fall

	Action	CTN4	Action	CTZ4	Spread
5/21/04	Sell	63.00	Buy	58.71	–4.29
6/23/04	Buy	47.95	Sell	53.19	5.24
Result		15.05		–5.52	
Spread net				9.53	9.53
Spread $ net				4,765.00	

Notice that the price of the July contract dropped 15.05 cents per pound, yet the spread widened by 9.53 cents. Of course this is true because both prices fell, but the new crop price fell only a little more than a third as much as the old crop price. Remember that a spread can widen if both prices rise but the deferred price rises more than the nearby price or if both prices fall but the deferred price falls less than the nearby price.

As a result of this spread widening, this spread trade would have earned $4,765 for every one-lot spread you bought—given these prices. More than that, this seems a useful demonstration that price direction is not the issue. This should not be the primary concern of a spread trader. Rather, the supply-demand situation and the resulting storage impulse are the crucial considerations for new crop–old crop spread traders. While most of the market obsesses about whether the current news will lead to higher or lower prices, the new crop–old crop spread trader will be asking whether this means crops will go into storage or be pulled out of storage. That is what shapes the spread.

A WORD OF CAUTION

In the face of all the misinformed talk about the safety of spread trades, it seems important to remember that, like any of the spreads discussed in this book, the new crop–old crop cotton spread is a speculative trade. If you forecast the storage situation incorrectly, you may find yourself buying the spread when you should have sold it or vice versa. When this happens, your trade will take a loss.

Because cotton is a world crop, not just a U.S. crop, your market outlook must have world scope. You may at times see a report in which analysts foresee a smaller U.S. cotton crop. This would seem to mean that you can anticipate higher prices and a narrowing of the new crop–old crop spread. Yet the next paragraph of the report may indicate that these analysts are predicting that world production will be significantly greater. Still another part of the report may say that China has placed big orders with Indian cotton merchants rather than with U.S. merchants.

All of this matters when you are formulating a cotton spread outlook. The easiest way to be wrong is to ignore any of the aspects of these reports and to focus only on the U.S. situation.

CHAPTER 5

Unleaded Gasoline and Heating Oil Spreads

Physical commodities exhibit seasonal patterns that create predictable storage impulses and trading opportunities. Grains (soybeans are an oilseed, technically, but informal usage lumps them with the grains) are in constant demand, but harvest is once a year. The energy market is different. The supply of crude oil is constant, but demand for unleaded gasoline and heating oil is seasonal.

These seasonal patterns have given rise to a rationing system that helps to make sure the supplies will be there when consumers need them, an important part of which are the month-to-month futures price spreads. These spreads help the markets build incentive for producers to store commodities or to draw them out of storage, as the case may be. You can find parallel examples in all the physical commodity markets, but for now consider only unleaded gasoline and heating oil futures.

TRADING SEASONALITY

On May 27, 2004, you could have seen the heating oil spreads shown in Exhibit 5.1. You can find similar price arrays in any quote source—print or screen. The table also shows the prices that you would have seen for the same contract months on May 29, 1998, and the month-to-month spreads.

Although many quote services give these prices in cents per gallon (the June 2004 price would be 98.78), this table converts the prices into dollars per gallon. The first thing you probably notice is how different the 2004 and 1998 prices are. More to the point, notice the spreads. In both

EXHIBIT 5.1

Heating Oil Futures Price Spreads

	5/27/04		5/29/98	
	Price	**Spread**	**Price**	**Spread**
Jun	0.9878		0.3910	
Jul	0.9930	0.0052	0.4037	0.0127
Aug	0.9970	0.0040	0.4167	0.0130
Sep	1.0020	0.0050	0.4312	0.0145

years, the prices climb higher the farther out they go. The July price in either case is higher than the June, and so on. This means that the market will pay, say, $0.0142 per gallon more for September 2004 delivery than for June 2004 delivery. The 2004 market is suggesting, in the mildest terms, that storage might be a good thing. The 1998 market is more nearly insisting on storage.

In the grain markets, this price pattern is called a *carry market.* In the New York energy and metals markets, it is called a *contango* market, or a market in *contango.* Regardless of what you call them, these positive spreads encourage storage. In 1998, as the summer wore on, some of the spreads widened to as much as 0.0160—that is 1.6 cents per gallon. The wider the spread, the more of the storage cost the market is paying. Grain and oil merchants can trade these spreads to lock in that payment and reduce their cost of carrying inventory. When the cost of carrying inventory decreases, it follows that it will be easier for those who have inventory to contemplate storing it.

The cost of carry consists of the storage, interest, shrinkage, and financing costs. The full cost of carry defines the upper limit of carry spreads. Whatever that cost is, positive spreads in that market will not widen more than that.

Contrast the May 27, 2004, heating oil market with the unleaded gasoline futures market on the same day and a month earlier as shown in Exhibit 5.2.

Notice that in this market, the nearby price is the highest one, and each subsequent price is lower, which results in negative spreads. In the grain markets, this is called an *inverted market.* In the New York markets, this is a *backwardated market,* or a *market in backwardation.* The message here is that gasoline demand is high relative to supply and that the

EXHIBIT 5.2

Unleaded Gasoline Futures Price Spreads

	5/27/04		4/27/04	
	Price	Spread	Price	Spread
Jun	1.3852		1.2017	
Jul	1.2806	–0.1046	1.1827	–0.0190
Aug	1.2286	–0.0520	1.1482	–0.0345
Sep	1.1751	–0.0535	1.0987	–0.0495

market will pay a premium for immediate delivery. And notice what happened to the premium in just one month. On April 27, the market was paying $0.1030 per gallon more for June delivery than for September delivery. By May 27, this premium had climbed to $0.2101 per gallon. You can see that while the spreads in a carry, or contango, market can widen only to the level of the full cost of carry, no such economic limit constrains spreads in an inverted, or backwardated, market. In effect, an inverted or backwardated market penalizes storage.

This only makes sense. Unleaded gasoline futures are likely to be in carry or contango mode, or only slightly inverted, in the winter months when people don't drive quite as much and gasoline demand slacks off. As summer approaches and the heavy driving season draws closer, the spreads become more and more negative to draw gasoline out of storage. The April 27–May 27 contrast shows the market getting ready for the summer driving season. This pattern will repeat in varying degree every year.

WIDER AND NARROWER

These negative gasoline spreads (and the same thing happens in the grains, metals, and other energy markets) create a bit of a problem in terminology. Start with the heating oil spreads in Exhibit 5.1. The August–September 1998 spread is $0.0145. If that spread is $0.0155 a month later, it is clearly widening. If it is $0.0135 a month later, it is clearly narrowing. Following the same logic, if this spread goes to –$0.0100 on some later date, it has narrowed even more. If it then goes to –$0.0500, it has narrowed yet more.

Granted there is more numerical space between –$0.0100 and –$0.0500 than there is between $0.0145 and $0.0135. However, both spread changes are in the same direction, and in the interest of spread logic, it seems useful to think of widening and narrowing in this way:

- When a positive spread becomes more positive, it is widening (0.0145 to 0.0155 is widening).
- When a positive spread becomes less positive, it is narrowing (0.0145 to 0.0135 is narrowing).
- When a negative spread becomes less negative, it is widening (–0.05 to –0.01 is widening).
- When a negative spread becomes more negative, it is narrowing (–0.05 to –0.10 is narrowing).

The last two bulleted items may take some getting used to, but they allow the claim that the June–July unleaded gasoline spread of 2004 narrowed by $0.0856 per gallon, from –$0.0190 to –$0.1046 during the month shown. This, in turn, will help keep track of spread trade structure in a sensible way.

MARKET BACKGROUND–UNLEADED GASOLINE, MAY 2004

If you remember the energy situation in the spring of 2004, this narrowing of the unleaded gasoline futures spreads should not seem surprising. The war in Iraq and the threat of terrorism elsewhere created concern that crude oil supplies could be interrupted at any moment. At the same time, demand for crude oil and refined oil products was at an all-time high. In addition to shifting American driving habits, demand from places such as China and India was rising sharply. This cast doubt on the adequacy of supplies, even without supply interruption.

These concerns about supply adequacy find ready expression in the price spreads. Because there is no economic constraint on these inverted spreads, a market will bid up the nearby price, or back off on the deferred prices, until gasoline (or corn or copper) begins to flow out of storage and into the spot market. The chart of Exhibit 5.3 makes it clear what was going on in late April and May of 2004.

You can see that all four prices move around during this period, but the July, August, and September prices move more or less horizontally, while the June price rises sharply. Clearly, the market was bidding up the price of gasoline for June delivery to a level that would induce those with inventory in storage to move it out. The chart makes it difficult to see that the August–September spread narrowed slightly (or became more inverted) during this period, and the July–August spread narrowed slightly more. But it

EXHIBIT 5-3

Unleaded Gasoline Spreads

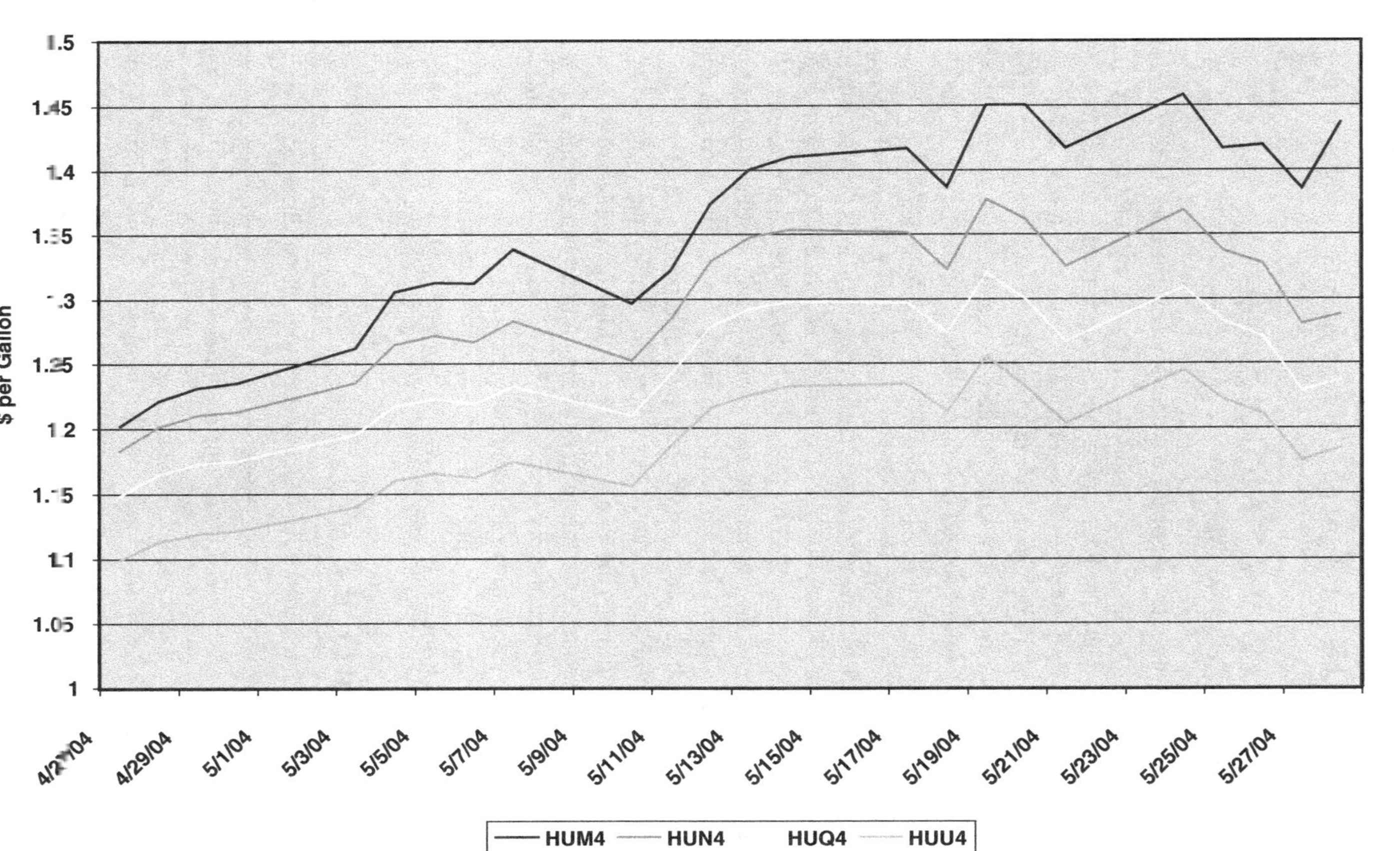

should be clear that the June–July spread narrowed considerably—from –0.0190 to –0.1492. Still, the principal message of this exhibit is that the market was bidding up the price of June gasoline to pull it out of storage.

STRUCTURING A GASOLINE SPREAD TRADE

The spread logic that applies to a gasoline spread trade is that you want to buy a thing you expect will gain in value and sell a thing you expect will lose value. That is, you buy a widening spread and sell a narrowing spread. You buy or sell these seasonal spreads in terms of what you do with the back, or deferred, month of the pair you are trading. Thus, anticipating a narrowing June–July spread, you sell the July contract (HUN4) and buy the June contract (HUM4). Based on the April 27 and May 27 prices shown in Exhibit 5.2, this trade would have earned $3,595.20 with the spread narrowing by $0.0856 per gallon, as Exhibit 5.4 shows.

The easiest way to calculate spread results is to first subtract the bought price of each contract from the sold price. The Result row shows the remainders generated by this subtraction. The number under HUN4 in the Spread net row sums the two results to show that this trade earned $0.0856 per gallon. The minus sign in the Spread net row under Spread indicates that the spread narrowed by that amount. The fact that the two Spread net numbers match is a useful check. Finally, the value in the Spread $ net row multiplies the Spread net by 42,000, the number of gallons in one contract. Among other things, calculating spread results this way makes it simple to calculate the results of larger positions. If you sold 100 spreads, you would simply move the decimal place.

You might think that trading an even more deferred contract than the July contract could generate even greater earnings. In theory, that is true.

EXHIBIT 5.4

Selling the June–July Unleaded Gasoline Spread

	Action	HUM4	Action	HUN4	Spread
4/27/04	Buy	1.2017	Sell	1.1827	–0.0190
5/27/04	Sell	1.3852	Buy	1.2806	–0.1046
Result		0.1835		–0.0979	
Spread net				0.0856	–0.0856
Spread $ net				3,595.20	

EXHIBIT 5.5

Selling the June–September Unleaded Gasoline Spread

	Action	HUM4	Action	HUU4	Spread
4/27/04	Buy	1.2017	Sell	1.0987	–0.1030
5/27/04	Sell	1.3852	Buy	1.1751	–0.2101
Result		0.1835		–0.0764	
Spread net				0.1071	–0.1071
Spread $ net				4,498.20	

Exhibit 5.5 illustrates how a June–September spread might have fared assuming Exhibit 5.2 prices.

A WORD OF CAUTION

Even though the June–September spread seems to generate a larger gain, you should check on the bid-ask spread before you make such a trade—in any market. In some markets, at some times, the deferred months are less frequently traded and less liquid as a result. This lesser liquidity makes itself felt in several ways, one key one being a wider bid-ask spread.

You should check this with your broker. If the bid-ask seems reasonable, the spread that uses contract months that are farther apart may be worth trading. If the back month bid-ask is very much wider than the nearby bid-ask, it will take a larger price move to overcome the back month bid-ask. Put another way, the bid-ask spread is your largest transaction cost. The larger the transaction cost, the less potential gain filters through to your account.

REVERSING THE SEASONAL SPREAD TRADE

Once the peak driving season arrives, the unleaded gasoline spreads will start to widen, or become less inverted. For example, the August–September unleaded gasoline spread was –0.0535 on May 27, 2004 (as Exhibit 5.2 shows). By July 30, 2004, it had widened enough to be slightly positive at 0.0054. This is a $0.0589 per gallon spread widening.

Knowing that something along these lines is bound to start happening around the end of May or early June, you can buy the August–September spread by buying September futures (HUU4) and selling August futures (HUQ4). Exhibit 5.6 shows how such a trade can be expected to perform assuming the May 27 and July 30, 2004, prices for these contracts.

EXHIBIT 5.6

Buying the August–September Unleaded Gasoline Spread

	Action	HUQ4	Action	HUU4	Spread
5/27/04	Sell	1.2286	Buy	1.1751	–0.0535
7/30/04	Buy	1.2995	Sell	1.3049	0.0054
Result		–0.0709		0.1298	
Spread net				0.0589	0.0589
Spread $ net				2473.80	

While it is true that carry, or contango, spreads can widen only to the limit of the full cost of carry, a deeply inverted market that is about to start motivating storage again can create a great deal of opportunity for spread buyers.

MARKET BACKGROUND–HEATING OIL

Naturally enough, the heating oil pattern is the reverse of the unleaded gasoline pattern. Winter is the peak usage time, and summer and fall are the inventory building time. That is, in summer and fall, you can expect to see a carry, or contango, market as futures prices adjust to motivate storage as the market strives to build up supplies against anticipated winter needs. When the first big cold snap hits in the northeastern United States, which is the primary heating oil consuming area, the market is likely to invert, or backwardate, sharply to draw these supplies out of storage. Actually, the winter month contracts may remain inverted during the inventory building period, but usually they are only slightly so.

Exhibit 5.7 charts the January and March 2004 prices (HOF4 and HOH4, respectively) and the January and March 2005 prices (HOF5 and HOH5, respectively) from September 2 to October 24 of 2003 and 2004.

The lower pair of lines represent the 2004 contracts in the early fall of 2003. You can see at a glance that the January–March spread was slightly inverted in 2003 and that this spread varied only slightly through this period.

The upper pair of lines represent the 2005 contracts in the early fall of 2004. The prices are much higher than those of a year earlier. What is more important, the spread was slightly narrower (more inverted) on September 2, 2004, than it was on September 2, 2003. While it was –0.0325 on that date in 2003, it was –0.0370 on that date in 2004.

It isn't hard to figure out how to account for the difference between the two years. In 2003, crude oil supplies were reasonably ample as were heating oil stocks. Also, the long-term weather forecast for the northeastern United States called for a mild winter. As a result, these spreads changed very little all heating season.

The 2004 heating oil market situation couldn't have been more different. Along with all the geopolitical concerns mentioned earlier, early fall hurricanes caused heavy damage to Gulf of Mexico oil drilling rigs. This exacerbated the crude oil supply problem and helped drive crude oil prices up to record levels (though not in inflation-adjusted terms). On the weather front, forecasters were calling for a harsh winter in the northeastern United States. In short, supply and demand forces were pulling in opposite directions, and you can see that in the 2004 plots of Exhibit 5.7. The January–March 2005 spread had already narrowed, or inverted, significantly by the end of October 2004.

This does not mean that heating oil spread traders had missed their opportunity, because they could count on the first cold snap of the season causing a major additional narrowing, or deepening of the inversion, of these heating oil spreads. Remember, an inverted market knows no limits. To cite but one example of what can happen to these spreads, consider the February–March 2000 spread as it appeared in December 1999 and January 2000. On December 28, 1999, February 2000 heating oil futures were trading at 0.6977, and March 2000 futures were trading at 0.6727. The spread was –0.0250. On January 28, 2000, the February–March spread was –0.1974 with February futures trading at 0.9251.

Even though the October 24, 2004, January–March 2005 spread was narrower (more inverted) than normal, a severe cold snap after the first of the year could have narrowed it more, especially if nothing happened to improve the heating oil supply situation.

If this had been your outlook, you might have sold the spread on October 24, 2004, by selling the March contract and buying the January contract. Assume that supplies remained tight and that right after the new year, the snows fell and frigid winds swept through the northeastern states. You might have seen results more or less like those shown in Exhibit 5.8. Based on these hypothetical January 5, 2005, prices, the January–March heating oil spread could have earned $7,236.60 on this $0.1723 per gallon spread narrowing.

A WORD OF CAUTION

The most obvious source of trouble for traders of seasonal spreads is an atypical season. When the economy is slumping or the threat of terrorism

EXHIBIT 5.7

2003 and 2004 Heating Oil Spreads

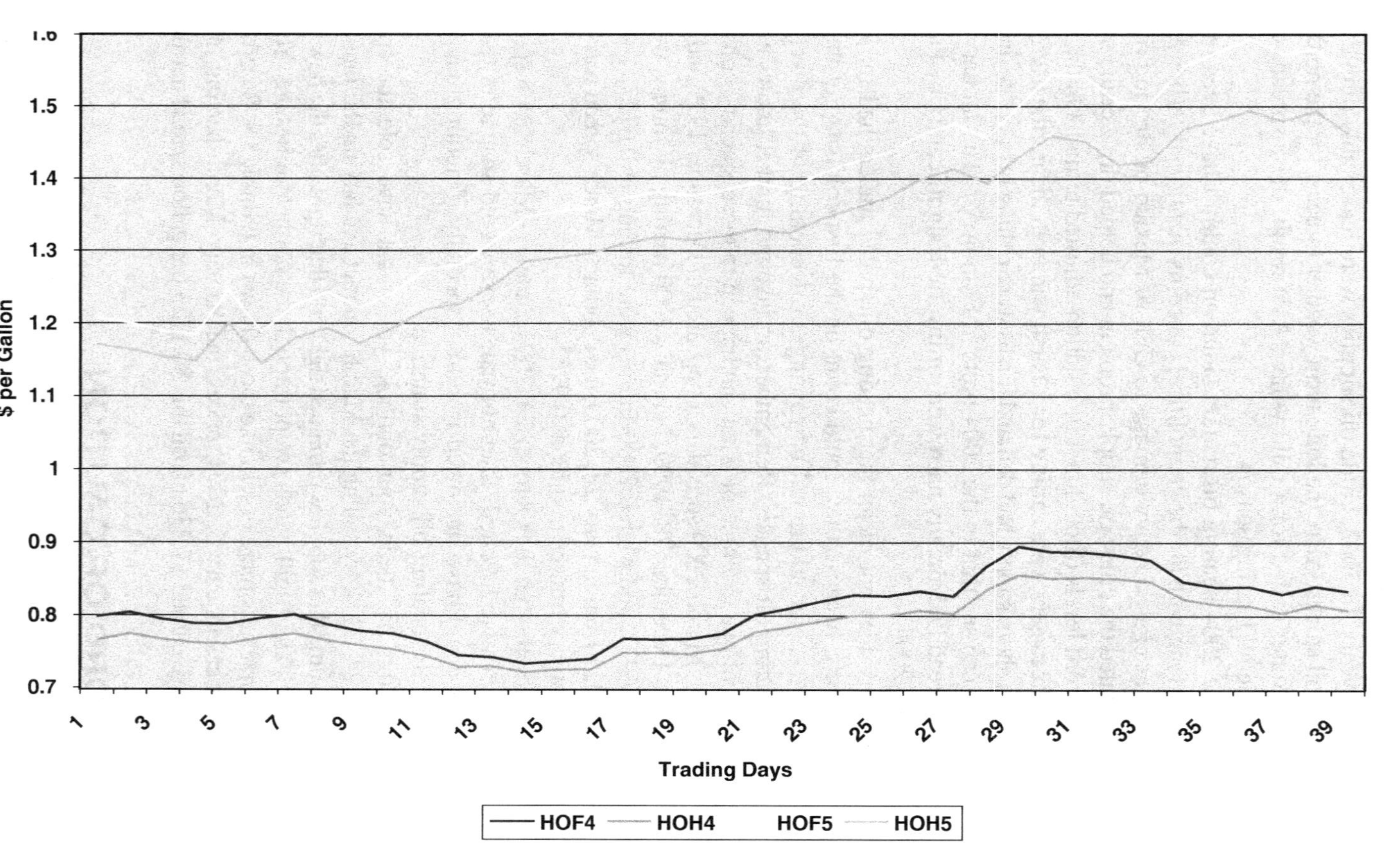

EXHIBIT 5.8

Selling the January–March Heating Oil Spread

	Action	HOF5	Action	HOH5	Spread
10/24/04	Buy	1.5425	Sell	1.4620	–0.0805
1/5/05	Sell	1.8452	Buy	1.5924	–0.2528
Result		0.3027		–0.1304	
Spread net				0.1723	–0.1723
Spread $ net				7,236.60	

weighs on people's minds, summer trip plans may be put on hold. The news media often cover what this does to airline revenues, but hard times and concerns about safety can affect automobile driving patterns as well. When this happens, gasoline demand may fall off. Similarly, the forecast of warmer than usual winter weather can lessen demand for heating oil.

Slack demand means lower prices in most cases, but it also means atypical spread behavior. What matters isn't that prices will be lower but that the spread will not narrow as it usually does because it is less imperative than usual to draw supplies out of storage. When that happens, trades that depend on this narrowing will at least underperform and most likely take losses. If the early signals suggest any of these possibilities, you may want to sit out this dance.

Another important cautionary note is to remember that these are increasingly international markets. It has long been true that international concerns affect supply—especially of the crude oil that refiners need. However, growing Asian demand for refined products can affect these spreads. It is becoming increasingly unwise to consider only the U.S. energy demand situation in planning these trades.

CHAPTER 6

Crude Oil Futures Calendar Spreads

A calendar spread balances a nearby contract in a given market against a deferred contract in the same market but typically not very deferred. The energy markets trade on a monthly cycle, so if the June crude oil futures contract is the one that's nearby, a calendar spread trader would typically balance that against the July crude oil contract, the next one out.

You will see references in trading literature to seasonal spreads, new crop–old crop spreads, and calendar spreads. In a way, these are all versions of the same thing. They all structure spread trades in one market—be it Treasury note futures, soybean futures, heating oil futures, or crude oil futures—and they structure these trades in terms of how traders believe one contract month will perform relative to another.

Apparently, when a market lacks the seasonality of the grains with their new crop–old crop dynamic or of the refined energy products with their peak demand seasons at opposite ends of the year, then these spreads are called calendar spreads. Thus you trade crude oil futures calendar spreads or Treasury futures calendar spreads. The supply-demand information of these spreads is similar to that of the grain markets or the refined energy product markets, but there is no seasonality to these spreads.

In structure, there is little or no difference between a calendar spread and the seasonal spreads or the new crop–old crop spreads of the heating oil, unleaded gasoline, or the various agricultural futures markets—apart from the fact that traders in the agricultural markets often trade contracts for relatively distant delivery—e.g., a December 2005–December 2004 corn spread.

TO STORE OR NOT TO STORE

At least in the physical commodities, all these futures spreads play a role in the operation of a market-driven rationing system. When supply is seasonal but demand is constant, as in the grains, these spreads signal the need to store supplies against future needs and, later, to draw supplies out of storage when demand motivates that. Other commodities are in constant supply but experience seasonal demand. Again, the price differentials of the spreads help the markets to regulate the flow of goods into and out of storage.

Consider the unleaded gasoline and heating oil markets. In late May 2004, heating oil was not much on anyone's mind, and the market wanted heating oil in storage to build supplies in readiness for the coming winter. Storage costs something, of course, so heating oil prices in spring and summer will typically look more or less as shown in Exhibit 6.1.

Notice that the July heating oil price is slightly higher than the June price and that the August price is higher yet. The stronger the storage impulse, the wider these spreads will be—to a point. These spreads will never widen beyond the full cost of storage, which is known as *full carry.*

The unleaded gasoline spreads go the other way. Each price is lower than the one before, which leads to negative spreads. The unleaded gasoline market is paying a premium for immediate delivery and penalizing storage. Notice that the differences between the gasoline prices are much greater than the differences between the heating oil prices. The more the market wants gasoline out of storage, the greater these differences will become. If the market senses a supply crisis in the offing, these spreads can increase a great deal.

A market with lower and lower prices, such as these unleaded gasoline futures prices, is called an *inverted market* in grain circles and a *backwardated market* in energy and metals circles. The terms are equivalent, but *inverted* seems more descriptive.

EXHIBIT 6.1

Signs of Seasonal Storage Impulses

	Unleaded Gasoline Futures	Spread	Heating Oil Futures	Spread
Jun	1.4165		1.0273	
Jul	1.3387	–0.0778	1.0307	0.0034
Aug	1.2827	–0.0560	1.0327	0.0020

Crude oil futures represent a somewhat special case in this context. For one thing, crude oil is in constant supply and, generally speaking, in constant demand. Consider that during the part of the year when unleaded gasoline demand is greatest, refiners must buy crude oil if they are to meet that demand. When heating oil demand is greatest, refiners must buy crude oil. Demand for the refined products may be seasonal, but crude oil demand is not. Furthermore, crude oil doesn't store well. Heating oil and unleaded gasoline store well, but crude oil does not—at least, not for long periods.

Because of the constant supply-constant demand situation in the crude oil market, crude oil futures spreads are typically inverted, or backwardated. When you pull up this market on a quote screen or look at a quote page, you will typically see a price array similar to that shown in Exhibit 6.2.

Keep in mind that these prices are dollars per gallon and that one NYMEX crude oil futures contract contains 1000 gallons. Accordingly, the Apr–Mar spread is –$1.50 per barrel. The May–Apr spread is –$0.73 per barrel, and so on. This is how the crude oil spread situation looks most of the time. That is not to say it is an invariable condition of this market. You can find positive spreads in this market from time to time, but this seems to be an unstable condition, and the spreads typically revert to their normal inverted condition after a short time.

Of course, the real interest in these spreads is not what they are at one moment but how that snapshot might compare with one taken at some later date. Consider what happens to the first two of the spreads in Exhibit 6.2 as time passes. Exhibit 6.3 shows the prices and relevant spreads on February 2 and February 20, 2004, the last trading day for the March 2004 contract, and on March 22, the last trading day for the April 2004 contract.

EXHIBIT 6.2

Crude Oil Futures Prices (2/2/04)

	Futures Price	Month-to-Month Spreads
Mar	34.98	
Apr	33.48	–1.50
May	32.75	–0.73
Jun	[illegible]	[illegible]
Jul	31.67	–0.51

EXHIBIT 6.3

Tracking the Crude Oil Futures Price Spreads

	2/2/04		2/20/04		3/22/04	
	Futures Price	Spread	Futures Price	Spread	Futures Price	Spread
Mar	34.98		35.60			
Apr	33.48	−1.50	34.26	−1.34	37.11	
May	32.75	−0.73	33.60	−0.66	37.05	−0.06

(Notice here and in what follows that crude oil futures contracts stop trading somewhere around the 20th of the month before the delivery date. Exchange contract specifications read like riddles. The official language concerning the last trading day for crude oil contracts says that they will stop trading "on the 3rd business day prior to the 25th calendar day of the month preceding the delivery month" and goes on to say that "if the 25th day is a nonbusiness day, trading shall cease on the 3rd business day prior to the business day preceding the 25th calendar day." In short, the March contract will stop trading in February, the April will stop trading in March, and so on.)

Notice that both the April–March spread and the May–April spread widened from month to month. A spread, remember, can widen if it is positive and becomes more positive (as when it goes from 0.05 to 0.20) or if it is negative and becomes less negative (as when the April–March spread goes from −1.50 to −1.34 as shown in Exhibit 6.3).

STRUCTURING A CRUDE OIL CALENDAR SPREAD TRADE

Logically enough, you want to buy this spread when you anticipate a widening and sell it when you anticipate a narrowing. You buy or sell this spread in terms of what you do with the more remote month. That is, to buy the Apr–Mar spread on February 2, 2004, you would have bought April futures (CLJ4) and sold March futures (CLH4). If you had unwound this trade on February 20, this spread would have performed as shown in Exhibit 6.4.

THE SPREAD IS THE THING

Breathes there a person with soul so dead, to butcher the Sir Walter Scott line, that he or she doesn't remember what happened to crude oil prices in 2004? They went up and then went up some more.

EXHIBIT 6.4

Buying the April–March Crude Oil Calendar Spread

	Action	CLH4	Action	CLJ4	Spread
2/2/04	Sell	34.98	Buy	33.48	–1.50
2/20/04	Buy	35.60	Sell	34.26	–1.34
Result		–0.62		0.78	
Spread net				0.16	0.16
Spread $ net				160.00	

It may seem odd to be selling crude oil futures in a year when prices rose and then rose some more. But this is rather like another market truism which suggests that almost everyone you meet who has any investments at all—even just a 401(k) plan—can tell you approximately where the Dow is trading but will have no idea where the S&P 500 is trading. Yet it is the S&P 500 that most investment professionals use to benchmark performance.

Similarly, almost everybody can tell you about crude oil prices, yet few people or no one can tell you anything about these spreads. Despite this general lack of awareness of the spreads on the part of most people, the spreads are the bread-and-butter trades of many a professional energy trader.

Still, you cannot simply trade these spreads mechanically. Suppose you generalized from the February and March spread data shown in Exhibits 6.1–6.3 and concluded that you could do well if you automatically bought the May–April spread on the day the March futures cease trading, or *go off the board* in market vernacular. A month later, on the day the April futures go off the board, you would unwind the May–Apr spread and buy the June–May spread, and keep doing this more or less in perpetuity. Exhibit 6.5 shows details and results for the April–March, May–April, June–May, July–June, and August–July spread trades covering the period from February 2 to June 22, 2004, the day the July contract went off the board.

Exhibit 6.6 calls attention to the spread change for each month and shows the sum of these five trade results in dollar terms.

You can see that the spread widened four of the five times shown. The –0.32 of trade C is the only narrowing, and this trade made a $320 loss because of this narrowing. Yet the net result of these five one-lot spread trades was a $1300 gain. That one loss, considered in this context may seem like no big deal.

EXHIBIT 6.5

A Sequence of Crude Oil Calendar Spreads

A

	Action	CLH4	Action	CLJ4	Spread
2/2/04	Sell	34.98	Buy	33.48	–1.50
2/20/04	Buy	35.60	Sell	34.26	–1.34
Result		–0.62		0.78	
Spread net				0.16	0.16
Spread $ net				160.00	

B

	Action	CLJ4	Action	CLK4	Spread
2/20/04	Sell	34.26	Buy	33.60	–0.66
3/22/04	Buy	37.11	Sell	37.05	–0.06
Result		–2.85		3.45	
Spread net				0.60	0.60
Spread $ net				600.00	

C

	Action	CLK4	Action	CLM4	Spread
3/22/04	Sell	37.05	Buy	36.27	–0.78
4/20/04	Buy	37.60	Sell	36.50	–1.10
Result		–0.55		0.23	
Spread net				–0.32	–0.32
Spread $ net				–320.00	

D

	Action	CLM4	Action	CLN4	Spread
4/20/04	Sell	36.50	Buy	36.06	–0.44
5/20/04	Buy	40.92	Sell	40.80	–0.12
Result		–4.42		4.74	
Spread net				0.32	0.32
Spread $ net				320.00	

EXHIBIT 6.5

A Sequence of Crude Oil Calendar Spreads (*Continued*)

E

	Action	CLN4	Action	CLQ4	Spread
5/20/04	Sell	40.80	Buy	40.40	–0.40
6/22/04	Buy	38.11	Sell	38.25	0.14
Result		2.69		–2.15	
Spread net				0.54	0.54
Spread $ net				540.00	

EXHIBIT 6.6

Highlighting Spread Results

Trade	Spread Net	Spread $ Net
A	0.16	160.00
B	0.60	600.00
C	–0.32	–320.00
D	0.32	320.00
E	0.54	540.00
Five-Month Total		1,300.00

But expand the context a few months, and you might draw a different conclusion. Exhibit 6.7 shows the September–August, October–September, and November–October spread trades. (The lettering begun in Exhibit 6.5 is continued in Exhibit 6.7.)

Exhibit 6.8 repeats the data from Exhibit 6.6 and adds the results of these last three calendar spread trades, again assuming that you automatically bought the spread each of these eight times.

The two additional losses are big ones, and they shrink the total gain from these eight trades to only $340. This hardly seems worth the trouble.

Yet suppose you had sold the September–August and October–September spreads. Change those two negatives to positives, and the eight trades would have gained $2,340. This raises the question of how anyone could know to sell the spread these two times when buying had been working so well for quite a few months.

Two things come to mind. First, it is important to remember that while crude oil futures spreads are normally inverted, or backwardated,

EXHIBIT 6.7

Expanding the Series of Trades

F

	Action	CLQ4	Action	CLU4	Spread
6/22/04	Sell	38.25	Buy	38.25	0.00
7/20/04	Buy	40.86	Sell	40.44	–0.42
Result		–2.61		2.19	
Spread net				–0.42	–0.42
Spread $ net				–420.00	

G

	Action	CLU4	Action	CLV4	Spread
7/20/04	Sell	40.44	Buy	39.88	–0.56
8/20/04	Buy	47.86	Sell	46.72	–1.14
Result		–7.42		6.84	
Spread net				–0.58	–0.58
Spread $ net				–580.00	

H

	Action	CLV4	Action	CLX4	Spread
8/20/04	Sell	46.72	Buy	46.34	–0.38
9/21/04	Buy	47.10	Sell	46.76	–0.34
Result		–0.38		0.42	
Spread net				0.04	0.04
Spread $ net				40.00	

they aren't always. It follows that while the spreads typically widen as the nearby contract approaches the end of trading, they won't always.

Second, in figuring out if a particular month is a normal one in which the spread can be expected to widen or one of the months in which the spread is likely to narrow, you can track the spread itself to derive useful information. Exhibit 6.9 shows the May–April spread from February 2, almost a month before the time to put on this spread trade, and the September–August spread from May 20, right at a month the before time to put on this version of the spread.

EXHIBIT 6.8

The Limitations of a Too Mechanical Trading Approach

Trade	Spread Net	Spread $ Net
A	0.16	160.00
B	0.60	600.00
C	–0.32	–320.00
D	0.32	320.00
E	0.54	540.00
F	–0.42	–420.00
G	–0.58	–580.00
H	0.04	40.00
Eight-Month Total		340.00

Exhibit 6.10 provides the prices and spread calculations that underlie the graphic presentation. (The contract symbol for April 2004, recall, is CLJ4, for May it is CLK4, for August it is CLQ4, and for September it is CLU4.)

Two aspects of these arrays seem to matter. Both spreads widen during the month prior to the putting on of the trades. The May–April spread moves from –0.73 on February 2 to –0.58 on February 19. That is 0.15 less negative, or wider. The September–August spread moves from –0.61 on May 20 to 0.03 on June 21. It has become 0.64 wider.

Apparently, the crucial difference between these two situations is not the amount of widening but the crossing over into positive territory. In the normal course of events, this positive spread seems what chemists might call an unstable condition—now you see it, now you don't. At any rate, in the crude oil market, positive spreads seem unlikely to remain in the market for long. When these spreads return to the more normal inverted (negative) condition, the spread will narrow. Therefore, this would seem an opportune time to be a spread seller.

Granted, two short data series don't make a case any more than two robins make a spring. However, these observations seem to hold for the eight spreads cited in this discussion. If another year's worth of similar data seemed to add support, you could gain more confidence that this is a valid way to decide whether to buy or sell the crude oil calendar spreads.

REFINING THE TRADING APPROACH

Tracking the calendar spreads can prove useful in at least one more way. The example trades provided here have assumed that you would unwind

EXHIBIT 6.9

Crude Oil Calendar Spreads

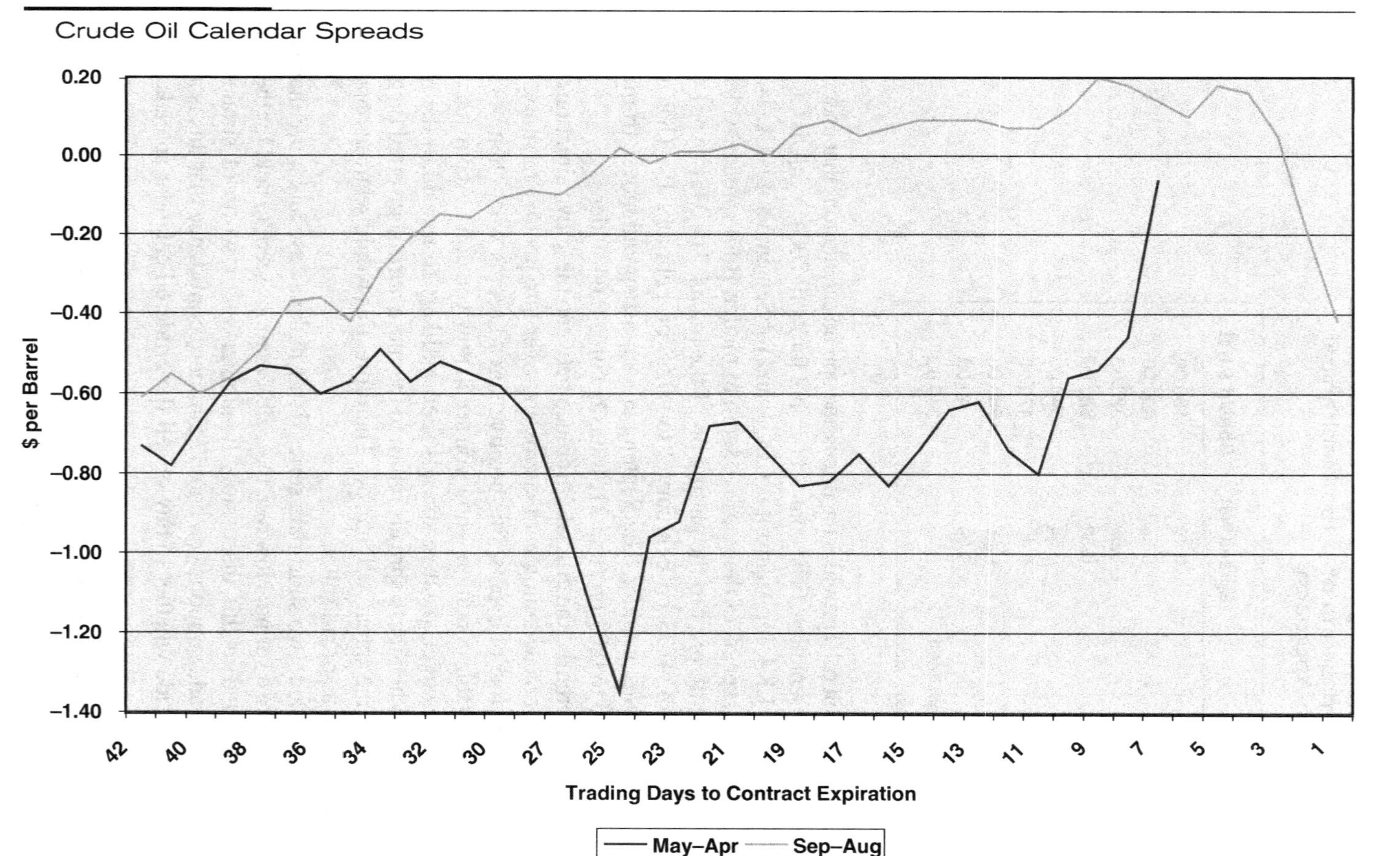

EXHIBIT 6.10

Tracking Two Crude Oil Futures Calendar Spreads

	CLJ4	CLK4	May–Apr Spread		CLQ4	CLU4	Sep–Aug Spread
2/2/04	33.48	32.75	–0.73	5/20/04	40.40	39.79	–0.61
2/3/04	32.82	32.04	–0.78	5/21/04	39.56	39.01	–0.55
2/4/04	31.99	31.32	–0.67	5/24/04	41.24	40.64	–0.60
2/5/04	32.17	31.60	–0.57	5/25/04	40.68	40.12	–0.56
2/6/04	31.74	31.21	–0.53	5/26/04	40.38	39.89	–0.49
2/9/04	32.03	31.49	–0.54	5/27/04	39.28	38.91	–0.37
2/10/04	33.01	32.41	–0.60	5/28/04	39.71	39.35	–0.36
2/11/04	33.21	32.64	–0.57	6/1/04	42.19	41.77	–0.42
2/12/04	33.38	32.89	–0.49	6/2/04	39.93	39.64	–0.29
2/13/04	34.10	33.53	–0.57	6/3/04	39.23	39.02	–0.21
2/17/04	34.86	34.34	–0.52	6/4/04	38.53	38.38	–0.15
2/18/04	34.48	33.93	–0.55	6/7/04	38.75	38.59	–0.16
2/19/04	34.64	34.06	–0.58	6/8/04	37.43	37.32	–0.11
2/20/04	34.26	33.60	–0.66	6/9/04	37.74	37.65	–0.09
2/23/04	34.35	33.47	–0.88	6/10/04	38.65	38.55	–0.10
2/24/04	34.58	33.45	–1.13	6/14/04	37.78	37.83	–0.05
2/25/04	35.68	34.33	–1.35	6/15/04	37.42	37.44	0.02
2/26/04	35.51	34.55	–0.96	6/16/04	37.65	37.63	–0.02
2/27/04	36.16	35.24	–0.92	6/17/04	38.81	38.82	0.01
3/1/04	36.86	36.18	–0.68	6/18/04	39.00	39.01	0.01
3/2/04	36.66	35.99	–0.67	6/21/04	37.77	37.80	0.03
3/3/04	35.80	35.05	–0.75	6/22/04	38.25	38.25	0.00
3/4/04	36.64	35.81	–0.83	6/23/04	37.57	37.64	0.07
3/5/04	37.26	36.44	–0.82	6/24/04	37.93	38.02	0.09
3/8/04	36.57	35.82	–0.75	6/25/04	37.55	37.60	0.05
3/9/04	36.28	35.45	–0.83	6/28/04	36.24	36.31	0.07
3/10/04	36.10	35.36	–0.74	6/29/04	35.66	35.75	0.09
3/11/04	36.78	36.14	–0.64	6/30/04	37.05	37.14	0.09
3/12/04	36.19	35.57	–0.62	7/1/04	38.74	38.83	0.09
3/15/04	37.44	36.70	–0.74	7/2/04	38.39	38.46	0.07
3/16/04	37.48	36.68	–0.80	7/6/04	39.65	39.72	0.07
3/17/04	38.18	37.62	–0.56	7/7/04	39.08	39.20	0.12
3/18/04	37.93	37.39	–0.54	7/8/04	40.33	40.53	0.20
3/19/04	38.08	37.62	–0.46	7/9/04	39.96	40.14	0.18
3/22/04	37.11	37.05	–0.06	7/12/04	39.50	39.64	0.14
				7/13/04	39.44	39.54	0.10

Continued

EXHIBIT 6.10

Tracking Two Crude Oil Futures Calendar Spreads (*Continued*)

CLJ4	CLK4	May–Apr Spread		CLQ4	CLU4	Sep–Aug Spread
			7/14/04	40.97	41.15	0.18
			7/15/04	40.77	40.93	0.16
			7/16/04	41.25	41.30	0.05
			7/19/04	41.64	41.44	–0.20
			7/20/04	40.86	40.44	–0.42

EXHIBIT 6.11

When Early Unwinding Produces Benefits

	Action	CLH4	Action	CLJ4	Spread
2/2/04	Sell	34.98	Buy	33.48	–1.50
2/20/04	Buy	35.19	Sell	34.86	–0.33
Result		–0.21		1.38	
Spread net				1.17	1.17
Spread $ net				1,170.00	

these trades on the last trading day of the front month and immediately put on the next spread. The results shown in Exhibit 6.8 suggest that this isn't a bad approach, yet there are times when unwinding the spread a few days earlier can be advantageous. There are other times when the behavior of the spread might suggest additional trades.

The Apr–Mar trade shown in Exhibit 6.4 earned $160 when the spread widened from –1.50 to –1.34 on the dates shown. However, on February 17, the spread was –0.33. If you had unwound at that price, the spread would have earned $1,170. Exhibit 6.11 shows the details.

Similarly, the July–June spread widened from –0.44 on April 20 to –0.12 on May 20 to earn $320. Yet, on May 19, this spread was slightly positive at 0.02. Unwinding on May 19 would have increased the earnings from $140 to $460. The August–July spread, which had widened by 0.54 between the dates shown, had actually been 0.21 wider on June 17.

Other kinds of opportunities exist as well. The September–August spread was zero on June 22, and prior spread behavior reinforced by news of possible crude oil supply interruptions might have prompted you to sell the

EXHIBIT 6.12

Finding Additional Opportunity to Trade

	Action	CLQ4	Action	CLU4	Spread
7/14/04	Buy	40.97	Sell	41.15	0.18
7/20/04	Sell	40.86	Buy	40.44	–0.42
Result		–0.11		0.71	
Spread net				0.60	–0.60
Spread $ net				600.00	

spread on that day in the expectation that it would narrow sharply. It did invert to –0.42, but before it did, it widened to 0.18 and then a bit more to 0.20.

This was either a signal for traders to panic or to sell more of this spread. Assume that you had sold another spread on July 14 with the spread at 0.18 and had unwound it on July 20. Exhibit 6.12 shows the details of this trade.

Opportunities such as the several pointed out don't always occur, but they do crop up often enough to reward diligent spread tracking.

A similar circumstance arose during the run of the May–April spread. On February 20, the spread was –0.66, and it ended at –0.06 on March 22. Before it widened, though, it narrowed a great deal. On February 25, it had dropped all the way to –1.35. Again, this is either a sign of impending disaster, or it is a buying opportunity. A bold trader who saw this as a time to buy more of this spread would have seen this second spread widen to 1.29 to gain $1,290.

A WORD OF CAUTION

The speculative nature of any spread trade cannot be stressed too much, and these crude oil calendar spread trades are no exception. The results highlighted in Exhibit 6.8 amply demonstrate what can happen when you make the wrong market call on these kinds of trades.

Even more, the results shown in Exhibit 6.8 seem to argue against taking this market for granted. Just because the spreads widen most of the time doesn't mean they always will. Because this is true, a mechanical trading approach is likely to bring disappointment. A long-time grain market analyst, where spread trading is a staple of trading life, said that to trade spreads, you have to know something about the market. You can't go only by technical factors. This seems no less true in the crude oil market.

To trade these crude oil calendar spreads effectively, you have to know, first, how these spreads are likely to behave. For this, there is no substitute for tracking the spreads. Second, you also have to know what news is in the market. Much of this is easy to find. A decision by the Saudi oil ministry to ship more oil will make headlines, after all. Fortunately, brokerage analysts can help you with this. They keep track of all the supply-demand information and generate helpful summaries in their reports.

That said, a crude oil calendar spread trading strategy that combines a systematic approach with careful market study and a dash of opportunism can generate solid results.

CHAPTER 7

Treasury Calendar Spreads

A Treasury futures calendar spread trade amounts to a synthetic money-market investment. As with a money-market investment—such as a certificate of deposit, a Treasury bill, commercial paper, or a money-market mutual fund—this trade offers modest returns but entails only small risk. More specifically, the returns these trades earn should come close to the 90-day repo rate. (*Repo* is short for repurchase agreement.) One important difference between a Treasury calendar spread and the repo market is that the repo market is open only to very large players such as the portfolio managers of pension funds and insurance company asset portfolios while Treasury calendar spreads are available to all futures traders.

A calendar spread is the easiest to build of all the interest rate spreads. Focusing on CBOT 10-year Treasury note futures, you trade the nearby contract and do the opposite with the next deferred contract. For example, in February, the March 10-year Treasury note futures contract is the nearby contract. If you buy that, you will sell the June 10-year contract, which is the next deferred contract. You can also use Treasury bond futures and five-year Treasury note futures to make these trades. The idea is the same.

WHAT'S IN THE NAME?

Treasury calendar spreads, sometimes called *calendar rolls,* probably generate their best results in the four roll months. The term *roll month* comes from the activity of risk managers who use these futures to hedge or otherwise manage interest rate risk. These people want nothing to do with the futures delivery process, yet they must often maintain their futures positions across the March, June, September, or December delivery months.

For example, a risk manager might buy June 10-year Treasury note futures in March and might need to maintain this coverage until sometime in July. To avoid getting tangled up in the June delivery process, this manager can roll the hedge in May. That is, he or she will sell the June futures and replace them by buying September futures. This action is *rolling the hedge*, hence the informal designation of February, May, August, and November as *roll months.*

Indeed, for many years, there has been a group of floor traders who emerge every roll month and make good livings by trading just during these four months. This activity helps to create deep and liquid markets for others—including spread traders.

CALENDAR SPREAD MARKET BACKGROUND

Calendar spread trades work the way they do for a variety of reasons. First, there is the matter of who might be operating in related markets that can affect the spreads and spread trades. The fact that risk managers often replace one hedge with another during the months before the delivery months contributes to how the calendar spreads perform. In addition to the risk managers, there are repo traders and cash-futures traders (loosely, basis traders). Second, there is the mechanics of fixed-income forward pricing. The spot price of the Treasury note from which the futures contract is derived responds to yield shifts. However, a futures price, even the nearby, is a kind of forward price, and forward prices are shaped by an interaction of the Treasury security coupon, the repo rate, and the amount of time to futures delivery.

RELATED TRADING ACTIVITY—THE REPO MARKET

Overnight and term repo rates are the financing benchmarks for all kinds of fixed-income transactions.Technically, a repo market participant sells a bond and agrees to buy it back the next day, or at some later time in the case of term repo, for a slightly higher price. On the other side of this trade is a reverse repo trader who initially buys the bond and subsequently sells it back for the slightly higher price.

The effect of the repo and reverse repo trade is to borrow money in the case of the repo and lend it in the case of the reverse repo. Significantly, these transactions are collateralized by the securities that are exchanged. If the borrower defaults, the lender still has the security to sell. This is in contrast to the fed funds markets or the commercial paper markets in which no collateral exchanges hands.

Repo traders think in terms of many millions of dollars at a time. No one wishing to repo or reverse the equivalent of one $100,000 par futures contract is welcome in their midst. Yet the fact that many hundreds of millions of dollars' worth of securities are reversed in and repoed out every day makes repo rates highly reliable benchmarks and contributes mightily to the formful performance of futures prices and Treasury calendar spreads.

RELATED TRADING ACTIVITY–A CASH-FUTURES STRATEGY

Cash-futures traders also help to create an atmosphere favorable to calendar spread trades. The trades these people make involve the delivery process, something best left to professionals who have the capital and information resources to make it work. What these people do is to buy the nearby Treasury contract and sell the next deferred contract (e.g., buy March and sell June). They hold this position into the delivery month (here, March) and take delivery of the cheapest-to-deliver Treasury security. This dissolves the nearby futures position. When the next delivery month rolls around, these traders make delivery of the Treasury security and so take themselves completely out of the market. The structure of this kind of trade locks in the Treasury prices and leaves only the risk that the relevant repo rate may change. This then is another kind of synthetic money-market investment. Tying the cash and futures prices together as it does, and done in substantial size as it typically is, this market activity also helps to ensure that the futures spreads will behave appropriately given current market conditions.

THE MECHANICS OF FORWARD PRICING (AN ADVANCED TOPIC)

A Treasury futures price is a forward price—a price today for delivery at a future date. Typically, given an upward sloping yield curve, delivery will take place at the last possible moment. Relative to September, this will be the last business day of September. This means that a September 10-year Treasury note futures price is a forward price based on the assumption of delivery at the end of September.

During the summer of 2004, both the September and December 10-year Treasury note futures contracts derived from the 5 percent of August 2011 Treasury note. That is, the 5 percent of August 2011 Treasury note was cheapest to deliver (CTD) into both those contracts (for more on CTD, conversion factors, and other relevant tools and concepts, see www.cbot.com). The September 10-year Treasury note futures price is a forward price for delivery on September 30, 2004, while the December futures price is a forward price for delivery on December 30, 2004. To arrive at the futures prices, the market computes the forward price of the CTD Treasury security and divides that price by the relevant conversion factor—0.9451 for September and 0.9468 for December.

The key here is the forward price of the CTD security. A fixed-income forward price is the spot price (the price for immediate delivery) minus carry. Carry, in turn, is the difference between the coupon, or interest, income earned for a given period and the cost of financing the security for that period.

Fixed-income securities pay interest twice a year, but a seller of such a security is entitled to the interest earned from the last coupon payment to the day of the sale. The 5 percent of August 2011 Treasury note pays coupon on February 15 and August 15 every year. In 2004, the February 15 to August 15 interval amounted to 182 days, so on July 15, 2004, to pick a date at random, an owner of this security would have earned \$0.013736 per day for every \$100 par of the security held (5/2 × 1/182 = 2.5 × 0.005495 = 0.013736). This is the daily coupon.

The daily financing calculation is slightly more complicated but still nothing more than basic arithmetic. The formula for daily financing is:

(spot price + accrued interest) × repo/100 × 1/360 = daily financing

On July 15, 2004, the spot price of the 5 percent of August 2011 Treasury note was 105.2375 (105-076 in points and 32nds), and the accrued interest was the daily coupon for the 151 days from February 15 to July 15, 2004, or 2.074176. The relevant repo rate was 1.30 percent, so daily financing was 0.003875 [(105.2375 + 2.074176) × 1.30/100 × 1/360]. (Note that repo rates are money-market rates and, by convention, the money-market year has 360 days.)

Given these two calculations, the daily carry was 0.009861 (0.013736 – 0.003875) for each \$100 par of the security. There were 77 days to delivery. The trouble is that there was a coupon payment after 31 days at this level of carry, and there were 184 days in the August 15, 2004. to February 15, 2005, coupon period. That tiny day-count change results in daily coupon of 0.013587 for the 46 days after August 15, assuming no repo change. This makes the total carry from July 15 to September 30 0.752441 for each $100 par. The forward price of the 5 percent of August 2011 Treasury note is the 105.2375 spot price minus the 0.752441 carry, or 104.485059. In conventional pricing terms, this is 104-15+. This, divided by the 0.9451 September conversion factor, yields a futures price of 110.5545, or 110-177.

Consider informally (no more arithmetic) what will happen to the futures price if the repo rate changes, assuming the same CTD security and no yield change. An increase in the repo rate will increase daily financing and lower daily carry (remember that daily coupon will not change). Lower carry results in a higher forward price relative to a given spot price, and a higher forward price results in a higher futures price. Leaving out all the interior steps, a higher repo rate results in a higher futures price—if all other factors are the same.

Consider next the relationship between the September and December 10-year Treasury note futures (but, really, between any such pair of contracts). Both July 15 prices derived from the 105.2375 spot price of the 5 percent of August 2011 Treasury note, which was CTD for both contracts during the summer of 2004. One difference was that, on July 15, where the September contract was 77 days away from futures delivery, the December contract was 168 days away from December 30, 2004, futures delivery—i.e., 91 more days of carry. One other difference was that financing for the December contract was based on a 1.55 percent repo rate. Skipping all the arithmetic, this leads to a 103.7265 (103-232 in points and 32nds) forward price for December 30 delivery of the 5 percent of August 2011 note. Given the 0.9468 conversion factor, this made the December futures price 109.5548 (109-178).

Based on this discussion of how the market derives these futures prices, it should be obvious that two primary factors drive changes in Treasury calendar spreads—the passage of time and changes in repo rates.

If nothing else changes, the passage of time will widen the spread. Based on the calculations in this discussion, the July 15 spread was 0.9997, barely less than 1-00. If, again, nothing else changes, the passage of 15 days will widen the spread to 1.0126—from barely under 1-00 to roughly 1-004 (one point and four-tenths of one thirty-second of a point).

Assuming no time change or change in the price of the CTD security and a 15 bp drop in the repo rate for the December forward price calculation (from 1.55 percent to 1.40 percent), the spread will also widen—from 0.9997 to 1.0791. In conventional pricing terms, this is from barely under 1-00 to 1-02+. Similarly, a higher repo rate will tend to narrow the spread.

Assuming no change to the July 15 price of the September futures contract and an instantaneous jump in the longer repo rate from 1.55 percent to 1.75 percent, the December futures price would climb to 109.6606. This would narrow the spread from 0.9997 to 0.8939.

Obviously, the various pricing factors do not change in isolation. Yields bounce around to change the CTD spot price. Time passes inexorably. And repo rates change. But, clearly, the most important factor in accounting for Treasury calendar spreads widening or narrowing is what is happening to repo rates.

THE REPO MARKETS AND THE FED FUNDS RATE

The 30-day and 90-day repo rates are the repo rates of greatest interest to Treasury calendar spread traders. Further, these rates bear an interesting relationship to the fed funds target rate. Exhibit 7.1 illustrates this relationship for the period from January 2, 2001 to August 19, 2004.

During much of 2002, 2003, and the first five months of 2004, the Fed was on hold at 1.75 percent, 1.25 percent, and 1.00 percent. During these long stretches, the 30-day and 90-day repo rates hovered close to each other and close to the fed funds target rate.

However, when the Fed lowered the target all through 2001 and began to raise the target at the end of June 2004, the repo rates parted company—from each other and from the fed funds target rate. Exhibit 7.2 shows the period from March 1 to August 19, 2004.

You can see that the two repo rates hugged the fed funds line until April 19. From March 1 until April 19, the difference between the 90-day and 30-day repo rates averaged six one-thousandths of a percentage point (0.006) as both of these repo rates hovered just under the 1.00 percent level.

You probably recall that at its May 4, 2004, meeting, the Fed left the target unchanged but warned the markets that it would soon start raising the fed funds target rate (the actual language was far less clear: "At this juncture, with inflation low and resource use slack, the Committee believes that policy accommodation can be removed at a pace that is likely to be measured"). From May 4 to May 28, the difference between the 90-day and 30-day repo rates averaged 0.138. Even before the May 4 statement, 90-day repo rates traded sharply higher, and they reached 1.21 percent on June 3 and crossed 1.25 percent on June 8, well in advance of the actual fed move.

EXHIBIT 7.1

30-Day and 90-Day Repo Rates and Fed Funds

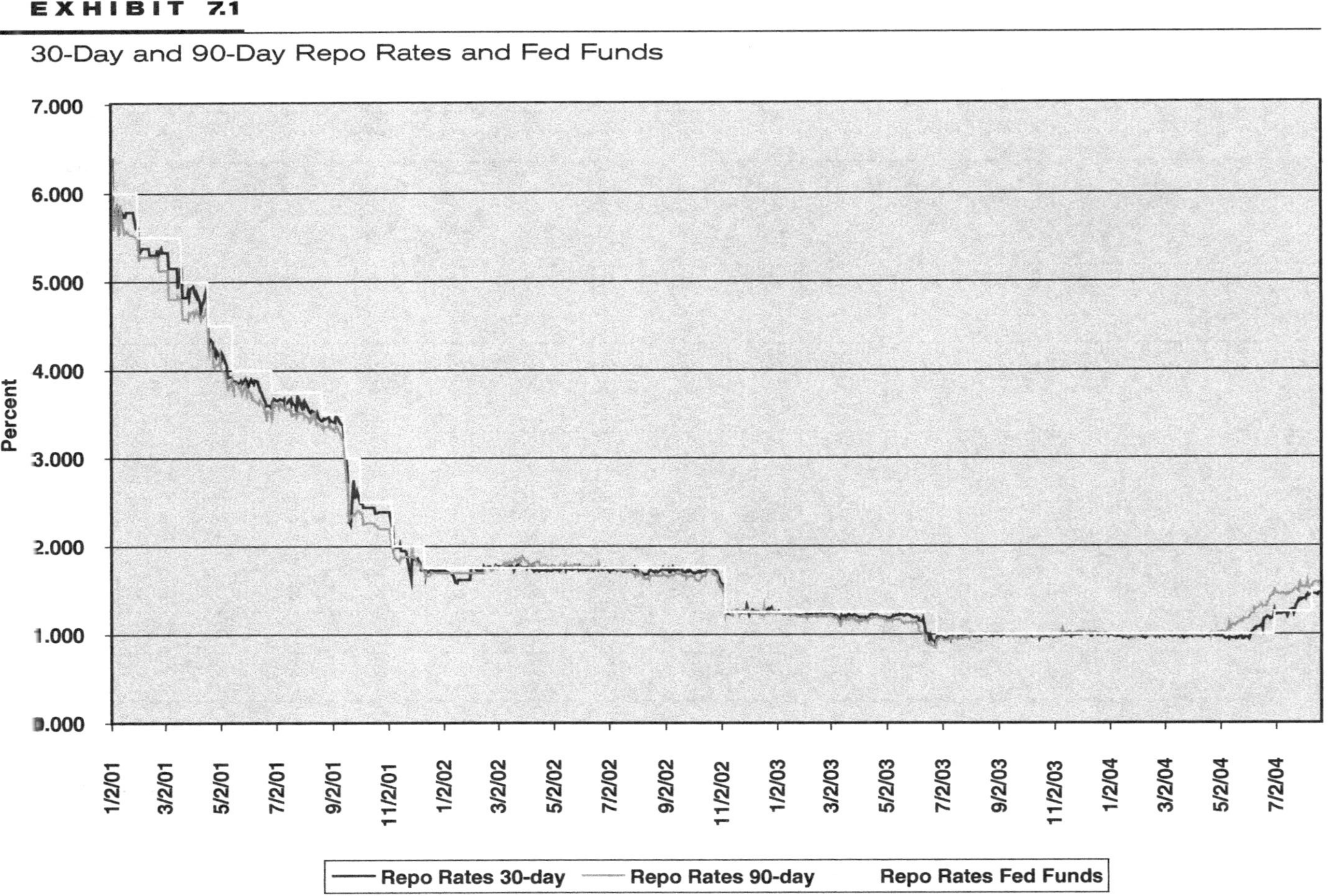

EXHIBIT 7.2

30-Day and 90-Day Repo Rates and Fed Funds (3/1/04 to 8/19/04)

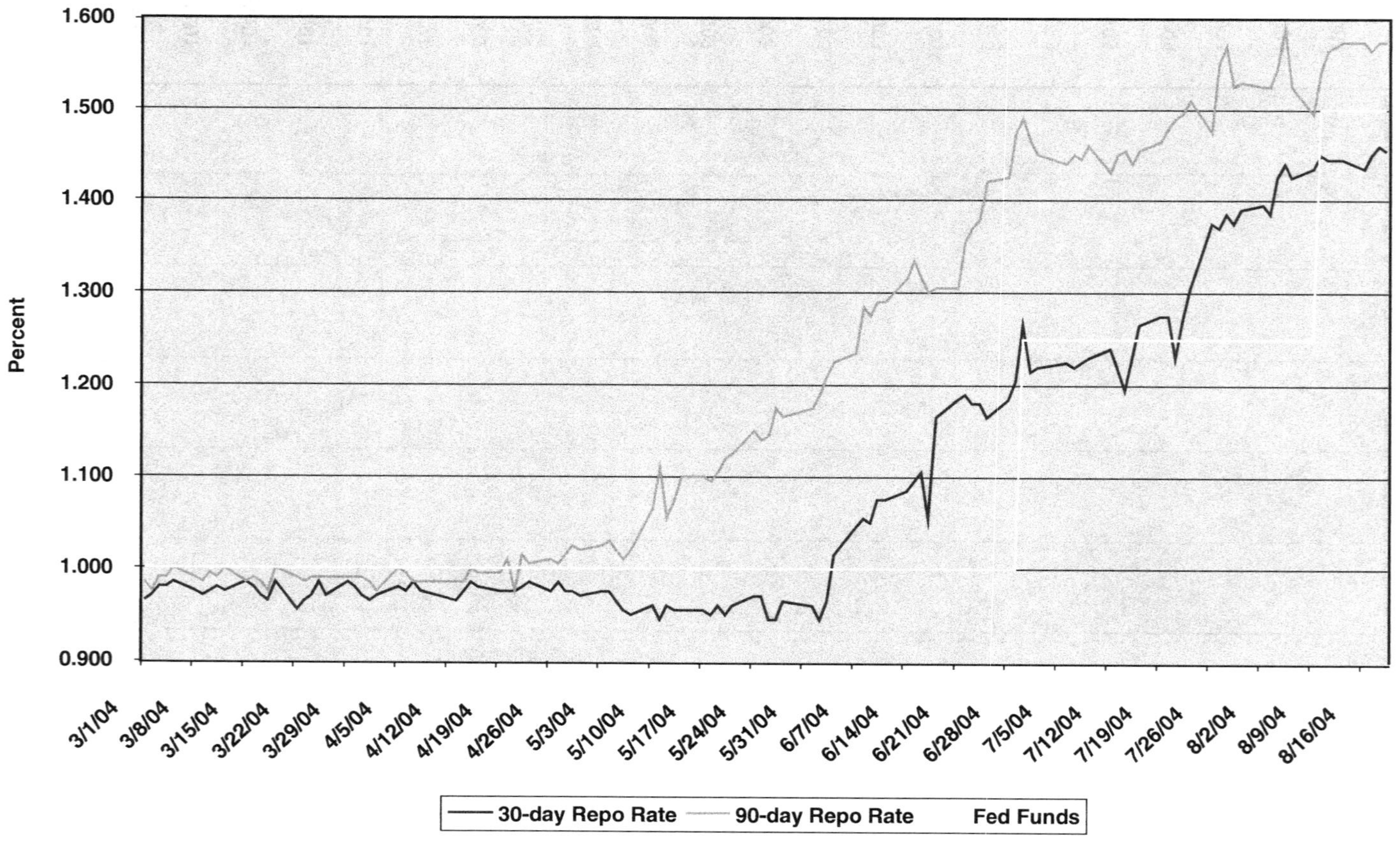

Percent

1.600
1.500
1.400
1.300
1.200
1.100
1.000
0.900

3/1/04
3/8/04
3/15/04
3/22/04
3/29/04
4/5/04
4/12/04
4/19/04
4/26/04
5/3/04
5/10/04
5/17/04
5/24/04
5/31/04
6/7/04
6/14/04
6/21/04
6/28/04
7/5/04
7/12/04
7/19/04
7/26/04
8/2/04
8/9/04
8/16/04

30-day Repo Rate
90-day Repo Rate
Fed Funds

The Fed raised the target 25 bps to 1.25 percent on June 30, 2004, a move that surprised nobody. During June 2004, the 30-day repo rate rose slowly from 0.96 percent on June 1 to 1.265 percent on June 30. The 90-day repo rate had reached 1.49 percent on June 30, and the average difference between these two repo rates for the month of June was 0.236. Clearly, the repo market was expecting yet another fed move and had already priced it into the 90-day repo rate.

Exhibit 7.3 shows the Fed lowering the target rate 11 times in 2001, 8 of them 50 bp moves. You can see that the 90-day repo rate ran ahead of the Fed almost the entire time. The exceptions came when the Fed made three unscheduled moves on January 2, April 18, and September 17. In every other instance, the 90-day repo rate led fed funds, often by rather a lot.

Obviously, attention to repo rates can provide early warning of fed moves. Conversely, attention to other fed tracking signals, such as fed funds futures, can provide hints about what to expect from repo rates.

TRACKING AND TRADING TREASURY CALENDAR SPREADS

Tracking Treasury calendar spreads requires only that you subtract the price of the deferred contract from the price of the nearby contract. This is easier if you do it in decimal terms.

Remember that converting a fraction like 0-16+, or 0-165 (which is the same thing) into decimals requires dividing the quote fraction by 32. Accordingly, 0-16+ becomes 16.5/32, which equals 0.515625. Some analysts break down prices exceedingly fine, so you might see a 110-062 quote. Here, the fraction is 6.2/32. which equals 0.19375, so 110-062 in decimals is 110.19375.

Exhibit 7.4 shows February 2004 10-year Treasury note futures prices for the March 2004 (TYH4) and June 2004 (TYM4) contracts in both conventional and decimal terms and the spread in decimals. [Note that you can convert back to 32nds by multiplying the decimal fraction by 32. Here, the 1.59375 February 2 spread is equivalent to 1-19 ($0.59375 \times 32 = 19$).]

An analysis such as the one shown in Exhibit 7.4 for the 12 roll months from November 2001 to August 2004 shows that the relevant 10-year Treasury note futures spread narrowed three times and widened nine times. Interestingly, widening and narrowing can happen regardless of what prices are doing. The spread can narrow or widen when prices are going up. It can narrow or widen when prices are going down. Exhibit 7.5 summarizes the data of 12 bodies of data like those in Exhibit 7.4.

EXHIBIT 7.3

Repo Rates and the Fed Funds Target Rate

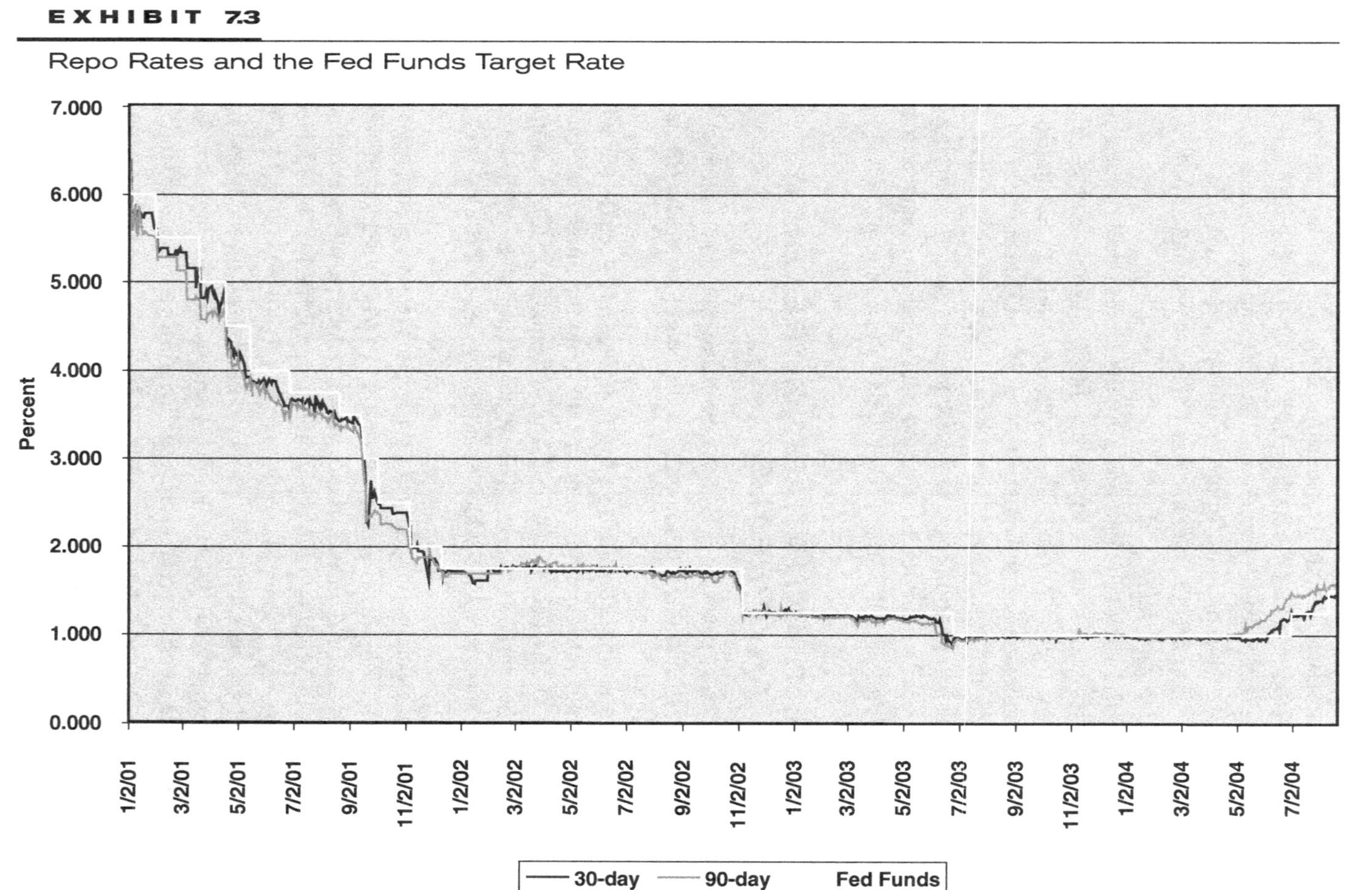

EXHIBIT 7.4

Tracking the March–June 2004 10-Year Treasury Note Calendar Spread

February 2004	TYH4	TYM4	TYH4	TYM4	Spread
2	113-12	111-25	113.375000	111.781250	1.593750
3	113-26+	112-07+	113.828125	112.234375	1.593750
4	113-22	112-03	113.687500	112.093750	1.593750
5	113-07+	111-20	113.234375	111.625000	1.609375
6	114-00	112-13+	114.000000	112.421875	1.578125
9	114-07	112-20+	114.218750	112.640625	1.578125
10	113-30	112-11+	113.937500	112.359375	1.578125
11	114-21+	113-03+	114.671875	113.109375	1.562500
12	114-15	112-29+	114.468750	112.921875	1.546875
13	114-26+	113-09	114.828125	113.281250	1.546875
17	114-25+	113-08+	114.796875	113.265625	1.531250
18	114-25	113-08+	114.781250	113.265625	1.515625
19	114-26	113-09+	114.812500	113.296875	1.515625
20	114-15	112-29	114.468750	112.062500	2.406250
23	114-28+	113-11+	114.890625	113.359375	1.531250
24	115-01+	113-16+	115.046875	113.515625	1.531250
25	115-04+	113-20+	115.140625	113.640625	1.500000
26	114-30	113-14	114.937500	113.437500	1.500000
27	115-12	113-28	115.375000	113.875000	1.500000

EXHIBIT 7.5

Futures Price and Calendar Spread Direction

Roll Month	Futures Prices (First to Last Trading Day)	Spread (First to Last Trading Day)
November 2001	Lower	Wider
February 2002	Higher	Wider
May 2002	Higher	Wider
August 2002	Higher	Wider
November 2002	Lower	Wider
February 2003	Higher	Narrower
May 2003	Higher	Narrower
August 2003	Higher	Wider
November 2003	Higher	Wider
February 2004	Higher	Narrower
May 2004	Lower	Wider
August 2004	Higher	Wider

STRUCTURING TREASURY CALENDAR SPREAD TRADES

Trading the Treasury calendar spread requires a spread logic similar to that used for the other spreads discussed in this book. If your analysis suggests that the spread will widen, you will want to buy the spread. If your analysis suggests that the spread will narrow, you will want to sell the spread. You buy or sell this spread in terms of what you do with the nearby, or front, month contract. That is, to buy the March–June 10-year Treasury note futures spread on February 2, 2004, you would have bought March futures and sold June futures. Conversely, to sell the spread on that day, you would have sold March futures and bought June futures. These spreads do not require ratioing, so you will buy and sell equal numbers of contracts.

In the actual case, your indicators would no doubt have prompted you to sell the 10-year spread on February 2, 2004, so your initial position would have been the one shown in Exhibit 7.6. If you had waited until February 27 to unwind this trade, you can see that one spread would have earned $93.75. While this may not seem like a great deal in dollar terms, keep in mind that the 90-day general collateral repo rate was 0.985 percent, and this $93.75 gives this trade a 1.191 percent annual rate of return. This is not a bad trade.

Calculating spread results is easier than perhaps Exhibit 7.6 makes it look. All you really have to do is subtract the spread value that you buy from the spread value that you sell. In this case, you sold at 1.59375 and bought at 1.50, so the result is 0.09375. To convert this into a dollar equivalent value, multiply by 1000. The sale of one spread on February

EXHIBIT 7.6

A Basic Calendar Spread Structure–Selling the Spread

	Action	TYH4	Action	TYM4	Spread
2/2/04	Sell	113.375	Buy	111.78125	1.59375
2/27/04	Buy	115.375	Sell	113.875	1.5
Result		–2.000		2.09375	
Spread Net				0.09375	0.09375
$ Result				93.75	

2, 2004, and the buying of it on February 27 would generate a $93.75 gain.

If you keep track of spread trades in terms of the individual futures prices as well as in terms of the spread values, you can tell at a glance which leg is making the money. Here it is the June leg, but it won't always be the same one.

The November 2001 and February 2002 roll months illustrate that the gains can come from different parts of the spread. In both cases, you would have no doubt bought the spread, and in both cases, the spread would have widened and showed a gain. Yet in November 2001, it was the deferred March leg that made the money, while in February 2002, it was the nearby March leg that made the money. The difference is that 10-year Treasury note futures prices were falling in November 2001, while in February 2002 they were rising. Exhibits 7.7a and b show the basic details of these two calendar spread trades.

EXHIBIT 7.7

Locating the Source of Calendar Spread Earnings

a

	Action	TYZ1	Action	TYH2	Spread
11/1/01	Buy	111.578125	Sell	110.484375	1.093750
11/30/01	Sell	108.250000	Buy	106.953125	1.296875
Result		−3.328125		3.531250	
Spread net				0.203125	0.203125
$ Result				$203.125	

b

	Action	TYH2	Action	TYM2	Spread
2/1/02	Buy	106.250000	Sell	104.953125	1.296875
2/28/02	Sell	107.250000	Buy	105.921875	1.328125
Result		1.0		−0.968750	
Spread net				0.031250	0.031250
$ Result				31.25	

TREASURY CALENDAR SPREAD TRADING STRATEGIES

Exhibit 7.8 shows the results of the simplest and most mechanical calendar spread strategy possible—buying or selling the spread on the first trading day of the roll month and unwinding the trade on the last trading day of that roll month—for the 12 roll months from November 2001 to August 2004.

For each of the roll months cited, the exhibit shows the initial and ending futures prices, in decimal form, for the two 10-year Treasury note futures contracts and the initial and ending spread value. In the Spread column, the exhibit then shows the Spread net, which is the difference between the spread sold and the spread bought. The next row shows the Spread net for one spread in dollars and the Repo Dollar Benchmark.

The Repo Dollar Benchmark assumes that you could have invested the dollar equivalent value of the initial front month futures price at the 90-day general collateral repo rate that was available on the first trading day of the roll month. The repo investment is held in place until the last trading day of the month.

Consider the November 2001 roll month for example. The December 2001 futures price was 111.578125, which is equivalent to $111,578.125 for one contract. The 90-day repo rate on November 1, 2001, was 2.195 percent, and this investment would have been for 29 days. To calculate such a money-market return, you use the formula:

$$\text{futures price} \times \text{repo}/100 \times \text{days}/360$$

Remember that, by convention, a money-market year contains 360 days. Substituting the cited values in the formula, you can discover that an investment of this amount at this repo rate for these 29 days would have earned $197.29.

$$111{,}578.125 \times 2.95/100 \times 29/360 = 197.29$$

Following the Repo Dollar Benchmark value, the exhibit shows the Annual rate of return for the futures trade. This again uses the dollar equivalent value of the front month futures price and the Spread net in dollars to solve for an annualized rate of return. Finally, the exhibit shows the actual 90-day repo rate and the difference between these two rates.

In the case of the November 2001 roll month, the futures trade was the better deal. This is not always the case. As you study Exhibit 7.8, you will see that, at times, this simple version of the trade outperforms the repo benchmark and at other times it does not.

EXHIBIT 7.8

Twelve Calendar Spread Trades

a. November 2001 Roll: Buy Spread

	TYZ1	TYH2	Spread	Repo $ Benchmark
11/1	111.578125	110.484375	1.093550	
11/30	108.250000	106.953125	1.296875	
Spread net			0.203125	
Spread $ net			203.125	197.29
Annual rate of return				2.260%
90-day repo (11/1/01)				2.195%
Difference (spread – repo)				0.065

b. February 2002 Roll: Buy Spread

	TYH2	TYM2	Spread	Repo $ Benchmark
2/1	106.250000	104.953125	1.296875	
2/28	107.250000	105.921875	1.328125	
Spread net			0.031250	
Spread $ net			31.25	134.67
Annual rate of return				0.392%
90-day repo (2/1/02)				1.690%
Difference (spread – repo)				–1.298

c. May 2002 Roll: Buy Spread

	TYM2	TYU2	Spread	Repo $ Benchmark
5/1	105.812500	104.515625	1.296875	
5/31	106.734375	105.281250	1.453125	
Spread net			0.156250	
Spread $ Net			156.25	157.40
Annual rate of return				1.772%
90-day repo (5/1/02)				1.785%
Difference (spread – repo)				0.013

Continued

EXHIBIT 7.8

Twelve Calendar Spread Trades (*Continued*)

d. August 2002 Roll: Buy Spread

	TYU21	TYZ2	Spread	Repo $ Benchmark
8/1	111.046875	110.484375	1.375000	
8/30	113.181875	111.781250	1.390625	
Spread net			0.015625	
Spread $ net			15.625	150.73
Annual rate of return				0.175%
90-day repo (8/1/02)				1.685%
Difference (spread – repo)				–1.510

e. November 2002 Roll: Buy Spread

	TYZ2	TYH3	Spread	Repo $ Benchmark
11/1	114.250000	112.984375	1.265625	
11/29	112.515625	111.109375	1.406250	
Spread net			0.140625	
Spread $ net			140.625	141.27
Annual rate of return				1.528%
90-day repo (11/1/02)				1.535%
Difference (spread – repo)				–0.007

f. February 2003 Roll: Sell Spread

	TYH3	TYM3	Spread	Repo $ Benchmark
2/3	113.968750	112.546875	1.421875	
2/28	116.718750	115.375000	1.343750	
Spread net			0.078125	
Spread $ net			78.125	92.99
Annual rate of return				0.987%
90-day repo (2/3/03)				1.175%
Difference (spread – repo)				–0.188

EXHIBIT 7.8

Twelve Calendar Spread Trades (*Continued*)

g. May 2003 Roll: Sell Spread

	TYM3	TYU3	Spread	Repo $ Benchmark
5/1	115.218750	114.312500	0.906250	
5/30	119.062500	116.437500	0.625000	
Spread net			0.281250	
Spread $ net			281.25	106.74
Annual rate of return				3.030%
90-day repo (5/1/03)				1.150%
Difference (spread – repo)				1.880

h. August 2003 Roll: Buy Spread

	TYU3	TYZ3	Spread	Repo $ Benchmark
8/1	110.546875	108.750000	1.796875	
8/29	111.531250	109.718750	1.812500	
Spread net			0.015625	
Spread $ net			15.625	86.83
Annual rate of return				0.175%
90-day repo (8/1/03)				0.975%
Difference (spread – repo)				–0.800

i. November 2003 Roll: Buy Spread

	TYZ3	TYH4	Spread	Repo $ Benchmark
11/3	111.781250	110.328125	1.453125	
11/28	112.406250	110.890625	1.515625	
Spread net			0.062500	
Spread $ net $			62.50	76.46
Annual rate of return				0.805%
90-day repo (11/3/03)				0.985%
Difference (spread – repo)				–0.100

Continued

EXHIBIT 7.8

Twelve Calendar Spread Trades (*Continued*)

j. February 2004 Roll: Sell Spread

	TYH4	TYM4	Spread	Repo $ Benchmark
2/2	113.375000	111.781250	1.593750	
2/27	115.375000	113.875000	1.500000	
Spread net			0.093750	
Spread $ Net			93.75	77.55
Annual rate of return				1.191%
90-day repo (2/2/04)				0.985%
Difference (spread – repo)				0.206

k. May 2004 Roll: Buy Spread

	TYM4	TYU4	Spread	Repo $ Benchmark
5/3	110.500000	109.093750	1.406250	
5/28	109.875000	108.375000	1.500000	
Spread net			0.093750	
Spread $ net			93.75	78.65
Annual rate of return				1.222%
90-day repo (5/3/04)				1.025%
Difference (spread – repo)				0.197

l. August 2004 Roll: Buy Spread

	TYU41	TYZ4	Spread	Repo $ Benchmark
8/2	110.812500	110.484375	1.093550	
8/31	113.475000	112.318750	1.156250	
Spread net			0.062700	
Spread $ net			62.70	131.44
Annual rate of return				0.702%
90-day repo (8/2/04)				1.590%
Difference (spread – repo)				–0.888

You can see that this trade clearly outperformed the repo benchmark four times, came close to matching it two times, and clearly underperformed it six times. This is not the most exciting result imaginable, but this can be dealt with in a variety of ways.

At certain times, your market analysis may suggest that you shouldn't even make the trade, that this is a good time to stay on the sidelines. However, an important difference between a money-market investment and a futures trade is that with futures you can take a more aggressive and opportunistic approach. After all, no law says that the simple mechanical strategy is the only way to trade calendar spreads.

The February and May 2003 roll months were times when a more aggressive and opportunistic approach would have been possible for calendar spread sellers. The November 2002 and May 2004 rolls provide examples of how a more aggressive and opportunistic trading approach might have rewarded calendar spread buyers.

ONE POSSIBLE TRADING PLAN

Assume that on February 3, 2003, the first trading day of that roll month, you had sold 100 March–June 10-year Treasury note futures spreads with the spread at 1.421875 (1-13+ in points and 32nds). One possible trading plan would have been to unwind half this position, 50 spreads, if the spread had narrowed 0.10 or more and to let the other 50 spreads ride until the end of the month. This means that with the initial spread at 1.421875, you would have bought back 50 spreads any time the spread narrowed to 1.321875 or to a level slightly below that.

Exhibit 7.9 shows the March 2003 (TYH3) and June 2003 (TYM3) 10-year Treasury note futures prices in conventional and decimal terms and the spread levels for the February 2003 roll month in decimal terms.

In the February 2003 case, the spread narrowed to 1.301339 after only two days. According to the plan that calls for buying back half the position any time the spread narrows 0.10 or more, this marks a time to buy 50 spreads. Suppose you had let the other 50 spreads ride until the last trading day of the month when the spread was 1.343750. These 100 spreads would have earned a total of $9,933.05. Exhibit 7.10 shows details.

Note that the dollar equivalent value of the result is the Result figure shown multiplied by 1000—e.g., 0.120536 × 1,000 is $120.536. This multiplied by 50 spreads is $6,026.80, the value in the Dollar Result column.

If you had invested $1,139,687.50 (the February 3, 2003, March 10-year Treasury note futures price multiplied by 100) at a 1.175 percent

EXHIBIT 7.9

February 2003 Futures Prices and Spread Levels

February	TYH3	TYM3	TYH3	TYM3	Spread
3	113-31	112-17+	113.968750	112.546875	1.421875
4	114-14	113-01	114.437500	113.031250	1.406250
5	113-29+	112-16+	113.785714	112.484375	1.301339
6	114-11	112-30	114.343750	112.937500	1.406250
7	114-18+	113-05+	114.578125	113.171875	1.406250
10	114-05+	112-24+	114.171875	112.765625	1.406250
11	114-12+	113-00	114.390625	113.000000	1.390625
12	114-26	113-14+	114.812500	113.453125	1.359375
13	115-11+	114-00	115.359375	114.000000	1.359375
14	114-26+	113-15	114.828125	113.468750	1.359375
18	114-28+	113-16+	114.890625	113.515625	1.375000
19	115-12+	114-00	115.390625	114.000000	1.390625
20	115-22+	114-10+	115.703125	114.328125	1.375000
21	115-10+	113-30	115.328125	113.937500	1.390625
24	115-22+	114-11	115.703125	114.343750	1.359375
25	115-28+	114-17	115.890625	114.531250	1.359375
26	116-06	114-26+	116.187500	114.828125	1.359375
27	116-10	114-30+	116.312500	114.953125	1.359375
28	116-23	115-12	116.718750	115.375000	1.343750

EXHIBIT 7.10

A Two-Step Trading Approach

Spread Level Sold	Spread Level Bought	Result	Number of Spreads	Dollar Result
1.421875	1.301339	0.120536	50	6,026.80
1.421875	1.34375	0.078125	50	3,906.25
			Total	9,933.05

90-day repo rate from February 3 until February 28, you would have earned $9,299.53. This is the benchmark you want the 100 spreads to match or improve on. While the basic mechanical strategy of Exhibit 7.8 underperforms this benchmark, the more aggressive strategy improves on it.

EXHIBIT 7.11

May 2003 Futures Prices and Spread Levels

May	TYM3	TYU3	TYM3	TYU3	Spread
1	115-07	114-10	115.218750	114.312500	0.906250
2	114-24+	113-27	114.765625	113.843750	0.921875
5	115-01	114-03+	115.031250	114.109375	0.921875
6	115-23	114-27+	115.718750	114.859375	0.859375
7	116-14+	115-21	116.453125	115.656250	0.796875
8	116-22	115-29	116.687500	115.906250	0.781250
9	116-23	115-29+	116.718750	115.921875	0.796875
12	116-31+	116-07	116.984375	116.218750	0.765625
13	117-02	116-10	117.062500	116.312500	0.750000
14	117-18	116-27+	117.562500	116.859375	0.703125
15	117-13+	116-23+	117.421875	116.734375	0.687500
16	118-01	117-12+	118.031250	117.390625	0.640625
19	118-06	117-18+	118.187500	117.578125	0.609375
20	118-23+	118-05	118.734375	118.156250	0.578125
21	118-14	117-27	118.437500	117.843750	0.593750
22	118-25+	118-08	118.796875	118.250000	0.546875
23	118-26	118-09	118.812500	118.281250	0.531250
27	118-17+	117-31+	118.546875	117.984375	0.562500
28	118-15	117-27+	118.468750	117.859375	0.609375
29	119-02+	118-16	119.078125	118.500000	0.578125
30	119-02	118-14	119.062500	118.437500	0.625000

The May 2003 roll month was another time when selling the spread would have seemed like the right thing to do. Exhibit 7.11 shows the relevant futures prices and spread levels.

Assume that you had sold 100 June–September 10-year Treasury note futures spreads on May 1, 2003, with the spread at 0.90625. Eight days later, the spread had narrowed to 0.796875. This is slightly beyond the 0.10 guideline, so you might have bought back 50 spreads at that level. After another 16 days, you could have bought back the remaining 50 spreads at 0.53125. Exhibit 7.12 shows the details of this trading sequence.

Alternatively, you could have let the remaining 50 spreads ride until the last trading day of the month when the spread was 0.625. Exhibit 7.13 shows the result of buying back the first 50 spreads at 0.796875 and the second 50 at 0.625.

EXHIBIT 7.12

An Early Quitting Time

Spread Level Sold	Spread Level Bought	Result	Number of Spreads	Dollar Result
0.90625	0.796875	0.109375	50	5,468.75
0.90625	0.53125	0.375	50	18,750.00
			Total	24,218.75

EXHIBIT 7.13

Holding on until the End of the Month

Spread Level Sold	Spread Level Bought	Result	Number of Spreads	Dollar Result
0.90625	0.796875	0.109375	50	5,568.75
0.90625	0.625	0.28125	50	14,062.50
			Total	19,531.25

The repo benchmark for May 2003 was $10,673.74. Either of these versions of the more aggressive strategy improve significantly on the repo benchmark, although in this case, the simple strategy does even better. What can be said for this more aggressive approach is that it provides at least some protection against an adverse spread move. Had the spread moved against your position, you would have held onto at least some gains.

The May 2003 data suggest an even more aggressive tactic that may seem viable at times. This approach assumes great confidence in your spread forecast, but given that confidence, it may be worth considering. Suppose that on May 1, 2003, you had sold 100 spreads as before. On May 2, the spread widened slightly to 0.921875. Suppose you had sold another 100 spreads, but your plan in this case was to buy back 50 if the spread narrowed by 0.20 or more. The second 50 would ride as before. At this point, you would have sold 200 June–December 10-year Treasury note futures spreads. Assume that you dealt with the first 100 as illustrated in Exhibit 7.12.

After 13 days, the spread narrowed to 0.703125. That is more than a 0.20 point narrowing from 0.921875, so you would have bought 50 spreads in keeping with your plan. Suppose you held the second 50 until the spread narrowed to 0.53125 and then sold them. Exhibit 7.14 shows the details of the trades involving the second 100 spreads.

EXHIBIT 7.14

Seizing the Day

Spread Level Sold	Spread Level Bought	Result	Number of Spreads	Dollar Result
0.921875	0.703125	0.21875	50	10,937.50
0.921875	0.53125	0.390625	50	19,531.25
			Total	30,768.75

In this case, the repo benchmark would have been $21,347.48, and this heavier trading strategy would have earned $54,987 in the aggregate. However, the basic strategy would have earned $56,987 for a 200-spread position. Again, the trade-off any trader must make involves deciding whether it is better to take some profit early to protect against adverse spread developments. Maybe it is. Maybe it isn't. The extra trading was certainly worth the trouble in the case of the February 2003 roll month, and the slightly weaker performance of the more aggressive strategies in the May 2003 example is still an extremely robust return.

When you buy the spread, a similar plan might work. In this case, you might decide that if the spread widens by 0.10 or more, you will sell half of your position and let the remainder ride. Another more aggressive plan is possible assuming, again, that you believe strongly in your spread forecast. If the spread narrows by 0.10 or more, you will buy 100 more spreads. Then, if the spread widens by 0.10 or more from that narrower level, you will sell half of these. The November 2002 roll month provided an opportunity for both parts of this trading plan, as the data of Exhibit 7.15 illustrate.

On November 1, 2002, you might have bought 100 spreads at a spread level of 1.265625. Eleven days later, the spread had narrowed to 1.10625. A trader who thought this was a sign of impending disaster and unwound the trade would have taken a $15,937.50 loss on 100 spreads. But suppose you took this to be a buying opportunity and bought another 100 spreads.

Two days later, the spread had widened to 1.25, so you might have sold 50 of the second 100 spreads for a 0.14375 gain (× 1000 = $143.75). The spread didn't reach the plus 0.10 level relative to the first 100 spreads until the next to last trading day of the month, but suppose you sold 50 of that first 100 just in case the spread backed up on you the next day — which has happened. The spread on that next-to-last day was 1.390625, so you would have gained 0.125 on that 50. On the last trading day of November 2002, the spread widened to 1.40625. The 50 from the first 100

EXHIBIT 7.15

November 2002 Futures Prices and Spread Levels

November	TYZ2	TYH3	TYZ2	TYH3	Spread
1	114-08	112-31+	114.250000	112.984375	1.265625
4	113-26	112-16+	113.812500	112.515625	1.296875
5	113-20	112-10	113.625000	112.312500	1.312500
6	113-27	112-16	113.843750	112.500000	1.343750
7	114-25	113-16+	114.781250	113.515625	1.265625
8	115-01+	113-27+	115.046875	113.859375	1.187500
12	115-02+	113-29	115.012500	113.906250	1.106250
13	115-08+	114-03	115.265625	114.093750	1.171875
14	113-30+	112-22+	113.953125	112.703125	1.250000
15	113-23+	112-15	113.734375	112.468750	1.265625
18	113-29	112-20+	113.906250	112.640625	1.265625
19	114-04+	112-28+	114.140625	112.890625	1.250000
20	113-10+	112-02	113.328125	112.062500	1.265625
21	112-27+	111-17+	112.859375	111.546875	1.312500
22	112-21	111-11	112.656250	111.343750	1.312500
25	112-21	111-09+	112.656250	111.296875	1.359375
26	113-14+	112-03	113.453125	112.093750	1.359375
27	112-05+	110-25	112.171875	110.781250	1.390625
29	112-16+	111-03+	112.515625	111.109375	1.406250

would have gained 0.140625 each, and the remaining 50 from the second 100 would have gained 0.30 each. Exhibit 7.16 shows the details.

The repo benchmark for 200 spreads during this month would have been $28,254.60. In hindsight, it would have been better not to have sold any spreads on the next-to-last day, but no trader could have known that on that day.

Furthermore, the August 2004 roll month makes the case for following the plan, even on the next-to-last day of the month. The September–December 10-year Treasury note futures spread started that month at 1.1375 and was trading at 1.203125 on the next-to-last day of August. On the last day, the spread dropped to 1.15625. Having sold half those spreads early would have seemed like a shrewd move.

The May 2004 roll month offered a curious opportunity to Treasury calendar spread traders. Given the 0.10 widening or narrowing guidelines discussed so far, there never was a time when the spread widened or narrowed that much. Exhibit 7.17 shows how the spread developed during that roll month.

EXHIBIT 7.16

Buying and then Buying More

Spread Level Sold	Spread Level Bought	Result	Number of Spreads	Dollar Result
1.265625	1.390625	0.125	50	6,250.00
1.265625	1.40625	0.140625	50	7.031.25
1.10625	1.25	0.14375	50	7,187.50
1.10625	1.40625	0.30	50	15,000.00
			Total	35,468.75

EXHIBIT 7.17

May 2004 Futures Prices and Spread Levels

May	TYM4	TYU4	TYM4	TYU4	Spread
3	110-16	109-03	110.500000	109.093750	1.406250
4	110-09.5	108-28.5	110.296875	108.890625	1.406250
5	110-02	108-19.5	110.062500	108.609375	1.453125
6	109-26.5	108-11.5	109.828125	108.359375	1.468750
7	108-15.5	107-00	108.484375	107.000000	1.484375
10	108-18	107-02	108.562500	107.062500	1.500000
11	108-22	107-06	108.687500	107.187500	1.500000
12	108-18	107-02.5	108.562500	107.078125	1.484375
13	108-06.5	106-23.5	108.203125	106.734375	1.468750
14	108-25	107-10	108.781250	107.312500	1.468750
17	109-16.5	108-02	109.515625	108.062500	1.453125
18	109-06.5	107-24.5	109.203125	107.765625	1.437500
19	108-23.5	107-09	108.734375	107.281250	1.453125
20	109-08.5	107-26	109.265625	107.812500	1.453125
21	108-30.5	107-15.5	108.953125	107.484375	1.468750
24	109-04	107-20.5	109.125000	107.640625	1.484375
25	109-08.5	107-26	109.265625	107.812500	1.453125
26	109-25	108-10	109.781250	108.312500	1.468750
27	110-12.5	108-29.5	110.390625	108.921875	1.468750
28	109-28	108-12	109.875000	108.375000	1.500000

Notice that there were two days at the beginning of the second week when the spread was 1.50, which was 0.09375 wider. Suppose you had relaxed the guideline on the second of those days and sold 50 spreads. At month's end, by an odd coincidence, the spread had climbed back to 1.50. As a result, you would have earned $93.75 for each spread traded, no matter when you sold them back to the market. The original 100-spread position would have earned $9,375. An equivalent 90-day repo investment would have earned $7,865.45 at then-prevailing repo rates. By selling the first 50 early, you could have matched the repo benchmark even if the spread had only widened back to 1.469809.

In sum, the basic rather mechanical trade, that Exhibit 7.8 reports, will generate satisfying results roughly half the time. Keep in mind that even a result that is slightly less than the repo benchmark is a good one for people who don't have access to the repo market. Yet it is possible during many, but not all, roll months to find opportunities to improve on the repo benchmark by somewhat more aggressive trading. To emphasize, a willingness to be aggressive assumes great confidence in your spread forecasts.

A WORD OF CAUTION

These Treasury calendar spread trades are some of the least risky trades available. A measure of how little risk the supercautious clearinghouse officials see in these trades is the fact that, as of the summer of 2004, the margins of the two contracts in a calendar spread offset each other. Treasury calendar spread traders did not have to post margin.

Yet any trade contains some risk, and it is good policy to think about what might be possible sources of risk ahead of time and to have a sense of what to watch out for.

Changing repo rates are one risk factor. Not only do repo rates trade close to the fed funds rate and even anticipate fed policy changes, but Treasury securities can go on special. Suppose general collateral repo is trading at 1.75 percent but that the CTD security is in short supply. If enough people need this security badly enough, they will offer to lend at a lower rate to draw this security out of hiding. It is possible in these cases to see the repo rate on a security that is on special drop significantly under the general collateral level. This can be a more severe problem when the two contracts in the calendar spread are tracking different CTD issues and one is on special while the other is not.

An even bigger risk factor in a calendar spread trade is the possibility of a change in CTD. On August 2, 2004, the September–December 10-year Treasury note futures spread was 1.1375 (the September price was 110.8125; the December, 109.625). An instantaneous 50 bp yield shift would have shifted CTD status for both contracts from the 5 percent of August 2011 Treasury note to the 4 1/4 percent of November 2013 Treasury note. The relevant conversion factors would have dropped from 0.9451 to 0.8797 for the September contract and from 0.9468 to 0.8821 for the December contract. Once the dust had settled, the futures prices would have been 107.28125 (Sep) and 106.1 (Dec), and the spread would have been 1.1825, which is 0.045 wider.

In this case, the same security is CTD throughout the term of the trade. That won't always be true. It is also possible for one to be on special while the other is not. That can affect the spread even more.

That said, Treasury calendar spread trades are simple to track and trade and entail relatively small risk. Also, because these are deep and liquid markets, if you see the spread moving against your position, you can unwind the trade quickly and for relatively small cost. An important factor to keep in mind is that your credit risk exposure in a futures trade is all but nonexistent. This cannot be said for all the money markets.

CHAPTER 8

Kansas City Wheat–Chicago Corn

Wheat-corn spreads have been traded since the beginning of futures trading time. At first glance, this might not make complete sense because these grains appear to serve different functions and not to be at all interchangeable.

The primary use for wheat, after all, is baking flour. Yet even here different kinds of wheat serve different purposes. The hard red wheat from which the Kansas City Board of Trade contract derives is a higher-protein grain used for bread flour. The soft red wheat from which the Chicago Board of Trade contract derives is a lower-protein grain used for cookie and cracker flour. So these two kinds of wheat cannot be substituted for each other, and corn is different yet.

One use of corn is for cornmeal, but that accounts for only a small fraction of corn use, and it certainly is not interchangeable with wheat flour. Corn sweeteners account for more corn than meal does, and the manufacture of ethanol fuel additives accounts for a growing share of the corn crop. Yet the largest use for corn is as a livestock feed.

A PROTEIN-DRIVEN SPREAD TRADE

People tend to forget that livestock feeders use major amounts of wheat, but it is this use of wheat as feed that accounts for a great deal of what happens to a spread such as the Kansas City wheat–Chicago corn trade. This also applies to the Chicago wheat-corn spread, but this discussion focuses on the higher-protein Kansas City variety.

AN INFORMAL LOOK AT THE KC WHEAT-CORN SPREAD

Exhibit 8.1 tracks a wheat-corn spread and its components. This graphic is based on the December 2004 Kansas City wheat contract (DWZ4) and the December 2004 Chicago Board of Trade corn contract (C Z4). While traders may well prefer to trade March, May, and July contracts during the early parts of the year, this graphic tells the same basic story as charts of the spread based on the other contacts would. Exhibit 8.1 also makes it possible to mention a few interesting features of the spread and of wheat-corn spread trades.

One way in which the agricultural markets differ from the financial markets is in their seasonality. One example of this seasonality at work on the spread is the dip that occurs in late June. This is mostly the effect of the wheat harvest. The winter wheat crop comes in three to four months ahead of the corn crop, so the postharvest wheat price drop is likely to narrow the spread during late May and June, as it seems to have done in the 2004 case.

In any market, participants strain to figure out in advance what might happen in the near future. Word was out early that the corn crop was likely to be big. U.S. Department of Agriculture reports highlighted a big switch from soybean acreage to corn acreage during the May 2004 planting period. From mid-June on, you could see the corn price trending downward, partly in anticipation of this. You can also see how this widened the spread in July.

Another factor that comes into play in this spread is that while corn is largely a U.S. crop, wheat is a global crop. Granted, other countries have corn corps, but the U.S. crop remains the dominant one. Not so with wheat. The Canadian, Australian, and European crops account for large fractions of world production. As a result of this, anything that happens in any of the other wheat-growing areas can affect U.S. wheat futures prices. The August trough in the spread shows the effect of news concerning the poor quality of the Canadian wheat crop, a condition that would drive most of it into livestock feed. That seems to have accelerated the downward trend of wheat prices and to have narrowed the spread until further confirmation of the giant size of the corn crop took hold.

Notice that the wheat-corn spread reached its widest levels of the year as wheat prices began to trade sideways while corn prices dropped even more because of growing certainty about the huge corn crop size.

STRUCTURING A WHEAT-CORN SPREAD TRADE

Staying with the logic that you want to buy a thing you expect to gain value and sell a thing you expect to lose value, you buy or sell the wheat-corn

EXHIBIT 8.1

KC Wheat-Corn Spread (1/2/04 to 10/15/04)

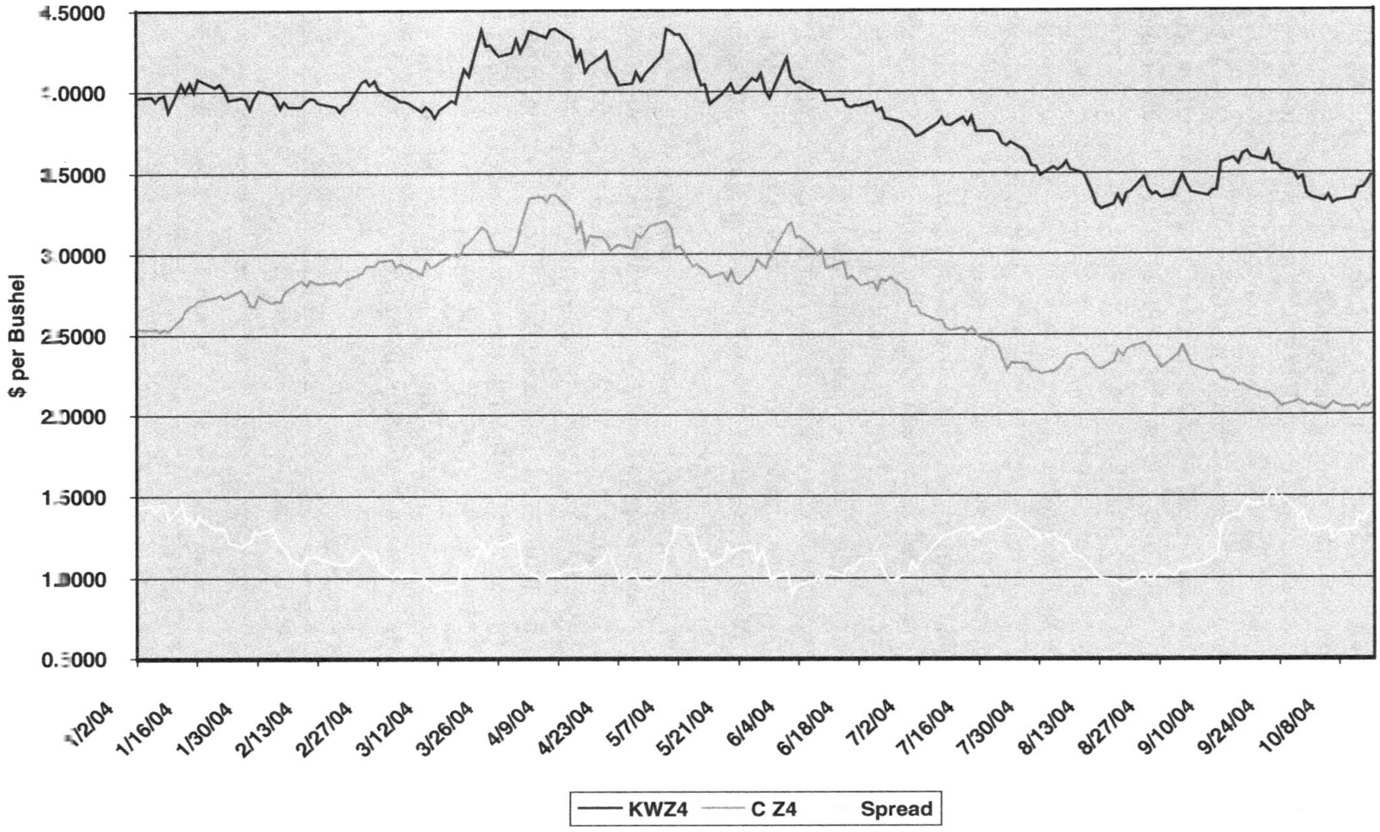

spread in terms of what you do with the wheat leg. To sell the spread, you sell wheat futures and buy corn futures, and, when the spread narrows as expected, you unwind by doing the opposite.

A look at the January through February segments of the wheat, corn, and spread plots of Exhibit 8.1 makes it obvious why you should do this. You can see that between January 16 and February 6, 2004, the spread narrowed. You can also see that the price of wheat was falling while the price of corn was rising. When this happens, selling wheat futures will gain as will buying corn futures. Had your market analysis prompted you to trade these contracts across this three-week span, the wheat leg of the trade would have earned $0.175 per bushel, the corn leg would have earned $0.075, but the spread would have earned $0.25 per bushel, or $1,250 per spread. Exhibit 8.2 shows the details of this trade.

The minus sign in the fourth row of the Spread column indicates a narrowing spread, and the Spread $ net value is the Spread net multiplied by 5,000 bushels. Note that if you invariably subtract bought wheat and corn prices from sold prices, the gains and losses always come out right (though perhaps not as you would prefer). Typically, spread trades involve a losing leg and a gaining leg. The situation where both legs gain occurs surprisingly often in the case of this wheat-corn spread, though by no means does this happen in every case.

Suppose that in late April, your market analysis suggested that this was a time to buy the spread—buy wheat and sell corn. Suppose further that you made this move on April 27 when the spread was trading at 1.0000 and unwound it on May 18 by which time the spread had widened 0.1875 cents per bushel to 1.1875. Exhibit 8.3 shows a more typical situation. The wheat leg lost $0.10, while the corn leg gained $0.2875 for a net gain of $0.1875 per bushel, or $937.50 per spread.

Notice that the fourth cell under Spread in this exhibit displays a positive value, which indicates spread widening.

EXHIBIT 8.2

Selling the KC Wheat-Corn Spread

	Action	KWZ4	Action	C Z4	Spread
1/6/04	Sell	4.0800	Buy	2.7100	1.3700
2/6/04	Buy	3.9050	Sell	2.7850	1.1200
Result		0.1750		0.0750	
Spread net				0.2500	–0.2500
Spread $ net				1,250.00	

EXHIBIT 8.3

Buying the KC Wheat-Corn Spread

	Action	KWZ4	Action	C Z4	Spread
4/27/04	Buy	4.1200	Sell	3.1200	1.0000
5/18/04	Sell	4.0300	Buy	2.8325	1.1875
Result		–0.1000		0.2875	
Spread net				0.1875	0.1875
Spread $ net				937.50	

You can trade this spread based on any of several approaches. You can be fairly mechanical about it, or you can base your moves on whatever sort of technical analysis you find helpful. But you will probably do better with a spread like this if you place your focus on the underlying economics of it. The key to this is the protein content of the various grains.

IT'S ABOUT PROTEIN

The primary difference between varieties of wheat and between wheat and corn, from a livestock feeding perspective as well as from a baking perspective, is in the protein content of each grain. According to a recent *Feedstuffs* reference issue, hard red wheat is 13.5 percent protein, soft red wheat is 10.8 percent protein, and corn is 7.9 percent protein. The protein content affects how each kind of wheat flour bakes.

Another factor that plays into the wheat picture is that the protein content of wheat can be adversely affected if, for instance, there are heavy rains shortly before harvest. When rains lower the protein content of the hard red varieties, it becomes ill-suited to baking use and gets shunted into the livestock feeding market.

THE CATTLE FEEDING BALANCING ACT

Basically, cattle feeders use corn for energy and soy meal for protein. A steer on feed can eat only so much dry matter each day, so the balancing act is to optimize protein content at the lowest possible cost given the dry bulk constraint.

Protein isn't the only part of the equation that matters, but assume for the moment that protein is the primary driver of a cattle feeder's decision making. Soy meal is about 45 percent protein. As noted above, corn is 7.9

EXHIBIT 8.4

Comparing the Cost of Protein

	Quoted Price	Price/Pound	Cost of 4.424 Pounds of Protein
Corn	2.9350	0.0524	0.2318
Hard red wheat	4.1100	0.0685	0.3030
Soybean meal	322.20	0.1611	0.7127

percent protein, and hard red wheat is 13.5 percent protein. Wheat provides as much energy as corn but not for the same cost.

A 56-pound bushel of corn that is 7.9 percent protein contains 4.424 pounds of protein, not that you can choose which of the 4.424 pounds of the corn to use. A 60-pound bushel of hard red wheat with 13.5 percent protein contains 8.10 pounds of protein. Soy meal trades by the ton, and at 45 percent protein, a ton contains 900 pounds of protein. Assume that corn is trading at $2.935 per bushel, hard red wheat at $4.11 per bushel, and soy meal at $322.20 per ton. Exhibit 8.4 shows the price per pound for each feed ingredient and the cost of 4.424 pounds of protein.

These prices change constantly, but the general idea holds. Soy protein costs far more than corn or wheat protein. So many commercial feeders use a linear program to find the lowest-cost mix that achieves their nutritional goals. The way these things work is that when you push up one factor in the equation, you push the others down but not out. That is, if the feeder adds a little wheat to the mix, that means that there will be somewhat less corn and soy meal.

A PRICE AT WHICH WHEAT AND CORN ARE EQUALLY ATTRACTIVE

One of the key questions in this balancing act is at what wheat price do feedlot operators become indifferent about whether they buy corn or wheat. A standard daily corn ration is 18 pounds (to achieve a 4.4 pound daily weight gain). This is slightly less than a third of a bushel, or 0.3214 bushel ($18 \div 56 = 0.3214$). At 7.9 percent protein, this 18 pounds contain 1.42 pounds of protein. Given the $2.9350 per bushel corn price shown in Exhibit 8.4, it will cost $0.9433 for that 18 pounds (0.3214×2.9350).

The next question concerns how much wheat it takes to match that 1.422 pounds of protein. That is, if 18 pounds of corn (with 7.9 percent of protein or 0.079 in decimal form) contains 1.42 pounds of protein, how many pounds of wheat (with 13.5 percent protein or 0.135) does it take to get 1.42 pounds of protein? More formulaically:

$$0.079 \times 18 = 1.42$$
$$0.135x = 1.42$$
$$x = 1.42 \div 0.135 = 10.52 \text{ lb/day of wheat}$$

Just as 18 pounds is 0.3214 of a 56-pound bushel corn, so 10.52 is 0.1753 of a 60-pound bushel of wheat (10.52 ÷ 60). Further, let the corn bushel fraction (in this example, 0.3214) be A, the corn price be B, the wheat bushel fraction be C, and the wheat price be D. So far, you have values for A, B, and C and need to solve for D, which will be the "indifference price" for wheat—that is, the price at which feedlot operators become indifferent about whether they buy corn or wheat.

The basic equation is A times B divided by C equals D, thus:

$$\frac{A \times B}{C} = D$$

Substituting actual numbers, this becomes:

$$\frac{0.3214 \times 2.935}{0.1753} = \frac{0.9433}{0.1753} = 5.38$$

You can see that $5.38 per bushel is the indifference price of wheat on that day.

In fact, the wheat price shown in Exhibit 8.4 was $4.11, so the cost of 10.52 pounds of wheat was actually $0.7205 (0.1753 × 4.11), well under the cost of 18 pounds of corn. This large disparity between the actual wheat price and the indifference price suggests that cattle feeders will be buying wheat. This increase in wheat demand should raise the price of wheat, while the decrease in demand for corn may slow the rate of the corn price increase or even lower the price of corn. Based on this, it seems logical to say that any time you see a sizable difference between the actual and indifference prices of wheat, it is probably a good time to buy the wheat-corn spread—that is, buy KC wheat and sell Chicago corn.

A question remains concerning what constitutes a "sizable difference." You can probably decide this in a number of ways, but one that might be useful is to use normal distribution statistics. Suppose you set up a spreadsheet to calculate the indifference price of wheat given the corn price on each day of June 2004. Exhibit 8.5 shows the prices for December 2004 wheat (KWZ4), corn (C Z4), the KC wheat-corn spread, the indifference price of wheat, and the difference between the indifference price and the actual price of wheat.

EXHIBIT 8.5

Tracking the KC Wheat-Corn Spread in June 2004

	KWZ4	C Z4	Spread	Indifference Price	Difference between Actual and Indifference Price (Ind-KW)
6/1/04	4.2075	3.1725	1.0350	5.8166	1.6091
6/2/04	4.0875	3.1925	0.8950	5.8532	1.7657
6/3/04	4.0500	3.1000	0.9500	5.6836	1.6336
6/4/04	4.0625	3.1075	0.9550	5.6974	1.6349
6/7/04	4.0125	3.0350	0.9775	5.5645	1.5520
6/8/04	4.0050	2.9925	1.0125	5.4865	1.4815
6/9/04	4.0075	3.0250	0.9825	5.5461	1.5386
6/10/04	3.9425	2.9075	1.0350	5.3307	1.3882
6/14/04	3.9525	2.9450	1.0075	5.3994	1.4469
6/15/04	3.9100	2.8425	1.0675	5.2115	1.3015
6/16/04	3.9025	2.8625	1.0400	5.2482	1.3457
6/17/04	3.9150	2.8325	1.0825	5.1932	1.2782
6/18/04	3.9125	2.8000	1.1125	5.1336	1.2211
6/21/04	3.9375	2.8225	1.1150	5.1749	1.2374
6/22/04	3.8825	2.7725	1.1100	5.0832	1.2007
6/23/04	3.8975	2.8425	1.0550	5.2115	1.3140
6/24/04	3.8325	2.8250	1.0075	5.1794	1.3469
6/25/04	3.8300	2.8550	0.9750	5.2344	1.4044
6/28/04	3.8075	2.7900	1.0175	5.1153	1.3078
6/29/04	3.7900	2.7750	1.0150	5.0878	1.2978
6/30/04	3.7650	2.6700	1.0950	4.8953	1.1303

You can see that the values in the Difference between Actual and Indifference Price column range from a high of 1.7657 on June 2 to a low of 1.1303 on June 30. The mean difference is 1.4017, and one standard deviation is 0.1682. The difference levels plus or minus one standard deviation from the mean are 1.5699 and 1.2335.

One possible definition of "sizable difference" is anything greater or less than one standard deviation—that is, any difference greater than 1.57 suggests a time to buy the spread because cattle feeders are likely to be buying wheat. Going the other way, any difference greater than 1.23 suggests a time to sell the spread.

Notice that the 1.7657 June 2 difference is slightly more than two standard deviations. Notice also that the 0.8950 spread level is the narrowest point for this spread for the entire period from January 2 to October 15, 2004. This makes June 2 look like the time to buy wheat and sell corn. Having made the trade, you can simply wait for the spread to widen, or you can take another look at the difference between the actual and indifference price of wheat.

By June 10, the spread had widened by 14 cents per bushel to $1.0350. To have unwound on that day would have been to have earned $700 per spread (0.14 × 5,000), as Exhibit 8.6 shows.

No law says you can't hold these spreads in place for longer. Having bought the spread on June 2, suppose you had waited until July 22 to unwind it. Exhibit 8.7 shows that the spread widened by 49.5 cents per bushel during the June 2–July 22 span—from 0.8950 to 1.3900, to earn $2,475 per spread.

At the $2.2775 per bushel July 22 corn price, the indifference level wheat price was $4.1756 per bushel, only $0.5081 more than the $3.6675 actual wheat price. That contrasts strongly with the $1.7657 per bushel difference of the actual and indifference prices of June 2.

Most traders probably find it easier to track the spread as a guide to trading it. Yet even these few examples seem to show a striking correspondence between large indifference and actual wheat price differences and relatively

EXHIBIT 8.6

A Buying Response to the Indifference Price of Wheat

	Action	KWZ4	Action	C Z4	Spread
6/2/04	Buy	4.0875	Sell	3.1925	0.8950
6/10/04	Sell	3.9425	Buy	2.9075	1.0350
Result		−0.1450		0.2850	
Spread net				0.1400	0.1400
Spread $ net				700.00	

EXHIBIT 8.7

Less Indifference—Better Spread Results

	Action	KWZ4	Action	C Z4	Spread
6/2/04	Buy	4.0875	Sell	3.1925	0.8950
6/10/04	Sell	3.6675	Buy	2.2775	1.3900
Result		−0.4200		0.9150	
Spread net				0.4950	0.4950
Spread $ net				2,475.00	

narrow spreads and small indifference—and actual wheat price differences and relatively wider spreads. This seems to support the hypothesis that the relative cost of protein is a major economic driver of the wheat-corn spread

DIFFERENT TIME, DIFFERENT PRICES? SIMILAR STORY

One month does not provide much of a statistical sample, and looking at a month when prices had changed a great deal might create a rather different impression. Exhibit 8.8 performs the exercise of Exhibit 8.5 with the prices recorded during September 2004 for these two December contracts.

EXHIBIT 8.8

Tracking the KC Wheat-Corn Spread for September 2004

	KWZ4	C Z4	Spread	Indifference Price	Difference between Actual and Indifference Price (Ind-KW)
9/1/04	3.4875	2.4275	1.0600	4.4506	0.9631
9/2/04	3.4200	2.3625	1.0575	4.3315	0.9115
9/3/04	3.3775	2.3100	1.0675	4.2352	0.8877
9/7/04	3.3550	2.2650	1.0900	4.1525	0.7977
9/8/04	3.3875	2.2675	1.1200	4.1573	0.7698
9/9/04	3.3900	2.2600	1.1300	4.1435	0.7535
9/10/04	3.5625	2.2225	1.3400	4.0748	0.5123
9/13/04	3.5900	2.2050	1.3850	4.0427	0.4527
9/14/04	3.5550	2.1800	1.3750	3.9969	0.4419
9/15/04	3.6150	2.1850	1.4300	4.0060	0.3910
9/16/04	3.6350	2.1650	1.4700	3.9694	0.3344
9/17/04	3.5975	2.1525	1.4450	3.9465	0.3490
6/20/04	3.5750	2.1275	1.4475	3.9006	0.3256
9/21/04	3.6325	2.1275	1.5050	3.9006	0.2681
9/22/04	3.5500	2.1025	1.5300	3.8548	0.3048
9/23/04	3.5475	2.0775	1.4725	3.8089	0.2614
9/24/04	3.5175	2.0525	1.4950	3.7631	0.2456
9/27/04	3.5000	2.0775	1.4225	3.8089	0.3089
9/28/04	3.4525	2.0850	1.3675	3.8227	0.3702
9/29/04	3.4750	2.0725	1.4025	3.7998	0.3248
9/30/04	3.3675	2.0550	1.3125	3.7677	0.4002

EXHIBIT 8.9

The Spread-Difference Relationship

	KW-C Spread	Difference
9/1/04	1.0600	0.9631
9/13/04	1.3850	0.4527
9/24/04	1.4950	0.2456

Notice that all the differences (Difference between Actual and Indifference Price) are smaller than the June differences. The range here is from a high of 0.9631 on September 1 to a low of 0.2456 on September 24. The mean is 0.4926, and one standard deviation is 0.2390. The September difference values vary significantly more than the June difference values (compare the 0.1682 June standard deviation). A 0.7316 difference is one standard deviation above the mean, so the 0.9631 September 1 difference is almost two standard deviations above the mean. Notice, too, that by September 10, the difference was 0.5123, and, by September 13, it was 0.4527—both values that are close to the September mean. Also, the 0.2456 September 24 difference is slightly less than one standard deviation below the mean.

In general, these differences seem to vary inversely with the wheat-corn spread. Exhibit 8.9 shows the September 1, 13, and 24 spread levels and difference values.

High difference values occur when the spread is relatively narrow, and low difference values occur when the spread is relatively wide, but this relationship is by no means perfect. The 1.4950 September 24 spread is almost 6 cents narrower than the 1.5300 of September 22, and the 1.0600 September 1 spread is a fourth of a cent higher than the 1.0575 spread of September 2. A scan of the data for other months will reveal more wobbles. Still, the indifference-actual numbers seem worth paying attention to.

FACTORING IN SPREAD STATISTICS

True spreads tend to be mean-reverting, and these data certainly suggest that this is true of the KC wheat-corn spread. Exhibit 8.10 shows how the December KC wheat-corn spread performed from September 1 to October 15, 2004. Overlaid on the spread plot is the spread mean for that period along with the plus or minus one standard deviation levels. This exhibit also shows the indifference-actual wheat price differences and the mean of the difference.

EXHIBIT 8.10

Wheat-Corn Spread (9/1/04 to 10/15/04)

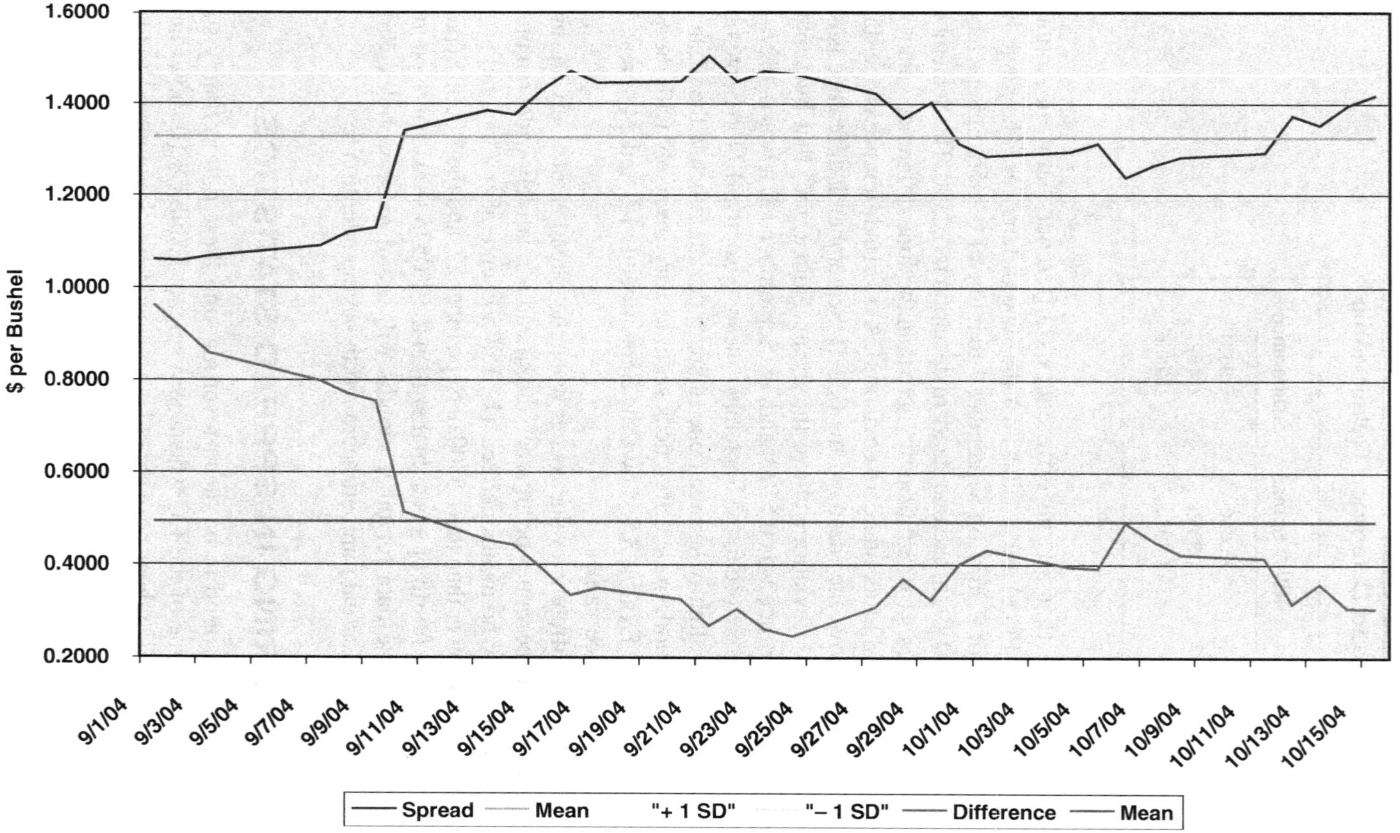

You can see at a glance that both series exhibit mean reversion. The obvious presence of mean reversion also suggests that this spread should generate both buying and selling opportunities. Further, it is possible to use the distribution statistics to develop a sense of trade potential. To see how this might work, consider a series of trades based on September and early October data and the statistics in Exhibit 8.11.

Suppose you saw the 0.9631 September 1 difference and the 1.0600 spread of that day. These values are both almost two standard deviations away from the mean and suggest a time to buy the spread.

By September 13, the indifference-actual wheat level was close to the September mean, and the spread traded at 1.3850, slightly higher than the spread mean. These both represent slightly more than two standard deviations of mean reversion. If your trading goal was to unwind at or close to the spread mean and you unwound on September 13, your trade would have earned $1,625 per spread as Exhibit 8.12 shows.

One interesting feature of this trade is that both legs gained. Recall that this was true of the trade depicted in Exhibit 8.2, although that trade involved selling the spread. It is worth emphasizing that, while you can't expect this to happen in every case, it happens surprisingly often with these wheat-corn spreads.

The 0.7535 September 9 difference was about one standard deviation greater than the September mean, and the 1.1200 wheat-corn spread was still about one and one-half standard deviations narrower than its mean. At this point, just a return to the mean level would generate solid

EXHIBIT 8.11

Spread and Difference Variability

			± 1 Std. Dev.	± 2 Std. Dev.
Sep. difference	Mean	0.4926	0.7316	0.9706
	Std. dev.	0.2390	0.2536	0.0146
	High	0.9631		
	Low	0.2456		
KW-C spread	Mean	1.3260	1.4636	1.6012
	Std. dev.	0.1376	1.1884	1.0508
	High	1.6000		
	Low	1.0575		

EXHIBIT 8.12

Buying the Spread in Response to a Strong Signal

	Action	KWZ4	Action	C Z4	Spread
9/1/04	Buy	3.4875	Sell	2.4275	1.0600
9/13/04	Sell	3.5900	Buy	2.2050	1.3850
Result		0.1025		0.2225	
Spread net				0.3250	0.3250
Spread $ net				1,625.00	

EXHIBIT 8.13

Less Than the Best Is Still Good

	Action	KWZ4	Action	C Z4	Spread
9/9/04	Buy	3.3900	Sell	2.2600	1.1300
9/13/04	Sell	3.5900	Buy	2.2050	1.3850
Result		0.2000		0.0550	
Spread net				0.2550	0.2550
Spread $ net				1,275.00	

gains. If you had bought the spread on September 9 and again unwound it on September 13, it would have earned $1,275, as Exhibit 8.13 shows.

Further, you could have had a different goal for this trade. Suppose you had bought the spread on either September 1 or September 9 and decided to hold onto either trade until the spread widened to at least one standard deviation above the mean. The four days from September 21 through September 14 all qualify as possible unwinding points in terms of this goal. September 24 was the day of the September difference low, so suppose you had unwound either trade on that day. Exhibits 8.14a and b show how these trades would have performed across this period.

Suppose the rule of thumb that guides your selling of the spread is that you will sell wheat and buy corn any time the indifference-actual wheat value is one or more standard deviations below its mean. This was the case on September 24, and it was also true that the wheat-corn spread was more than one standard deviation wider than its 1.3260 September–early October mean. On October 5, the wheat-corn spread had narrowed to 1.3125, slightly narrower than its mean. The difference reached 0.4898, almost its mean, on October 6. Exhibits 8.15a and b show how the spread would have performed

EXHIBIT 8.14

Waiting to Make a Good Buy Better

a

	Action	KWZ4	Action	C Z4	Spread
9/1/04	Buy	3.4875	Sell	2.4275	1.0600
9/24/04	Sell	3.5175	Buy	2.0525	1.4650
Result		0.0300		0.3750	
Spread net				0.4050	0.4050
Spread $ net				2,025.00	

b

	Action	KWZ4	Action	C Z4	Spread
9/9/04	Buy	3.3900	Sell	2.2600	1.1300
9/24/04	Sell	3.5175	Buy	2.0525	1.4650
Result		0.1275		0.2075	
Spread net				0.3350	0.3350
Spread $ net				1,675.00	

EXHIBIT 8.15A

Selling the Spread for a Solid Gain

	Action	KWZ4	Action	C Z4	Spread
9/24/04	Sell	3.575	Buy	2.0525	1.4650
10/5/04	Buy	3.3575	Sell	2.0450	1.3125
Result		0.1600		–0.0075	
Spread net				0.1525	–0.1525
Spread $ net				762.50	

if you had sold it on September 24 and unwound the trade on either October 5 or October 6.

MECHANICS OR ECONOMICS

This attention to means, standard deviations, and mean reversion may seem like just another mechanical trading approach. Keep in mind that the spread levels cited seem to relate rather closely, though not perfectly, to

EXHIBIT 8.15B

What a Difference a Day Made

	Action	KWZ4	Action	C Z4	Spread
9/24/04	Sell	3.575	Buy	2.0525	1.4650
10/6/04	Buy	3.3100	Sell	2.0725	1.2375
Result		0.2075		0.0200	
Spread net				0.2275	–0.2275
Spread $ net				1,137.50.00	

what is happening to the difference between the indifference and actual prices of wheat. Further, that seems tied to the livestock feeders' balancing act with regard to optimizing protein content at minimal cost. In short, this approach to the Kansas City wheat–Chicago corn spread trade appears to have a strong basis in the economics of livestock feeding.

CHAPTER 9

White and Yellow: The Platinum-Gold Spread

The metals markets should not be overlooked by spread traders. While the gold-silver spread has enjoyed reasonable popularity for some time, an even more interesting spread is the one between platinum and gold.

What makes these two markets interesting in terms of spread potential is that both these precious metals serve a variety of functions. Gold has an obvious jewelry and decorative function, and so does platinum. In addition, gold has long served an investment function. Basically, when inflation rages or when financial investments do not generate reasonable rates of return, gold becomes an inflation hedge for many—or at least a solid alternative investment. Promoters of platinum tout its investment potential also, but this seems never to have become a major role for platinum.

Platinum is more of an industrial metal than is gold. To be sure, gold has important uses in electronics and in the manufacture of space equipment and aircraft, yet it remains hard for most people to think of gold as an industrial metal. Not so, platinum. The automotive industry uses platinum in catalytic converters. Platinum serves as a catalyst in petroleum refining and in the manufacture of a variety of chemicals and of fuel cells for power generation. And it is used to make computer hard disks, spark plugs, and pollution-control devices. This is not an exhaustive list, but it gets across the idea.

DEVELOPING A SPREAD OUTLOOK

In thinking about how such a spread might perform, you can develop a general idea by thinking, first, about how the general economy is performing and how it might perform in the near future. To a first approximation, it seems fair to think that during any period when the U.S. economy is growing at a healthy pace and inflation seems largely under control, the platinum-gold spread should widen. That is, platinum futures should outperform gold futures. Conversely, during periods of very low investment returns or periods when inflation threatens, or both, the spread should narrow. That is, gold futures should outperform platinum futures.

The July 2004 Congressional testimony of U.S. Federal Reserve Chairman Alan Greenspan seemed to indicate a situation in which you might well expect the spread to widen going forward. Chairman Greenspan said, among other things, that "market-based indicators of inflation, after rising earlier in the year, have receded," and that "the growth of aggregate demand [was] looking more sustainable and . . . employment [was] expanding broadly." In short, the U.S. economy was poised to grow and inflation seemed not to threaten, which seemed to suggest an economic climate in which platinum futures would gain relative to gold futures. You may take exception to the chairman's outlook in a case like this, but that's the beauty of trading spreads. You can express the contrary opinion.

The general economic outlook can point in a general direction, but you should also look at more particular factors which can affect the performance of the spread. One economic sector to watch is the automotive sector. When cars and trucks are selling, platinum demand is likely to be rising. For example, demand for platinum for catalytic converters grew by 23 percent from 2002 to 2003. Also, a thriving computer industry will elevate platinum demand.

Another important question involves the availability of supplies of these metals. During much of 2002, the automotive industry was able to draw down existing stocks of platinum. During 2003, these users had to come to market for supplies. That boosted platinum prices. Further, demand for platinum had exceeded supply for several years. By early 2004, that seemed to have changed, which might be expected to ease upward pressure on platinum prices to some extent. What the balance between upward and downward forces may be is an important consideration.

Information about the prospects for these metals is easy to find. Your broker no doubt has access to helpful analyst reports covering these topics. Also, you can find excellent resources online.

METALS MARKET BACKGROUND

While gold futures trade on numerous exchanges around the world, the Commodity Exchange (COMEX) contract seems the one to use for this spread because platinum is a New York Mercantile Exchange (NYMEX) market, and COMEX is a division of NYMEX. The gold and platinum contracts differ more in appearance than in substance. Both are priced in terms of dollars per troy ounce (a troy ounce is 1/12 of a pound, whereas a conventional ounce is 1/16 of a pound). However, the COMEX gold contract contains 100 troy ounces, while the NYMEX platinum contract contains 50 troy ounces.

Also, these contracts trade on different cycles. A look at the contract specifications will give you a somewhat different idea of which months are available than will a look at a commodity quote page. What matters is that COMEX gold uses a February, April, August, and October cycle along with various nearby and far distant months. NYMEX platinum uses a January, April, July, and October cycle along with various more transitory months. The times of overlap are the April and October contracts, which should suffice for spread trading purposes.

The platinum-gold spread is simply the platinum futures price minus the gold futures price:

$$\text{Platinum price} - \text{gold price} = \text{spread}$$
$$787.20 - 390.80 = 396.40$$

These prices make the difference between the two contracts seem greater than it really is. Given that one platinum contract contains 50 troy ounces while one gold contract contains 100 troy ounces, the spread here is between a contract valued at \$39,360 (787.20 × 50) and another valued at \$39,080 (390.80 × 100).

Exhibit 9.1 uses October 2004 platinum and gold futures prices (i.e., PLV4 and GCV4) to illustrate how this spread performed during the first 10 months of 2004. You can pretty well track the degree of market concern for inflation or the belief that the U.S. economy would grow by watching the widening and narrowing of this spread.

STRUCTURING THE SPREAD

By calculating the spread this way (platinum futures price minus gold futures price), the platinum-gold spread will widen whenever platinum prices gain relative to gold and narrow whenever gold prices gain relative to platinum. Accordingly, the logic of this spread is that you buy or sell the spread in terms of what you do with the platinum leg.

Suppose that in late July 2004 you agreed with Chairman Greenspan that the U.S. economy was poised to grow during the rest of 2004 and that

EXHIBIT 9.1a

Platinum-Gold Spread

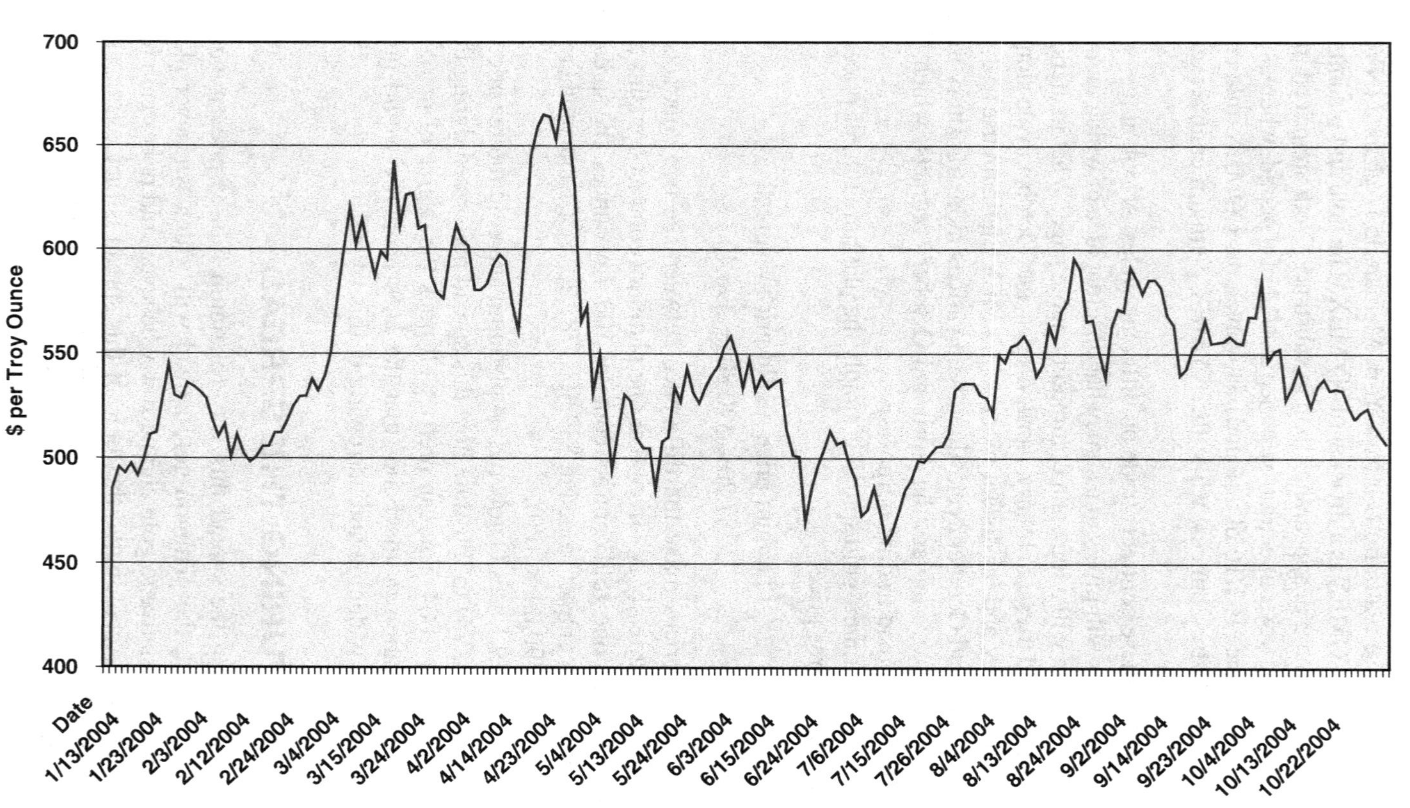

EXHIBIT 9.1b

Platinum-Gold Spread (Contract Values)

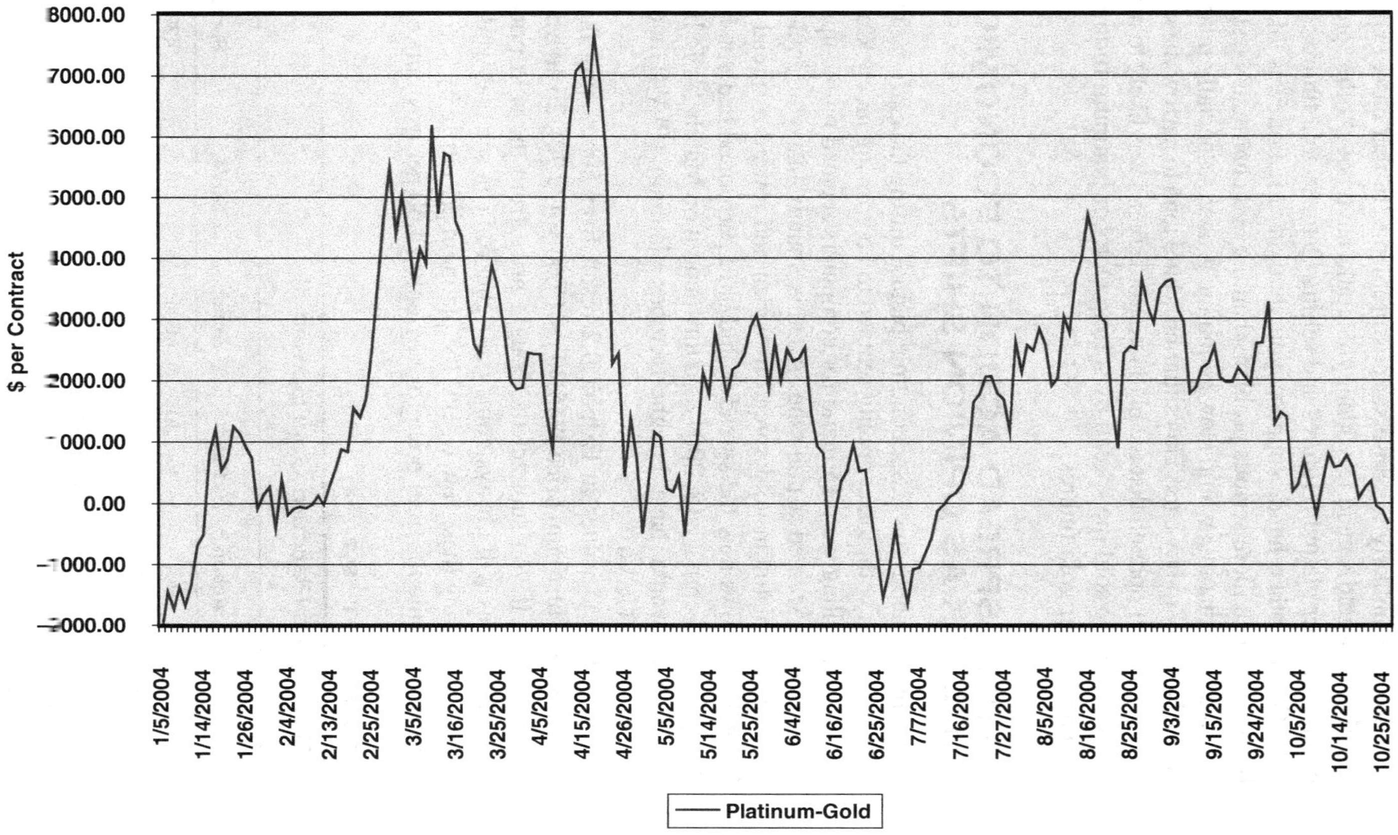

inflation was unlikely to cause serious problems. In that case, expecting the platinum-gold spread to widen, you could have bought the spread by buying October platinum futures and selling October gold futures.

On the other hand, suppose you thought inflation was likely to become a much more serious problem than the Fed chairman's testimony indicated and that this would slow economic growth, especially relative to people's ability to buy cars. This situation would tend to narrow the spread. To express your opinion that the platinum-gold spread was likely to narrow, you could have sold the spread by selling October platinum futures and buying October gold futures.

FITTING SPREAD ACTION TO ECONOMIC OUTLOOK AS OPINION SHIFTS

Think briefly about the U.S. economic picture during the early months of 2004. To begin with, the economy seemed to be growing nicely. Cars and trucks were selling well. Demand for computers seemed on the upswing. And inflation seemed a nonissue. All this sounds like you could have expected the platinum-gold spread to widen and reward a spread buyer. Exhibit 9.2 shows how the spread would have performed had you bought the spread on February 18, 2004, and unwound it on March 24. To buy the spread, you would have bought October platinum (PLV4) and sold October gold (GCV4)

The Spread values in Exhibit 9.2 result from subtracting the gold price from the platinum price (845.30 – 415.60 = 429.70). To arrive at the Result values, if you subtract the bought price from the sold price, the gains and losses will always come out right. You can see that while both prices rose during these few weeks, the platinum price rose by $56.50 per troy ounce, while the gold price rose by only $4.60 per troy ounce. Also,

EXHIBIT 9.2

Buying the Platinum-Gold Spread

	Action	PLV4	Action	GCV4	Spread
2/18/04	Buy	845.30	Sell	415.60	429.70
3/24/04	Sell	901.80	Buy	420.20	481.60
Result		56.50		–4.60	
$ Result		2,825.00		–460.00	
Spread net				51.90	51.90
Spread $ net				2,365.00	

since you initially sold gold, the price rise results in a loss. The $ Result row multiplies the platinum result by 50, there being 50 troy ounces in one platinum contract, and multiplies the gold result by 100, there being 100 troy ounces in that contract. The Spread net row entry in the GCV4 column is the sum of the platinum and gold results, while the Spread net entry in the Spread column is the March 24 spread value minus the February 18 spread value. By doing both these calculations, you create a useful check, for, apart from a possible positive-minus difference, these numbers should match. Finally, the Spread $ net value is the sum of the two $ Result values. This 51.90 spread widening resulted in a $2,365.00 gain.

HERE COMES INFLATION TALK

Starting in mid to late April 2004, talk about inflation moved more to the forefront. The market consensus was that the Fed would have to start raising its fed funds target rate sometime during the summer, and this talk created an economic speed bump that promised to narrow the platinum-gold spread. That is, this might well have seemed a good time to reverse strategy and sell the platinum-gold spread. Exhibit 9.3 shows that while both prices fell during the April 21 to May 12, 2004, period, the platinum price fell more to narrow the spread and benefit the spread seller.

Notice the minus sign on the Spread net value in the Spread column. This indicates a spread narrowing. For spread sellers, as in this case, this should result in a gain—hence the positive value in the GCV4 column.

It may be worth noting that the positive results in both Exhibits 9.2 and 9.3 come from the platinum leg of the spread. Even though you sell the spread with the expectation that gold will outperform platinum, outperformance can take the form of losing less. In this case, the sold leg will gain

EXHIBIT 9.3

Selling the Platinum-Gold Spread in Response to Inflation Talk

	Action	PLV4	Action	GCV4	Spread
4/21/04	Sell	874.50	Buy	393.50	481.00
5/12/04	Buy	775.00	Sell	379.80	395.20
Result		99.50		–13.70	
$ Result		4,975.00		–1,370.00	
Spread net				85.80	–85.80
Spread $ net				3,605.00	

more than the bought leg will lose. Spread trading is rather an *Alice in Wonderland* kind of world at times, and it takes some getting used to.

The situations outlined in Exhibits 9.2 and 9.3 are not the only situations that can widen or narrow this spread, of course. Exhibits 9.4 and 9.5 illustrate two interesting possibilities.

Exhibit 9.4 shows that if you had bought the spread on February 18, as in Exhibit 9.2, but unwound it on March 17 rather than a week later, the spread would have still widened, but it would have done so because the two legs had headed in opposite directions. Thus, both would have shown positive results. The higher platinum price would have rewarded having bought that leg, and the falling gold price would have rewarded having sold that leg.

Exhibit 9.5 shows a situation in which both prices rose, but the gold price rose significantly more than the platinum price. In this case, the platinum leg of the spread booked a loss, but the gold gain prevailed to reward a seller of the spread.

EXHIBIT 9.4

When the Two Markets Head in Opposite Directions, Both Legs Gain

	Action	PLV4	Action	GCV4	Spread
2/18/04	Buy	845.30	Sell	415.60	429.70
3/17/04	Sell	887.80	Buy	409.90	477.90
Result		42.50		5.70	
$ Result		2,125.00		570.00	
Spread net				48.20	48.20
Spread $ net				2,695.00	

EXHIBIT 9.5

Selling the Spread When Rising Prices Cause a Narrowing

	Action	PLV4	Action	GCV4	Spread
3/17/04	Sell	887.80	Buy	409.90	477.90
3/31	Buy	890.20	Sell	430.30	459.90
Result		–2.40		20.40	
$ Result		–120.00		2,040.00	
Spread net				18.00	–18.00
Spread $ net				1,920.00	

A WORD OF CAUTION

As always, it is good to remember that the platinum-gold spread is a speculative trade. If you misread the economic situation or for any other reason get on the wrong side of this spread, you can suffer a loss.

Also, because of the contract size difference, it is a good idea to translate the futures prices and results of platinum-gold spreads that you contemplate making into dollar values, as has been done with Exhibits 9.2, 9.3, 9.4, and 9.5. Here's why. You can be right about this spread and wrong about the trade. To illustrate, suppose that for some reason you had bought the platinum-gold spread on March 29 and unwound it two days later. Exhibit 9.6 shows the details of the trade except for the dollar conversions. These are left out.

Notice that the platinum leg gained more than the gold leg lost as the spread widened by nine points. This seems like it should be a good enough trade. The spread widened, and both Spread net values are positive. Exhibit 9.7 tells the whole story.

EXHIBIT 9.6

When You Are Right about the Spread . . .

	Action	PLV4	Action	GCV4	Spread
3/28/04	Buy	870.90	Sell	420.00	450.90
3/31/04	Sell	890.20	Buy	430.30	459.90
Result		19.30		–10.30	
Spread net				9.00	9.00

EXHIBIT 9.7

. . . and Wrong about the Trade

	Action	PLV4	Action	GCV4	Spread
3/28/04	Buy	870.90	Sell	420.00	450.90
3/31/04	Sell	890.20	Buy	430.30	459.90
Result		19.30		–10.30	
$ Result		965.00		–1,030.00	
Spread net				9.00	9.00
Spread $ net				–65.00	

Whoops! The larger size of the gold contract creates a situation in which the gold loss overwhelms the platinum gain. This is rather a special case, but it does illustrate that it is possible to be right about how the spread will change and still suffer a loss. This spread will achieve breakeven when the platinum gain doubles the gold loss (e.g., if the March 31 platinum price had been 891.50, the platinum gain would have been 20.60 and created a wash trade).

In practice, situations like this seem rare. It took a lot of looking to find one. Still, it is good to be aware of the possibility, however remote.

CHAPTER 10

The Soybean Crush Spread

Processing Soybeans into Soybean Meal and Soybean Oil

The soybean crush spread is one of several interesting process spreads available to futures traders. These spreads capture the basic economics of processes that add value to one or more raw materials—in this case, soybeans. A *crusher* (as soybean processors are called) buys soybeans, crushes them, and sells soybean meal and soybean oil. The business plan calls for the product output to sell for more than the cost of the soybean input. This doesn't invariably work out according to plan, but that's the basic idea.

Regardless of whether things work out in keeping with the crushers' business plans, soybean crush traders can find opportunity to generate healthy gains.

THE BASIC ECONOMICS OF THE SOYBEAN CRUSH SPREAD

The primary use for soybean meal is as a high-protein livestock feed. Soybean oil serves in a variety of industrial and food uses. Normally, according to traders and analysts who specialize in the soy complex, meal drives the spread, and it is news when oil seems to dominate the spread. Obviously, this is too simple, but this is the general idea.

During years when the soybean crop has been disappointing, soybean prices will trade higher, and this can narrow the spread. When that happens, strong livestock feed demand can more or less save the day. However, if a soybean shortage coincides with a period of very low livestock prices, feed demand may fall off sharply. When that happens, it will take bodacious demand for soy oil to "save" the spread.

When the spread margin is relatively wide and promises to widen even more, crushers will step up crushing activity. That can increase supply relative to demand and ultimately narrow the spread. When supply exceeds demand, people don't have to bid as aggressively, and prices tend to fall. Conversely, when the spread margin is narrow and promises to narrow yet more, crushers will curtail crushing activity. That will tend to decrease supply relative to demand and ultimately widen the spread when product users begin to bid up the prices.

CALCULATING THE SOYBEAN CRUSH SPREAD

The three contracts of the CBOT (Chicago Board of Trade) soy complex use different pricing systems and weights. Consider the March 15, 2004, prices for the May crush spread and its components, which are shown in Exhibit 10.1. Soybeans are typically quoted in cents per bushel, and one contract contains 5000 bushels. Thus, a quote of 978.25 (traditionally, 978 1/4) is 978 and 1/4 cents, easily convertible into $9.7825. Soybean meal (or more simply soy meal) is quoted in dollars per ton, and one contract contains 100 tons—e.g., $297.80 per ton. Soybean oil (or soy oil) is quoted in cents per pound, and one contract contains 60,000 pounds. Thus a quote of 33.75 translates into $0.3375. To calculate the soybean crush spread, you can use two conversion factors to convert the meal and oil prices to dollars per bushel.

CONVERTING TO DOLLARS PER BUSHEL

To convert the $297.80 soy meal price into dollars per bushel, multiply by 0.022. To convert the $0.3375 soy oil price into dollars per bushel, multiply by 11. Exhibit 10.1 shows the results of converting these March 15 prices of the May contracts and further shows that the August crush spread that

EXHIBIT 10.1

Soy Complex Price Conversions and the Crush Spread Value (August Contracts)

Contract	Quoted Price	Conversion Factor	Converted Price
Soy meal	297.80	0.022	6.5516
Soy oil	0.3375	11.0	3.7125
Soybeans	9.7825		9.7825
Crush spread			0.7868

day was $0.4816 per bushel. Incidentally, the crush spread formula is: [(Soy meal price × 0.022) + (Soy oil price × 11)] – Soybean price = Crush spread in dollars per bushel, and a good ballpark breakeven for crushers is $0.40 per bushel.

LIVESTOCK FEEDERS AND FOREIGN MARKETS

Clearly, informed soybean crush spread traders must keep track of several kinds of information. One large market that deserves the attention of soybean crush spread traders is the livestock feeding market. Livestock feeders use soy meal to boost the protein content of their feed, but soy meal isn't the only source of protein for this purpose. In addition, if dietary fads cause people to shun red meat, as has happened in recent memory, demand for soy meal can fall off, and this will narrow the spread—all else remaining equal.

Even when livestock feeders are running at full capacity, soy meal prices can come under threat. When alternative protein sources (such as wheat) become relatively inexpensive, demand for soy meal can drop, and this can have a domino effect.

Suppose demand for soy oil is strong, but demand for soy meal is relatively weak. Crushers can't produce one or the other. Crush a bean and you get both—like it or not. If the demand for meal is greater than the demand for oil, no problem. Oil is easy to store. The crushers can hold the oil until the market for it improves. The catch is that meal doesn't store well. Because this is true, when the crush is driven by demand for oil, the crushers have to find a way to unload the meal they generate. That way is lower and lower prices. At some price, the stuff will move.

That situation may please livestock feeders, but it can narrow the crush spread margin in a cruel way—cruel for the crushers. Obviously, this presents a good opportunity for crush spread traders.

Soybean crush spread traders cannot ignore the export markets, and it is important to know whether the importers are buying soybeans or soy products. In the early spring of 2004, for example, Chinese soybean crushers were buying soybeans. This bid up the price of soybeans enough to narrow the spread and to keep it relatively narrow. In late April 2004, these buyers dropped out. As a result, soybean prices dropped enough to widen the spread dramatically.

TRACKING THE SOYBEAN CRUSH SPREAD

Exhibit 10.2 tracks the May 2004 soybean crush spread and its components from mid-March to the end of April.

EXHIBIT 10.2

Tracking the May 2004 Crush Spread and Its Component Contracts

	S K4	SMK4	BOK4	Crush Spread
3/15/04	9.7825	297.80	0.3375	0.4816
3/16/04	9.8900	302.10	0.3357	0.4489
3/17/04	9.9400	304.90	0.3339	0.4407
3/18/04	10.1800	313.20	0.3416	0.4680
3/19/04	10.2400	314.20	0.3411	0.4245
3/22/04	10.5575	325.50	0.3485	0.4370
3/23/04	10.5200	325.50	0.3480	0.4690
3/24/04	10.2350	317.80	0.3390	0.4856
3/25/04	10.2850	319.70	0.3370	0.4554
3/26/04	10.1300	316.90	0.3337	0.5125
3/29/04	10.1300	315.50	0.3339	0.4839
3/30/04	10.1625	316.50	0.3311	0.4426
3/31/04	9.9500	314.30	0.3223	0.5099
4/1/04	10.2950	329.40	0.3277	0.5565
4/2/04	10.4550	336.00	0.3264	0.5274
4/5/04	10.2450	326.50	0.3274	0.5394
4/6/04	10.0900	321.80	0.3241	0.5547
4/7/04	10.1600	324.50	0.3267	0.5727
4/8/04	9.8800	316.80	0.3188	0.5964
4/12/04	9.6700	309.50	0.3122	0.5732
4/13/04	9.7150	310.30	0.3149	0.5755
4/14/04	10.1300	322.00	0.3283	0.5653
4/15/04	9.6300	303.40	0.3171	0.5329
4/16/04	9.6500	304.90	0.3227	0.6075
4/19/04	9.6900	304.00	0.3237	0.5587
4/20/04	9.5275	297.30	0.3228	0.5639
4/21/04	9.3500	294.50	0.3265	0.7205
4/22/04	9.4700	299.10	0.3287	0.7259
4/23/04	9.6700	303.40	0.3301	0.6359
4/26/04	9.6450	301.20	0.3293	0.6037
4/27/04	10.0300	308.20	0.3426	0.5190
4/28/04	9.9650	306.50	0.3358	0.4718
4/29/04	10.1450	310.70	0.3457	0.4931
4/30/04	10.3400	318.10	0.3403	0.4015

Notice that during much of April, the May crush was trading plus or minus a few cents of 0.55. On April 21, the crush widened dramatically to $0.72 per bushel. This would seem to be, at least in part, a reaction to the Chinese news.

The spread narrowed back fairly soon after that because the market isn't just one group. The point is that a change of behavior by one group of participants can strongly influence the spread, and the relevant groups are not all domestic.

The Chinese story of the spring of 2004 continues. A short while after the Chinese crushers stopped buying soybeans, Chinese meal users came to the U.S. market. But these buyers don't have crushing facilities, so they were soy meal buyers. This tended to widen the spread.

Exhibit 10.3 shows the July 2004 crush spread and its components during June 2004.

Notice that while July soybean prices trended slightly higher during this month and July soy oil prices held fairly steady, July soy meal prices rose sharply toward the end of June. Between June 1 and June 17, the crush spread, meanwhile, traded in the mid fifties—the average crush level

EXHIBIT 10.3

Tracking the July 2004 Crush Spread and Its Component Contracts

	S N4	SMN4	BON4	Crush Spread
6/1/04	8.6400	273.70	0.2951	0.6275
6/2/04	8.4950	266.20	0.2896	0.5470
6/3/04	8.0600	254.50	0.2790	0.6080
6/4/04	8.3850	263.70	0.2841	0.5415
6/7/04	8.4900	268.70	0.2853	0.5597
6/8/04	8.5200	268.70	0.2842	0.5176
6/9/04	8.5200	272.50	0.2821	0.5781
6/10/04	8.4700	271.30	0.2783	0.5599
6/11/04	8.4700	271.30	0.2811	0.5907
6/14/04	8.7250	279.50	0.2734	0.4314
6/15/04	8.8400	283.20	0.2736	0.4000
6/16/04	8.6950	279.50	0.2724	0.4504
6/17/04	8.6300	280.70	0.2748	0.5682
6/18/04	8.7200	283.00	0.2823	0.6113
6/21/04	8.8850	293.00	0.2827	0.6707
6/22/04	8.8700	296.20	0.2827	0.7561
6/23/04	9.1750	304.60	0.2921	0.7393
6/24/04	9.2150	306.00	0.2940	0.7510
6/25/04	9.2050	308.00	0.2924	0.7874
6/[illegible]/04	[illegible]	294.00	0.2852	0.7552
6/29/04	8.9450	293.30	0.2875	0.6701
6/30/04	8.9300	297.50	0.2818	0.7148

for that time being 0.5369. But when the meal prices jumped, the spread widened remarkably. The average for the last eight trading days of June was 0.7306.

Exhibit 10.4 makes it easier to see the relationship between these two spreads.

News about livestock feeding trends or foreign participation in the markets tends to filter into the market well in advance of the decisive event. There will be talk that this or that buyer is running out of funding and may have to withdraw. Brokerage house analysts will notice that alternative protein feeds are becoming relatively cheap and are able to predict a switch. In short, the potential impact of this news on the soybean crush spread should be easy to figure out—often well in advance. So traders should be able to take effective action.

BUYING AND SELLING THE SOYBEAN CRUSH SPREAD

Sticking with the same spread logic that you want to buy a thing that you expect to increase in value and sell a thing that you expect to decrease in value, you buy or sell the soybean crush spread in terms of what you do with the product legs.

To buy the spread, you initially buy the products and sell soybeans. To unwind the spread, you sell products and buy soybeans. If the spread has widened in the interval, this trade will post a gain.

The situation as you might have seen it on April 1, 2004, provides an example of a time when you might have bought the May soybean crush spread, given the news that was starting to emerge.

Actually, you can trade the 1-1-1 crush spread directly. (Note that the 1-1-1 crush spread involves trading one contract each of soybean, soy meal, and soy oil futures.) You don't have to leg into it. *Legging in* is trade jargon for trading the spread components, or legs, individually. So, you can tell your broker to buy or sell the spread (or choose the equivalent on-screen button). You don't have to indicate that you want to buy one contract of May soy meal (SMK4), buy one contract of May soy oil (BOK4), and sell one contract of May soybeans (S K4).

Still, it's good to be able to analyze the crush in terms of its components. This allows you to figure out where your profit came from—or your loss. Exhibit 10.5 shows what would have happened had you bought 10 May crush spreads on April 1 and sold them on April 21, 2004.

If you subtract the bought price from the sold price, the gains and losses will always come out right. The Result row does this for the three

EXHIBIT 10.4

Soybean Crush Spreads

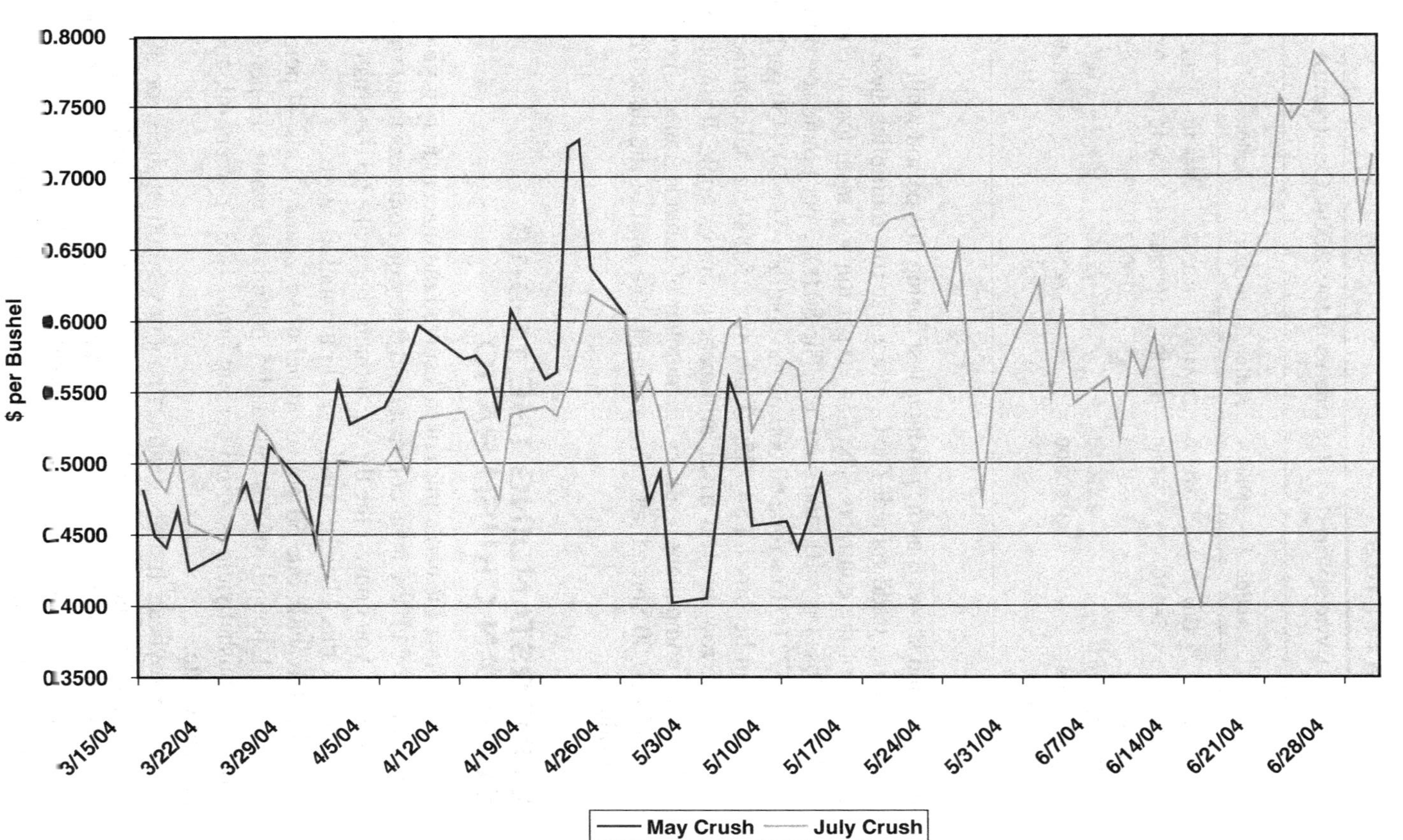

EXHIBIT 10.5

Buying a Widening 1-1-1 Spread (May 2004 Contracts)

	Action	SMK4	Action	BOK4	Action	S K4
4/1/04	Buy 10	329.40	Buy 10	0.3277	Sell 10	10.2950
4/21/04	Sell 10	294.50	Sell 10	0.3265	Buy 10	9.3500
Result		–34.90		0.0012		0.9450
Contract size		–3,490.00		–72.00		4,725.00
Position size		–34,900.00		–720.00		47,250.00
Spread net						11,630.00

contracts and shows that the products lost during this period while the soybean leg of the trade gained. The Contract size row multiplies these results by the size of the contracts. The $34.90 per ton soy meal loss becomes a $3,490.00 loss for a 100-ton contract. The $0.0012 per pound soy oil loss becomes a $72.00 loss for a 60,000-pound contract. The $0.9450 per bushel soybean gain becomes a $4,725.00 gain for a 5,000-bushel contract. The Position size row involves trivial arithmetic in this example. It simply multiplies each component result by the number of spreads traded—here, 10. The $11,630.00 Spread net value is simply the sum of the three Position size values.

UNDERSTANDING THE 11-9-10 SOYBEAN CRUSH RATIO

You can capture the economics of this spread more accurately if you trade it in a ratio of 11 soy meal contracts and 9 soy oil contracts to 10 soybean contracts. If you convert the three contracts that make up the crush spread into pounds, this 11-9-10 crush spread ratio makes sense.

To start with, one 60-pound bushel of soybeans yields 44 pounds of soy meal, 11 pounds of soy oil, and 5 pounds of waste. In percentage terms, the bushel yield is 73.33 percent meal, 18.33 percent oil, and 8.33 percent waste.

One soybean futures contract contains 5,000 bushels, or 300,000 pounds at 60 pounds per bushel (5,000 × 60). One soy meal contract contains 100 tons, or 200,000 pounds at 2,000 pounds per ton (100 × 2,000). And one soy oil contract contains 60,000 pounds. Exhibit 10.6 multiplies these weights by the numbers of contracts for each spread component.

EXHIBIT 10.6

Balancing the Weights of the Soybean Crush Components

Futures	Contract Weight (lbs)	Number of Contracts	Spread Weight (lbs)	Percentage (Prod./Soybean)
Soy meal	200,000	11	2,200	73.33
Soy oil	60,000	9	540,000	18.00
Soybeans	300,000	10	3,000,000	

From this, you can see that the 2.2 million pounds of 11 soy meal contracts amounts to 73.33 percent of the 3 million pounds of 10 contracts of soybeans. The 540,000 pounds of 9 contracts of soy oil comes close to the 18.33 percent of the soybean weight. Clearly, the volumes of the ratioed spread reflect the bushel yield of soybeans more accurately than a 1-1-1 spread does.

A REASON TO BOTHER WITH THE RATIO

The 11-9-10 crush spread ratio might seem like an extra bother in a way. Maybe the bother is worth it.

The bother is that you can trade nine 1-1-1 spreads directly, but then you must buy or sell two extra soy meal contracts and one extra soybean contract. What might make it worth it to do this is that the ratioed spread typically makes slightly more money. Exhibit 10.7 shows how the May 11-9-10 spread performed across the April 1 to April 21, 2004, interval.

EXHIBIT 10.7

Buying the Ratioed Soybean Crush Spread (May 2004 Contracts)

	Action	SMK4	Action	BOK4	Action	S K4
4/1/04	Buy 11	329.40	Buy 9	0.3277	Sell 10	10.2950
4/21/04	Sell 11	294.50	Sell 9	0.3265	Buy 10	9.3500
Result		–34.90		0.0012		0.9450
Contract size		–3,490.00		–72.00		4,725.00
Position size		–38,390.00		–648.00		47,250.00
Spread net						8,212.00

Granted, this seems like a much worse result than the $11,630 gain from the unratioed spread. The extra soy meal contract in the case of the ratioed spread adds $3,490 to the loss and accounts for most of the Spread net difference that you see. It doesn't always come out like this.

ONE FOR THE RATIO

Suppose that you had decided to buy the spread on hearing talk that Chinese buyers were coming back, but this time into the soy meal market. Suppose further that you delayed taking action until June 14, 2004, when the prices were those shown in Exhibit 10.7 and the July soybean crush spread was trading at 0.4314 (see Exhibit 10.3 for these data). Exhibit 10.7 shows how the ratioed spread would have performed if you had put it on on June 14 and unwound it on June 25, 2004. Exhibit 10.8 shows how 10 of the unratioed spreads would have performed given the same data on the same days.

You can see that the change in soy meal prices generated a large gain, the soy oil leg of the spread generated a gain that is one-third the size of the meal gain, and the soybean leg generated a hefty loss. The net result of the spread, though, is a $17,610 gain.

The unratioed spread would have done somewhat less well, as Exhibit 10.9 shows.

In this case, the soybean leg performed exactly as it did in the ratioed case, but the product legs are different. The soy oil leg gained an extra $1,140, but the soy meal leg gained $2,850 less. The $1,710 difference between those two gains is the difference between the two spread results (17,610 – 15,900 = 1,710).

EXHIBIT 10.8

Buying the Ratioed Soybean Crush Spread (July 2004 Contracts)

	Action	SMN4	Action	BON4	Action	S N4
6/14/04	Buy 11	279.50	Buy 9	0.2734	Sell 10	8.7250
6/25/04	Sell 11	308.00	Sell 9	0.2924	Buy 10	9.2050
Result		28.50		0.0190		–0.4800
Contract size		2,850.00		1,140.00		–2,400.00
Position size		31,350.00		10,260.00		–24,000.00
Spread net						17,610.00

EXHIBIT 10.9

Buying the Unratioed Soybean Crush Spread (July 2004 Contracts)

	Action	SMN4	Action	BON4	Action	S N4
6/14/04	Buy 10	279.50	Buy 10	0.2734	Sell 10	8.7250
6/25/04	Sell 10	308.00	Sell 10	0.2924	Buy 10	9.2050
Difference		28.50		0.0190		–0.4800
Contract size		2,850.00		1,140.00		–2,400.00
Position size		28,500.00		11,400.00		–24,000.00
Spread net						15,900.00

SELLING THE MAY SOYBEAN CRUSH SPREAD

Markets often overreact to news events. Going back to the April situation and the May contracts, suppose that seeing the remarkably wide crush spread on April 21 and 22, you had decided that the market would shortly come to its senses and that the spread would narrow at least somewhat. Based on this outlook, you might have decided to sell the soybean crush spread.

To sell the soybean crush, you initially sell the products and buy soybeans. To unwind, you reverse that. Such a position should post a gain any time the spread narrows.

Suppose you had decided to sell the spread on April 22, 2004, when the spread was trading at 0.7259 and ultimately decided to unwind this trade on April 30, when the spread had narrowed to 0.4015. The ratioed spread, based on these assumptions, would have generated a $16,336 gain. Exhibit 10.10 shows that the soybean leg of the spread was the source of the gain.

When you compare the leg results with those of the unratioed spread trade illustrated in Exhibit 10.11, you can see that the smaller loss of the soy meal leg, moving from the ratioed to the unratioed results, overcame the larger loss of the soy oil leg. This accounts for the difference in the results, just as it did in the prior example.

If you could know in advance which legs of the spread would do what, choosing between ratioed or unratioed versions would be simple. You cannot know this, so balancing simplicity against economic accuracy is an interesting choice. Try this. Using the data of the three trades shown in this discussion, find the differences among the spreads on the first and

EXHIBIT 10.10

Selling the Ratioed Soybean Crush Spread (May 2004 Contracts)

	Action	SMK4	Action	BOK4	Action	S K4
4/22/04	Sell 11	299.10	Sell 9	0.3287	Buy 10	9.4700
4/30/04	Buy 11	318.10	Buy 9	0.3403	Sell 10	10.3400
Result		–19.00		–0.0116		0.8700
Contract size		–1,900.00		–696.00		4,350.00
Position size		–20,900.00		–6,264.00		43,500.00
Spread net						16,336.00

EXHIBIT 10.11

Selling the Unratioed Soybean Crush Spread (May 2004 Contracts)

	Action	SMK4	Action	BOK4	Action	S K4
4/22/04	Sell 10	299.10	Sell 10	0.3287	Buy 10	9.4700
4/30/04	Buy 10	318.10	Buy 10	0.3403	Sell 10	10.3400
Result		–19.00		–0.0116		0.8700
Contract size		–1,900.00		–696.00		4,350.00
Position size		–19,000.00		–6,960.00		43,500.00
Spread net						17,540.00

last days of the trades shown. Then divide the ratioed and unratioed dollar results by 50,000 (the number of bushels in ten soybean contracts). See which spread structure more nearly captures that difference. For example, Exhibit 10.12 shows the details for the April 22 to April 30 trade of Exhibits 10.10 and 10.11.

Clearly, the ratioed spread more nearly reflects what happened to the spread—for better or for worse. If this matters to you, you will want to trade the ratioed spread. If simplicity of execution is the overriding consideration for you, you will want to trade the unratioed spread. Based on a small sample of possible trades, it looks as though each side will come out ahead about half the time.

EXHIBIT 10.12

An Economic Reality Check

	Crush Spread		Dollar Result	Divided by 50,000
4/22/04	0.7259	Ratioed	16,336	0.3267
4/30/04	0.4015	Unratioed	17,540	0.3508
Difference	0.3244			

A WORD OF CAUTION

This discussion has mentioned only a few of the factors that shape the soybean crush spread. Much has been made of the Chinese situation because the influence of foreign buyers is too often overlooked and this anecdote makes the point that it matters whether these buyers are in the market. And it also matters what they are buying—soybeans or products. Yet, even in the spring of 2004, this wasn't all that was going on in terms of spread-influencing factors. What is happening with the South American soybean crops and who is buying them will have its effect on the U.S. crush spread. The price levels of alternative sources of protein will affect the crush spread. And that's just the tip of the iceberg.

Brokerage house analysts and other analysts study the current situation, compare it to similar situations in the past, and generate volumes of useful insight. A study of that body of opinion can help you decide what factors seem to matter most at a given time.

CHAPTER 11

Crack Spreads

Turning Crude Oil into Unleaded Gasoline and Heating Oil

Crack spreads encapsulate the economics of refining crude oil. The term *crack* refers to the chemical process of breaking complex molecules, in this case crude oil, into simpler molecules, such as unleaded gasoline and heating oil, by means of heat. The traditional picture of a refinery includes a forest of tall narrow structures called *cracking towers*. Early refiners applied heat to crude oil, and the various products cracked out at higher and higher temperatures—literally, for this was a noisy process. The heat process has given way to chemical processes, but the term remains.

BASIC REFINING ECONOMICS DRIVES THE CRACK SPREAD

A barrel of crude oil yields such aromatics as benzene, unleaded gasoline, jet kerosene, diesel fuel, heating oil, bunker fuel, and asphalt. The only two products of crude oil for which there are U.S. futures contracts are unleaded gasoline and heating oil. Yet these two product contracts, along with the crude oil contract, all of which trade on the New York Mercantile Exchange (NYMEX), allow traders to build what is sometimes referred to as a paper refinery.

Consider the basic refining process. Refiners buy crude oil, add value by refining it, and sell the products. The spread ratio derives from the approximate yield of a barrel of crude oil. Depending on the type of crude oil, the yield will be roughly 67 percent gasoline to 33 percent heating oil or 60 percent gasoline to 40 percent heating oil. Thus the common 3-2-1 crack spread balances three units of crude oil against two units of gasoline and one of heating oil. Less common is the 5-3-2 spread which balances five units of crude oil against three units of gasoline and two units of heating oil. This larger spread (in terms of the number of contracts required) more nearly reflects the 60 percent–40 percent barrel yield of the heavier mideastern crude oils.

While it is difficult to say exactly what refining breakeven might be because no two refineries have quite the same process costs, it seems fair to assume that breakeven lies somewhere in the \$0.08 to \$0.095 per gallon range. These values are equivalent to \$3.36 and \$4.00 per barrel.

TO CALCULATE THE 3-2-1 CRACK SPREAD

At first glance, the product contracts seem to differ from the crude oil contract. The crude contract specifies 1,000 barrels, and prices are in dollars per barrel. The product contracts specify 42,000 gallons, and prices are in cents per gallon. In fact, one barrel contains 42 gallons, so the contracts turn out to be the same size. Each contains 1,000 barrels or 42,000 gallons which turns out to be one New York harbor barge load.

Two simple conversions ease the calculation of the spread. First, the cents per gallon of the product contracts can be converted into dollars per gallon by shifting the decimal point two places to the left (note that some quote sources already list these contracts in these terms). Thus, 101.85 becomes \$1.0185, and 77.11 becomes \$0.7711. Second, the dollars per barrel of the crude oil contract can be converted into dollars per gallon by dividing that price by 42. Thus, 33.29 becomes 0.7926. This allows the crack spread to be quoted in dollars per gallon.

Using these dollars per gallon prices, you can calculate the 3-2-1 crack spread in terms of this formula:

$$\{[(\text{gasoline price} \times 2) + \text{heating oil price}] - 3(\text{crude price}/42)\}/3 = \text{crack spread}$$

Substituting the April 1, 2004, values from Exhibit 11.1, you can calculate the spread for that day and discover that it was \$0.1434 per gallon.

$$\{[(1.0185 \times 2) + 0.7711] - 3(33.29/42)\}/3 = 0.1434$$

Exhibit 11.1 repeats this calculation for each trading day of April 2004. Because refining takes time, good policy is to use the crude oil contract for one month and the product contracts for the next month. If you use the July crude oil contract (CLN4), as shown in Exhibit 11.1, you will use August unleaded gasoline (HUQ4) and August heating oil (HOQ4). Exhibit 11.6 on page 151 plots the spread in terms of November crude oil (CLX4) and December products (HUZ4 and HOZ4).

The crack spread widened fairly steadily throughout April 2004, but it zoomed sharply wider during the last week of that month. One glance

EXHIBIT 11.1

Calculating the July–August 3-2-1 Crack Spread for April 2004

	HUQ4 ($/gallon)	HOQ4 ($/gallon)	CLN4 ($/barrel)	3-2-1 Crack Spread ($/gallon)
4/1/04	1.0185	0.7711	33.29	0.1434
4/2/04	1.0154	0.7890	33.44	0.1437
4/5/04	1.0084	0.7883	33.44	0.1388
4/6/04	1.0242	0.7991	33.91	0.1418
4/7/04	1.0564	0.8095	35.07	0.1391
4/8/04	1.0889	0.8208	36.05	0.1412
4/12/04	1.1141	0.8276	36.72	0.1443
4/13/04	1.0966	0.8237	36.26	0.1423
4/14/04	1.0987	0.8273	36.09	0.1489
4/15/04	1.1175	0.8398	36.74	0.1502
4/16/04	1.1144	0.8393	36.63	0.1506
4/19/04	1.1102	0.8278	36.40	0.1494
4/20/04	1.1026	0.8261	36.06	0.1519
4/21/04	1.0863	0.8147	35.34	0.1543
4/22/04	1.1197	0.8303	36.28	0.1594
4/23/04	1.1130	0.8228	36.01	0.1589
4/26/04	1.1289	0.8322	36.60	0.1586
4/27/04	1.1482	0.8446	37.23	0.1606
4/28/04	1.1647	0.8427	37.17	0.1724
4/29/04	1.1728	0.8390	37.05	0.1827
4/30/04	1.1754	0.8504	37.08	0.1842

tells you that all prices rose. Obviously, product prices rose relative to crude oil prices. One way to get a handle on what was driving the widening or narrowing of this spread is to compare price changes in percentage terms. Some calculators allow you to do this in one step, but it is easy to do even without such an aid.

Start with the April 1 prices, and compare the April 24 prices. Exhibit 11.2 lays out the steps.

The row marked by the first date simply lays out the prices from Exhibit 11.1. The second row value under Unleaded Gasoline is the gasoline price doubled, while the second row value under Crude Oil is that price divided by 42. The third row value under Heating Oil is the sum of the doubled gasoline price and the heating oil price. The third row value under Crude Oil triples the gallon price from row two. The next set of numbers does the same thing for the next date. Finally, the percent change

EXHIBIT 11.2

Relating Crude Oil and Product Price Changes–April 1 to April 23, 2004

	Unleaded Gasoline	Heating Oil	Crude Oil
4/1/04	1.0185	0.7711	33.29
	2.0370		0.7926
		2.8081	2.3779
4/23/04	1.1130	0.8228	36.01
	2.2260		0.8574
		3.0488	2.5721
	Percent change	8.57	8.17

EXHIBIT 11.3

Relating Crude Oil and Product Price Changes–April 26 to April 30, 2004

	Unleaded Gasoline	Heating Oil	Crude Oil
4/26/04	1.1289	0.8322	36.60
	2.2578		0.8714
		3.0900	2.6143
4/30/04	1.1754	0.8504	37.08
	2.3508		0.8829
		3.2012	2.6486
	Percent change	3.60	1.31

can be found by subtracting the first product sum from the second product sum (3.0488 – 2.8081 = 0.2407) and dividing the result by the first product sum (0.2407 ÷ 2.8081 = 0.0857). That times 100 is the percent change. Next, follow the same steps for the crude oil values. Exhibit 11.2 shows that while the product prices rose by 8.57 percent, the crude oil price rose by only 8.17 percent. This widened the spread.

Exhibit 11.3 shows the same exercise for the last week in April 2004.

What matters here is not that 8.57 percent is greater than 3.60 percent but that the 3.60 percent to 1.31 percent gap is greater than the 8.57 percent to 8.17 percent gap. The product rise relative to the crude oil rise during the last week was much greater.

STRUCTURING A CRACK SPREAD TRADE

If you had been tracking the July–August crack spread in early April 2004, seen this steady spread widening, and decided that the widening would continue, you could have bought the 3-2-1 crack spread. You buy or sell this spread in terms of what you do with the products. Thus, to buy the spread, you buy two unleaded gasoline contracts and one heating oil contract, and you sell three crude oil contracts.

The use of single-gallon prices makes spread tracking easy, but it doesn't tell you how much the spread might make. For that you need the dollar value of the contract, or at least the dollar value of the price change. The crude oil contract contains 1,000 barrels, so the dollar value is the current price times 1,000. The unleaded gasoline contract contains 42,000 gallons, so the dollar value is the current price times 42,000. Exhibit 11.4 does the arithmetic for the crude oil and unleaded gasoline prices of April 1 and April 30, 2004, calculates the difference, and shows the values of price changes for a three-contract crude oil position and a two-contract unleaded gasoline position.

EXHIBIT 11.4

Converting Quoted Prices into Dollar Values

	Crude Oil Price	1,000/Barrels/Contract	Contract $ Value
4/1/04	36.72	1,000	36,720
4/30/04	37.99	1,000	37,990
		Difference (36,720 – 37,990)	–1,270
		Three-contract position	–3,810
	Unleaded Gasoline Price	**42,000/Gallons/Contract**	**Contract $ Value**
4/1/04	1.0966	42,000	46,057.20
4/30/04	1.1959	42,000	50,215.20
		Difference (50,215.2 – 46,057.2)	4,158
		Two-contract position	8,316

EXHIBIT 11.5

Calculating a Crack Spread Result

	Action	HUQ4	Action	HOQ4	Action	CLN4
4/1/04	Buy 2	1.0185	Buy 1	0.7711	Sell 3	33.29
4/30/04	Sell 2	1.1754	Sell 1	0.8504	Buy 3	37.08
One-contract result		0.1569		0.0793		–3.79
Position $ result		13,179.60		3,330.60		–11,370
Spread $ net						5,140.20

You can calculate spread results that way, but it seems less laborious to deal in terms of single-contract prices and move up to position size nearer the end of the process as illustrated in Exhibit 11.5. The trade illustrated in Exhibit 11.5 assumes that you bought one spread on April 1 and unwound it on April 30. To buy the spread, you would have bought two contracts of August unleaded gasoline futures (HUQ4) and one contract of August heating oil futures (HOQ4) and sold three contracts of July crude oil futures (CLN4).

The easiest way to handle this calculation is to, first, subtract the bought price of each contract from the sold price. The One-contract result row shows these remainders. The Position $ result row takes that up to contract size in this way: The unleaded gasoline contract contains 42,000 gallons, or 84,000 gallons for two contracts, so multiply the 0.1569 price change by 84,000 to get 13,179.60; the heating oil result is 42,000 (one contract) times 0.0793, or 3,330.60; the crude oil contract contains 1,000 barrels or 3,000 barrels for three contracts, so multiply –3.79 by 3,000 to arrive at –11,370. The Spread $ net is the sum of the three Position $ result values.

Among other things, this makes it simple to calculate the results of larger positions. If you bought 100 spreads, no need to sort out what happened to 200 gasoline contracts, 100 heating oil contracts, and 300 crude oil contracts. You can simply multiply the single-spread result by the number of spreads traded. On these assumptions, a 100-spread position would have earned $514,020, while a 75-spread position would have earned $385,515 (5,140.20 × 75).

HIGH PRICES MAY NOT BE WHAT THEY SEEM

The summer and early fall of 2004 were an interesting time in many markets, none more so than oil. The unsettled situation in Iraq, an election campaign going on in the United States, and concerns about terrorism everywhere combined to create an ongoing concern about whether crude oil supplies would be cut off or would be adequate. High product prices didn't seem to curtail demand, and crude oil prices flirted with the $50 per barrel mark until September 28, 2004, when the NYMEX nearby futures price actually broke through to $50.47, though it settled slightly lower that day.

The November–December 3-2-1 crack spread history during August 2004, as set forth in Exhibit 11.6, hammers home the point that crude oil is not the whole story—the financial media notwithstanding. Notice that the 3-2-1 crack spread narrowed fairly steadily throughout that month. The move from 0.1663 on August 2 to 0.1310 on August 31 amounts to a –19.66 percent change.

EXHIBIT 11.6

Tracking the November–December 3-2-1 Crack Spread in August 2004

	HUZ4 ($/gallon)	HOZ4 ($/gallon)	CLX4 ($/barrel)	3-2-1 Crack Spread ($/gallon)
8/2/04	1.1763	1.1912	42.63	0.1663
8/3/04	1.1850	1.2075	43.14	0.1654
8/4/04	1.1440	1.1809	41.84	0.1601
8/5/04	1.1870	1.2167	43.22	0.1679
8/6/04	1.1782	1.2003	43.00	0.1618
8/9/04	1.1952	1.2146	43.96	0.1550
8/10/04	1.1887	1.2002	43.60	0.1544
8/11/04	1.2004	1.2023	43.89	0.1560
8/12/04	1.2164	1.2231	44.50	0.1591
8/13/04	1.2433	1.2432	45.61	0.1573
8/16/04	1.2212	1.2361	45.29	0.1478
8/17/04	1.2310	1.2526	45.81	0.1475
8/18/04	1.2379	1.2564	45.93	0.1505
8/19/04	1.2669	1.2935	47.23	0.1512
8/20/04	1.2269	1.2622	46.34	0.1353
8/23/04	1.2132	1.2463	45.71	0.1359
8/24/04	1.2045	1.2271	44.86	0.1439
8/25/04	1.1515	1.1780	43.15	0.1330
8/26/04	1.1320	1.1728	42.15	0.1277
8/27/04	1.1400	1.1754	42.75	0.1331
8/30/04	1.1203	1.1509	42.98	0.1279
8/31/04	1.1259	1.1440	42.11	0.1310

Notice also that all three prices peaked on August 19. November crude oil (CLX4) reached $47.23 per barrel, December unleaded gasoline (HUZ4) reached $1.2669 per gallon, and December heating oil (HOZ4) reached $1.2935 per gallon. All three prices then sagged off to end the month lower.

It is interesting to contemplate what drove the spread steadily narrower despite the up and down flow of the component prices. What squeezed the spread from August 2 to August 19, during which period the spread narrowed by slightly more than 9 percent, was that the price of crude oil rose more in percentage terms than the product prices. Yet from August 19 to August 31, the product prices fell more than the crude oil price. This runs contrary to what you might expect.

IN DEFIANCE OF THE COMMON WISDOM

Some time during every summer, refiners switch their processes from maximizing gasoline production to maximizing heating oil production. Refiners can't do one or the other. Every barrel produces both products, so this is more a shift of emphasis. Product prices ordinarily reflect that shift with deferred heating oil prices rising relative to nearby to encourage the buildup of stocks. How much higher they go, in relative terms, will largely be a function of the weather outlook for the northeastern United States, the primary heating oil market. These August prices seem inconsistent in terms of that shift in refining emphasis—and in terms of almost all else that seems usually to drive these markets.

The common wisdom is that product prices adjust quickly when crude oil prices are rising and get sticky at the top when crude oil prices are falling. Falling crude oil prices, then, should ordinarily widen the spread. In this regard, August 2004 seems an odd month. What is clear is that to understand what is happening to the crack spread, traders must consider both ends of the process, not just the crude oil input.

The price shifts of August do illustrate the advantage of trading spreads. Suppose that your market analysis suggested that the November–December 3-2-1 crack spread would narrow and that you had decided to sell this spread. To sell one spread, you sell two December unleaded gasoline contracts (HUZ4) and one December heating oil contract (HOZ4) and buy three November crude oil contracts (CLX4).

To make the point, consider two trades. One is put on at the August 2 prices of Exhibit 11.6 and unwound at the August 19 prices. The other is put on at the August 19 prices and unwound at the August 31 prices. Exhibits 11.7 and 11.8 show the details of these trades.

You can see that the trade illustrated in Exhibit 11.7 earned $1,893 and that it was the crude oil side that made the gain.

EXHIBIT 11.7

Anticipating a Spread Narrowing–Sell the November–December 3-2-1 Crack Spread

	Action	HUZ4	Action	HOZ4	Action	CLX4
8/2/04	Sell 2	1.1763	Sell 1	1.1912	Buy 3	42.63
8/19/04	Buy 2	1.2669	Buy 1	1.2935	Sell 3	47.23
One-contract result		–0.0906		–0.1023		4.60
Position $ result		–7,610.40		–4,296.60		13,800.00
Spread $ net						1,893.00

EXHIBIT 11.8

Anticipating a Spread Narrowing–Sell the November–December 3-2-1 Crack Spread

	Action	HUZ4	Action	HOZ4	Action	CLX4
8/19/04	Sell 2	1.2669	Sell 1	1.2935	Buy 3	47.23
8/31/04	Buy 2	1.1259	Buy 1	1.1440	Sell 3	42.11
One-contract result		0.1410		0.149		–5.12
Position $ result		11,844		6,279		–15,360.00
Spread $ net						2,763.00

In this case, the spread narrowing was greater, which made the gain larger. What is interesting is that here the product side generated the gain.

REASSERTING THE COMMON WISDOM

Curiously, the market from August 31 to September 28, 2004, the day that November crude oil futures broke through the $50 per barrel mark, behaved more in keeping with the common wisdom. That is, even as crude oil prices soared, the product prices raced ahead to widen the spread. Soaring crude oil prices may not always narrow the crack spread. When product supply and demand allow those prices to keep pace or even outpace crude oil prices, refining becomes more profitable despite the higher input cost.

EXHIBIT 11.9

Anticipating a Spread Narrowing–Sell the November–December 3-2-1 Crack Spread

	Action	HUZ4	Action	HOZ4	Action	CLX4
8/31/04	Sell 2	1.1259	Sell 1	1.1440	Buy 3	42.11
9/28/04	Buy 2	1.3257	Buy 1	1.3911	Sell 3	50.47
One-contract result		0.1998		0.2471		–8.36
Position $ result		16,783.20		10,378.20		–25,080.00
Spread $ net						2,081.40

Consider what would have happened if you had bought the November–December 3-2-1 crack spread on August 31 and unwound the trade on September 21 at the daily highs for all three contracts. Exhibit 11.9 shows the trade details.

The product prices in this case widened the spread to 0.1458—enough to generate a $2,081.40 gain even with crude oil at $50.47 per barrel. As it turned out, the crude oil price dropped back to a $49.90 settlement price. And while the product prices retreated slightly—HUZ4 to 1.3240 and HOZ4 to 1.3849—they exhibited the well-known stickiness as the spread widened to 0.1562. The same trade unwound at the September 28 settlement prices would have gained $3,388.20. Notice where the crack spread is in these examples relative to the 0.0950 breakeven estimate.

A WORD OF CAUTION

You can see from the examples cited that the crack spread does not always perform in keeping with the common wisdom—the common wisdom having, often, a large folklore component. These markets require consideration of a range of factors—among them market economics, the world political situation, and consumer psychology. Any of these factors can throw a wrench into the best-laid trading plans. That said, crack spread trades are extremely interesting and can be rewarding.

CHAPTER 12

A NASDAQ 100–S&P 500 Futures Spread

Pitting the Small Caps against the Large Caps

The stock index markets provide a rich source of spread trading opportunities. Thinking only of U.S. markets, the Chicago Mercantile Exchange offers contracts on the S&P 500, the S&P Midcap 400, the NASDAQ 100, the Russell 2000, and the Russell 1000. The Chicago Board of Trade offers contracts based on the Dow Jones Industrial Average. Further, the S&P 500, the NASDAQ 100, and the Dow contracts come in both full-size and small-size versions. In addition, exchanges around the world offer contracts on indexes that represent the British, the Japanese, and the Euro zone markets—to mention only the most widely traded stock index contracts.

Even this abbreviated listing suggests that these markets offer a variety of spread trading opportunities, but this discussion focuses on the relationship between the NASDAQ 100 and the S&P 500. The S&P 500 consists of the stocks of 500 companies that have the largest market capitalization. This index has become perhaps the most frequently cited benchmark for measuring the performance of institutional portfolio managers. The NASDAQ 100 consists of only a fifth as many stocks. Further, the companies represented in this index are mostly smaller and have smaller market capitalizations. Also, the NASDAQ 100 has a heavy concentration of tech stocks—both electronic, or high tech, and biotech. This discussion refers to the e-mini versions, both of which are available on-screen exclusively, to illustrate the challenges and opportunities these markets present.

DEFINING THE SPREAD AND STRUCTURING THE TRADE

The first challenge is to define the spread. A glance at a quote screen or newspaper commodities page shows these indexes to vary greatly in size as well as in index composition. The names tell you that the S&P 500 contains five times as many stocks as the NASDAQ 100. Stock index futures size is the product of the futures price in index points and the multiplier. The e-mini S&P 500 multiplier is $50, while the NASDAQ 100 multiplier is $20. So given a quote of 1,000 points in both markets, the S&P contract size (or dollar value) will be $50,000 (1,000 index points times the $50 multiplier) and the NASDAQ 100 contract size will be $20,000 (1,000 index points times the $20 multiplier). Actual quotes might be 1,113.75 for the S&P 500 and 1,493.00 for the NASDAQ 100. These translate into dollar values of $56,587.50 and $29,870, respectively.

It makes sense to calculate the spread in terms of dollar values rather than in terms of quotes, but translating into dollar values makes the size difference even more obvious. The way to bring the two contracts into approximate balance is to determine a spread ratio by dividing the S&P 500 value by the NASDAQ 100 value. Given these dollar values, the spread ratio is 1.89 (56,587.50 ÷ 29,870). This spread ratio indicates that, to put on a spread trade on the day these quotes were current, you would have traded 189 e-mini NASDAQ 100 contracts for every 100 e-mini S&P 500 contract traded.

Curiously, no market convention has emerged regarding this spread. You cannot call a broker and say you want to buy 100 spreads as you can with the soybean crush or other spreads for which market convention is well established. The spread ratio also allows for a meaningful definition of the spread, and it seems intuitively right to define the spread by subtracting the S&P 500 value from the ratioed NASDAQ 100 value:

$$\text{Spread} = (\text{NASDAQ 100 value} \times \text{ratio}) - \text{S\&P 500 value}$$
$$134 = (29{,}870 \times 1.89) - 56{,}788$$

Although the spread ratio shifts constantly, it is simpler in tracking the spread to take the ratio on the first day of the tracking period and to hold that constant. Exhibit 12.1 shows June contract prices for the NASDAQ 100 (NQM4) and the S&P 500 (ESM4), dollar values for both, the ratio, the ratioed NASDAQ 100 value using the 1.85 January 21 ratio throughout, and the spread. This exhibit shows snapshots at weekly intervals.

You won't always see negative numbers in the Spread column. Exhibits 12.2a and b show a continuation of these prices but offer two views of the spread. The Spread column in 12.2a continues the sequence

EXHIBIT 12.1

Tracking the NASDAQ 100 Minus the S&P 500 Spread

	NQM4	ESM4	NQ × $20	ES × $50	Ratio	NQ × 1.85	Spread
1/21/04	1,549.50	1,145.00	30,990	57,250	1.85	57.332	82
1/28/04	1,495.00	1,128.30	29,940	56,415	1.88	55,389	–1,026
2/4/04	1,466.00	1,122.90	29,320	56,145	1.91	54,242	–1,903
2/11/04	1,515.60	1,154.30	30,310	57,715	1.90	56,074	–1,642
2/18/04	1,514.50	1,150.20	30,290	57,510	1.90	56,037	–1,474
2/25/04	1,475.50	1,141.90	29,510	57,095	1.93	54,594	–2,502

EXHIBIT 12.2a

Tracking the Spread Using the 1.85 Spread Ratio

	NQM4	ESM4	NQ × $20	ES × $50	Ratio	NQ × 1.85	Spread I
3/17/04	1,431.50	1,122.50	28,630	56,125	1.96	52,966	–3,160
3/24/04	1,386.50	1,091.50	27,730	54,575	1.97	51,301	–3,275
3/31/04	1,441.50	1,124.90	28,830	56,245	1.95	53,336	–2,910
4/7/04	1,490.00	1,142.30	29,800	57,115	1.92	55,130	–1,985
4/14/04	1,483.50	1,129.70	29,670	56,485	1.90	54,890	–1,596
4/21/04	1,448.50	1,122.60	28,970	56,130	1.94	53,595	–2,535
4/28/04	1,458.00	1,123.40	29,160	56,170	1.93	53,946	–2,224
5/5/04	1,432.00	1,122.00	28,640	56,100	1.96	52,984	–3,116
5/12/04	1,419.00	1,098.70	28,380	54,935	1.94	52,503	–2,432

of spread calculations using the January 21 1.85 spread ratio. The Spread column in 12.2b uses the March 17 1.96 spread ratio and holds that constant the rest of the way.

SPREAD BEHAVIOR

Whether the spread is negative or positive makes no difference in the message of the spread. What you want to know as a spread trader is not the particular spread level so much as whether the spread is narrowing or widening. Basically, when the NASDAQ 100 outperforms the S&P 500, the spread will widen. When the S&P 500 outperforms the NASDAQ 100,

EXHIBIT 12.2b

Tracking the Spread Using the 1.95 Spread Ratio

	NQM4	ESM4	NQ × $20	ES × $50	Ratio	NQ × 1.96	Spread II
3/17/04	1,431.50	1,122.50	28,630	56,125	1.96	56,115	–10
3/24/04	1,386.50	1,091.50	27,730	54,575	1.97	54,350	–224
3/31/04	1,441.50	1,124.90	28,830	56,245	1.95	56,507	262
4/7/04	1,490.00	1,142.30	29,800	57,115	1.92	58,408	1,293
4/14/04	1,483.50	1,129.70	29,670	56,485	1.90	58,153	1,668
4/21/04	1,448.50	1,122.60	28,970	56,130	1.94	56,781	651
4/28/04	1,458.00	1,123.40	29,160	56,170	1.93	57,154	984
5/5/04	1,432.00	1,122.00	28,640	56,100	1.96	56,134	34
5/12/04	1,419.00	1,098.70	28,380	54,935	1.94	55,625	690

the spread will narrow. Because negative spread values are possible, it is important to remember that widening and narrowing can happen in a variety of ways. The spread will narrow if:

- Given a negative initial value, the spread becomes more negative.
- Given a positive initial value, the spread becomes negative.
- Given a positive initial value, the spread becomes less positive.

The spread will widen if:

- Given a negative initial value, the spread becomes less negative.
- Given a negative initial value, the spread becomes positive.
- Given a positive initial value, the spread becomes more positive.

Consider the spread change from March 31 to April 7. Using the 1.85 ratio, the spread starts at –2,910 and goes to –1,985. When the spread goes from negative to less negative, it is widening. Using the 1.95 ratio, the spread goes from 262 to 1,293. When the spread goes from positive to more positive, it is also widening. Both exhibits convey the same message about the way the spread changes during this one-week period.

Consider next the spread change from April 28 and May 5. Using the 1.85 ratio, the spread goes from –2,224 to –3,116. When the spread goes from negative to more negative, it is narrowing. Using the 1.95 ratio, the spread goes from 984 to 34. When the spread goes from positive to less positive, it is also narrowing. Again, both exhibits convey the same message about this one-week period.

RESISTING MARKET FOLKLORE

Another challenge is to resist the lure of market folklore. You may hear traders say with great conviction that small cap stocks typically outperform large cap stocks in a rally. Often this appears to be true, but there are enough exceptions that you should be wary of such talk. One notable case involves the long bull market of the 1990s. That was led by the big, blue-chip stocks for the most part. Even in recent times, it is possible to find short-term situations where the NASDAQ 100 outperforms in both rising and falling markets and other situations where the S&P 500 outperforms in both directions. Exhibit 12.3 shows four situations taken from 2004 markets that illustrate the four possibilities (note that Exhibits 12.3 b, c, and d quote the June contracts; Exhibit 12.3a quotes the September contracts).

EXHIBIT 12.3a

Both Markets Up; Spread Narrows

	NASDAQ 100	S&P 500	Spread
Jan 14	1,542.50	1,128.8	16
Jan 26	1,559.50	1,152.10	–526

EXHIBIT 12.3b

Both Markets Up; Spread Widens

	NASDAQ 100	S&P 500	Spread
Feb 4	1466.00	1122.90	–1,903
Feb 11	1515.60	1154.30	–1,642

EXHIBIT 12.3c

Both Markets Down; Spread Narrows

	NASDAQ 100	S&P 500	Spread
Apr 14	1,483.60	1,129.70	1,668
Apr 21	1,448.50	1,122.60	651

EXHIBIT 12.3d

Both Markets Down; Spread Widens

	NASDAQ 100	S&P 500	Spread
May 5	1,432.00	1,122.00	34
May 12	1,419.00	1,098.00	690

What this tells you is that you'd better base your spread outlook on more than folkloric rules of thumb. The NASDAQ 100 tends to outperform the S&P 500 when the electronic technology sectors (mostly telecom and computer chip makers) and biotechnology firms seem poised to make big gains. The S&P 500 will outperform the NASDAQ 100 when a strongly growing economy promises to produce benefits for the larger companies. On the downside, the larger companies may at times have more cushion against the effects of a slowing economy.

Perhaps a more accurate observation is that small-cap companies tend to outperform larger companies during the first stages of a rally. After a certain point, though, investors begin to think in terms of quality. At this point, the large-cap stocks begin to outperform the small caps. This is basically what seems to have happened in the long bull run of the 1990s.

BUYING AND SELLING THE STOCK INDEX SPREAD

Based on the way this spread is defined (ratioed NASDAQ 100 value minus S&P 500 value), you can buy or sell this spread in terms of what you do with the NASDAQ 100 leg. Expecting the NASDAQ 100 to outperform the S&P 500 and widen the spread, you can buy the spread by buying the ratioed number of NASDAQ 100 contracts and selling the appropriate number of S&P 500 contracts. Expecting the S&P 500 to outperform the NASDAQ 100 and narrow the spread, you can sell the spread by selling the ratioed number of NASDAQ 100 contracts and buying the appropriate number of S&P 500 contracts. The logic behind this is the same as that behind the other spreads discussed so far. You generally want to buy anything that you expect to see increase in value and sell anything that you expect to see decrease in value.

The four situations shown in Exhibit 12.3 serve to demonstrate what happens when you buy a widening spread and sell a narrowing spread—regardless of price direction. Exhibit 12.4 sets out the four trades based on the dollar values of the two contracts on the relevant days and the spread ratio for the first day of each trade (not the ratio used for spread calculation). Assume in each case that you buy or sell 100 e-mini S&P 500 contracts and the ratio times 100 contracts of e-mini NASDAQ 100 futures.

The values in the Spread column are the differences between the NASDAQ 100 positions and the S&P 500 positions (e.g., in Exhibit 12.4a, 5,645,550 – 5,544,000 = 1,550). Also, since these are dollar values to begin with, if you subtract the initial spread value from the ending spread value, you will see that the result in the Spread net row is negative when the spread narrows and positive when the spread widens. Also, this value should match the Spread net value in the S&P 500 column. In calculating the values in the Result row, you should always subtract the bought price from the sold price. This way, the gains and losses will always come out right. Finally, the Spread net is simply the sum of these two results (e.g., –62,220 + 116,500 = 54,280).

A look at the results for each leg of each spread tells you where the gains, or losses, come from. Notice that where this happens varies from

EXHIBIT 12.4a

Both Markets Up; Spread Narrows; Sell the Spread

	Action	NASDAQ 100 (value × 183)	Action	S&P 500 (value × 100)	Spread
Jan 14	Sell 183	5,645,550	Buy 100	5,644,000	1,550
Jan 26	Buy 183	5,707,770	Sell 100	5,760,500	–52,730
Result		–62,220		116,500	
Spread net				54,280	–54,280

EXHIBIT 12.4b

Both Markets Up; Spread Widens; Buy the Spread

	Action	NASDAQ 100 (value × 183)	Action	S&P 500 (value × 100)	Spread
Feb 4	Buy 191	5,600,120	Sell 100	5,614,500	–14,380
Feb 11	Sell 191	5,789,210	Buy 100	5,771,500	18,710
Result		189,090		–156,000	
Spread net				33,090	33,090

EXHIBIT 12.4c

Both Markets Down; Spread Narrows; Sell the Spread

	Action	NASDAQ 100 (value × 183)	Action	S&P 500 (value × 100)	Spread
Apr 14	Sell 190	5,637,300	Buy 100	5,648,500	–11,200
Apr 21	Buy 190	5,504,300	Sell 100	5,613,000	–108,700
Result		133,000		–35,500	
Spread Net				97,500	–97,500

EXHIBIT 12.4d

Both Markets Down; Spread Widens; Buy the Spread

	Action	NASDAQ 100 (value × 183)	Action	S&P 500 (value × 100)	Spread
May 5	Buy 196	5,613,440	Sell 100	5,610,000	3,440
May 12	Sell 196	5,562,480	Buy 100	5,493,500	68,980
Result		–50,960		116,500	
Spread net				65,540	65,540

trade to trade. When you sell the spread in a rising market and the spread narrows, the S&P 500 leg generates the gain (Exhibit 12.4a). Yet, when you sell the spread in a falling market and the spread narrows, the NASDAQ 100 leg generates the gain (Exhibit 12.4c).

The opposite is true when you buy the spread, assuming that the spread widens. Here, the NASDAQ 100 leg generates the gain in a rising market (Exhibit 12.4b), while the S&P 500 leg generates the gain in a falling market (Exhibit 12.4d).

These four examples demonstrate once again that it is spread behavior, not price direction, that matters in these trades.

SCALING THE TRADE TO YOUR COMFORT LEVEL

The moderately large size of the trades in Exhibit 12.4 makes the results big enough to be obvious, but this trade size may or may not suit your trading needs. You can scale these trades up or down easily enough to trade this spread within your comfort level. The 1.96 spread ratio for the May 5 trade is actually 1.9588 when carried out to four decimal places. To trade a larger size, you can use 1959 NASDAQ 100 contracts for every 1000 S&P 500 contracts.

You can just as easily adjust in the other direction, but when you trade in smaller sizes, the rounding of the spread ratio becomes more of a factor. Suppose you feel comfortable in the 10-lot range. Given this 1.96 ratio, you can use either 19 or 20 NASDAQ 100 contracts for every 10 S&P 500 contracts you trade. You can take this ratio all the way down to 2-to-1.

Exhibit 12.5 shows how trades based on 19-to-10, 20-to-10, and 2-to-1 spread ratios would have performed during the May 5 to May 12 interval.

To fit the spread to other sizes, another approach is to decide how many S&P 500 contracts you are comfortable with and multiply that by

EXHIBIT 12.5a

Using a 19-to-10 Spread Ratio

	Action	NASDAQ 100 (value × 183)	Action	S&P 500 (value × 100)	Spread
May 5	Buy 19	544,160	Sell 10	561,000	–16,840
May 12	Sell 19	539,220	Buy 10	549,350	–10,130
Result		–4,940		11,650	
Spread net				6,710	6,710

EXHIBIT 12.5b

Using a 20-to-10 Spread Ratio

	Action	NASDAQ 100 (value × 183)	Action	S&P 500 (value × 100)	Spread
May 5	Buy 20	572,800	Sell 10	561,000	11,800
May 12	Sell 20	567,600	Buy 10	549,350	18,250
Result		–5,200		11,650	
Spread net				6,450	6,450

EXHIBIT 12.5c

Using a 2-to-1 Spread Ratio

	Action	NASDAQ 100 (value × 183)	Action	S&P 500 (value × 100)	Spread
May 5	Buy 2	57,280	Sell 1	56,100	1,180
May 12	Sell 2	56,760	Buy 1	54,935	1,825
Result		–520		1,165	
Spread net				645	645

EXHIBIT 12.6

Scaling a Spread Structure

Number of S&P 500 Contracts	Spread Ratio	Product of S&P Size and Ratio	Spread Structure (NASDAQ 100 to S&P 500 Contracts)
15	1.96	29.40	29-to-15
20	1.96	39.20	39-to-20
35	1.96	68.60	69-to-35
15	1.85	27.75	28-to-15
20	1.85	37.00	37-to-20
35	1.85	64.75	65-to-35

the spread ratio. Exhibit 12.6 shows what trade structures would result for two spread ratios given three S&P 500 sizes.

The greater the rounding, the greater the amount of directional exposure remaining in the spread position. When one of these trades retains a fairly large amount of directional exposure, two less-than-ideal results may occur. The worst case is that a large directional move can overwhelm a small spread change. You might have forecast the spread change correctly, but the trade will still generate a loss. The less damaging result is that if you had bought the spread, your position might perform differently in one direction than in the other. A widening spread in a falling market might generate a smaller gain than the same amount of widening in a rising market.

Suppose you were to calculate a spread ratio and it turned out to be 1.60. In this case, 16 NASDAQ 100 contracts to 10 S&P 500 contracts is an obvious possibility, but you should probably concede the minimum possible size to be 3-to-2 in such a case as this.

STRATEGIC CONSIDERATIONS FOR STOCK INDEX SPREAD TRADING

In late March of 2004, the economic news was generally good, but it seemed that telecom stocks were poised to stage a comeback after a long period of less-than-stellar performance. Suppose you had bought the spread on March 31 and planned to leave it in place for a month or a little more. The anticipation here was that continuing good news would pump up earnings in the small-cap sectors leading to a widening of the spread when the NASDAQ 100 outperformed the S&P 500 during this period.

By April 14, as Exhibit 12.2b shows, the spread had widened remarkably. Yet unwinding the trade on any of the dates shown except for May 5 would have generated positive results. Given the 262 initial spread value, only the narrowing to 34 on May 5 would have produced a loss. Exhibit 12.7 illustrates the kinds of opportunities, and dangers, that await traders of this spread in terms of three possibilities. In all three, you bought the spread on March 31. In one case, you unwound on April 14, in another on May 5, and finally on May 12.

TO BE ACTIVE OR NOT TO BE ACTIVE

Looking at a sequence of spread values such as the one in Exhibit 12.7b, it is tempting to say that when a spread widens as much as this one did from March 31 to April 14, you should rebalance it and take at least some profit. On a closer look, rebalancing probably doesn't pay in many cases. One way to rebalance is to note that by April 14, the spread ratio was 1.90

EXHIBIT 12.7a

Unwinding the Spread on April 14 Generates a Gain

	Action	NASDAQ 100	Action	S&P 500	
March 31	Buy 195	5,621,850	Sell 100	5,624,500	–2,650
April 14	Sell 195	5,785,650	Buy 100	5,684,500	101,150
Result		163,800		–60,000	
Spread net				103,800	103,800

EXHIBIT 12.7b

Unwinding the Spread on May 5 Generates a Loss

	Action	NASDAQ 100	Action	S&P 500	
March 31	Buy 195	5,621,850	Sell 100	5,624,500	–2,650
May 5	Sell 195	5,584,800	Buy 100	5,610,000	–25,200
Result		–37,050		14,500	
Spread net				–22,550	–22,550

EXHIBIT 12.7c

Unwinding the Spread on May 12 Generates a Gain

	Action	NASDAQ 100	Action	S&P 500	
March 31	Buy 195	5,621,850	Sell 100	5,624,500	–2,650
May 12	Sell 195	5,534,100	Buy 100	5,493,500	40,600
Result		–87,750		131,000	
Spread net				43,250	43,250

and to conclude that it would be good to cash out the extra five NASDAQ 100 contracts. In fact, that would result in a $4,000 gain. This would reduce the gain at any other point in the sequence, and the loss that would result from unwinding on May 5 would overwhelm that small gain.

The one kind of move that might make sense, seeing the large widening on April 14, would be to unwind a large fraction of the initial position. Other possibilities exist, but consider what might have happened if you had unwound approximately half of the spread by selling 95 NASDAQ 100 contracts and buying 50 S&P 500 contracts. Exhibit 12.8 illustrates.

Had you made the trade of Exhibit 12.8a and then the one of 12.8b, the net gain to the pair of trades would have been $38,050 (49,800 – 11,750). Had you made the trades of Exhibits 12.8a and 12.8c, the net gain would have been $70,300 (49,800 + 20,500). This makes far more sense than the bit-by-bit unwinding of the NASDAQ 100 leg of the spread.

Yet it might make the most sense of all to try to resist the impulse to do too much. Ultimately, what moves you do make depend on what kinds of news is in the market. It might be that, even though the spread is widening nicely, you are hearing rumblings that another big scandal in the bio-tech

EXHIBIT 12.8a

Unwinding Half the Spreads to Preserve a Gain

	Action	NASDAQ 100	Action	S&P 500
March 31	Buy 95	2,738,850	Sell 50	2,812,250
April 14	Sell 95	2,818,650	Buy 50	2,842,250
Result		79,800		–30,000
Spread net				49,800

EXHIBIT 12.8b

Unwinding the Rest of the Spreads Preserves Some of the Gain

	Action	NASDAQ 100	Action	S&P 500
March 31	Buy 100	2,883,000	Sell 50	2,812,250
May 5	Sell 100	2,864,000	Buy 50	2,805,000
Result		–19,000		7,250
Spread net				–11,750

EXHIBIT 12.8c

Waiting to Unwind at this Time Increases the Gain

	Action	NASDAQ 100	Action	S&P 500
March 31	Buy 100	2,883,000	Sell 50	2,812,250
May 12	Sell 100	2,838,000	Buy 50	2,746,750
Result		–45,000		65,500
Spread net				20,500

sector or in the telecom sector might be about to cloud the small-cap markets. If such a thing materializes, it might be a major setback for NASDAQ 100 performance, and for the spread if you have bought it.

What you do next will depend on how convincing you find the rumblings. If you find them very convincing, and are looking at the spread of April 14, you might decide to unwind the spread that you bought on March

31 and turn right around and sell it. Alternatively, if you think any setback is likely to be only temporary, you might still unwind the trade and wait for a few weeks. After seeing how the market digests whatever news there may be, you might buy the spread again or sell it—depending on what seems to be happening.

A WORD OF CAUTION

This kind of stock index spread trade is a view-driven trade. You buy or sell based on your opinion concerning which kind of index is likely to outperform during the term of the trade.

Two dangers lie in wait. First, if your opinion is wrong, these spreads can make losses. Second, it is possible to overtrade a position. Even professional stock traders seem a jittery lot. The financial headlines record their knee-jerk reactions to every bit of news and wisp of rumor.

The best policy in trading these spreads, it would seem, is to resist the temptation to adjust your positions at every news flash. If the trade makes sense to begin with, leave it alone. If the situation has definitely changed for the worse, unwind it. A calm approach seems likely to produce the best results.

CHAPTER 13

Stock Index–Single Stock Futures Spreads

Structure a Trade to Match Your Outlook

Single stock futures open up interesting possibilities for spread traders. One Chicago, an exchange dedicated to these markets, offers contracts on a broad range of these trading tools, and you can structure an entire family of spreads between a stock index futures contract, such as CBOT minisized Dow futures, and the single stock futures contracts representing a particular market sector such as pharmaceuticals, telecommunication, computers, financial services, or any of several others.

Two kinds of strategies suggest themselves. In one case, you may believe that the U.S. stock market will do well during the next week or two, or longer, but that one market sector may underperform. This outlook might lead you to want to own the stock market, in the form of CBOT mini-sized Dow futures, but not, say, the pharmaceutical sector. The Dow Jones Industrial Average (DJIA) contains three pharmaceutical stocks: Johnson and Johnson (JNJ), Merck and Co. (MRK), and Pfizer, Inc. (PFE). (Note that the One Chicago ticker symbols are the stock exchange symbol plus 1C—e.g., JNJ1C.) You can structure a spread such that you buy CBOT mini-sized Dow futures and sell the three pharmaceuticals. This way, you will have tailored your holding to fit your stock market outlook.

A second possibility arises if you decide that one sector, such as computers, will outperform the market as a whole. The DJIA contains four stocks that have various connections to the computer business: Hewlett-Packard Co., IBM Corp., Intel Corp., and Microsoft Corp. Even if the market as a whole rallies, you may believe that this sector will do better in relative value terms. The market may rally, that is, but these stocks may seem likely to rally more. Conversely, the market may fall, but these stocks may seem likely to fall less. If this is what you believe, you can sell CBOT mini-sized Dow futures and buy the single stock futures of the four computer-related companies.

WHEN YOU WANT TO OWN THE STOCK MARKET BUT NOT . . .

On September 28, 2004, CBOT mini-sized Dow futures were trading at 10,065, Johnson and Johnson futures (JNJ1C) were trading at $57.10 per share, Merck futures (MRK1C) were trading at $44.92, and Pfizer futures (PFE1C) were trading at $30.08. If your market analysis suggested that this was a good time to own the market but not pharmaceuticals, you could have sold out that part of your exposure.

Although the stock index futures contracts and single stock futures contracts seem very different on the surface, you can arrive at the appropriate trade sizes if you think in terms of dollar equivalent values for each contract. This way you can balance the legs of your spreads such that the spread will perform the task that you want it to perform.

The dollar equivalent value of one CBOT mini-sized Dow futures contract is the index times the $5 multiplier. With the index trading at 10,065, one contract gives you exposure to a $50,325 holding of the 30 Dow stocks.

Each One Chicago single stock futures contract gives you exposure to 100 shares of that stock, so the dollar equivalent value of one futures contract is the stock price times 100. With Johnson and Johnson stock trading at $57.10 per share, for example, one JNJ1C futures contract has a dollar equivalent value of $5,710. One important feature of these single stock futures contracts is that the margin is 20 percent of this dollar equivalent value—in this example, $1,142. Also, the contract specifications say, "Certain offsets may apply." This margin level makes it possible to trade five futures contracts for the same money that it will take to buy 100 shares.

STRUCTURING THE SPREAD TRADE

To structure this kind of multilegged spread, you must first figure out what fraction of the $50,325 stock index value each of those three stocks accounts for. A listing of the DJIA component stocks (available at www.averages.dowjones.com) gives the weightings for all the stocks. Johnson and Johnson accounts for 4.275 percent of the index, Merck accounts for 1.872 percent, and Pfizer accounts for 1.943 percent. Exhibit 13.1 uses this information to arrive at the number of shares of each stock that it takes to account for that company's share of the total index value.

EXHIBIT 13.1

To Find the Number of Shares of the Three Pharmaceutical Stocks (9/28/04 Prices)

Stock	CBOT Minisized Dow $ Value	Index Component Weight (%)	Component $ Weight	Share Price	Number of Shares	To Balance 10-Stock Index Contracts
JNJ	50,325	4.275	2,151.39	57.10	37.68	377
MRK	50,325	1.872	942.08	44.92	20.97	210
PFE	50,325	1.943	977.81	30.08	32.51	325

What Exhibit 13.1 tells you is that if the value of one December CBOT mini-sized Dow futures contract is $50,325, then 4.275 percent of that is $2,151.39. Further, at a $57.10 share price, 37.68 shares of Johnson and Johnson stock have that dollar value, and it will take 377 shares of this stock to account for the exposure that 10 CBOT mini-sized Dow contracts have to this stock.

Of course, you must trade single stock futures in whole numbers of contracts. The balancing of 10 CBOT minisized Dow contracts requires rounding up or down to achieve this. In this case, you might buy the 10 CBOT mini-sized Dow contracts and sell four JNJ1C futures contracts, two MRK1C futures contracts, and three PFE1C contracts.

Consider how this trade could have performed during several short intervals during the fall of 2004. Exhibit 13.2 assumes that you put on this trade on September 28 and unwound it a week later on October 5 at the prices shown in the exhibit.

The Dow gained 113 index points during this span. That 113 times the $5 multiplier and times 10 contracts results in a $5,650 gain. Merck stock dropped by $11.49 per share. This multiplied by the 100 share futures contract size and the two contracts sold results in a $2,298 gain. In contrast, the Johnson and Johnson and Pfizer stocks both gained slightly, so the short positions on these single stock futures suffered small losses. The Spread net is the sum of these four results—a handsome $7,441 gain. In effect, this is how CBOT mini-sized Dow futures would have performed during this week had the index not contained these three stocks.

Suppose you had held this trade in place for two weeks, until October 12, 2004. Exhibit 13.3 shows how this trade would have performed based on the September 28 and October 12 prices.

EXHIBIT 13.2

Buying the Market but Selling Pharmaceuticals

	Action	Dow	Action	JNJ1C	Action	MRK1C	Action	PFE1C
9/28/04	Buy 10	10,065	Sell 4	57.10	Sell 2	44.92	Sell 3	30.08
10/5/04	Sell 10	10,178	Buy 4	57.46	Buy 2	33.43	Buy 3	31.29
Result		113		–0.36		11.49		–1.21
One contract		565		–36.00		1,149.00		–121.00
Position		5,650		–144.00		2,298.00		–363.00
Spread net								7,441.00

EXHIBIT 13.3

When Everything Follows the Plan

	Action	Dow	Action	JNJ1C	Action	MRK1C	Action	PFE1C
9/28/04	Buy 10	10,065	Sell 4	57.10	Sell 2	44.92	Sell 3	30.08
10/12/04	Sell 10	10,068	Buy 4	56.82	Buy 2	30.85	Buy 3	29.86
Result		3		0.28		14.07		0.22
One Contract		15		28.00		1,407.00		22.00
Position		150		112.00		2,814.00		66.00
Spread net								3,142.00

In this case, the CBOT mini-sized Dow futures position gained only three index points for a tiny $150 gain for the 10-contract position. However, the positions short four JNJ1C, two MRK1C, and three PFE1C contracts all show positive results because all three stock prices moved lower. All in all, this makes for a $3,142 Spread net.

When you decide to own the stock market, of course, you must be prepared to accept that the market does not always rise. From September 28 to October 21, in fact, the Dow dropped 203 points, causing a 10-contract position long CBOT mini-sized Dow futures to lose $10,150. Exhibit 13.4 shows how the Dow minus pharmaceuticals spread would have performed across this 23-day interval.

Notice that the Johnson and Johnson stock gained $0.68 per share. Because this is a short position in that futures contract, this shows up as a loss in the exhibit. On the other hand, the Merck stock lost $13.66 per share and the Pfizer stock lost $1.64 per share, and these show up as gains because these are short positions. In fact the two MRK1C contracts gained $2,732 and the three PFE1C contracts gained $492. As a result of these gains the Spread net is minus $7,198, a far better result than the $10,150 index futures loss.

WHEN ONE SECTOR PROMISES TO OUTPERFORM THE MARKET

At times, your market research may alert you to the possibility that one market sector may outperform the broad market in relative terms. That is, your belief may be that:

- In a rallying market, this sector may rally more than the market as a whole.
- In a falling market, this sector may rally.
- In a falling market, this sector may fall less far.

In all three of these situations, you can benefit from a spread in which you initially sell CBOT mini-sized Dow futures and buy the single stock futures representing the companies in the sector that you expect to see outperform the market as a whole.

Within the 30 stocks of the Dow Jones Industrial Average, several market sectors have enough representation to be interesting candidates for such a trade. Computer-related stocks include Hewlett-Packard (HPQ), Intel (INTC), IBM (IBM), and Microsoft (MSFT). The financial services stocks in the index are American Express (AXP), Citigroup (C), and JP Morgan-Chase

EXHIBIT 13.4

Buying the Broad Market, Selling Pharmaceuticals

	Action	Dow	Action	JNJ1C	Action	MRK1C	Action	PFE1C
9/28/04	Buy 10	10,065	Sell 4	57.10	Sell 2	44.92	Sell 3	30.08
10/21/04	Sell 10	9,862	Buy 4	57.78	Buy 2	31.26	Buy 3	28.44
Result		–203		-0.68		13.66		1.64
One Contract	–1,015		–68.00		1,366.00		164.00	
Position		–10,150		–272.00		2,732.00		492.00
Spread net								–7,198.00

(JPM). Basic industrial and manufacturing stocks include 3M (MMM), General Electric (GE), Honeywell International (HON), General Motors (GM), Caterpillar (CAT), United Technologies (UTX), Alcoa (AA), and Boeing (BA). Any of these sectors, wholly or in part, are candidates for this kind of spread trade, but concentrate for now on the four computer-related stocks.

STRUCTURING THE SPREAD TRADE

This kind of spread requires a different structure from the one in which you simply want to eliminate the sector. Because one of the possibilities is that both the CBOT mini-sized Dow futures and the sector futures can rally, you must have an aggregate sector position such that the stock index leg of the spread cannot overwhelm it. The way to do this is to make the sum of the dollar values of the three or four single stock futures legs approximately match the dollar value of the CBOT mini-sized Dow leg. Exhibit 13.5 illustrates one good way to accomplish this dollar value balance, based on a spread between CBOT mini-sized Dow futures and the four computer-related single stock futures prices that were in the market on September 28, 2004.

EXHIBIT 13.5

To Find the Number of Shares of the Four Computer Stocks 9/28/04

Number of CBOT Mini-sized Dow Contracts	Futures Price	Position Dollar Value	Sum of Single Stock Futures Prices	Number of Single Stock Contracts	Position Dollar Value	Dollar Value Difference
1	10,065	50,325	14,967	3.36	44,901	5,424
2	10,065	100,650	14,967	6.72	104,769	–4,119
3	10,065	150,975	14,967	10.09	149,670	–1,305
4	10,065	201,300	14,967	13.45	194,571	6,729
5	10,065	251,625	14,967	16.81	254,439	–2,814
6	10,065	301,950	14,967	20.17	299,340	–2,610
7	10,065	352,275	14,967	23.54	359,208	–6,933
8	10,065	402,600	14,967	26.90	404,109	–1,509
9	10,065	452,925	14,967	30.26	449,010	3,915
10	10,065	503,250	14,967	33.62	508,878	–5,628

The first column shows a possible number of CBOT mini-sized Dow contracts. The second column is simply the stock index futures quote for the day in question. The Position Dollar Value column multiplies the futures quote by the $5 multiplier and by the number of contracts (e.g., 10,065 × 5 × 3 = 150,975).

Next, multiply the four stock prices by 100 shares to find the prices of single contracts of each, and sum the futures contract values. On September 28, the four futures contract dollar values were $1,824 for HPQ1C, $8,448 for IBM1C, $1,968 for INTC1C, and $2,727 for MSFT1C. The sum of these is $14,967.

Divide the series of stock index values for the various numbers of those contracts by the sum of the dollar values of the single stock futures. That is, to find the number of single stock futures contracts that it will take to balance the dollar value of four CBOT mini-sized Dow contracts, divide 201,300 (from the Position Dollar Value column) by 14,967 to discover that you will need to use 13.45 contracts of each of the four single stock futures contracts. This result is shown in the Number of Single Stock Contracts column. Ultimately, you must round to the nearest whole number of contracts, thus 13.45 must become 13.

Finally, multiply the rounded numbers by 14,967 (in the Sum of Single Stock Futures Prices column) to find the dollar value of a position consisting of that number of contracts of each of the single stock futures (e.g., the $149,670 value of 10 contracts of each of the four computer single stock futures comes close to matching the $150,975 value of three stock index contracts).

The Dollar Value Difference column subtracts the dollar value of the aggregate single stock futures position from the dollar value of the specified number of stock index futures. Obviously, the smaller the amount of rounding, the closer the single stock futures side of the spread will come to matching the dollar value of the specified number of stock index contracts and the smaller the number in the Dollar Value Difference column. On September 28, 2004, the best matches were to the three-, six-, and eight-contract stock index positions.

Obviously, when you sell CBOT mini-sized Dow futures, you are selling a certain amount of exposure to these four computer stocks. If you perform an exercise similar to the one displayed in Exhibit 13.1, you will find that one CBOT mini-sized Dow futures contains Hewlett-Packard exposure equivalent to 38 shares of the stock. A six-contract CBOT mini-sized Dow position, then, includes exposure to 228 shares. The 20-contract HPQ1C leg of the spread is equivalent to 2,000 shares of the stock. Less the 228 shares in the index, this spread is net long the equivalent of 1,772 shares of Hewlett-Packard stock. By the same arithmetic, it is net long 1,760 shares of IBM, 1,754 shares of Intel, and 1,766 shares of Microsoft.

ASSESSING POSSIBLE RESULTS

Exhibit 13.6 shows how this spread could have performed if you had put it on at the September 28 prices shown and unwound it a week later at these October 5, 2004, prices.

Notice that the Dow did rally 113 index points during this week. The One contract row multiplies this result by $5 to show that one contract would have lost $565 on this price move, because it was sold initially. The six CBOT mini-sized Dow contracts would have lost $3,390 dollars at this point as you can see by looking at the Position row. The three computer stocks all gained at least a small amount. The One contract row multiplies by 100 to take these amounts up to futures contract size, and the Position row multiplies by the number of contracts—20 in each of the four cases. The four single stock futures would have gained $12,660. That minus the $3,390 stock index futures loss leaves a spread net of $9,270. In this case, the stock market as a whole rallied, but the computer sector rallied more.

By late October 2004, the stock market had sold off for a variety of reasons—the ongoing middle East war, crude oil, and the impending U.S. presidential election among them. Not daunted by any of this, the computer stocks rallied. Exhibit 13.7 shows how this spread could have performed if you had let it ride until October 21.

The 203 index point drop in the price of CBOT mini-sized Dow futures turned this six-contract short position into a solid gainer. The 20

EXHIBIT 13.6

When Both Parts of the Spread Rally

	Action	Dow	Action	HPQ1C	IBM1C	INTC1C	MSFT1C
9/28/04	Sell 6	10,065	Buy 20	18.24	84.48	19.68	27.27
10/5/04	Buy 6	10,178	Sell 20	18.98	87.32	21.32	8.38
Result		–113		0.74	2.84	1.64	1.11
One contract		–565		74.00	284.00	164.00	111.00
Position		–3,390		1,480.00	5,680.00	3,280.00	2,220.00
Single stock net							12,660.00
Spread net							9,270.00

EXHIBIT 13.7

When the Stock Index Falls but the Computer Stocks Rally

	Action	Dow	Action	HPQ1C	IBM1C	INTC1C	MSFT1C
9/28/04	Sell 6	10,065	Buy 20	18.24	84.48	19.68	27.27
10/21/04	Buy 6	9,862	Sell 20	18.36	88.10	21.69	28.56
Result		203		0.12	3.62	2.01	1.29
One contract		1,015		12.00	362.00	201.00	129.00
Position		6,090		240.00	7,240.00	4,020.00	2,580.00
Single stock net							14,080.00
Spread net							20,170.00

EXHIBIT 13.8

To Find the Number of Shares of the Four Computer Stocks, 10/21/04

Number of CBOT Minisized Dow Contracts	Futures Price	Dollar Value	Sum of Single Stock Futures Prices	Number of Single Stock Contracts	Dollar Value	Dollar Value Difference
1	10,068	50,340	15,284	3.29	45,852	4,488
2	10,068	100,680	15,284	6.59	106,988	–6,308
3	10,068	151,020	15,284	9.88	152,840	–1,820
4	10,068	201,360	15,284	13.17	198,692	2,668
5	10,068	251,700	15,284	16.47	244,544	7,156
6	10,068	302,040	15,284	19.76	305,680	–3,640
7	10,068	352,380	15,284	23.06	351,532	848
8	10,068	402,720	15,284	26.35	397,384	5,336
9	10,068	453,060	15,284	29.64	458,520	–5,460
10	10,068	503,400	15,284	32.94	504,372	–972

futures contract IBM position did even better—all by itself. Yet the three other computer stocks gained, and the four single stock futures put together a $14,080 gain during this three-week period. Added to the stock index futures gain, this spread trade earned a total of $20,170.

As futures prices shift, so must the position sizes for a spread trade of this kind. Exhibit 13.8 replicates the calculations of Exhibit 13.5 except that it uses October 21, 2004, prices.

EXHIBIT 13.9

A Spread Trade that Catches the Early November 2004 Rally

	Action	Dow	Action	HPQ1C	IBM1C	INTC1C	MSFT1C
10/12/04	Sell 7	10,068	Buy 23	18.53	86.00	20.28	28.03
11/11/04	Buy 7	10,475	Sell 23	19.25	94.79	23.17	29.98
Result		–407		0.72	8.79	2.89	1.95
One contract		–2,083		72.00	879.00	289.00	195.00
Position		–14,245		1,656.00	20,217.00	6,647.00	4,485.00
Single stock net							33,005.00
Spread net							18,760.00

In this case, the three closest fits result from balancing 7 CBOT mini-sized Dow futures contracts against 23 contracts each of the four computer single stock futures, 10 CBOT mini-sized Dow futures contracts against 33 contracts each of the four computer single stock futures, or 3 CBOT mini-sized Dow futures contracts against 10 contracts each of the four computer single stock futures.

Suppose you had been watching this spread but hadn't decided to put it on until October 12. Exhibit 13.9 shows how this spread would have performed if, on October 12, you had sold seven CBOT mini-sized Dow futures and bought 23 contracts each of the four computer-related single stock futures. The exhibit assumes that you subsequently unwound the spread on November 11 at the prices shown.

The 407 postelection stock market rally made this seven-contract short position in CBOT mini-sized Dow futures a $14,245 loser, but the four computer stocks more than made up for that. Their outperformance of the market resulted in an $18,760 net gain for this spread.

This 7-23-23-23-23 trade size achieved the best dollar match, as Exhibit 13.8 shows. However, the smaller 3-10-10-10-10 spread of Exhibit 13.10, using the same October 12 and November 11 prices, shows that a smaller-scale spread trade can also produce solid results.

Finally, Exhibit 13.11 shows how this spread would have performed across this interval if you had initially sold 5 stock index contracts and bought 16 each of the four single stock futures.

This 5-16-16-16-16 trade earned $12,875, which seems a good result. Note that, based on the evidence of Exhibit 13.8, this is the worst fit of the 10 position sizes shown. Yet the result is hardly terrible.

EXHIBIT 13.10

Proving That Smaller Position Sizes Can Be Effective

	Action	Dow	Action	HPQ1C	IBM1C	INTC1C	MSFT1C
10/12/04	Sell 3	10,068	Buy 10	18.53	86.00	20.28	28.03
11/11/04	Buy 3	10,475	Sell 10	19.25	94.79	23.17	29.98
Result		–407		0.72	8.79	2.89	1.95
One contract		–2,083		72.00	879.00	289.00	195.00
Position		–6,249		720.00	8,790.00	2,890.00	1,950.00
Single stock net							14,350.00
Spread net							8,245.00

EXHIBIT 13.11

Even Imperfect Spread Ratios Can Perform Well

	Action	Dow	Action	HPQ1C	IBM1C	INTC1C	MSFT1C
10/12/04	Sell 5	10,068	Buy 16	18.53	86.00	20.28	28.03
11/11/04	Buy 5	10,475	Sell 16	19.25	94.79	23.17	29.98
Result		–407		0.72	8.79	2.89	1.95
× Multiplier		–2,083		72.00	879.00	289.00	195.00
× Contracts		–10,175		1,152.00	14,064.00	4,624.00	3,120.00
Single stock net							22,960.00
Spread net							12,785.00

One way to check the fit of these spread ratios is to multiply the One contract results for the four computer contracts in Exhibits 13.9, 13.10, and 13.11 using the unrounded numbers in the Number of Single Stock Contracts column of Exhibit 13.8. In Exhibit 13.10, multiply by 9.88 rather than by 10. In Exhibit 13.11, multiply by 16.47 rather than by 16. You will find that, based on these prices, rounding introduced only $674.45 of slippage to the trade illustrated in Exhibit 13.11. The other position sizes experience less slippage, of course. Still, this seems to indicate that you can trade whatever position size fits your trading budget and your appetite for risk with reasonable confidence of a satisfactory result. The single stock futures position size rounding does not introduce debilitating slippage.

A WORD OF CAUTION

The satisfactory results, of course, depend crucially on your getting your market call right. Like any spread trade, these stock index-single stock futures spreads are based on your market analysis and opinion. No one gets it right every time.

These stock index-single stock futures spreads involve another kind of risk that you must not overlook. Even though the example trades shown all involve screen-traded contracts, which many people think reduce execution risk, these spreads use contracts traded on two exchanges. This can, at times, cause timing problems. Carefully monitored, though, even this source of potential execution risk should be manageable.

CHAPTER 14

Yield Curve Spread Background

When interest rates are on the move, the U.S. Treasury yield curve is likely to change shape, and these yield curve shifts create opportunities for yield curve spread traders. A yield curve spread focuses on two points along the yield curve—for example, the 5-year Treasury and 10-year Treasury note yields—and attempts to capitalize on the relative difference between the shifts in these two yields.

An outright futures trade, as when you simply buy or sell 10-year Treasury note futures, expresses an opinion about the future direction of interest rates. The futures buyer, obviously, expects the 10-year yield to fall and the futures price to rise while the futures seller expects the opposite. In contrast, a properly structured yield curve spread trade, in which you buy one maturity and sell the other, enables you to express an opinion, not about the direction of a yield or price change, but about how the yield curve is likely to change shape during a given time period—how one maturity is likely to change relative to the other, regardless of the direction of the yield changes. The assumption going in is that one leg of the spread will gain while the other loses. The reason to do both is that the projected shape change can take place in a variety of ways, and the spread structure allows you to benefit from any of them.

It follows that successful yield curve trading requires a yield curve outlook based on a sense of how yield curves respond to economic stimuli. Also, because yields and prices at different maturities will respond differently to a given interest rate change, these trades must be carefully structured. This discussion reviews yield curve dynamics and suggests what must go into the formation of a yield curve outlook. Further, because it is important to think about how a given trade might perform given a variety of yield shifts, the discussion shows how to build a simple spreadsheet estimator that will help you explore a variety of possible outcomes—to do a series of "what if" exercises.

With this groundwork in place, subsequent chapters show how to structure three kinds of yield curve spread trades:

- CBOT 5-year Treasury note futures against CBOT 10-year Treasury note futures, sometimes called the *FYT spread*
- CBOT 2-year Treasury note futures against CBOT 10-year Treasury note futures, sometimes called the *TUT spread*
- CBOT fed funds futures against CBOT 10-year interest rate swap futures, sometimes called the *bank credit spread*

THE INFORMATION CONTENT OF YIELD CURVE SHIFTS

A yield curve is simply a plot of yields at a range of key maturities. The U.S. Treasury yield curve, which is probably the most frequently mentioned yield curve, plots the yields of 3- and 6-month Treasury bills, 2-, 3-, 5-, and 10-year Treasury notes, and 30-year Treasury bonds. Even though the U.S. Treasury yield curve is the one most people think of when they hear the term, the swap curve has emerged as the benchmark for business lending and corporate, municipal, and mortgage security issuance in recent years. Swap rates derive from LIBOR (London Inter Bank Offered Rate) and these rates are available on a variety of quote systems and on the Federal Reserve Web site in its H.15 reports. Also, the Wall Street Journal displays the swap curve alongside its Treasury yield curve graphic.

Discussions of interest rate movement often assume a parallel yield curve shift. That is, the assumption is that all yields will change by the same amount. In practice, parallel shifts seldom occur, and what makes yield curves interesting to economists and futures traders alike is that shifting interest rates typically cause changes in the shape of the yield curve. That is, no two yields are likely to respond in quite the same way to given economic or political stimuli.

When yield curve analysts refer to a normal yield curve, they mean a situation in which the longer the maturity, the higher the yield. Exhibit 14.1 shows the January 9, 2004, and May 7, 2004, U.S. Treasury yield curves both to have been normal.

When the yield curve inverts, shorter-term yields are higher than longer-term yields. The Treasury yield curve inverted in the late summer of 2000, as Exhibit 14.2 illustrates.

EXHIBIT 14.1

Normal U.S. Treasury Yield Curves

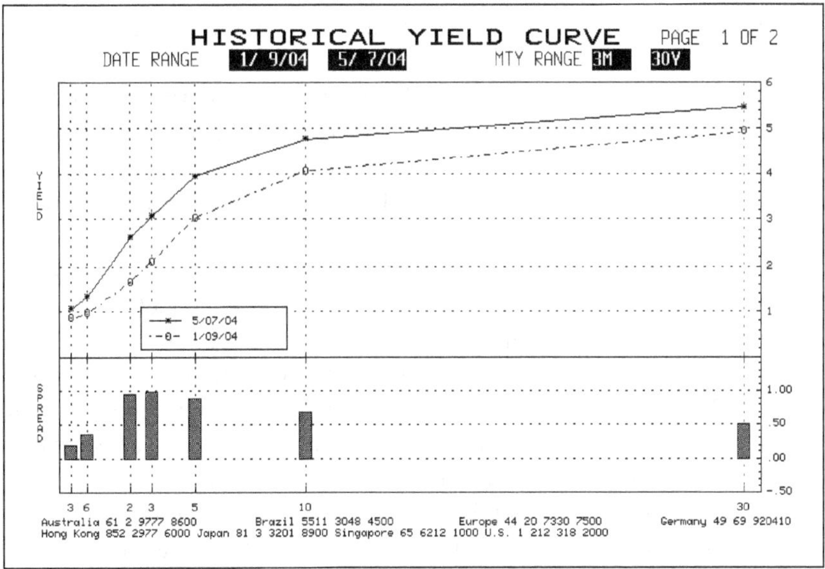

EXHIBIT 14.2

Inverted U.S. Treasury Yield Curves

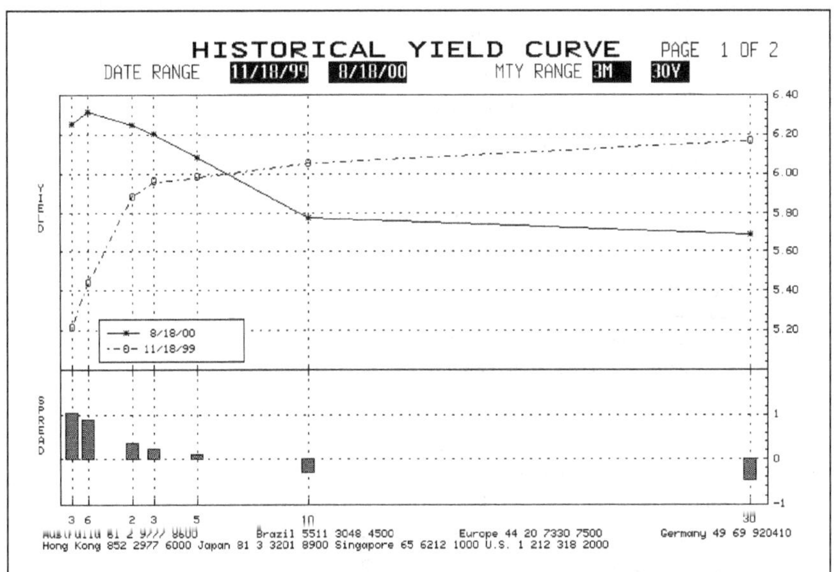

Notice that between November 18, 1999, and August 18, 2000, the 3-month yield rose by 103.5 bps, the 5-year yield rose by 10 bps, and the 10-year yield fell by 27.9 bps. The contrast between the normal November 1999 yield curve and the inverted August 2000 yield curve should be clearly apparent.

The typical comment about yield curves is that a normal yield curve indicates a healthy economy, while an inverted yield curve signals an impending recession, or at least a period of slower economic growth. This oversimplifies. The yield curve doesn't have to invert to signal periods of economic slowing.

Yield curve analysts often speak in terms of whether the slope of the yield curve is flat or steep. To measure this, you choose the yield curve segment that interests you and subtract the shorter yield from the longer. You can see from Exhibit 14.1 that during the 4-month period from January 9 to May 7, 2004, all yields rose, but 2-year yields rose more than 10-year yields. Exhibit 14.3 displays the arithmetic for the 2-year to 10-year segment.

On January 9, the 10-year minus 2-year difference was 2.42, or 242 basis points (bps). (1 bp, recall, is 1/100 of a percentage point, or 0.01%.) On May 7, it was 215 bps. This yield curve segment had flattened 27 bps (242 – 215 = 27).

The crucial observation is not the absolute yield curve shape at a given moment but whether it is flattening or steepening. The dynamics are what are important. In general, a steepening yield curve indicates an accommodative credit policy. The Fed is trying to nurture economic growth by making credit relatively easy. A flattening yield curve indicates a restrictive Fed policy. The Fed is trying to slow growth and curb the buildup of inflation by tightening the credit reins.

The graphic representation of Exhibit 14.1 lends itself to talk about steepness or flatness. A numerical presentation like the one in Exhibit 14.3 lends itself to talk about spread widening or narrowing. A widening yield

EXHIBIT 14.3

The Shifting Slope of the 2-Year to 10-Year Yield Curve Segment

Maturity	1/9/04	5/7/04
2-year Treasury note yields	1.66%	2.62%
10-year Treasury note yields	4.08%	4.77%
Yield curve slope, or spread	2.42	2.15

curve spread is equivalent to a steepening yield curve, and a narrowing yield curve spread is equivalent to a flattening yield curve.

UNDERSTANDING YIELD CURVE SHIFTS

It is important to remember that while longer-term Treasury prices are more volatile than shorter-term Treasury prices, shorter-term yields are more volatile than longer-term yields. Because futures trade in price terms, options on Treasury note futures price in terms of price volatility, not yield volatility. In price volatility terms, the longer the maturity, the higher the volatility relative to the other Treasury futures contracts. A 10-year Treasury note price will change more given a 1 bp yield shift than a 2-year Treasury note price will.

Yield volatility is the opposite. Shorter-term yields show greater responsiveness to a given stimulus than longer-term yields do. Exhibit 14.4 shows the yield volatility–price volatility contrast for representative 2-year, 5-year, and 10-year Treasury notes on June 3, 2004. Keep in mind that these are actual Treasury note volatilities, not futures volatilities. The general idea is the same.

ANOTHER APPROACH TO FIXED-INCOME PRICE VOLATILITY

Options traders think of volatility in terms of an annualized percentage value as Exhibit 14.4 illustrates. The bond market has introduced two other measures of price volatility—modified duration and dollar value of a basis point (DV01). Another common term is basis point value (BPV), which is exactly equivalent. A modified duration and a DV01 deliver the same message once you work through the details of the story.

Assume the existence of two Treasury notes both paying 5 percent coupon but one maturing May 15, 2009, the other May 15, 2014. Assume

EXHIBIT 14.4

The Yield Volatility–Price Volatility Contrast

	Yield Volatility	Price Volatility
2 3/8% of Aug 6 Treasury note	49.71%	2.93%
3 7/8% of May 9 Treasury note	36.63%	6.38%
4 3/4% of May 14 Treasury note	23.89%	8.91%

EXHIBIT 14.5

The Price Effect of a 100 Basis Point Yield Increase at Two Maturities

	Price @ 4.5%	Price @ 5.5%	Difference	% Change
5 year	102.2166	97.8400	4.3766	4.28
10 year	103.9909	96.1932	7.7977	7.50

further that on May 15, 2004, both were priced to yield 4.5 percent. Given these data, a bond calculator will show the price of the five-year note to be 102.2166 (approximately 102-09 in points and 32nds). The price of the 10-year note would be 103.9909 (approximately 103-31+). Now suppose that these yields instantaneously rose to 5.5 percent. Both prices would fall, but Exhibit 14.5 shows that the 10-year price would fall more.

Note that the percent change values are the difference divided by the price at the 4.5 percent yield.

The fixed-income world incorporates this observation (and actually quite a bit more) in its modified duration values. Note that modified duration (dollar duration in some discussions) is always thought of in years. A modified duration of 6.52 years indicates that an instantaneous 100 bp yield shift will cause the price of this security to move 6.52 percent in the opposite direction. The approach of Exhibit 14.5 is not how these values are calculated, but it gives a rough and ready idea about the content of modified duration values. For coupon bearing securities, the modified duration is always at least somewhat shorter than the maturity. Modified durations tell you that the price of a 5-year note will necessarily respond less to a given yield change than the price of a 10-year note. Said another way, the price of the 10-year note will be more volatile than the price of the 5-year note.

Another, and often more convenient, way to capture this difference in price volatility across maturities is to use DV01s. These derive from modified durations and full prices [a full price is the quoted price plus accrued interest—for an excellent discussion of this, see Berghardt and Belton (1994)]. The formula for deriving a DV01 is:

$$[(0.01 \times \text{modified duration}) \times \text{full price}] \times 0.01 = \text{DV01}$$

Assume that the security for which you want a DV01 is trading at the full price of \$110,460 and has a 6.52 modified duration. Using the formula, you can discover that it has a \$72.02 DV01.

$$[(0.01 \times 6.52) \times \$110{,}460] \times 0.01 = \$72.02$$

This indicates that a 1 bp drop in yield will raise the price by $72.02, to $110,532.

FOCUSING ON THE RIGHT SECURITY

Yield curve analysts typically base their opinions on the most recently issued Treasury security at each maturity, which is known as the *on-the-run* note or bond. The Treasury note futures contracts do not often derive from the on-the-run note, however. Rather, they take their character from the cheapest-to-deliver (CTD) security. The on-the-run and CTD can be very different securities. Consider that on May 21, 2004, the on-the-run 10-year Treasury note was the 4.75 percent coupon maturing in May 2014 (familiarly, the 4.75 percent of May 14) with a yield-to-maturity of 4.76 percent. The CTD on that day was the 5 percent of February 11 with a yield-to-maturity of 4.32 percent. (For helpful discussions of CTD, see Burghardt, et al., *The Treasury Bond Basis*, revised edition, McGraw-Hill, 1994, or www.cbot.com).

Because this is true, the modified duration and full price of the on-the-run are not what you want to look at in trying to understand how a futures contract will respond to yield changes. Rather, you want to look at the modified duration and full price of the CTD in calculating the relevant DV01.

Having performed this exercise for the CTD Treasury security, however, you still do not have a futures DV01. By convention, the futures DV01 is the CTD DV01 divided by the CTD conversion factor. Assuming that $72.02 is the CTD DV01 and that the conversion factor is 0.9451, you can discover that the futures DV01 is $76.20 (72.02 ÷ 0.9451).

Notice that 6.52 percent of $110,460 is $7,201.99. That is based on a 100 bp yield change, so divide by 100. This indicates that a 1 bp yield change will move the security price by $72.02, which is the same thing the DV01 tells you. You can find both modified durations and DV01s on many of the more full-service quote screens. Lacking access to this kind of resource, your broker should be able to supply these values. Using DV01s saves several steps, so DV01s are the tool of choice for assessing fixed-income price volatility.

A HANDY SPREADSHEET ESTIMATOR

DV01s provide a quick way to estimate in very approximate terms the dollar effect of a yield shift. Assume the 10-year Treasury note futures are trading at 110-22+, or $110,703.125, and have a $71.94 DV01. Suppose you would like to know what will happen to this futures price if yields rise or fall by 10 bps. Simply multiply the DV01 by the yield shift and add or subtract that to or from the dollar futures price, as is done in Exhibit 14.6.

EXHIBIT 14.6

Using DV01s to Estimate a Futures Price Change

DV01	Yield Change	DV01 × YC	Initial Futures	Final Futures	
71.94	10	–719.40	110,703.125	109,983.725	109-31+
71.94	–10	719.40	110,703.125	111,422.525	111-13+

EXHIBIT 14.7

A Spread Results Calculator

Futures Contract	DV01	Yield Change	Number of Contracts	Result
5-year Treasury note	42.42	10	10	–4,241
10-year Treasury note	71.94	5	10	–3,597

Some brokerages compute the actual price changes, but that is a long and complicated calculation. For trade planning purposes, these DV01 estimates do very well.

This way of using DV01s suggests a handy way to estimate spread results. Assume that 5-year Treasury note futures have a $42.41 DV01, while 10-year futures have a $71.94 DV01. Suppose you would like to know approximately how much the values of 10 contracts of each futures contract will change if the five-year yield rises by 10 bps, while the ten-year yield rises 5 bps.

Using a spreadsheet, you can build a simple calculator. Enter the relevant values under DV01, Yield Change, and Number of Contracts. To find the Results, multiply across, as is done in Exhibit 14.7.

Of course, if you buy futures, rising yields result in a loss, while falling yields result in a gain. If you sell futures, the converse is true. In setting up the Result cell, you can assure yourself of the right sign if, as a final step, you multiply by minus one.

BACK TO YIELD CURVE SHIFTS

Given the nature of yield volatility, the normal expectation is that when yields are on the rise, shorter-term yields will rise more than longer-term yields. Exhibit 14.8 shows what you might expect to see if the 2-year yield were to rise by 25 bps. Note that the 5-year and 10-year yields also rise but progressively less, and this narrows the yield curve spreads.

When a shift such as this one happens, yield curve analysts speak in terms of the yield curve flattening. Yield curve spread traders speak in terms of the spread narrowing. In this example, the 2–10 yield curve segment flattened by 15 bps, and, what is the same thing, the 2–10 spread narrowed by 15 bps. The 5–10 spread also narrowed, but only by 5 bps.

Conversely, when yields are falling, shorter-term yields normally fall more than longer-term yields. This steepens the yield curve or widens yield curve spreads as Exhibit 14.9 demonstrates.

These exhibits illustrate the normal expectation, but you shouldn't automatically assume this is what will happen. For example, prior to the June 2003 Fed meeting, the market consensus was that the U.S. economy was limping badly enough that the Fed needed to drop its Fed funds target rate by 50 bps, from 1.25 percent to 0.75 percent. In fact, the Fed dropped the rate by only 25 bps, to 1.00 percent. Alarmed by this, the market

EXHIBIT 14.8

A Normal Yield Curve Spread Reaction to Rising Yields

	2-Year Yield	5-Year Yield	10-Year Yield	2-10 Spread	5-10 Spread
Initial	2.70	3.83	4.83	2.13	1.00
Yield change	0.25	0.15	0.10		
Ending	2.95	3.98	4.93	1.98	0.95
Spread change				–0.15	–0.05

EXHIBIT 14.9

A Normal Yield Curve Spread Reaction to Falling Yields

	2-Year Yield	5-Year Yield	10-Year Yield	2-10 Spread	5-10 Spread
Initial	2.70	3.83	4.83	2.13	1.00
Yield change	–0.25	–0.15	–0.10		
Ending	2.45	3.68	4.73	2.28	1.05
Spread change				0.15	0.05

pushed 5-year and 10-year yields sharply higher just when the normal expectation would have been for them to fall slightly.

In the late spring of 2004, with the Fed having announced its readiness to begin raising its Fed funds target rate, at least some interest rate market analysts feared that the Fed wasn't planning to do enough to control a rapid buildup of inflationary forces. Given this concern, it seemed entirely possible to these analysts that 10-year yields would rise more than 2-year and 5-year yields. This would widen yield curve spreads when, normally, you would expect Fed tightening—that is, the raising of the Fed funds target rate—to narrow them.

DEVELOPING A YIELD CURVE OUTLOOK

When formulating a yield curve outlook, you need to ask what would be the normal yield curve reaction and then ask what economic or political factors could force a variation from the norm.

Consider the interest rate situation you would have seen in late May 2004. From March 12 to May 28, Treasury yields had been rising. The 5-year Treasury constant maturity yield had climbed from 2.72 percent to 3.83 percent, a 111 bp increase. The 10-year Treasury yield had climbed from 3.75 percent to 4.68 percent, a 93 bp increase. The 5-year to 10-year spread had narrowed by 18 bps, from 103 bps (3.75 – 2.72 = 1.03) to 85 bps (4.68 – 3.83 = 0.85). (Note that the Federal Reserve Web site keeps track of Treasury yield history in terms of these constant maturity yields, which are theoretical constructs and not quite what you can find in the market. However, for the purposes of tracking spread history and developing a yield curve outlook, they serve well.)

This is normal for a rising yield situation. The shorter-term yield rises relative to the longer-term yield, causing the spread to narrow.

The question to consider, in thinking about a yield curve trade, is whether this narrowing will continue or whether the inflation numbers that come out in the month before the June 30 Fed meeting will alarm the market enough to widen the spread. Spreads do tend to be mean-reverting. For example, from January 3, 2003, to May 28, 2004, the mean 5-year to 10-year spread was 103 bps. From March 12 to May 28, 2004, the spread narrowed below this mean. In the normal course of events, you can expect the spread to widen back toward its 103 bp mean. When you find the spread wider than its mean, you can expect it to narrow back to the mean. This is mean reversion at work.

But you don't want to depend blindly on that. You should ask whether anything on the horizon promises to make this other than "the normal course of events." In late May and early June 2004 there was something—in the form of questions about signs of stronger than expected inflation buildup and about whether the Fed seemed ready to do enough to control these inflation forces. If the Fed were to raise its Fed funds target rate less than the market thought necessary, that could drive the 10-year yield higher relative to the 5-year yield and widen this yield curve spread rather than narrow it.

In fact, the Fed seems to have been aware of these market concerns, for Chairman Greenspan mentioned in several speeches that, although he and his colleagues believed that they could take a gradual approach to raising the Fed funds target rate, they were prepared to take stronger action if new evidence suggested the need.

It is possible for thoughtful people to disagree on matters of this kind. This is why there are markets. But this outlines the kinds of considerations that go into the formulation of yield curve outlooks.

CHAPTER 15

The 5-Year to 10-Year Treasury Yield Curve Spread

The FYT Spread

A good yield curve spread for the purpose of showing how to structure yield curve spread trades is the one that balances a CBOT 5-year Treasury note futures position against a CBOT 10-year Treasury note futures position. This spread is sometimes called the *FYT* (*FY* being the most common ticker symbol for the 5-year contract, and *T* being the first letter of the 10-year symbol TY). The $100,000 par size of these two contracts makes structuring this trade slightly less complicated than structuring some of the other yield curve spreads.

Exhibit 15.1 plots the constant maturity Treasury yields at the 5-year and 10-year maturities using weekly data. Even when the spread seems to be trending, this exhibit shows that this spread creates ample trading opportunity—on both sides of the spread market.

TRADING RESPONSES TO AN OUTLOOK

In general, anticipating a widening yield curve spread, you will want to buy the spread. Anticipating a narrowing spread, you will want to sell it. The logic of buying and selling is straightforward. If you expect a thing to increase in value, you typically want to buy it. If you expect its value to decrease, you typically want to sell it.

You buy or sell a yield curve spread in terms of what you do on the short maturity leg of the trade. To sell the 5-year to 10-year spread, you will sell 5-year Treasury note futures and buy 10-year Treasury note futures. To buy this spread, you will buy 5-year and sell 10-year Treasury note futures.

EXHIBIT 15.1

10-Year–5-Year Spread (Constant Maturity Treasuries, Weekly Data)

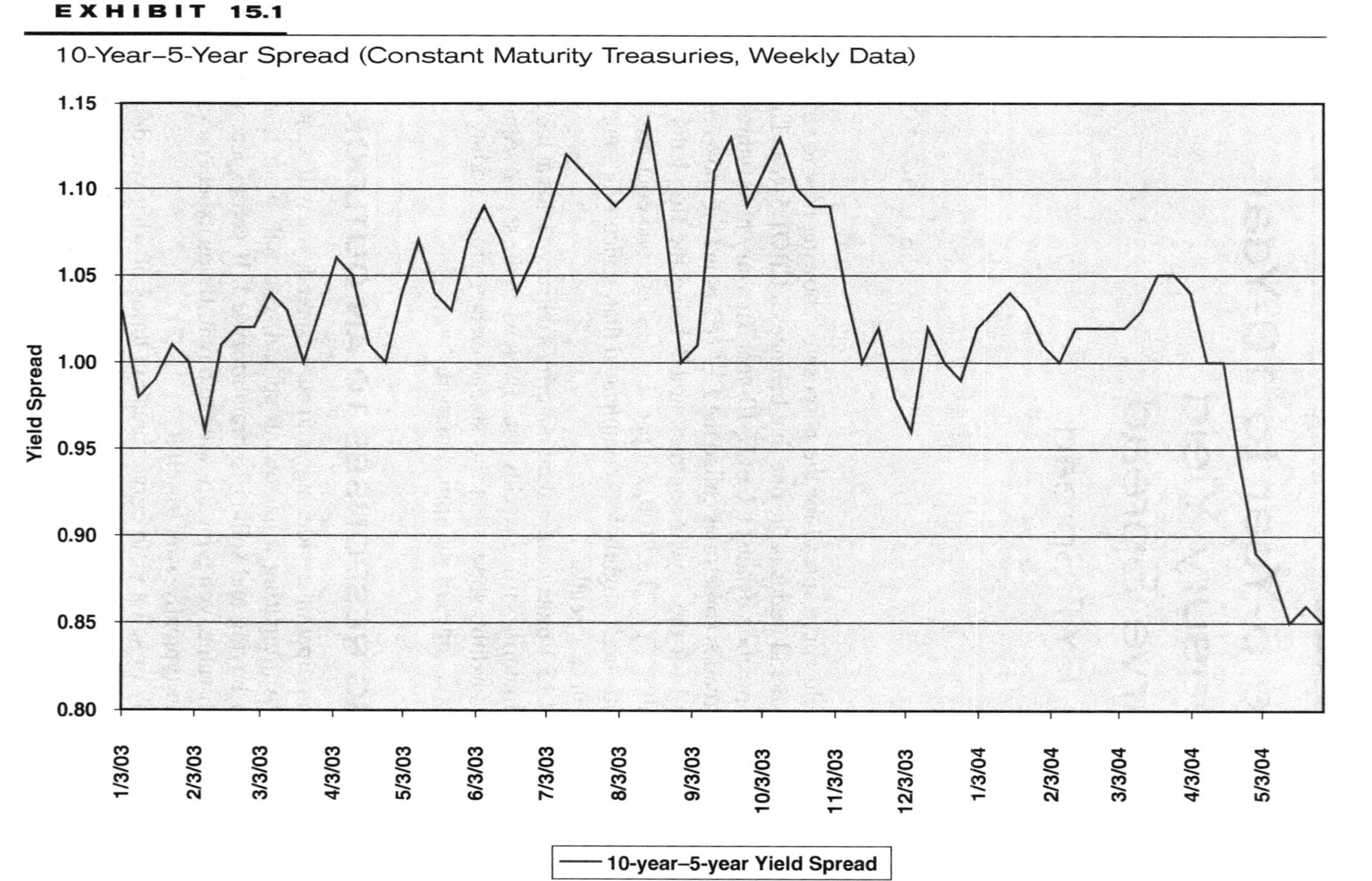

The advantage of trading this kind of spread is that it gives you three ways to be right. If you sell the spread, you gain any time the spread narrows, as it will when:

1. Both yields rise, but the 5-year rises more than the 10-year.
2. Both yields fall, but the 5-year falls less than the 10-year.
3. The 5-year yield rises, while the 10-year yield falls.

Similarly, if you buy the spread, you gain any time the spread widens, as it will when:

1. Both yields rise, but the 5-year rises less than the 10-year.
2. Both yields fall, but the 5-year falls more than the 10-year.
3. The 5-year yield falls, while the 10-year yield rises.

How much your trade will gain depends on how much the spread narrows or widens.

Keep in mind that these are directional trades. However, it is the direction of the spread change, not the direction of the yield or price change, that matters. Because these are directional trades, negative results are possible. If you sell the spread and experience any of the three spread widening events, the trade will lose, as it will if you buy the spread and experience any of the three spread narrowing events.

THE IMPORTANCE OF STRUCTURE

The idea of a yield curve spread is that it will isolate one factor—spread widening or narrowing—and filter out the effects of changes in yield or price direction. A yield curve spread trade achieves this focus by ratioing the two legs.

To see why structure matters, consider two hypothetical situations, both resulting in a 5 bp narrowing of the 5-year to 10-year spread. Suppose that, given your opinion that this yield curve spread will narrow, you sell 1,000 contracts of 5-year Treasury note futures and buy 1,000 contracts of 10-year Treasury note futures in the expectation that a narrowing spread will cause your trade to gain.

Assume, first, that both yields rise but that the 5-year yield rises 15 bps while the 10-year yield rises only 10 bps. So far, so good. The spread is now 5 bps narrower. The trouble is that a trade that balances two 1,000 contract legs will show a loss rather than a gain, as Exhibit 15.2 demonstrates.

EXHIBIT 15.2

Rising Yields Narrow the Spread 5 bps

Futures	DV01	Yield Change	Number of Contracts	Result (to Nearest $)
5-year	45.20	15	–1,000	678,000
10-year	69.90	10	1,000	–699,000
Spread net				–21,000

EXHIBIT 15.3

Falling Yields Narrow the Spread 5 bps

Futures	DV01	Yield Change	Number of Contracts	Result (to Nearest $)
5-year	45.20	–10	–1,000	–452,000
10-year	69.90	–15	1,000	1,048,500
Spread				596,500

Reading across Exhibit 15.2, you can see the two DV01s. Under Yield Change, the positive numbers indicate that the yields have risen by these numbers of basis points. Under Number of Contracts, the minus 1,000 indicates that this number of 5-year contracts is being sold, while the positive number in the 10-year row indicates that this number is being bought.

All that remains is to multiply across to come up with the results for each leg. Remember that if yields rise and you are selling futures, the result will be positive. If yields rise and you are buying futures, the result will be negative. Conversely, if yields fall and you are selling futures, the result will be negative, but if yields fall and you are buying futures, the result will be positive. You can see that, given the assumptions underlying Exhibit 15.2, this trade lost $21,000.

The spread could also narrow if both yields fell, so assume that the 5-year yield fell 10 bps while the 10-year yield fell 15 bps to narrow the spread by 5 bps. Alarmingly, Exhibit 15.3 shows that the 1,000 to 1,000 position will now generate a huge gain.

This shouldn't be. It's hard to say that a large gain is a bad result, but if the spread narrowed by 5 bps each time, it seems reasonable to expect a true yield curve spread to generate similar results in each case. The problem with this trade is that it has a large directional exposure as signaled by the difference between the DV01s of the two futures contracts. As a result, when yields rise, the 1,000 10-year contracts that you bought will lose more than the 1,000 5-year contracts will gain. Conversely, when yields fall, the 10-year position will gain more than the 5-year position will lose.

A trade with two equal sized legs such as this one is not a yield curve spread. Granted, it buys at one point of the yield curve and sells at another, but it has nothing about it that filters out directional effect. It does nothing to isolate spread change.

CALCULATING A SPREAD RATIO

A yield curve spread does filter out directional effect to create a futures position that will react only to changes in the spread. Further, it will react more or less equally no matter the direction of the yield shift. As long as the spread narrows or widens a certain amount, a true yield curve spread will generate a result you can count on.

To structure a trade that will respond only to yield curve shape change, you can calculate a spread ratio by dividing the 5-year DV01 by the 10-year DV01. Given the $45.20 5-year DV01 and the $69.90 10-year DV01 of Exhibits 15.2 and 15.3, the appropriate ratio in this case is 0.6466 (45.20 ÷ 69.90). This indicates that for every 1,000 5-year contract you sell, in the expectation that the spread will narrow, you should buy 647 10-year contracts. Exhibits 15.4a and b show how you can expect this ratioed spread to react to the same yield shifts shown in Exhibits 15.2 and 15.3.

In both cases, the spread narrowed by 5 bps, and the spread trade generated almost equal gains. The direction of the yield change made no difference to the size of the result. The slight mismatch is the result of rounding in the calculation of the spread ratio. Notice that a 15 bp change causes a $678,000 gain in the 5-year leg in Exhibit 15.4a but a $678,380 gain in the 10-year leg in Exhibit 15.4b. The 10 bp change causes similar slight mismatches in the two legs. This is because 0.6466 was rounded to 0.647. Given the scale of the trade, this slight mismatch is of no consequence.

This should make the case for structuring yield curve spread trades. The unratioed trade is not a yield curve spread. It isolates nothing of interest as far as yield curve shifts go. Only a ratioed spread is truly a yield curve spread.

EXHIBIT 15.4

Ratioed Yield Curve Spreads Respond Only to Spread Change

a

Futures	DV01	Yield Change	Number of Contracts	Result (to Nearest $)
5-year	45.20	15	–1,000	678,000
10-year	69.90	10	647	–452,253
Spread net				225,747

b

Futures	DV01	Yield Change	Number of Contracts	Result (to Nearest $)
5-year	45.20	–10	–1,000	–452,000
10-year	69.90	–15	647	678,380
Spread net				226,380

WHERE YIELD CURVE THEORY MEETS FUTURES REALITY

Keep in mind that when yields are on the move, DV01s will change, and different Treasury securities may become cheapest to deliver (CTD). Because of this, spread ratios can change—sometimes rather drastically.

Exhibit 15.5 shows which Treasury securities were cheapest to deliver into the June 2004 5-year and 10-year Treasury note futures for a sequence of six Fridays in May and June 2004. It also shows the futures DV01s, the June futures prices, and the 5-year and 10-year constant maturity Treasury yields. Based on these DV01s and yields, the exhibit also shows the spread ratios and yield spreads on each of the six days.

Notice that three different securities were CTD into the June 10-year Treasury note futures contract during the first three weeks in May, and their maturities ranged over 21 months. During this same six-week period, only one Treasury security was CTD into the June 5-year Treasury note futures contract. Yields trended higher but not in a straight line. The 5-year yield traded across a 24 bp range, while the 10-year yield traded across a 19 bp range. The yield spread narrowed fairly steadily from 88 bps to 82 bps.

Partly because of this fluid CTD situation, the spread ratios ranged from a high of 0.602 on May 7 to a low of 0.562 on May 21, and the June 10 ratio is close to the low at 0.563. That is, to balance a 1,000 position in

EXHIBIT 15.5

How Shifting CTD, DV01s, and Yields Affect Spread Ratios

5/7/04

	June 5-Year Treasury Note Futures	June 10-Year Treasury Note Futures	Yield Spread	Spread Ratio
CTD	3.25 of Aug 08	4.875 of Feb 12		
DV01	43.19	71.70		0.602371
Price	108-15	108-156		
CM yield	3.74	4.62	0.88	

5/14/04

	June 5-Year Treasury Note Futures	June 10-Year Treasury Note Futures	Yield Spread	Spread Ratio
CTD	3.25 of Aug 08	4.25 of Aug 13		
DV01	43.28	75.92		0.570074
Price	108-29+	108-28+		
CM yield	3.96	4.81	0.85	

5/21/04

	June 5-Year Treasury Note Futures	June 10-Year Treasury Note Futures	Yield Spread	Spread Ratio
CTD	3.25 of Aug 08	4.25 of Nov 13		
DV01	42.74	76.04		0.562073
Price	108-31	108-31+		
CM yield	3.88	4.74	0.86	

Continued

EXHIBIT 15.5

How Shifting CTD, DV01s, and Yields Affect Spread Ratios (*Continued*)

5/28/04

	June 5-Year Treasury Note Futures	June 10-Year Treasury Note Futures	Yield Spread	Spread Ratio
CTD	3.25 of Aug 08	4.875 of Feb 12		
DV01	42.56	73.42		0.579679
Price	109-18	109-30		
CM yield	3.83	4.68	0.85	

6/4/04

	June 5-Year Treasury Note Futures	June 10-Year Treasury Note Futures	Yield Spread	Spread Ratio
CTD	3.25 of Aug 08	4.875 of Feb 12		
DV01	42.36	74.38		0.569508
Price	108-30	109-02+		
CM yield	3.91	4.74	0.83	

6/10/04

	June 5-Year Treasury Note Futures	June 10-Year Treasury Note Futures	Yield Spread	Spread Ratio
CTD	3.25 of Aug 08	4.875 of Feb 12		
DV01	41.81	74.24		0.563173
Price	108-272	109-022		
CM yield	3.98	4.80	0.82	

5-year Treasury note futures, you would have needed to use 602 10-year contracts on May 5 but only 562 contracts on May 21.

Exhibit 15.6 shows analogous data for the September futures contracts for a span of six Fridays in July and August 2004.

Notice that during this period, the CTD situation is stable. The same Treasury securities are CTD for all six Fridays. Also, yields trend down, but they rise and then fall rather sharply at both maturies. The high-low range for the 5-year yield is 37 bps, while for the 10-year yield it is 23 bps. The yield spread narrows by 5 bps during the first three weeks and then widens by 4 bps by August 20, 2004.

Finally, contrast the smaller variation in the spread ratio for this period relative to the variation in May and June. Exhibit 15.7 shows how many

EXHIBIT 15.6

How Shifting CTD, DV01s, and Yields Affect Spread Ratios

7/16/04

	September 5-Year Treasury Note Futures	September 10-Year Treasury Note Futures	Yield Spread	Spread Ratio
CTD	3.375 of Nov 08	5 of Aug 11		
DV01	42.22	71.30		0.592146
Price	110-016	111-104		
CM yield	3.64	4.47	0.83	

7/23/04

	September 5-Year Treasury Note Futures	September 10-Year Treasury Note Futures	Yield Spread	Spread Ratio
CTD	3.375 of Nov 08	5 of Aug 11		
DV01	41.93	70.01		0.598914
Price	109-16	110-23		
CM yield	3.67	4.46	0.79	

7/30/04

	September 5-Year Treasury Note Futures	September 10-Year Treasury Note Futures	Yield Spread	Spread Ratio
CTD	3.375 of Nov 08	5 of Aug 11		
DV01	41.87	70.72		0.592053
Price	109-162	110-22		
CM yield	3.78	4.56	0.78	

Continued

EXHIBIT 15.6

How Shifting CTD, DV01s, and Yields Affect Spread Ratios (*Continued*)

8/6/04

	September 5-Year Treasury Note Futures	September 10-Year Treasury Note Futures	Yield Spread	Spread Ratio
CTD	3.375 of Nov 08	5 of Aug 11		
DV01	42.44	70.99		0.597831
Price	110-316	112-23+		
CM yield	3.61	4.41	0.80	

8/13/04

	September 5-Year Treasury Note Futures	September 10-Year Treasury Note Futures	Yield Spread	Spread Ratio
CTD	3.375 of Nov 08	5 of Aug 11		
DV01	42.40	70.59		0.600652
Price	110-306	112-23+		
CM yield	3.47	4.28	0.81	

8/20/04

	September 5-Year Treasury Note Futures	September 10-Year Treasury Note Futures	Yield Spread	Spread Ratio
CTD	3.375 of Nov 08	5 of Aug 11		
DV01	42.43	70.69		0.600226
Price	111-002	112-236		
CM yield	3.41	4.23	0.82	

10-year Treasury note futures contracts would be required to balance a 1,000 contract position in 5-year Treasury note futures on each of the six Fridays during these two periods.

These spread ratios need careful watching at times, and Exhibits 15.5, 15.6, and 15.7 show why.

EXHIBIT 15.7

To Isolate Spread Change

Week	Number of June Contracts	Number of September Contracts
1	602	592
2	570	599
3	562	592
4	580	598
5	570	601
6	563	600
High-low difference	40	9

SCALING POSITION SIZE TO YOUR COMFORT LEVEL

The position sizes of Exhibit 15.6 and of the trade illustrations that follow all use large positions to reduce the rounding effect in the spread ratio calculation. These spreads can easily be scaled down to fit your risk tolerance level and your trading budget. Consider the six June ratios in Exhibit 15.7.

The first ratio balances 1,000 5-year Treasury note futures against 602 10-year Treasury note futures. This can easily be adjusted downward to 100 to 60, 10 to 6, or even 5 to 3. None of these smaller positions involves significant rounding or directional exposure. The second ratio is 1,000 to 570. A 100 to 57 ratio is obviously going to work well, but at the level of 10 5-year Treasury note futures, you face a choice—10 to 6 or 10 to 5. Either way you turn, this much rounding error allows a fair amount of directional exposure to creep into your trade. This can affect results to a significant degree. Most of the June ratios in Exhibit 15.7 introduce a similar Hobson's choice.

An easy way to scale these trades is to choose the size of the five-year leg that feels comfortable and multiply that by the spread ratio as Exhibit 15.8 illustrates. The references Week 1 and Week 5 the Exhibit 15.5 spread ratios for those weeks in the sequence.

You can see that the smaller position sizes of the Week 1 sequence introduce very little rounding error. As a result, trades made using these numbers should not experience much slippage from directional exposure. The position sizes of the Week 5 sequence do introduce a good bit of rounding error, and trades using these numbers may experience quite a bit of slippage.

You can either decide to live with that (after all, it can go in your favor as well as against you), or you can make slight adjustments to your five-year

EXHIBIT 15.8

Scaling Spread Ratios

Week 1			Week 5	Week 5 adjusted		
Number of 5-Year Contracts	Spread Ratio	Number of 10-Year Contracts	Spread Ratio	Number of 10-Year Contracts	Number of 5-Year Contracts	Number of 10-Year Contracts
10	0.602371	6.02	0.569508	5.70	9	5.13
15	0.602371	9.04	0.569508	8.54	14	7.97
25	0.602371	15.06	0.569508	14.24	23	13.10
50	0.602371	30.12	0.569508	28.48	51	29.04
75	0.602371	45.18	0.569508	42.71	74	42.14

position size. The sequence headed Week 5 adjusted in Exhibit 15.8 shows how a series of one- and two-contract adjustments can improve the resolution of the spread ratio filter (e.g., 5.13 = 9 × 0.569508).

HOW YIELD CURVE SPREAD TRADES MIGHT PERFORM

Ultimately, you must trade futures prices, not DV01s. A few examples of trades that might have been made during these two periods shows how rewarding these trades can be—even when the spread widens or narrows only slightly. The final example makes even clearer the need to pay careful attention to the details of which security is CTD and spread ratio change.

Consider the situation facing a yield curve spread trader on May 14, 2004. In its May 4, 2004, statement, the Fed had issued a clear signal that it was ready to begin raising its fed funds target rate, and 5-year and 10-year Treasury yields had already risen quite a bit. Between May 4 and 14, the 5-year yield had risen from 3.66 percent to 3.96 percent, a 30 bp increase. The 10-year yield had risen from 4.56 percent to 4.81 percent, a 25 bp increase. Obviously, these yield increases had narrowed the yield spread, as typically happens when yields are on the rise. This might well have seemed an opportune time to sell the spread.

Going back to Exhibit 15.5, you can see that the spread ratio on May 14 was 0.570, so, to sell the spread, you might have sold 1,000 June 5-year Treasury note futures (FVM4) and bought 570 June 10-year Treasury note futures (TYM4). Exhibit 15.9 shows that, had you unwound this trade on June 4 at the futures prices shown in Exhibit 15.5, this trade would have earned $91,250.

In analyzing these spread results, the arithmetic is easier if you do most of the work for a single contract and factor in the position size at the last possible stage. Also, if you always subtract the bought price from the sold price, you'll always get the gains and losses right. In Exhibit 15.9, the five-year price rose to generate a loss for a short position, and the minus sign pops up in the right place here. From May 14 to June 4, the five-year loses only $15,625. This is a 1,000 contract position, so that becomes minus $15,625. In this example, the 10-year leg is the one that makes the money—$187.50 per contract multiplied by 570 contracts becomes $106,875. The spread gains $91,250 (106,875 − 15,625).

Exhibit 15.10 shows that, given the same spread outlook, a similar trade made on May 28 and unwound on June 10 would have been considerably more rewarding—given the price data of Exhibit 15.5. This trade, using a 0.580 spread ratio, would have earned $208,625.

EXHIBIT 15.9

Anticipate Spread Narrowing–Sell June Spread

	Action	FVM4	Action	TYM4
5/14/04	Sell 1,000	108.921875	Buy 570	108.890625
6/4/04	Buy 1,000	108.9375	Sell 570	109.078125
One-contract result		−0.015625		0.1875
One contract in $		−15.625		187.50
Position $ result		−15,625		106,875
Spread $ net				91,250

EXHIBIT 15.10

Anticipate Spread Narrowing–Sell June Spread

	Action	FVM4	Action	TYM4
5/28/04	Sell 1,000	109.5625	Buy 580	109.9375
6/10/04	Buy 1,000	108.85	Sell 580	109.06875
One-contract result		0.7125		−0.86875
One contract in $		712.50		−868.75
Position $ Result		712,500		−503,875
Spread $ net				208,625

EXHIBIT 15.11

Anticipate Spread Narrowing–Sell June Spread

	Action	FVM4	Action	TYM4
5/7/04	Sell 1,000	108.46875	Buy 602	108.4875
5/14/04	Buy 1,000	108.921875	Sell 602	108.890625
One-contract result		–0.453125		0.403125
One contract in $		–453.125		403.125
Position $ result		–453,125		242,681.25
Spread $ net				–210,443.75

In both these cases, the spread change was small—2 bps from May 14 to June 4 and 3 bps from May 28 to June 10—yet both trades generated solid returns. Notice that while the spread narrowed both times, prices rose in the first case and fell in the second. An interesting fact about the Exhibit 15.10 trade is that one 10-year contract lost more than one 5-year contract gained, but the spread ratio took care of that.

Consider one more trade from this period, this one leading to an unhappy result. Suppose that, based on the same outlook as in the other two cases, you had sold the spread on May 7, when the ratio was 0.602, and unwound it on May 14. Exhibit 15.11 shows that this trade would have resulted in a $210,443.75 loss.

The spread actually narrowed as much or more during this week than it did in the other two cases, yet the result isn't what you would think it should be. The key, here, is the change in CTD. When CTD changes, the futures contract derives its price from a different source and maybe a *very* different source. The only one of these three trades that is not affected by that is the May 28 to June 10 trade. The only one that turns out to be a loser is the one in Exhibit 15.11, but the May 14 trade is also affected by the CTD shift.

In general, the period after the June 30, 2004, Fed meeting would have looked like a good time to sell the FYT spread. Yields were rising, inflation threats had abated, and yield curve spreads promised to narrow.

Exhibit 15.12 shows a trade covering the July 16 to July 30, 2004, period to have earned $166,350 on a 5 bp spread narrowing.

Often, during a trending period traders can find opportunities to capitalize on shifts in spread direction, much as they can find buying opportunities in the dips in a rallying single-contract market. Assuming that your market analysis would have tipped you off to the possibility of such a spread-widening countermove, you might have decided to buy the September FYT

EXHIBIT 15.12

Anticipate Spread Narrowing–Sell September Spread

	Action	FVU4	Action	TYU4
7/16/04	Sell 1,000	110.05	Buy 592	111.325
7/30/04	Buy 1,000	109.50625	Sell 592	110.6875
One-contract result		0.54375		–0.6375
One contract in $		543.75		–637.50
Position $ result		543,750		–377,400
Spread $ net				166,350

EXHIBIT 15.13

Anticipate Spread Widening–Buy September Spread

	Action	FVU4	Action	TYU4
7/30/04	Buy 1,000	109.50625	Sell 592	110.6875
8/20/04	Sell 1,000	111.00625	Buy 592	112.7375
One-contract result		1.5		–2.05
One contract in $		1,500.00		–2,050.00
Position $ result		1,500,000		–1,213,600
Spread $ net				286,400

spread on July 30, 2004. Had you done so and subsequently unwound the trade on August 20, this trade could have earned $286,400 as Exhibit 15.13 illustrates.

The trades illustrated in Exhibits 15.12 and 15.13 benefit from the stable CTD situation in both contracts and also from the stability of the spread ratio during these weeks.

A WORD OF CAUTION

The common wisdom in the futures markets holds that spread trades are safer than outright futures trades. This may well be. Certainly, a yield curve spread gives you more ways to be right than an outright trade does.

Nevertheless, you can decide that the spread will narrow only to see it widen, or vice versa. In short, these are still speculative trades, and you can suffer a loss when your market call is wrong.

Worse yet, you can be right about what the spread will do and still suffer a loss. Treasury note futures derive from the CTD Treasury issue, and CTD status can change, as Exhibit 15.5 demonstrates. It is especially likely to change when yields are active and when yields are close to the 6 percent yield level that is used in calculating conversion factors. These changes can alter the spread ratio significantly and can cause the affected futures contract to behave in unexpected ways. When this happens, your trade can suffer a loss even when you have made the right spread call, as Exhibit 15.11 shows. However, careful monitoring of your yield curve spread positions can alert you to the need to adjust your positions. This can help you prevent, or at least greatly reduce, possible losses.

That said, the majority of the exhibits in this chapter demonstrate that a carefully structured and closely monitored yield curve spread trade can generate solid gains.

CHAPTER 16

The 10-Year Treasury Note under 2-Year Treasury Note Futures

The TUT Spread

A commonly traded yield curve spread uses 2-year Treasury note futures at the short end and 10-year Treasury note futures at the long end. On the exchange floor, this is the TUT spread (tens under twos).

This is a solid kind of trade for several reasons. For one, many yield curve spread traders and analysts consider the 2-year to 10-year yield curve segment to be the curve. The more people who come to the party, the greater the liquidity and the easier it is to trade this spread. For another thing, when the yield curve is changing shape, you can expect this spread to narrow or widen by more than the 5-year to 10-year spread. To the extent this is true, the 2-year to 10-year spread, the TUT spread, offers the opportunity for larger gains.

At the same time, the TUT spread introduces a special wrinkle that requires care when it comes to structuring trades. Where the 5-year and 10-year Treasury note futures contracts have a $100,000 par contract size, the 2-year Treasury note has a $200,000 par contract size. Not all quote sources take his into account when posting DV01s. In the final analysis, this can be dealt with easily. Also developing an outlook for this spread requires a bit of caution.

TUT SPREAD BACKGROUND AND OUTLOOK

One thing that makes the TUT different from other yield curve spreads is that the two-year Treasury yield tends to march to the beat of a different drummer from the one longer-dated yields march to. A primary driver of

5-year and 10-year yields is the market perception concerning inflation. These yields respond to other stimuli as well, but the longer the maturity, the greater the influence of inflation concerns.

The two-year yield is less subject to inflation concerns than the longer-dated yields. After all, inflation will erode a 2-year or shorter investment far less than it will a 10-year investment. As a result, the two-year yield will respond more directly to Fed policy shifts than will the longer maturities—as a general rule.

Exhibit 16.1 tracks the TUT spread and the yields of the 2-year and 10-year Treasury issues (using weekly constant maturity Treasury yields from the Federal Reserve H.15 reports) from the beginning of 2003 to almost the end of October 2004.

Notice that between late March and mid-May 2004 both yields rose sharply. On March 26, 2004, the 10-year yield was 3.76 percent. By May 14, it had climbed to 4.81 percent. The two-year yield climbed from 1.53 percent to 2.62 percent during this stretch. Then, part way through June, the 10-year yield began a fairly pronounced downward trend to end at 4.03 percent on October 22, 2004. In contrast, the two-year yield bounced up somewhat higher but then settled down to trade at around the 2.50 percent level. On October 22, this yield was 2.55 percent. Clearly, the two-year market found the inflation news of only mild interest. What matters to TUT spread traders is that the reaction of the 10-year market and the lack of reaction of the 2-year market caused a 71-basis-point narrowing of the TUT spread—from 219 bps on May 14 to 148 bps on October 22.

This is not to say that 2-year Treasury notes are immune to inflation concerns nor that 10-year Treasury notes are immune to shifts in Fed policy. It is only to assign relative weights to the factors that shape yields in the normal case. These markets abound with special cases, as many traders have learned, to their regret.

In terms of formulating a TUT spread outlook, you can expect a Fed policy shift to cause more of a response at the 2-year point on the yield curve and relatively less response at the 10-year point. If the Fed is in a quiet period, as it was during the first five months of 2004, and concerns about inflation were building, you might well expect to see the 2-year yield respond relatively little while the 10-year yield responds a great deal. For example, on March 17, 2004, the TUT spread was 221 bps (3.75 percent 10-year Treasury constant maturity yield minus 1.54 percent 2-year Treasury constant maturity yield). By April 7, the spread had widened 12 bps to 233 bps. During this three-week period, the 10-year yield rose by 46 bps to a 34 bp rise on the part of the 2-year yield, and this seems to be a typical response to inflation concerns. Participants in the market for 10-year Treasury

EXHIBIT 16.1

The TUT Spread

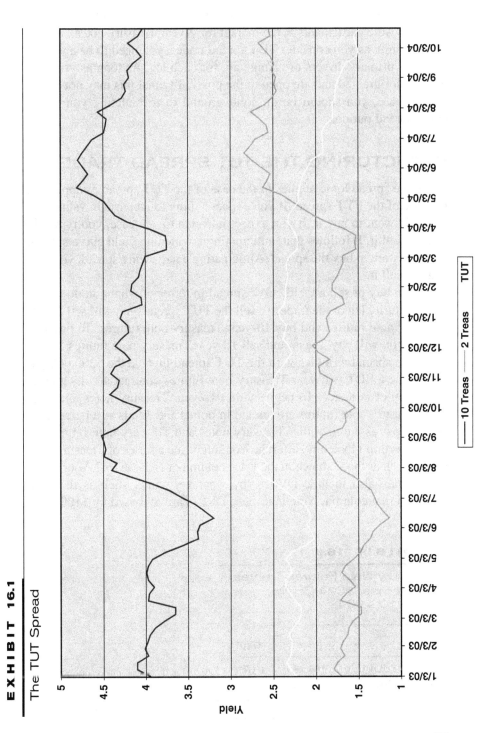

notes were more concerned about the possibility of a major buildup of inflation than were participants in the market for 2-year Treasury notes.

In sum, as you consider TUT spread trades, you need to be aware of what the primary drivers of change are for each leg. As long as you take nothing for granted and are open to the possibility that this may not be the normal case, you should be on solid ground in formulating your yield curve spread outlook.

STRUCTURING THE TUT SPREAD TRADE

The same spread logic applies in the case of the TUT spread as applies in the case of the FYT spread. If you expect a thing to increase in value, you typically want to buy it. If you expect its value to decrease, you typically want to sell it. It follows that, anticipating a widening yield curve spread, you will want to buy the spread. Anticipating a narrowing spread, you will want to sell it.

You buy or sell a yield curve spread in terms of what you do on the short maturity leg of the trade. To sell the TUT spread, you will sell 2-year Treasury note futures and buy 10-year Treasury note futures. To buy this spread, you will buy 2-year and sell 10-year Treasury note futures.

The special wrinkles with the TUT spread involve the $200,000 par size of the CBOT two-year Treasury note futures contract and its greater frequency of issuance. To begin with, two-year Treasury notes and two-year Treasury note futures are quoted in points and 32nds as a percentage of $100 par as are the other Treasury notes and Treasury note futures, so the quotes don't look any different. You might see a series of Treasury note quotes such as those shown in the Price column of Exhibit 16.2. Your quote source may also include DV01s (by whatever name) such as the ones shown in that column. Note that these DV01s are all based on $100 par.

EXHIBIT 16.2

Treasury Note Futures Quotes (September 2004 Contracts on June 10, 2004)

	Price	DV01
2-Year (TUU4)	104-28	0.0219
5-Year (FVU4)	107-16	0.0449
10-Year (TYU4)	107-18+	0.0694

The trouble with this is that all three prices and DV01s are based on $100 par. To convert them into dollar equivalent values that reflect the sizes of the futures contracts, you can divide the fraction by 32 to find the decimal version ($28 \div 32 = 0.875$, $16 \div 32 = 0.5$, $18.5 \div 32 = 0.578125$) and add the decimal version to the full points. That is, 107-16 translates into $107.50. To take this five-year Treasury note futures price up to the $100,000 par futures contract size, multiply by 1,000 to arrive at a $107,500.00 dollar equivalent value for one futures contract. But where this 107.50 five-year Treasury note futures price is 107.5% of $100,000 par, the 104.875 two-year Treasury note futures price is 104.875 percent of $200,000 par. You must multiply by 2,000 to find the $209,750.00 dollar equivalent value for one $200,000 par contract.

Suppose that on this day, the cheapest-to-deliver (CTD) two-year Treasury note had a 2.09-year modified duration and a $99.59 full price for $100 par. This leads to a 0.0208 DV01 $\{[(2.09 \times 0.01) \times 99.59] \times 0.01 = 0.0208\}$. To get from this to the futures DV01, the conventional approach is to divide this DV01 by this issue's conversion factor, which, relative to the September 2004 futures contract, was 0.9467. This generates a 0.02197 futures DV01. Where you would multiply this by 1,000 to scale the 10-year Treasury note futures DV01 up to the $100,000 par contract size, you must multiply by 2,000, just as in the case of finding the dollar equivalent value given the price quote. Thus the futures DV01 in this case is $43.94 which you can round to $43.90 for spread ratio purposes. As long as you remember to adjust prices and DV01s to the two-year Treasury note contract size, or to check to see that your quote source has done so, you should not have trouble structuring TUT spread trades.

Using the 10-year DV01 from Exhibit 16.2 and this $43.90 2-year DV01, you can divide the 2-year DV01 by the 10-year DV01 to see that the spread ratio on that day would have been 0.633 ($43.90 \div 69.40 = 0.63256$). That is, to buy the TUT spread, you would have sold 633 10-year Treasury note futures for every 1,000 2-year Treasury note futures that you bought.

FITTING TRADING STRATEGY TO YIELD CURVE OUTLOOK

Contemplating the yield curve situation from the vantage point of July 12, 2004, you would have seen a changing interest rate picture. The most obvious change was the Fed's long anticipated 25 bp hike in its Fed funds target rate on June 30. Less obvious, but equally important, the market seemed to be accepting the view that inflation was not about to flare out of control. Several key market indicators seemed to support this, among them the spreads between the 10-year swap rate and the 10-year Treasury yield and the spread between the nominal 10-year Treasury yield and the 10-year TIPS (Treasury inflation protected security) yield. The narrowing of these two spreads signaled an easing of inflation concerns. Accordingly, you might have decided that the TUT spread was likely to narrow and that this was a good time to sell the spread.

On July 12, the 10-year Treasury constant maturity yield was 4.46 percent, the two-year Treasury constant maturity yield was 2.53 percent, and the TUT yield spread was 193 bps. The September two-year Treasury note futures contract was trading at 105-22+ and had a $35.52 DV01 (correctly allowing for the $200,000 par contract size). The September 10-year Treasury note futures contract was trading at 110-23 and had a $71.94 DV01. These DV01s give rise to a 0.4937 spread ratio (35.52 ÷ 71.94), so you might have sold 100 2-year contracts and bought 49 10-year contracts.

Yields had been rising for some time, so you might have wondered how this spread would perform if the 2-year yield rose 20 bps while the 10-year yield rose 15 bps. Exhibit 16.3 uses the DV01s to estimate a possible result given such a 5 bp spread narrowing.

By July 23, the 2-year Treasury constant maturity yield had climbed 16 bps to 2.69 percent, while the 10-year Treasury constant maturity yield had fallen 1 bp to 4.45 percent. This narrowed the spread 17 bps—from 193 bps to 176 bps. Further, the September 2-year Treasury note futures price dropped from 105-22+ to 105-16, and the September 10-year Treasury note futures price dropped from 110-23 to 110-20. (It might seem curious that a 1 bp drop in the 10-year Treasury yield would drop the futures price. This can happen from time to time because a futures price is a forward price and the crucial carry calculation that goes into determining the forward price involves a repo rate that will sometimes change in anticipation of a future

EXHIBIT 16.3

Estimating TUT Spread Performance

Futures Contract	DV01	Yield Change (in bps)	Number of Contracts	Result (to Nearest Dollar)
2-year Treasury note (TUU4)	35.52	20	−100	71,040
10-year Treasury note (TYU4)	71.94	15	49	−52,875
Spread Net				18,164

EXHIBIT 16.4

Selling the TUT Spread

	Action	TUU4	Action	TYU4	Spread
7/12/04	Sell 100	105.703125	Buy 49	110.71875	193
7/23/04	Buy 100	105.500000	Sell 49	110.62500	176
1 Contract Result		0.203125		−0.09375	
1 Contract $ Result		406.25		−93.75	
Position $ Result		40,625.00		−4,594	
Spread $ Net				36,031	−17

Fed move where the 10-year yield will not be affected.) Exhibit 16.4 shows that, based on these price changes, a TUT spread seller would have earned $36,031.

Note that the $406.25 2-year One-contract $ result reflects the use of the 2,000 multiplier, while the 10-year One-contract $ result derives from the use of 1,000 multiplier. The values in the Position $ result row multiply that by the number of contracts shown in the two Action columns, and the Spread $ net is the sum of the two Position $ results. This $36,031 spread result reflects the fact that the yield spread actually narrowed by 17 bps, not by the estimated 5 bps of Exhibit 16.3.

BUYING THE TUT SPREAD IN ANTICIPATION OF SPREAD WIDENING

Of course, yield curve spreads can widen as well as narrow. By July 26, the economic situation seemed to have changed, at least temporarily. The current economic reports suggested a sudden slowing of economic growth. In that case, demand for credit might ease somewhat, and that would cause yields to drop. The normal expectation would be for the 2-year yield to drop by more than the 10-year yield, which would widen the spread. Given this possibility, this might be a good time to buy the TUT spread—that is, buy 2-year Treasury note futures and sell 10-year Treasury note futures.

On July 26, 2004, 2-year Treasury note futures were trading at 105-13, 10-year Treasury note futures were trading at 110-16, and the TUT spread was 174 bps. The $35.41 2-year DV01 and the $70.10 10-year DV01 generated a 0.505136 spread ratio (35.41 ÷ 70.10), so you could have bought 100 2-year Treasury note futures contracts and sold either 50 or 51 10-year Treasury note futures contracts.

You can use these DV01s to explore several possibilities. After all, yields may not fall, and even if they do, the spread might not widen. It's important to know what can happen and to have Plan B ready. Among the possibilities are the ones illustrated in Exhibit 16.5, which assumes that you bought the spread and that among the possibilities are situations such that:

- Yields fall, but the spread narrows.
- Yields continue to rise, and the spread narrows.
- Yields fall, and the spread widens.

EXHIBIT 16.5

Estimating Possible TUT Spread Results

a: Yields Fall, Spread Narrows

Futures Contract	DV01	Yield Change (in bps)	Number of Contracts	Result (to Nearest Dollar)
2-year Treasury note (TUU4)	35.41	−5	100	17,705
10-year Treasury note (TYU4)	70.10	−10	−50	−35,050
Spread Net				−17,345

b: Yields Rise, Spread Narrows

Futures Contract	DV01	Yield Change (in bps)	Number of Contracts	Result (to Nearest Dollar)
2-year Treasury note (TUU4)	35.41	10	100	−35,410
10-year Treasury note (TYU4)	70.10	5	−50	17,525
Spread Net				−17,885

c: Yields Fall, Spread Widens

Futures Contract	DV01	Yield Change (in bps)	Number of Contracts	Result (to Nearest Dollar)
2-year Treasury note (TUU4)	35.41	−10	100	35,410
10-year Treasury note (TYU4)	70.10	−5	−50	−17,525
Spread Net				17,885

The first two possibilities illustrated are unpleasant to think about, but they can happen. Spreads are not riskless trades. Because these results are possible, it is important to have decided ahead of time how large a loss you would be willing to absorb and to monitor these trades carefully. In the event that the 10-year yield starts to fall more than the 2-year yield, you might want to pull the plug on this trade any time the spread narrows by a certain amount—say, 2 bps. Based on these DV01s, this would hold the loss to something close to $7,000, given this 100-to-50 ratio.

The third example in Exhibit 16.5 is the predicted yield change, and it can result in a solid gain. Suppose you had watched this trade run until August 2. By this time the 2-year constant maturity Treasury yield had dropped by 9 bps to 2.66 percent, while the 10-year constant maturity Treasury yield had dropped only 1 bp to 4.49 percent. This widened the yield spread 8 bps, from 174 bps to 182 bps. As a result of these yield changes, September 2-year Treasury note futures were trading at 105-20, and September 10-year Treasury note futures were trading at 110-28 on August 2. Exhibit 16.6 shows that this TUT spread trade would have earned $25,000 on this 8 bp spread widening.

Depending on your yield curve spread outlook, you can treat these yield curve spread trades as relatively long-term propositions. As long as the yield curve seems to be changing in keeping with your market analysis, you may want to let these trades ride.

Staying with the idea that you bought the spread on July 26, 2004, at the prices shown in Exhibit 16.6, suppose you had let it ride until August 23, when 2-year Treasury note futures were trading at 106-02+ and 10-year Treasury note futures were trading at 112-13. Alternatively, you could have let it ride until August 31, just before the start of the September delivery month. On that day, 2-year Treasury note futures were

EXHIBIT 16.6

Buying the TUT Spread in Anticipation of a Spread Widening

	Action	TUU4	Action	TYU4	Spread
7/26/04	Buy 100	105.40625	Sell 50	110.500	174
8/2/04	Sell 100	105.62500	Buy 50	110.875	182
1 Contract Result		0.21875		−0.375	
1 Contract $ Result		437.50		375.00	
Position $ Result		43,750.00		−18,750.00	
Spread $ Net				25,000.00	8

EXHIBIT 16.7

When Waiting Can Be Worthwhile

	Action	TUU4	Action	TYU4	Spread
7/26/04	Buy 100	105.406250	Sell 50	110.50000	174
8/23/04	Sell 100	106.078125	Buy 50	112.40626	178
1 Contract Result		0.671875		−1.90625	
1 Contract $ Result		1,343.75		−1,906.25	
Position $ Result		134,375.00		−95,312.50	
Spread $ Net				39,062.50	4

EXHIBIT 16.8

The Spread Ratio and Contract Size Advantage Illustrated

	Action	TUU4	Action	TYU4	Spread
7/26/04	Buy 100	105.406250	Sell 50	110.50000	174
8/31/04	Sell 100	106.296875	Buy 50	113.46875	172
1 Contract Result		0.890625		−2.96875	
1 Contract $ Result		1,781.25		−2,968.75	
Position $ Result		178,125.00		−148,437.50	
Spread $ Net				29,687.50	-2

trading at 106-09+, and 10-year Treasury note futures were trading at 113-15. Exhibits 16.7 and 16.8 show the details of these trades.

At first glance, these results seem to run contrary to the laws of spread gravity or some such thing. The trade of Exhibit 16.6 seems sensible enough. The spread widened, and the trade showed a gain. The spread also widened between July 26 and August 23 but only half as much as between July 26 and August 2. This makes it seem decidedly odd that the Exhibit 16.7 trade earned a great deal more than the Exhibit 16.6 trade. Odder yet is the Exhibit 16.8 trade in which the spread actually narrowed by 2 bps, yet this trade earned more than the Exhibit 16.6 trade.

The first thing to look at in a situation such as this is which securities are CTD. The U.S. Treasury auctions 2-year notes monthly, and CTD status can become unstable at times as new issues become deliverable. Chapter 15 points out a period in May and June of 2004 when 10-year CTD status shifted around quite a bit. Curiously, CTD status didn't change for either the 2-year or 10-year Treasury note futures contract during the period from July 26 to August 31.

What did change is the term repo rate that was being used to finance two-year Treasury note holdings in the cash market. (Repo rates and forward pricing are discussed in greater detail in Chapter 7. Burghardt, et al. has an excellent discussion of this as well.) This financing rate is the major variable in determining fixed-income carry. (Note that carry refers to the difference between the coupon income and the financing cost for a given number of days.) This is relevant to futures pricing because the forward price of the CTD Treasury security is the spot price minus carry. And the futures price is the forward price divided by the conversion factor of the CTD issue. All else being the same, the higher the repo rate, the lower the carry, and the higher the futures price.

Exhibit 16.9 shows the term repo rates and the carry for the CTD 2-year and 10-year Treasury notes on the four dates that appear in Exhibits 16.6, 16.7, and 16.8.

Note that the carry values are 32nds, so the 9.25 July 26 carry for the two-year Treasury note is nine and one-fourth thirty-seconds.

Carry diminishes with the passage of time, as the 10-year carry values show. A rising repo rate will diminish it even more. The lower the carry, the higher the futures price—all else being the same.

Based on these repo rates and carry changes for the two-year Treasury note, it seems that what happened to the TUT spread trade in the late August iterations resulted from these repo changes. They were apparently large enough to overwhelm the small spread change. This seems technical, but it is an important part of futures pricing and something to watch out for.

The trade illustrated in Exhibit 16.8 is also interesting in that the One-contract result row makes it seem that the loss in the 10-year leg must

EXHIBIT 16.9

Relevant Term Repo Rates and Carry Values

	2-Year CTD Treasury Note		10-Year CTD Treasury Note	
	Term Repo Rate	Carry	Term Repo Rate	Carry
7/26/04	1.20%	9.25	1.30%	20.42
8/2/04	1.25%	8.03	1.30%	18.18
8/20/04	1.35%	4.95	1.30%	11.52
8/31/04	1.40%	3.85	1.30%	9.00

surely overwhelm the gain in the 2-year leg. This appears to be true of the trades in Exhibits 16.6 and 16.7 also, but not to the same extent. In the case of Exhibit 16.8, once you multiply the 0.890625 2-year gain by 2,000 and then by 100 contracts and multiply the 2.96875 10-year loss by 1,000 and then by 50 contracts, you can see that this first appearance was deceptive. The net of the two legs would have been a very solid $29,687.50 gain.

Also interesting is the final result shown in Exhibit 16.7. Notice that here, the 2-year leg earned less than the 2-year leg of the Exhibit 16.8 trade, but the 10-year leg in Exhibit 16.7 lost considerably less than the 10-year leg of the Exhibit 16.8 trade. As a result, the Exhibit 16.7 trade earned almost $10,000 more.

A WORD OF CAUTION

This discussion of the TUT spread points out several details of this trade in particular and yield curve spread trades in general that can cause grief to the unwary. The use of the two-year Treasury note futures contract in structuring the TUT spread requires care because of its $200,000 par size and also because the greater frequency of two-year Treasury note auctions can cause CTD status to shift.

At times, futures prices can be more sensitive to changes in repo rates than they are to changes in Treasury yields—or so it seems in cases like the July 26 to August 31, 2004, trade of Exhibit 16.8. This is a factor that spread traders must be aware of and have a general understanding of. Forewarned may not be forearmed, but at least forewarned gives you time to take evasive action.

Despite these potential trouble spots, the TUT spread, along with the other yield curve trades, can be a useful part of your trading repertoire.

CHAPTER 17

A 10-Year Interest Rate Swap–Fed Funds Futures Spread

Since swap rates have become the benchmarks for all manner of commercial lending and since the Fed funds rate defines banks' cost of credit, at least as far as reserves are concerned, the 10-year interest rate swap and the Fed funds rate form an interesting yield curve.

THE BANK CREDIT YIELD CURVE SPREAD

Looked at one way, as this spread widens, lending should be more profitable, and credit should be more readily available. A widening spread should indicate an expanding economy. If that is the glass-half-full interpretation, the glass-half-empty view might be that a widening spread (especially if the swap rate is rising a great deal) is sounding an alarm to the effect that:

- Lenders are concerned about inflation and are building an inflation premium into the swap rate.
- Lenders have concerns about borrowers' ability to meet their obligations and are building that kind of risk premium into the swap rate.

Once you have sorted out the details of the situation and formed an opinion—half full or half empty—you can use CBOT Fed funds futures and CBOT 10-year swap futures to trade the bank credit yield curve.

STRUCTURING A SWAP–FED FUNDS SPREAD

As always when trading yield curve spreads, you must ratio this spread to ensure that it will respond to changes in the spread and nothing else. Given that the Fed funds contract has a $5 million notional principal while the 10-year swap futures has a $100,000 notional principal, there appears to be a major mismatch in contract size. (In this context, *notional principal* refers to a hypothetical amount of principal that is used as a basis for determining an interest payment. This amount does not actually change hands as the principal payment in a bond deal does.) Don't be fooled. That mismatch quickly goes away.

The Fed funds futures DV01 is given implicitly in the contract specifications. The Fed funds futures contract trades in half basis points (0.005), and one-half basis point has a $20.835 value. This gives Fed funds futures an invariable $41.67 DV01.

The swap futures DV01 might take a little more work. At least some quote sources give swap futures DV01s, and most brokers should be able to provide them. Lacking access to these sources, however, you can calculate the swap DV01s you need by using the futures pricing formula given in contract salient features summary or in the *CBOT Interest Rate Swap Futures Reference Guide* (both documents are available at www.cbot.com/swap). Calculate the futures prices for swap rates 1 bp below and 1 bp above the swap rate currently implied by the futures contract. The difference between these two prices divided by 2 is the DV01. Given the 5 percent June 14 swap rate, Exhibit 17.1 shows how you can arrive at a $81.63 DV01 for the September swap futures contract.

Based on these DV01s, the June 14, 2004, bank credit yield curve spread ratio was 0.510 (41.67 ÷ 81.63). To buy this spread, you would sell 51 10-year swap futures contracts for every 100 fed funds futures contracts that you buy.

A SPREAD OUTLOOK AND A SPREAD TRADE

Exhibit 17.2 contrasts the bank credit yield curve spread and the TUT spread for a roughly 14-month stretch beginning July 2, 2003 and ending September 8, 2004.

EXHIBIT 17.1

Calculating a Swap Futures DV01–Swap Rate, 5%

Swap Rate	Swap Futures Price
4.99	107,876.25
5.01	107,712.99
	163.25
	81.63

EXHIBIT 17.2

Bank Credit and TUT Yield Curve Spreads (7/2/03 to 9/8/04)

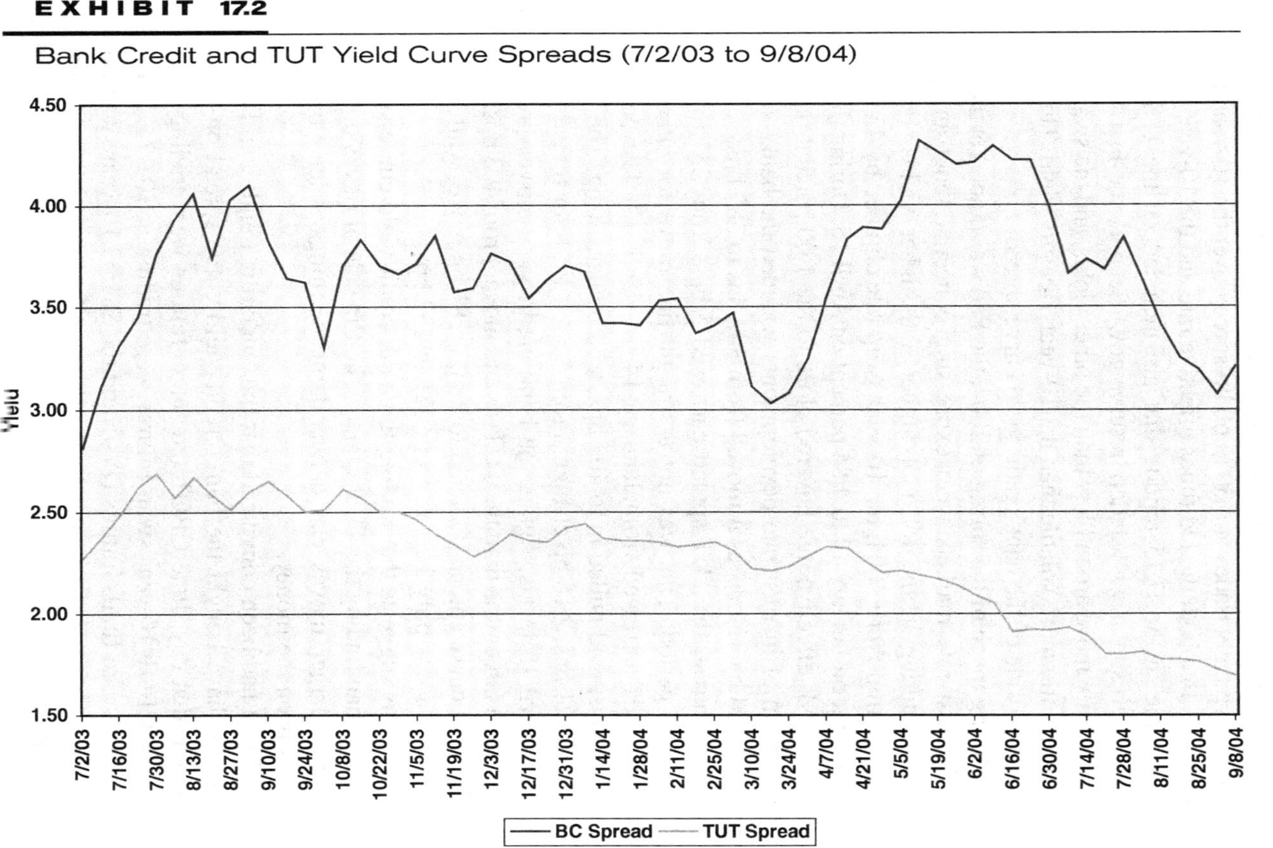

Two factors contribute to the different look of these two spread plots. First, the bank credit yield curve spread is wider because of the maturity difference between the 2-year Treasury note and the fed funds and because the swap rate typically trades at a 30 to 60 bp spread over the 10-year Treasury yield. (Note that both the fed funds effective rate and the 10-year swap rate are available in the H.15 reports that are included on the U.S. Federal Reserve Web site at www.federalreserve.gov.) Second, the Fed funds rate will ordinarily move around less than the other yields, and the swap rate can be significantly more volatile than the 10-year Treasury yield. This leads to the bumpier ride of the bank credit yield curve spread.

During much of the spring of 2004, the Fed was quiet. Yet the longer-term interest rate markets were expressing concerns about an apparent inflation buildup in the form of higher and higher yields. From mid-January to mid-April 2004, the 10-year swap rate climbed by 43 bps, from 4.41 percent on January 14 to 4.84 percent on April 15. During this period, the Fed funds effective rate hovered close to the 1.00 percent target. This combination of interest rate developments widened the bank credit yield curve spread by 41 bps, as it moved from 342 bps to 383 bps.

In contrast, the TUT spread narrowed 5 bps, from 237 to 232 bps, during this period. This was not a straight-line move for either spread. Both spreads narrowed from January 14 to March 17. The bank credit yield curve spread pulled in to 403 bps, a 38 bp narrowing. The TUT narrowed to 221 bps, a 16 bp change. From March 17, both spreads widened to their April 15 levels. Again, the bank credit yield curve spread move was a much larger one than the TUT spread move. From 403 bps, the bank credit yield curve spread widened to 484, an 81 bp move, while the TUT spread move was only 11 bps, from 221 to 232 bps.

All this suggests that trading the bank credit yield curve spread can be riskier than trading the TUT spread. The flip side of risk is opportunity, and these larger moves can deliver larger earnings when your spread analysis is on the money.

If you had been convinced that this widening trend would continue, you could have bought the bank credit yield curve spread on April 28, 2004. On that day, June CBOT fed funds futures were trading at 98.97, and June CBOT 10-year swap futures were trading at 107-24. The standard $41.67 Fed funds futures DV01 and the $81.63 10-year swap futures DV01 of Exhibit 17.1 produced a 0.510 spread ratio which indicates that you would have sold 51 swap futures contracts for every 100 Fed funds futures contracts that you bought.

Assume that, after putting on this trade on April 28, you unwound the trade two weeks later on May 12 when June Fed funds were trading at

EXHIBIT 17.3

Buying the Bank Credit Yield Curve Spread

	Action	FFM4	Action	DIM4
4/28/04	Buy 100	98.97	Sell 51	107.75
5/12/04	Sell 100	98.975	Buy 51	104.8125
1 Contract Result		0.005		2.9375
1 Contract in $		20.835		2,937.50
Position $ Result		2,083.50		149,812.50
Spread $ Net				151,896.00

98.975 and June 10-year swap futures were trading at 104-26. Exhibit 17.3 shows the details of this trade.

If you always subtract the bought price from the sold price when you calculate spread results, you'll always get the gains and losses right. In Exhibit 17.3, the Fed funds price rose half a basis point to generate a $20,835 one-contract gain, or $2,083.50 for 100 contracts. The swap futures contract gained 2.9375 (2-30 in conventional fixed-income notation) for a $2,937.50 one-contract gain. The 51-contract swap futures position gained $149,812.50. The Spread $ net is the sum of the two Position $ results, and this is a rare instance when both legs of the spread show positive results to generate a $151,896 spread gain.

ANOTHER TIME, ANOTHER OUTLOOK

Consider the economic situation on June 14, 2004. This was 16 days before the next Fed meeting. After the May 4 meeting, the Fed released a statement that contained two sentences that attracted the notice of economists and interest rate traders.

At the end of a paragraph indicating a belief that the U.S. economy was growing nicely, the statement says, "Although incoming inflation data have moved somewhat higher, long-term inflation expectations appear to have remained well contained."

The next paragraph contains the now-notorious sentence: "At this juncture, with inflation low and resource use slack, the Committee believes that policy accommodation can be removed at a pace that is likely to be measured."

Many comments have been made on the badness of Fed prose. The phrase about the removal of policy accommodation is the Fed's way of saying that the Fed funds target rate will begin to rise. The reference to a measured pace indicates a belief that this tightening sequence can go forward in mild 25 bp steps.

A fairly large number of economists and traders responded to both those fed claims with skepticism. The threat of inflation picking up seemed more serious than the Fed statement indicated. Every week in May and early June brought more indications of at least the potential for a fairly severe inflation buildup. Because of this, numerous market users believed that the Fed would have to take stronger steps than the measured pace language indicated.

By June 14, trading activity in the September Fed funds futures contract had dropped the futures price from 98.605 on May 4 (the day of the last fed meeting) to 98.150. The May 4 price implies a 1.395 percent Fed funds rate by the September futures expiration (implied rate = 100 – Fed funds futures price: 100 – 98.605 = 1.395), while the June 14 price implies a 1.85 percent fed funds rate by the September futures expiration.

Given that the Fed funds target in mid-June was 1.00 percent, this June 14 Fed funds futures price tells you that the market expected to see at least a 75 bp increase in the Fed funds target rate by the end of September. That implied something more than a measured pace.

Interestingly, several market indicators suggested that the Fed was right about inflation being essentially under control. Even though the 10-year swap rate rose by over 27 bps from May 4 to June 14, the spread between the credit risky swap rate and the credit risk-free Treasury yield had narrowed slightly. Also, the spread between 10-year nominal Treasury yields and 10-year TIPS (the U.S. Treasury's inflation-protected securities) had narrowed.

Both these spread narrowings suggested that the market's inflation fears would be abating. In terms of trading the bank credit yield curve spread, you might have decided, on June 14, that easing inflation fears would allow the Fed to maintain its measured pace and the swap-Fed funds spread would narrow.

ANOTHER TRADE

Assume that you had sold the bank credit yield curve spread on June 14, 2004, with September Fed funds futures (FFU4) trading at 98.15 and September 10-year swap futures (DIU4) trading at 103-21 (103.65625). Given a $77.77 swap futures DV01 on that day, the spread ratio would have been 0.535811. That ratio indicates that you would have needed to buy 54 10-year swap futures for every 100 Fed funds futures that you sold.

Assume further that you unwound this trade on June 30, after the Fed meeting, with September Fed funds futures trading at 98.335 and

EXHIBIT 17.4

Anticipating the June 30, 2004, Fed Meeting

	Action	FFU4	Action	NIU4
6/14/04	Sell 100	98.150	Buy 54	103.65625
6/30/04	Buy 100	98.335	Sell 54	106.0625
1 Contract Result		−0.205		2.40625
1 Contract in $		−854.235		2,406.25
Position $ Net		−85,423.50		129,937.50
Spread Result				44,514.00

EXHIBIT 17.5

A Closer Look at the Bank Credit Yield Curve Spread

	Fed Funds Rate	10-Year Swap Rate	Bank Credit Yield Curve Spread
7/7/04	1.28	4.94	3.66
7/14/04	1.25	4.98	3.73
7/21/04	1.25	4.93	3.68
7/28/04	1.26	5.10	3.84
8/4/04	1.27	4.90	3.63
8/11/04	1.36	4.77	3.41
8/18/04	1.42	4.67	3.25
8/25/04	1.51	4.70	3.19

September swap futures trading at 106-02 (106.0625). Exhibit 17.4 shows that this trade would have earned $44,514.

As the summer of 2004 unfolded, the markets seemed more and more to buy into the Fed's opinion that inflation was under control. At any rate, the bank credit yield curve continued to flatten as the 10-year swap rate fell and the Fed funds rate rose in measured steps.

This yield curve spread trade could have been repeated on numerous occasions with gratifying results. It could have been repeated on certain other occasions with unhappy results. Exhibit 17.2 shows that the bank credit yield curve spread narrowed precipitously after May 12. Exhibit 17.5 breaks out the weekly data underlying the Exhibit 17.2 graphic to show both the rates and the resulting spread.

Notice that on May 12 (Exhibit 17.2), the bank credit yield curve spread was the widest shown on this chart at 432 bps. By September 1, it had narrowed to 307 bps, a 125 bp narrowing. But that isn't the whole story. From May 12 to July 7, the spread narrowed to 366 bps, a 66 bp narrowing. For the rest of that month, the spread widened until, on July 28, the spread was at 384 bps. Note that both the chart and this description of events are based on the weekly data of the Fed H.15 report.

Suppose that you had sold the bank credit yield curve spread on July 7, 2004, with the expectation that the narrowing would continue. Exhibit 17.6 shows that you would have sold 100 September fed funds futures and bought 51 September swap futures. If you had unwound this trade a week later, you would have lost $6,864, as the exhibit shows.

In contrast, suppose that you had sold this spread near the end of July—again with the expectation that waning inflation fears would narrow the spread. If you had put on the trade on July 28, 2004, at the prices shown in Exhibit 17.5 and unwound it on August 25 at the prices shown, this trade would have earned $172,958. Exhibit 17.7 shows the details of this trade.

EXHIBIT 17.6

A Trade that Misfired

	Action	FFU4	Action	NIU4
7/7/04	Sell 100	98.410	Buy 51	107.375
7/14/04	Buy 100	98.415	Sell 51	107.28125
1 Contract Result		−0.005		−0.09375
1 Contract in $		−20.835		−93.75
Position $ Result		−2,083.50		−4,781.25
Spread $ Net				−6,864

EXHIBIT 17.7

A Trade that Worked as Expected

	Action	FFU4	Action	NIU4
7/28/04	Sell 100	98.425	Buy 52	106.53125
8/25/04	Buy 100	98.435	Sell 52	109.9375
1 Contract Result		−0.010		3.40625
1 Contract in $		−41.67		3,406.25
Position $ Result		−4,167.00		177,125
Spread $ Net				172,958

A WORD OF CAUTION

The bank credit yield curve spread, because it uses Fed funds futures at the short end and 10-year interest rate swap futures at the long end, seems to offer more opportunity than the other commonly traded yield curve spreads. Partly this is because of the wider range between maturities, and partly it is because of the fact that swap rates can be rather volatile at times when the Fed funds rate tends to hover around the Fed funds target rate or, when the Fed is on the move, around the market consensus of what that rate will be.

The contrast between this spread and the TUT spread, shown in Exhibit 17.2, should alert you to another possible source of risk. There are moments when the bank credit yield curve seems to have contrarian tendencies relative to the Treasury yield curves. This is a danger only if you are not aware of the possibility, or if you mistakenly assume that an analysis of the Treasury yield curve situation will suffice for all yield curves.

Remember that this is still a speculative trade and that you can make the wrong call. When you do that, as Exhibit 17.6 illustrates, the trade can lose. For all that, trading the bank credit yield curve spread can generate solid gains for those who take the trouble to study the relevant situations.

CHAPTER 18

A Review of Basic Options Features

Often called strategies in options texts, option spreads offer colorful names—*bull call spread, put butterfly, condor, strangle*—and very real trading opportunity.

A common saying is that where many stock traders are comfortable only with a rallying market, futures traders feel equally at home with rising and falling markets. Option spread traders can similarly handle both the ups and the downs, and they can find ways to benefit from markets that are doing little or nothing.

Option spreads can also be tailored to fit any risk-reward profile. Successful trading over the long haul requires staying power. Traders can't always make winning trades, so it is important to position yourself such that the losses don't put you out of the game. Option spreads can help you do this. For one thing, when you trade a bull call spread or buy a strangle, you know at the outset what the maximum possible loss is. Option spreads, in many cases, allow you define the worst case. Yet these trades offer the possibility of solid, if modest, rewards.

True, options make use of some special terminology and depend on some factors that need not concern futures traders. At the same time, options are options. What you know about stock index options translates readily to options on Treasury futures or on soybean futures. So options are well worth learning about.

In general, then, options expand trading opportunity. However, options also require awareness of several factors that don't enter into futures spread planning.

Like futures traders, option traders must have an opinion about where futures prices are going, for option prices respond to changes in futures prices. At the same time, option traders must keep in mind that option prices do not move one-for-one with futures prices. They move in a ratio. Where a futures price moves 10 cents, the related option may move only 5 cents or even 3.5 cents.

Also, option prices are subject to time decay. If the underlying market moves a certain amount, futures prices will move with it. It doesn't matter whether the move happens next week or next month. With options, the futures move that happens next month may be completely or at least largely undercut by time decay. So the time factor needs to be part of the trade planning.

Finally, along with an opinion about the direction of prices, option traders must also have an opinion about volatility. This includes an awareness of whether volatility is currently higher or lower than normal and of what drives volatility in this market.

For those who can use an informal review of option basics, this chapter reviews these key points about options in a nontechnical way. At the close of this discussion, you will find brief definitions of the more formal option risk parameters—the *greeks*. The discussions of spreads that follow will, for the most part, proceed in these informal terms. Readers who are well versed in options will probably want to skip this.

STARTING AT SQUARE ONE

When you buy a call, you have the right, but not the obligation, to buy the underlying futures contract for a specified price—the strike price. If December corn is trading at $2.32 per bushel, you might buy a December 240 call. This 240 is the strike price, and this option gives you the right to buy December corn futures at $2.40 per bushel any time up to option expiration—even if futures are trading at $2.55 per bushel.

When you buy a put, you have the right, but not the obligation, to sell the underlying futures contract for a specified price—the strike price. If March crude oil is trading at $46 per barrel, you might buy a March 44 put. The 44 is the strike price, and this option gives you the right to sell March crude oil futures any time up to option expiration—even if futures are trading at $39 per barrel.

In either case—call or put—you pay a price for this right, often called the *option premium*. This discussion sticks with price. For option buyers, this price defines the maximum possible loss. For option sellers, it defines the maximum possible gain.

This may seem abstract, but it describes situations we deal with all the time in our everyday lives. Everyone who has a mortgage has bought a call option. Every mortgage holder has the right, but not the obligation, to refinance at a lower interest rate. If interest rates rise, the holder has no obligation to do anything other than continue with the existing mortgage.

Suppose you buy replacement value insurance coverage on your new car, and a truck totals your car on a mall parking lot the day after the coverage goes into effect. Your insurance policy gives you the right to sell your car to the insurance company for full value. Of course, if nothing happens to your car during the term of the policy, you don't have to do anything. That is, when you buy an insurance policy, you are buying a put option.

To apply this to the markets in options on futures, suppose December CBOT DJIA futures are trading at 10,065, and you buy a December 10,100 call. Consider only two of the possible outcomes.

First, a week later, the futures are trading at 9,790. This call gives you the right to buy the futures at 10,100. It makes no economic sense to buy them at 10,100 when you can buy them at a lower price in the futures market. So, in the absence of obligation, you can ignore the option.

Second, another week later, the futures are trading at 10,500. This option gives you the right to buy futures at 10,100. Theoretically, you can turn right around and sell the futures at 10,500. This looks like a sure profit. Given that, you might consider exercising your right to buy futures at this price.

These examples hint at two of the three ways you can exit an option position. First, you can ignore the option and let it expire valueless. Second, you can exercise your right to buy futures (if you bought a call in the first place) or sell futures (if you bought a put). The third alternative is to offset your option position any time before option expiration. If you bought the December 10,100 call, you offset by selling a December 10,100 call. If you bought a December 9,900 put, you offset that by selling a December 9,900 put.

Offset is by far the best way to exit option positions no matter where the futures price is relative to the option strike price. Indeed, it is possible to demonstrate that this option is never economically optimal.

ONE REASON TO TRADE OPTIONS

You might wonder why you should go to all the trouble of learning about options when you can more easily buy or sell futures. One important reason involves the difference between a stock market or futures market risk exposure and an options market risk exposure.

Suppose that December CBOT mini-sized Dow futures are trading at 10,065 and you are bullish on the stock market. To express this opinion, you can:

- Buy December CBOT minisized Dow futures at 10,065.
- Buy a December 10,100 call on these futures at 210.

Both actions allow you to control a similar exposure to the stock market—the futures position has a $50,325 value (10,065 × $5 futures multiplier) while the option controls a position with a $50,500 value (10,100 × $5). Here the similarities end.

For one, when you trade futures, you must post margin. During the fall of 2004, the initial margin for CBOT mini-sized Dow futures was $2,500. The maintenance margin was $2,000. When you buy an option on futures, you must pay the full price—in this example $1,050 (210 × $5). You can see that the initial cost of this option right is $950 less than the maintenance margin on the futures position.

For another, the risk-reward profiles look very different. Exhibit 18.1 shows the gains or losses for the long futures and 9,300 call positions after two weeks have passed. (Note that this set of examples assumes 60 days to option expiration initially and a constant 14 percent implied volatility.)

With futures, you can plainly see, the losses pile up as long as the market drops. These hypothetical futures prices represent one standard deviation increments. The 10,342 futures price is plus one standard deviation from the 10,065 initial futures price. The 9,790 futures price is minus one standard deviation from the initial futures price. The 8,959 futures price represents a four standard deviation drop from the initial price and is right at an 11

EXHIBIT 18.1

Comparing Futures and Call Option Outcomes

CBOT Mini-sized Dow Initial Price	Ending Price	Result	10,100 Call Initial Price	Ending Price	Result	Dollar Result
10,065	10,342	1385	210	345	135	675
10,065	9,790	−1375	210	80	−130	−650
10,065	9,513	−2760	210	27	−183	−915
10,065	9,236	−4145	210	7	−203	−1,015
10,065	8,959	−5530	210	1	−209	−1,045

percent drop in percentage terms. In market vernacular, a 10 percent drop is officially a correction. Whatever the terminology, a $5,530 loss is a major jolt on a position that began with a $50,325 value. The $1,045 loss on the call, while unpleasant, is not nearly so damaging to the trading account as the futures loss. Notice also that the call position has essentially reached its loss limit. If the market had fallen to 8,682 or even to 8,405, the futures losses would continue to pile up, but the call would lose only $1,050 at either of those levels (given the market data and assumptions behind these examples).

This example shows that futures have a symmetrical risk-reward profile. That is, if the underlying index rises or falls, the futures price will rise and fall with it. The same is true with every futures market. If actual soybeans, crude oil, Treasury note, or stock index prices rise or fall, the related futures prices will rise or fall one-to-one with the underlying commodity, security, or index.

In contrast, options have asymmetrical risk-reward profiles. For a call buyer, the option can lose only the price paid. As the underlying market falls, the option will fall only to the extent of the price paid and no more. But, if the market rallies, the option will gain without limit, although the gain will be reduced by the amount of the price paid for the option. For a call seller, the price paid by the buyer and collected by the seller limits the potential gain. No matter how far the underlying market falls, that amount is the most the seller can make. If the market rallies, the call seller can lose without limit. Put buyers can lose only the amount of the price paid if the market rallies against their option positions. They can gain when the market falls as long as the underlying market keeps falling. Put sellers gain only when the underlying market rallies and then only to the extent of the price collected for selling the put option. When the underlying market falls, put sellers can lose seemingly without limit. The market can only go to zero, of course, but it will seem worse than that long before the market reaches zero. This is the asymmetry of option risk and reward.

OPTION PRICES DIFFER FROM FUTURES PRICES

Futures prices respond to a variety of economic and political factors in rather obvious ways. When political unrest or even war in the oil or copper producing parts of the world threatens supplies, it follows that crude oil or copper futures prices will rise. When timely rains in the U.S. and Argentine soybean growing regions create the promise of bumper crops, it follows that soybean futures prices will fall. When the governors of the U.S. Federal Reserve Board begin to mention in speeches that it may be time to start raising the fed funds target rate to control the threat of rising inflation, it follows that yields will rise and that interest rate futures prices will fall. Ultimately, even technical indicators will respond to these factors.

Option Pricing Factors

Option prices respond to these economic stimuli as well, but several additional factors enter into the pricing of options. The pricing models—Black-Scholes being the most frequently cited—that generate option prices make options seem exceedingly technical. On one level, they are. But you can trade options effectively without going deeply into the math. A homely analogy may create a useful perspective. Just as you don't need to know how to build an internal combustion engine to drive a car, so you don't need to know the math of the pricing models to trade options. Still, it is helpful to understand the general idea of how your car works, and it is useful to understand that option prices depend on five bits of information:

- The underlying futures price
- The strike price
- Time to expiration
- A financing rate
- Implied volatility

The first four factors are relatively cut and dried. The futures price comes from a quote source. You choose the strike prices you want to trade. The relevant exchange publishes an option expiration calendar on its Web site from which you can determine days to expiration (although many quote sources do this for you). The financing rate is usually close to the fed funds rate. Implied volatility is more complex, hence the somewhat more extensive discussion later in this chapter.

Option Prices Change on a Sliding Scale

When you look at a page of option quotes on-screen, the display will probably include at least the information given in Exhibit 18.2 (note that the exchange Web sites and the newspaper quote pages tend to offer little but strike prices and option prices). Although formats vary, you can usually find the futures price, the number of days to option expiration, a range of strike prices, the option prices for each strike price, and a value called *delta*. With corn futures trading at 300 cents per bushel, 52 days to option expiration, and 30 percent implied volatility, the strike prices and deltas of a range of call options will be those of Exhibit 18.2.

EXHIBIT 18.2

Prices and Deltas for a Series of Calls on Corn Futures

Corn Futures	300	
Days to Expiration	52	
Strike Price	**Call Price**	**Delta**
290	18 ⅞	0.638
300	13 ½	0.522
310	9 ¾	0.407
320	6 ¼	0.303
330	4	0.216

EXHIBIT 18.3

How Options Respond to Futures Price Changes

Futures Price		300	305 ¼	
Days to Expiration		52	51	
Strike Price	**Call Price**	**Call Price**	**Call Price Change**	**Call Change/ Futures Change**
290	18 ⅞	22 ¼	3 ⅜	0.643
300	13 ½	16 ¼	2 ¾	0.524
310	9 ¾	11 ½	2 ⅛	0.405
320	6 ¼	7 ¾	1 ½	0.288
330	4	5 ⅛	1 ⅛	0.214

Your quote screen may include more data, but this will do for now. Notice that these quotes indicate that on this day you could have bought the 320 corn call for 6 ¼ cents per bushel. That is, you would have paid 6 ¼ cents for the right, but not the obligation, to buy corn futures for 320 cents per bushel any time during the next 52 days. Obviously, if corn prices rise much at all, this call option will gain value. So will the futures and all the other options. The question is by how much.

Suppose that one day later, this corn futures contract is trading at 305 ¼ cents per bushel and, except for the one-day time and 5 ¼ cent futures price differences, all the other pricing factors remain unchanged. In that case, you will see the call prices shown in the third column of Exhibit 18.3.

Notice that the larger the delta, the greater the price change. Also notice that option price change as a percent of the futures price change, in the fifth column, shows values that are close to the deltas.

A Rough and Ready Definition of Delta

This should make clear what an option delta is. The delta of an option derives from the pricing formula and tells you how much the prices of a range of options will change for a given futures price change. Where the 300 call price will change by 52 percent, the 330 call price will change by 21.6 percent.

Option prices change in a ratio to futures price changes, and the delta of the option defines the ratio.

Options traders often talk about where a given option price is relative to the money. The money is the futures price of the moment, and "moniness" is a useful informal idea.

When the option strike price is the same as the futures price, the option is *at the money*. In Exhibit 18.2, the 300 call is at the money. When a call strike price is lower than the futures price, the call is *in the money*. Here, the 290 call is in the money. When the call strike price is higher than the futures price, the option is *out of the money*. The 310, 320, and 330 calls are all out of the money with futures trading at 300 or 305 ¼, but notice that with futures at 305 ¼, the 300 call is slightly in the money.

If these were put options, the moniness would be reversed. The 300 put would still be at the money, but the 290 put would be out of the money and the 310 put would be in the money.

In the case of calls, the deltas range from 0 to 1. Put deltas range from 0 to –1. You can also see from Exhibits 18.2 and 18.3 that at-the-money deltas will be close to 0.5. The farther out of the money, the smaller the delta. The farther in the money, the larger the delta. Futures, by definition, have deltas of 1.0. The closer an option delta, put or call, is to 1, the more the option will trade like the futures contract and the less like an option. As a general rule, options professionals trade out-of-the-money options and avoid in-the-money options.

Delta Can Help You Decide Which Option to Buy

Suppose you are thinking about buying a call on corn futures and have narrowed the choice to either the 310 call or the 330 call. Keep in mind that this gives you the right to buy a futures contract at the strike price. In practice, you will be more likely to offset your call. If you initially buy the 330 call, you offset by selling the 330 call for the same expiration.

EXHIBIT 18.4

Comparing Option and Futures Price Changes after 14 Days

		Initial Price	Ending Price	Price Change	ROI
Futures price		300	325	25	
Call strike	310	9 ⅜	21 ⅛	11 ¾	125%
prices	330	4	10 ¼	6 ¼	156%

A natural reaction might be to say that you'd rather pay 4 cents per bushel than 9 ⅜ cents per bushel. Everybody likes a bargain. The trick here is deciding what constitutes a bargain. In deciding this, it's important to ask what you might get for what you pay—whether the extra 5 ⅜ cents per bushel might be worth paying.

Consider what would happen to these option prices if the only pricing factors that change are the passage of 14 days and a futures price increase to 325 cents per bushel. Exhibit 18.4 shows the results of these changes.

Notice that the 310 call netted 11 ¾ cents per bushel while the 330 call netted 6 ¼ cents per bushel. Veteran options traders are fond of saying that with options you get what you pay for. This is probably true, but there are two ways to look at this.

In absolute dollar terms, certainly the 310 call looks like the better deal. However, in terms of return on investment (ROI), the 330 call gives you more bang for your buck. To calculate ROI, divide the net gain by the initial option price. The 330 call has a 156 percent ROI (6 ¼ ÷ 4), while the 310 call has a 125 percent ROI. This is a trade-off each trader must make. The factors to consider are how much the option will cost, of course, and how much it will make. Next, you have to decide whether you want to shoot for the most absolute dollars or the most bang for your buck. Obviously, the price paid for the option defines the maximum possible loss. Either choice is defensible.

With option spreads, you will face similar choices with regard to whether to trade at or away from the money and also with regard to how to space the strike prices in spreads involving two calls or two puts.

Additional Reasons to Know about Delta

An awareness of delta can help you in other ways as you think about options. In addition to telling you how much the option price will change for a given futures price change, the option delta indicates the probability that an option will expire in the money. If December corn is trading at

$2.10 per bushel with 28 days to December option expiration, you might notice that a December 220 call has a 0.25 delta. This indicates a 25 percent probability that this option will expire in the money. Remember that to expire in the money is not the same as being profitable. Suppose you paid 3 cents per bushel for this option and the futures price at expiration was $2.21 per bushel. This option will have been 1 cent in the money, but it will have made a 2-cents-per-bushel loss.

Another use for delta is in the definition of hedge ratios. This 0.25 delta indicates that it will take four of these December 220 calls to have the same responsiveness to price change that one futures contract will have. For spread traders, this often doesn't matter, but it is a useful option feature to keep in mind because there are situations in which it does matter.

WITH OPTIONS, IT'S ABOUT TIME

When you buy an option, you are, in large part, buying time—specifically, time to make up your mind about whether to buy or sell a market. Suppose that crude oil futures are trading at $44 per barrel and that your market analysis has defined $48 per barrel as a key resistance level. Your idea is that if the crude oil futures price breaks through this level, it might soar far higher. Based on this reasoning, you might like to buy crude oil at $46, but only if you see that $48 resistance level being broken through. With futures, you're stuck. You can buy futures at your $46 target price or wait to see whether the price breaks through this key resistance level. You can't have it both ways.

With options, you can buy a 46 call option. Now you can afford to wait, because if the futures price breaks through any time between the moment your option trade clears and option expiration, you have the right to buy futures at $46 per barrel—even if the price has already broken through the $50 level. If the futures price never goes higher than $46 per barrel, you will lose what you paid for the option, but that is the price you pay to be able to wait and see. This is how buying an option can buy you time. But there's a catch. Options experience time decay.

The Futures-Options Time Difference

This matter of time, and especially time decay, is a big part of what makes options different from futures. If you sell NYMEX crude oil futures and the price of crude oil drops, you will show a gain as well. If the price of crude oil does little or nothing, you'll probably be close to breakeven (ignoring transaction costs). Further, if the price of crude oil drops by $5 per barrel on the first day of the trade, the gain is the same as when it drops by $5 per barrel by the 21st day of the trade, or at any other time. With futures, time isn't a factor (except that futures contracts do eventually stop trading—*go off the board*, in market vernacular).

Options traders cannot be indifferent to time. Suppose that December NYMEX crude oil futures are trading at $43.87 per barrel and there are 63 days left until the expiration of the December options. Your quote screen might include, in part, the data shown in the first two columns of Exhibit 18.5.

After the passage of 21 days, assume that the crude oil futures price remains at $43.87 per barrel, or is back to that level. If all the other pricing factors except days to expiration also remain unchanged, you will see the put prices with 42 days left to expiration that are shown in the Ending Price column. And, as the Price Change column shows, the December 43.5 put will have lost $0.55, the 43.0 put will have lost $0.52, and so on. Even though the futures price is the same on both the initial day and the ending day, the options have all lost value.

This is option time decay at work. This is an important difference between futures and options. It is a negative factor for option buyers but a positive factor for option sellers.

Exhibit 18.6 shows a similar situation involving November puts on crude oil futures. On the same day that the December options had 63 days remaining to expiration (Exhibit 18.5), the November options had 31 days remaining.

EXHIBIT 18.5

Time and December Put Options on NYMEX Crude Oil Futures

		Initial Price	Ending Price	Price Change
December NYMEX crude oil futures		43.87	43.87	
Days to expiration		63	42	
December put strike prices	43.5	2.73	2.20	−0.55
	43.0	2.48	1.96	−0.52
	42.5	2.25	1.74	−0.51
	42.0	2.03	1.53	−0.50

EXHIBIT 18.6

Time and November Put Options on November NYMEX Crude Oil Futures

		Initial Price	Ending Price	Price Change
November NYMEX crude oil futures		44.34	44.34	
Days to expiration		31	10	
November put strike prices	43.5	1.79	0.87	−0.92
	43.0	1.57	0.68	−0.89
	42.5	1.36	0.52	−0.84
	42.0	1.33	0.50	−0.83

Again assuming the passage of 21 days and no other pricing factor changes, you can make five observations:

- The initial prices of the November puts are much less than the initial prices of the December puts on the same date.
- All four puts suffered losses even though the futures price remained unchanged.
- The November puts lost more, in both nominal and percentage terms, than the December puts over the same 21-day period.
- The rate of time decay accelerates as expiration approaches, especially during the last month before expiration.
- The nearer-the-money 43.5 put lost more to time than the farther out-of-the-money calls.

Time Affects Trading Results

Exhibit 18.7 offers another way to look at the effect of time on an option trade. It contrasts a December 42.5 crude oil put with a November 42.5 put and looks at what will happen to each if the futures price drops to $40 per barrel after 1 day or after 21 days. The assumption is that all other pricing factors remain the same.

Note that the $3.87 December futures price change and the $3.91 November futures price change are both 8.82 percent changes.

Several things should be obvious from this. First, both options made money after 1 day and after 21 days. However, while the November option made $0.04 per barrel less than the December option after 1 day, it made a $0.34 per barrel less after 21 days. Second, while the extra 20 days cost the

EXHIBIT 18.7

The Effect of Time on Two Option Positions

	Initial Price		Ending Price	Price Change	Ending Price	Price Change
December NYMEX crude oil futures price	43.87		40.00	−3.87	40.00	−3.87
Days to December expiration	63		62		42	
Strike Price	**Put Price**	**Delta**	**Put Price**	**Price Change**	**Put Price**	**Price Change**
December 42.5 put	2.25	0.39	4.16	1.91	3.72	1.47
November NYMEX crude oil futures price	44.34		40.43		40.43	
Days to November expiration	31		30		10	
November 42.5 put	1.36	0.34	3.23	1.87	2.49	1.13

December option $0.44 (4.16 – 3.72), the passing of those 20 days cost the November option $0.74 (3.23 – 2.49). These differences in the options results are due, as purely as possible, to time decay.

Given the examples of Exhibit 18.7, a useful rule of thumb might be that you should consider buying options with more time to expiration to reduce the ravages of time decay.

The mirror image rule of thumb is that you should consider selling options with less time to expiration to maximize the effect of time decay, preferably a month or less.

One way to express a bearish opinion is to buy a put. Conversely, one way to express a bullish opinion is to sell a put. The converse is true of calls—buy when bullish; sell when bearish. Remember, when you buy options, time decay is an enemy. When you sell options, time decay is a friend.

To illustrate how time decay can help an option seller, assume that you considered selling both of these 42.50 crude oil puts at the initial put prices shown in Exhibit 18.6. Consider three possible outcomes. After 21 days, the crude oil futures prices:

- Rise by 4.56 percent
- Stay the same
- Fall by 4.56 percent.

EXHIBIT 18.8

Time Decay Can Help Option Sellers

	Initial Price	Futures Up	Price Change	Futures Same	Price Change	Futures Down	Price Change
December futures	43.87	45.87	2.00	43.87	0.00	41.87	−2.00
December 42.5 put	2.25	1.10	1.15	1.74	0.51	2.64	−0.39
November futures	44.34	46.36	2.02	44.34	0.00	42.32	−2.02
November 42.5 put	1.36	0.17	1.19	0.52	0.84	1.29	0.07

Exhibit 18.8 shows the results given the same pricing assumptions as in previous examples, other than these three ending futures price assumptions.

Keep in mind that to sell a put is to express a somewhat bullish opinion. You expect crude oil prices to rise or at least stay about the same. The down move which helps the put buyer is an adverse move for the put seller.

Notice that as a seller of the November 42.50 put, you can expect to do better than the seller of the December 42.50 put in each situation. Also, while the December put loses $0.39 per barrel when the futures price drops $2.00 per barrel, the November 42.50 put makes a little money even when the market moves against this position. This should make it obvious how the shorter-dated put benefits from its greater sensitivity to time decay.

It is important to remember when contemplating the selling of options that option sellers can suffer unlimited losses when the market moves against them. In contrast, the loss to option buyers is always limited to the option price paid, exclusive of transaction costs.

Even more important, when you buy options you must consider the effect of time decay because time decay will reduce the potential gain. It can even overcome favorable futures market moves, unless they are quite large.

IMPLIED VOLATILITY IS A CRUCIAL FACTOR IN OPTIONS PRICING

Volatility is probably the most important single options pricing factor. Informally, this term refers to how agitated the market is and, in general, serves as an indicator of how risky an option might be. The higher the volatility, the higher the risk, and the higher the option price. In thinking about volatility, it is important to distinguish between historical volatility and implied volatility, although most of what goes into options trade planning involves implied volatility.

Historical volatility values make claims about the history of the futures price and are based on statistical analyses of daily futures price differences for a specified period—10 days and 30 days are common. This value is then annualized and expressed as a percent. A 5 percent volatility claims a 68 percent probability that the futures price one year forward will fall within a range plus or minus 5 percent of the current price. If the 10-year Treasury note futures price now is 100-00, this 5 percent volatility says that the price in a year is likely to fall somewhere between 95-00 and 105-00. Note that the 68 percent probability is plus or minus one standard deviation.

Backing into a Definition

Often, you will see option prices quoted in the market that seem at odds with what you think they should be, given historical volatility. Suppose that with September 10-year Treasury note futures trading at 116-14 and 40 days to the September option expiration, an option calculator shows that the September 116 put should cost 0-42 (42/64) at a 5.6 percent historical volatility. Yet when you look at an option quote screen, you might see that this option is trading at 0-57. This option price implies a 7.1 percent volatility. To arrive at that price, that is, you would have to use a 7.1 percent volatility in the pricing process, not the 5.6 percent historical volatility reading.

This example underscores that implied volatility is simply the expected volatility that the option price quote implies and that it is not necessarily equal to historical volatility. The professional traders at the major trading houses estimate what they think the volatility will be between the option transaction date and option expiration. This implied volatility estimate forms the basis for their pricing of the options. When these market professionals consider the situation to be especially risky, the implied volatility will be several points higher than the historical volatility. In this 10-year Treasury note example, the 15/64 price difference represents a risk premium that option market makers—traditionally, the traders on the exchange floor but, increasingly, screen-based traders—charge to compensate themselves for making a market in risky circumstances. At other times, these traders may see less risk, and the implied volatility will be lower than the historical volatility.

Isolating the Implied Volatility Factor

A series of what-if exercises can help you begin to appreciate what options traders mean when they say that implied volatility is the most important option-pricing factor. The summer of 2003 was a time of huge volatility shifts in the Treasury markets—especially in the 10-year sector.

On July 16, 2003, 38 days to the September options expiration, September 10-year Treasury note futures settled at 114-23. Two weeks later, on July 30, the September futures settled at 111-30. At-the-money implied volatility was 7.5 percent on July 16 but had climbed to 10.8 percent by July 30. Had you priced September 113, 112, and 111 put options on 10-year Treasury note futures based on the 114-23 futures price, the 7.5 percent implied volatility, and 38 days to expiration, the option prices would have been those of the Initial Options Prices column in Exhibit 18.9.

Treasury futures are priced in points and 32nds. A futures quote of 114-23 indicates a price that is 114 and 23/32 percent of par, with par for one contract being $100,000. The related options are quoted in points and 64ths, so an options quote of 1-32 indicates a price that is 1 and 32/64 percent of par. Exhibit 18.9 converts the 113 put price in Scenario 3 from 1-32 (or 1'32 on some screens) to 96 (64 + 32) to make it easier to eyeball the arithmetic. A notation such as 96 – 28 = 68 seems more accessible than 1-52 – 0-28 = 1-04, although they are equivalent.

You know enough about time decay to know that if the only change was the passage of 14 days and that if the futures price and the implied volatility remained the same, these puts would all lose value—a good thing if you'd sold them, bad if you'd bought them. This result is shown in the Scenario 1 column of Exhibit 18.9.

But now suppose that, after the passage of 14 days, the futures price stayed the same but the implied volatility soared to 10.8 percent. As the put prices under Scenario 2 show, all these options would have made a little money. A big enough volatility change can overcome the effect of time decay. Note also that the closer to the money the option strike price (the closer the strike price is to the initial futures price), the greater the effect of a given volatility change.

Notice that the first three columns of the lower segment of Exhibit 18.9 repeat the initial data of the upper segment. The option prices under

EXHIBIT 18.9

Illustrating the Value of Implied Volatility

Scenarios 1 and 2

Strike Price	Initial 7/16/03 Put Price (64ths)	Delta	Scenario 1 (7/30/03) Put Price (64ths)	Scenario 1 (7/30/03) Change (64ths)	Scenario 2 (7/30/03) Put Price (64ths)	Scenario 2 (7/30/03) Change (64ths)
111	7	0.08	2	−5	11	4
112	15	0.16	7	−8	21	6
113	28	0.26	17	−11	37	9
			Dollar Equivalents			
111	109.375			−78.125		62.500
112	234.375			−125.000		93.750
113	437.500			−171.875		140.625

Scenarios 3 and 4

Strike Price	Initial 7/16/03 Put Price (64ths)	Delta	Scenario 3 (7/30/03) Put Price (64ths)	Scenario 3 (7/30/03) Change (64ths)	Scenario 4 (7/30/03) Put Price (64ths)	Scenario 4 (7/30/03) Change (64ths)
111	7	0.08	30	23	52	45
112	15	0.16	57	42	81	66
113	28	0.26	96	68	118	90
			Dollar Equivalents			
111	109.375			359.375		703.125
112	234.375			656.250		1,031.250
113	437.500			1,062.500		1,406.250

Scenario 3 illustrate the effect of a favorable futures price change when there is no change in volatility. (While it is difficult to imagine a case in which a futures price change of this magnitude would not cause a volatility shift, this artificial example makes a useful point.) Puts increase in value when futures prices fall, and the Scenario 3 put prices are based on a futures price drop to 111-30, the passage of 14 days, and no change in volatility.

Approaching the Options Trading Real World

When describing how options work, it is convenient to isolate such factors as time, futures price, and implied volatility to the extent possible, as has been done in Scenarios 1, 2, and 3 of Exhibit 18.9. This helps you see how much influence these pricing factors can exert on the price of the option.

The reality is that these pricing factors interact. They can work against each other—as in Scenarios 2 and 3 where the positive effects (positive from the point of view of an option buyer) of volatility change and futures price change, respectively, can overcome the negative effect of time decay. Scenario 4 shows what can happen when several of these factors work together.

The assumptions behind Scenario 4 are that the futures price has dropped by 2-25, from 114-23 to 111-30, and the implied volatility has soared from 7.5 percent to 10.8 percent. This futures price-implied volatility interaction can drive large option price increases. Indeed, the Scenario 4 results appear to be greater than the sum of the parts.

Consider Exhibit 18.10, which shows the percent change in the put prices in these four scenarios. (Note that percent changes result from dividing the values in the change columns by the initial option price. Consider the 111 put in Scenario 1: –5 price change ÷ 7 initial price = –0.71429, or –71.4%.)

The percent changes for Scenario 4 are much larger than those for Scenario 3. Notice that the options that were initially farther out of the money outperformed, in percentage terms, the options that were closer to the money. This will always be the case.

These exhibits underscore the importance of a notion common among options trades: While a futures trader must have an opinion about price direction, an options trader must also have an opinion about the direction of implied volatility.

EXHIBIT 18.10

Percent Changes in Put Prices

	Scenario 1	Scenario 2	Scenario 3	Scenario 4
111 put	–71.4	57.1	329	643
112 put	–53.3	40.0	280	440
113 put	–39.3	32.1	243	321

DEVELOPING A VOLATILITY OUTLOOK

A good starting place in formulating a volatility outlook is to develop at least a basic idea about possible sources of volatility in a given market.

Traders often seem to live by series of rules of thumb. Talk about volatility is no different. Rules of thumb abound. It is always a good idea to step cautiously in the presence of these. They wouldn't exist if they didn't embody at least a measure of truth, but they don't always apply. So it is a good idea to think about whether these are normal times, when the given rule might apply, or exceptional times, when the given rule might better be ignored.

Finally, even though historical volatility represents memories and implied volatility represents a prediction, it is important to consider where the prediction lies relative to the memories.

By the time you have considered these factors, you should have developed a useful idea about volatility.

Sources of Volatility

A customary view relates volatility shifts to price changes. Rising prices increase volatility in the physical commodities markets while falling prices tend to decrease volatility in these markets. In the stock or stock index markets, the opposite holds true as a general rule. Falling prices tend to elevate volatility, while rising prices tend to reduce volatility. The longer-term interest rate markets resemble the stock markets in this one way. Falling prices and rising interest rates go together, of course, and a period of falling fixed-income prices will tend to drive volatility higher. Rising prices and falling yields will reduce volatility in these markets.

This customary view is accurate as far as it goes. Successful trading depends on anticipating market developments, and these customary price-volatility links raise questions concerning why prices will go up or down and why volatility responds as it does when these things happen. A few high-level generalizations are possible and may serve the purpose for most traders.

In a way, volatility measures market uncertainty about supply in the physical markets, or about future profits in the stock market, or about the threat of rising inflation in the longer-term interest rate markets.

You can easily see what general conditions will create uncertainty. In the physical commodities, supply shocks are a major factor. Unfriendly weather at crucial stages in the development of a crop will threaten crop yield, and this supply uncertainty will drive prices and volatility higher.

Weather can make a difference in the energy markets, too. But in these markets, this often seems more of a demand factor. For example, an unexpectedly cold winter in New England can create demand for heating oil. Yet even here it works around to uncertainty about the adequacy of heating oil supplies. This kind of uncertainty will cause volatilities and prices to rise.

The energy markets and the metals are also subject to political factors. Political unrest in producing regions obviously threatens supplies. A striking recent example involves crude oil and gasoline prices. During the spring of 2004, with the situation in Iraq up for grabs and the Saudis talking about cutting back on crude oil shipments, crude oil and unleaded gasoline futures prices and volatilities climbed steadily. Part way through May 2004, inventory concerns abated, and prices and volatilities subsided, only to rise again later as new uncertainties emerged.

Demand shifts can drive volatility higher as well. An increase in manufacturing activity means an increase in demand for copper, aluminum, and the other industrial metals. Factories require energy also. If you think about it, this is only likely to drive volatility higher if the market view is that this increase in activity will strain supplies. If stockpiles are large, demand can increase and drive up prices with no visible volatility change. If stockpiles have not been replenished during a slack period, increasing demand will elevate both prices and volatility.

So really, uncertainty about the adequacy of supplies is what drives volatility higher in the physical commodities. When supplies are considered adequate, volatility tends to subside, even when demand increases.

Also, once the uncertainty goes away, volatility tends to abate. Not surprisingly, volatility in the crop markets has a seasonal aspect. Corn and soybean volatility tends to peak in midsummer when the crops are in the ground but less than fully developed. No one can know for certain about yields at this time because weather problems can still affect crop development. At harvest, this uncertainty will largely go away, and volatility tends to drop even when yields are poor. This phenomenon is a good reminder that it is uncertainty about supply more than supply itself that boosts volatility.

Moving on to the financial markets, it seems fair to say that rising stock prices bother no one. They signal a growing economy, and growing economies generate healthy corporate profits. There can be exceptions. Individual companies or certain sectors may do badly, even when most companies and sectors are thriving. But stock indexes reflect the general rule, not the exceptions. So in general, rising prices should calm stock index volatility. Conversely, falling stock prices create uncertainty about future profits and drive stock index volatility higher.

Rising interest rates can also boost stock index volatility. Corporations borrow vast sums in the corporate bond markets, and rising interest rates can squeeze margins. Obviously, if corporations can increase prices of finished goods, rising interest rates will not be a problem. When they have no room to raise prices, then rising interest rates can threaten profits, and you can expect to see volatility rise to the extent that market analysts are uncertain about how this will affect future profits.

Falling prices in the long-term interest rate markets will also elevate volatility. The reason for this is similar to the reason for stock market volatility. Falling fixed-income prices result from rising yields. Rising interest rates are a response to two factors apart from the obvious interest in what the Fed may or may not be doing at the time: institutional investors' estimates of how much credit risk the securities in question contain and how much rising inflation is likely to erode returns to these investments. Obviously, the Treasury markets do not contain credit risk, so rising inflation is the primary factor that drives longer-term yields higher. And uncertainty about these factors will drive up implied volatility.

Taking Exception to Rules of Thumb

Volatility tends to be mean-reverting. This means that when you see an implied volatility value that is higher or lower than the median historical value for that market, the normal expectation is that the implied volatility will work back toward the median.

The long-term median wheat historical volatility tends to hover at around 20 percent during the spring and summer months. Yet it can go as high as 35 or 40 percent or as low as 10 percent during these months (in the odd case, it has gone even higher). Because volatility is normally mean-reverting, if you see a 35 percent implied volatility for options on May wheat futures in early March, the normal expectation is that this volatility will drift back at least closer to the 20 percent median. Similarly, if the early March implied volatility is 8 percent, your normal expectation is for the implied volatility to drift higher.

A word of caution: Markets aren't always "normal."

Consider 10-year Treasury note futures volatility. Historical records might show the median historical volatility to hover around 7 percent. Toward the middle of May 2004, with September 10-year Treasury futures trading around 107-28, implied volatilities for July out-of-the-money 10-year Treasury note puts ranged between 8.3 and 9 percent, well over the median.

The temptation in a case like this is to think that this is an ideal time to sell volatility. You might argue that declining volatility helps an option seller and that, because of the mean-reverting property of volatility, this implied volatility is almost sure to move back to the median or even lower. Convinced by this logic, you might decide to sell a strangle or to trade a bear call spread.

In many situations, this could be the right thing to do, but it might not have been in May 2004. The Fed had met on May 4, 2004, and issued a statement that indicated a readiness to start raising their fed funds target rate at future meetings. Also in May 2004, almost all the economic indicators foretold a strong inflation buildup.

Normally, when the Fed raises its Fed funds target rate 25 basis points (bps), longer-term yields rise, but they rise less. If the Fed moves 25 bps, the 10-year Treasury note yield might rise only 10 bps, for example. However, fixed-income investors fear rising inflation above all else because it erodes future earnings from these investments. If these investment professionals decide the Fed isn't doing enough to control inflation, the 10-year yield increase could be more like 40 or 50 bps. In May 2004, this kind of larger long-term yield increase seemed at least a possibility.

Because of this, May 2004 had the look of a time when, even though Treasury implied volatilities looked high, these volatilities could easily go higher. That is, this might have been a better time to buy volatility than to sell it. A sequence rather like this did play out during the summer of 2003. In early June of that year, Treasury note implied volatilities seemed relatively high. Then at the end of June, the Fed eased 25 bps when the market thought they should have eased 50 bps. During the next several weeks both yields and implied volatilities shot sharply higher.

Rules of thumb are helpful, but careful traders ask themselves whether there is anything about the current situation that might violate the normal situation that the rule of thumb addresses. If there isn't, then the rule of thumb applies. If there is, then the rule of thumb should be ignored.

Similarly, in the grain and oilseed markets, volatility tends to peak in June or early July when the crops are still in doubt. By September, the harvest will have begun, and all those concerned should have a good idea about crop yields. Then, whether yields are bad or good, volatilities in these markets tend to calm down.

In early October 2003, though, soybean analysts were saying they had no idea about the size of the soybean crop. One analyst said she expected a dollar a bushel move in soybean futures prices but couldn't figure out if it would be up, because the crop yield was poor, or down, because yields were great. This kind of uncertainty about supplies drives volatility higher. Any trader who had sold soybean volatility based on a thoughtless assumption about normal patterns in these markets might well have been sorely disappointed.

Technical Factors Can Affect Volatility

At times, futures markets enter into trading ranges. You might see S&P 500 futures climb to 1,150 only to fall back to 1,110 a few days later and continue to bounce around between these levels for several weeks. This can happen in any of the futures markets. The range may be a little wider or a little narrower, but the market seems unable to break out of this range in either direction.

This range trading phenomenon tends to suck the volatility right out of a market. It often seems that the longer the range persists, the lower implied volatilities go, especially for strike prices that lie beyond the range boundaries. Seeing a market like this, you can be reasonably sure that a long option position will get no help from rising volatility regardless of where the volatility is relative to the long-term median. On the other hand, this is a situation that should prove ideal for straddle and strangle sellers and other strategies that involve selling options. Both time decay and falling implied volatilities will help straddle and strangle sellers.

The Term Structure of Volatility

Another common rule of thumb in options trading is that you should try to buy options when implied volatility is relatively low and to sell options when volatility is relatively high. The idea is that when you do this, the mean reverting character of volatility will work for your trading positions, not against them. The trick is to define high or low in a useful way. Many quote systems allow you to chart implied volatility and historical volatility so you can see where implied volatility is trading relative to historical volatility. This may be a good first step, but a richer analysis is possible with volatility cones.

A volatility cone does for historical volatility more or less what a yield curve does for yields. It displays the term structure. Consider the price volatility cone for 10-year Treasury note structures displayed in Exhibit 18.11a. The accompanying table (Exhibit 18.11b) may help in locating key volatility levels at the various times to expiration.

This graphic summarizes a study of every 10-year Treasury note option that traded during the two-year term of the study. It takes observations of

EXHIBIT 18.11a

Treasury 10-Year Note Futures Volatility, April 2001 to March 2003

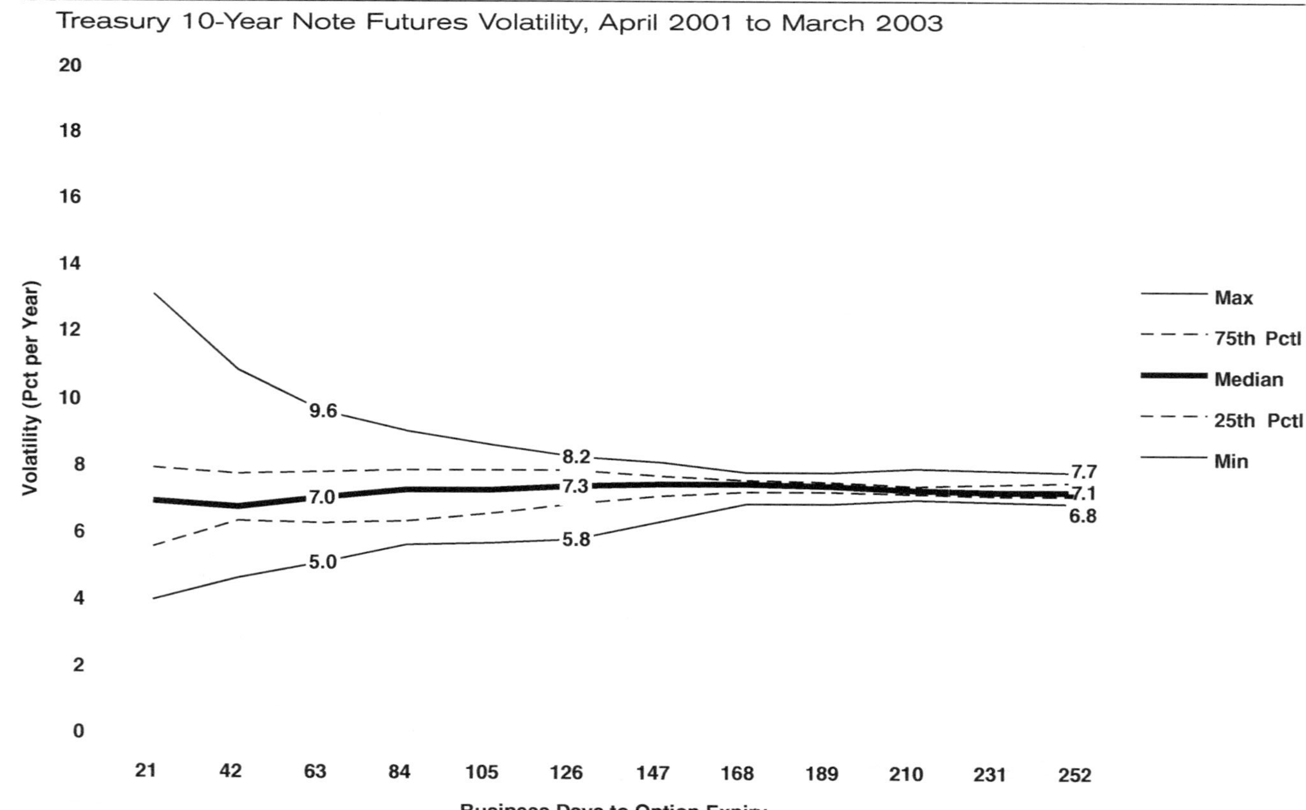

Source:CBOT

EXHIBIT 18.11b

10-Year Volatility Levels

Days to Expiration	21	42	63	84	105	126	147	168	189	210	231	252
Maximum	13.08	10.81	9.57	8.96	8.57	8.22	8.02	7.73	7.77	7.84	7.78	7.74
75th percentile	7.83	7.67	7.75	7.77	7.78	7.79	7.63	7.48	7.43	7.34	7.40	7.47
Median	6.89	6.69	6.89	7.22	7.20	7.33	7.37	7.38	7.31	7.23	7.17	7.14
25th percentile	5.49	6.25	6.23	6.28	6.54	6.81	7.02	7.16	7.17	7.10	7.05	7.02
Minimum	3.94	4.57	5.02	5.60	5.63	5.76	6.28	6.78	6.80	6.91	6.87	6.83

historical volatility at every point starting with 252 days to option expiration. Just as a yield curve moves from the shortest yields on the left to the longer-term yields on the right, so a volatility cone moves from option expiration on the left to 252 days to expiration on the right.

The heaviest, almost flat line shows the median historical volatility during the two years of the study to be approximately 7 percent, regardless of the time until option expiration. The uppermost and bottommost lines define the maximum and minimum volatilities observed at each moment. Given the volatility cone graphic, you can easily plot the implied volatility that is in the market and see how it compares with these observations of historical volatility.

For example, assume that with 126 days to option expiration, an option that interests you is trading at 8.1 percent implied volatility. The cone shows you that the median is 7.3 percent and the maximum that has been observed at this time is 8.2 percent. Given that, this 8.1 percent implied volatility seems very high. Going back to the rule of thumb that instructs you to buy low volatilities and to sell high volatilities, you might conclude that this is a good time to be a volatility seller. If this is a normal market, that may be right. The mean-reverting character of volatility may well pull this high volatility down closer to the 7.3 percent median or even lower.

Before you get too comfortable with an outlook based on the mean-reverting character of volatility, think back. There are times when mean reversion seems not to hold. If the Fed is raising interest rates or if the markets find inflation developments alarming, this high volatility may go yet higher.

Also, notice that the range of volatility observations is relatively narrow until approximately 168 days from expiration. From that time on, the range of volatility observations begins to widen. Thus a volatility cone gives you a rough and ready way to consider the volatility of volatility.

For the first 84 days (that is, from 252 days to expiration to 168 days), the readings range between a 7.7 percent maximum and a 6.8 percent minimum. At 126 days, the maximum is a half point higher (8.2 percent). and the minimum is a full point lower (5.8 percent). At 63 days, the range has widened from the initial 0.9 percentage points (7.7-6.8) to 4.55 percentage points (9.57-5.02), and by 21 days, it stretched out to 9.14 points (13.08-3.94). That is, as options approach expiration, volatility itself becomes more volatile. The 8.1 percent volatility that seems high at 126 days is only a 75th percentile reading at 63 days. The volatility cone shows that, given this 8.1 percent reading, the upside potential for volatility increases markedly as option expiration draws closer.

This expansion of the range of volatilities should warn you to accept rules of thumb only after careful thought. When formulating a volatility outlook, you should consider what factors may make the current situation abnormal. Maybe there are none, and then the rules of thumb may well hold. But don't assume that blindly.

Also, what you know about volatilities in one market may not have much to do with volatilities in another—even in another that seems closely related. Consider Exhibit 18.12a which presents a volatility cone for 5-year Treasury note futures that covers the same period of time as the cone of Exhibit 18.11a.

In many ways, the two graphics seem similar. The general pattern is certainly the same, but the levels of volatility shown at the various times to expiration are very different. While the 10-year volatility median ranges around 7 percent, the 5-year volatility median ranges around 5 percent, and there is far less variation among the 5-year medians than there is among the 10-year medians.

In short, it is important to consider each market on its own terms when you set out to formulate an opinion about implied volatility and where the current implied volatility quote is in relation to the term structure of historical volatility.

THE OPTION GREEKS IN BRIEF

Professional options traders pay careful attention to four risk parameters, which are derivatives of the option pricing models—delta, gamma, theta, and vega. These are referred to as the greeks because the first three are Greek letters. Vega derives from Arabic. For the purpose of trading the spreads that are discussed in this book, it suffices to have a rough and ready idea about delta and theta and to know that gamma and vega are out there and influencing your positions. Only the two volatility spread chapters make explicit use of vega in ratioing positions. Briefly, then:

- *Delta* indicates how much the option price will change for a small change in the underlying futures price.
- *Gamma* indicates how much the option delta will change for a small change in the underlying futures price.
- *Theta* defines the rate at which an option price will fall with the passing of time.
- *Vega* defines how much the option price will change for a small implied volatility change.

EXHIBIT 18.12a

Treasury 5-Year Note Futures Volatility, April 2001 to March 2003

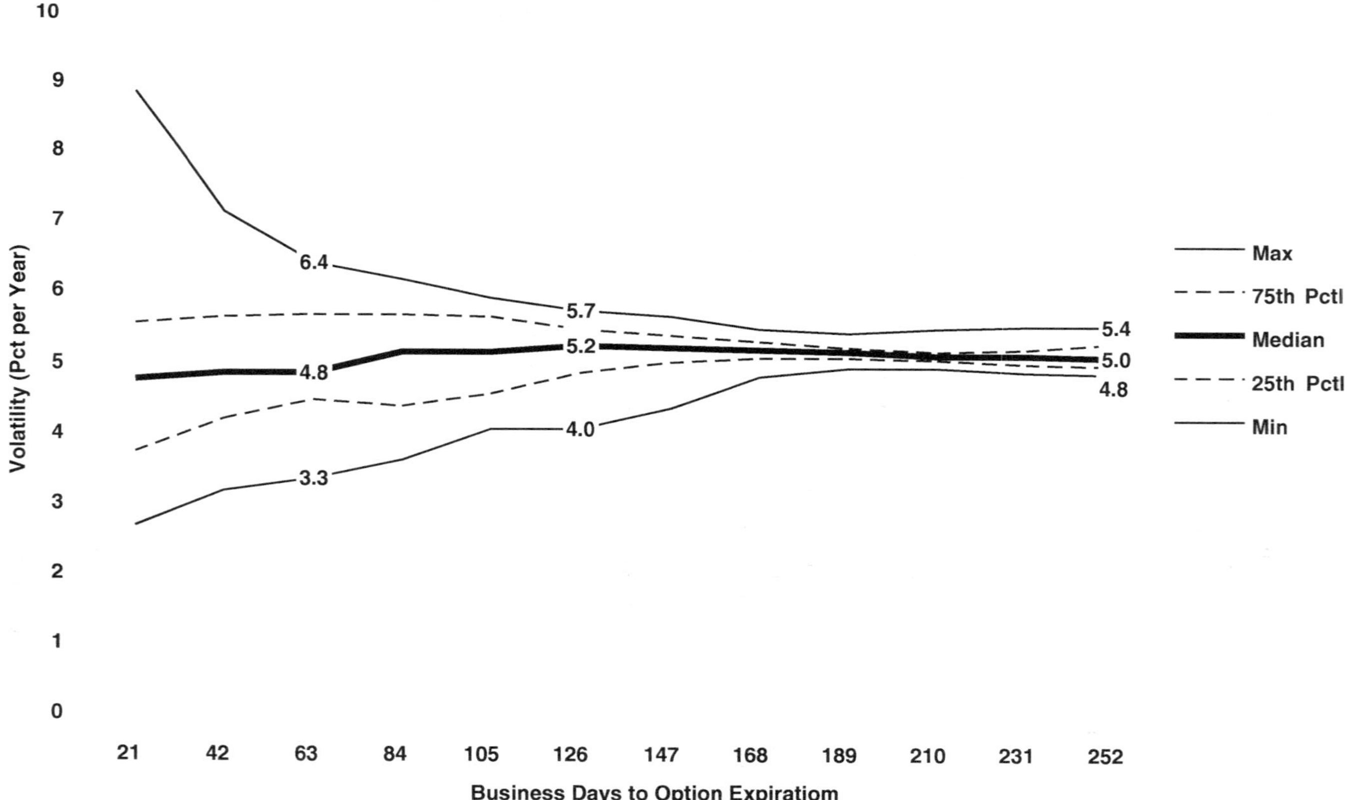

Source:CBOT

EXHIBIT 18.12b

5-Year Volatility Levels

Days to Expiration	21	42	63	84	105	126	147	168	189	210	231	252
Maximum	8.82	7.11	6.38	6.12	5.87	5.70	5.62	5.41	5.36	5.42	5.47	5.45
75th percentile	5.51	5.61	5.62	5.63	5.61	5.44	5.33	5.25	5.17	5.11	5.13	5.21
Median	4.73	4.81	4.80	5.10	5.10	5.20	5.17	5.13	5.10	5.06	5.03	5.00
25th percentile	3.69	4.17	4.42	4.33	4.53	4.81	4.96	5.00	5.03	4.99	4.94	4.90
Minimum	2.65	3.15	3.33	3.58	4.02	4.02	4.32	4.75	4.87	4.87	4.82	4.77

CHAPTER 19

Bull Call and Bear Put Option Spreads

With Options, There Is No Free Lunch

Some traders insist that, when they trade options spreads, they want the sold options to pay for the bought options, or at least pay for most of the cost of the bought options. These people seem to have an aversion to paying up-front money. Be wary of such an attitude, for slightly more astute option traders point out that in the options markets, there are no free lunches. You get pretty much what you pay for. The unwiseness of the former attitude and the wisdom of the latter bit of advice become especially clear in the consideration of such option spreads as bull call or bear put spreads.

In structuring these option spreads, traders typically buy an at-or near-the-money option and sell an option that is farther from the money. Given a bullish outlook, both options will be calls. Given a bearish outlook, both will be puts. However, when traders sell an option that is too close to the money, in order to let the sold option pay for most of the cost of buying the other option and reduce the initial cost of the trade, they also limit the profit potential of the trade.

CURTAILING PARTICIPATION

A useful way to illustrate the truth of this contention is to look at a bull call spread in corn options. Suppose that the relevant corn futures contract is trading at 295.25 cents a bushel, at-the-money implied volatility is 32.9 percent, and 39 days remain to options expiration. Given these initial market conditions, the options array on a quote page might include the data of Exhibit 19.1.

EXHIBIT 19.1

A Range of Corn Options

Futures Price		295.25
Implied volatility		33%
Days to expiration		40
Strike price	**Call price**	**Delta**
300	10.75	0.46
310	7.125	0.35
320	4.5	0.25
330	2.75	0.17

Given these options prices and deltas, the possible bull call spreads include:

A: Buy the 300 call; sell the 310 call.

B: Buy the 300 call; sell the 320 call.

C: Buy the 300 call; sell the 330 call.

The textbook description of a bull call spread usually includes a statement to the effect that the maximum possible profit amounts to the difference between the strike prices less the net cost of the spread.

Spread A costs 3.625 cents per bushel (–10.75 + 7.125). The difference between the strike prices is 10 cents per bushel. That 10 cents minus 3.625 is 6.375 cents per bushel. It is important to remember that this is the potential of this trade at expiration.

In contrast, Spread B costs 6.25 cents per bushel (–10.75 + 4.5), so this spread has a 13.75 cents per bushel potential (the 20-cent per bushel strike price difference minus the 6.25 cents per bushel initial cost)—to emphasize, at expiration. It costs more to put on, but the potential gain is much larger.

It is important to remember that this textbook profit potential derives from an expiration analysis. This eliminates the time value factor. The classic hockey stick diagrams similarly depict the situation at expiration. Graphs of the futures price-options price relationship based on longer times to expiration show a curved line rather than two straight lines. The longer the time to expiration, the shallower the curve.

One way to evaluate the wisdom of selling an option that is relatively closer to or farther from the money is to consider what might happen to spreads A, B, and C if the futures reach prices ranging from 305 to 330 cents per bushel at expiration. (Note that volatility ceases to be relevant at expiration. Further, volatility shifts matter less with call or put spreads than they do with many other kinds of option spreads.)

Exhibit 19.2 assumes the initial prices shown in Exhibit 19.1 and takes the futures price up in 5-cent increments. At expiration, of course, these calls will be worth the difference between the futures price and the strike price or nothing. That is, at a futures price of 310 cents per bushel, the 300 call is worth 10 cents per bushel, but the 320 and 330 calls are worth nothing.

The spread value at expiration is the net expiration value less the initial cost. That is, at a 305 cents per bushel futures price, the net spread value for all three spreads is 5 cents per bushel. In the case of spread A, 5 cents minus the 3.625 initial cost amounts to a 1.375 cents per bushel gain.

You can see that spreads B and C lost money at the 305 cents per bushel futures price but made money after that. You can also see that spread A flatlined at its 6.375 cents per bushel potential at a futures price of 310 cents per bushel and gained no more regardless of how high the futures price climbed. The other two spreads peaked at their upper strike price—just as the textbooks say they should.

Even though the textbook focus is on the expiration analysis, the expiration situation isn't especially realistic. It is almost always better to unwind trades of this kind well in advance of option expiration. Exhibit 19.3 provides the means to consider how these same three spreads might perform given futures price increases to 315 and 325 cents per bushel.

This series of examples illustrates the wisdom of paying more up front. The wider spreads outperformed the narrower both in terms of dollars earned and in terms of return on investment. You can let the sold option pay for more of the bought option if you like, but you limit the potential of your trade if you do—often by quite a lot.

WHEN INTEREST RATES ARE ABOUT TO RISE

In many cases, the situation that suggests the appropriateness of an option spread will lend itself to the use of longer-dated options. CBOT 10-year Treasury note options provide a useful example.

In the late spring of 2004, the market was poised for the Federal Reserve to start raising its fed funds target rate. Anticipating higher yields, and therefore lower fixed-income prices and rising implied volatility, bearish traders might have considered putting on bear put spreads. These

EXHIBIT 19.2

Expiration Results for Three Bull Call Spreads

a

Futures	295.25	305	310	315	320	325	330	335
300 Call	Buy –10.75	Sell 5	Sell 10	Sell 15	Sell 20	Sell 25	Sell 30	Sell 35
310 Call	Sell 7.125	Buy –10.70	Buy 0	Buy –5	Buy –10	Buy –15	Buy –20	Buy –25
Net	–3.625	5	10	10	10	10	10	10
Result		1.375	6.375	6.375	6.375	6.375	6.375	6.375

b

Futures	295.25	305	310	315	320	325	330	335
300 Call	Buy –10.75	Sell 5	Sell 10	Sell 15	Sell 20	Sell 25	Sell 30	Sell 35
320 Call	Sell 4.5	Buy 0	Buy 0	Buy 0	Buy 0	Buy –5	Buy –10	Buy –15
Net	–6.25	5	10	15	20	20	20	20
Result		–1.25	3.75	8.75	13.75	13.75	13.75	13.75

c

Futures	295.25	305	310	315	320	325	330	335
300 Call	Buy –10.75	Sell 5	Sell 10	Sell 15	Sell 20	Sell 25	Sell 30	Sell 35
330 Call	Sell 2.75	Buy 0	Buy 0	Buy 0	Buy 0	Buy 0	Buy 0	Buy –5
Net	–8	5	10	15	20	25	30	30
Result		–3	2	7	12	17	22	22

EXHIBIT 19.3

Evaluating the Performance of Three Corn Bull Call Spreads

Spread A

	Initial	Ending I	Result	ROI	Ending II	Result	ROI
Futures	295.25	315.00			325.00		
Days to exp.	40	26			26		
Implied volatility	33%	33%			33%		
300 Call	–10.75	19.875	9.125		27.75	17.00	
310 Call	7.125	–13.625	–6.50		–20.25	–13.125	
Net	–3.625	6.25	2.625	72.41%	7.50	3.875	106.90%

Spread B

	Initial	Ending I	Result	ROI	Ending II	Result	ROI
Futures	295.25	315.00			325.00		
Days to exp.	40	26			26		
Implied volatility	33%	33%			33%		
300 Call	–10.75	19.875	9.125		27.75	17.00	
320 Call	4.50	–8.875	–4.375		–14.00	–9.50	
Net	–6.25	11.00	4.75	76.00%	13.75	7.50	120.00%

Spread C

	Initial	Ending I	Result	ROI	Ending II	Result	ROI
Futures	295.25	315.00			325.00		
Days to exp.	40	26			26		
Implied volatility	33%	33%			33%		
300 Call	–10.75	19.875	9.125		27.75	17.00	
310 Call	2.75	–5.375	–2.625		–9.125	–6.375	
Net	–8.00	14.50	6.50	81.25%	18.627	10.625	132.81%

EXHIBIT 19.4

Prices and Risk Parameters for Five Puts on 10-Year U.S. Treasury Note Futures

Futures Price	Implied Volatility	Days to Expiration
109-06	8.3%	101

Strike price	Put price (64ths)	Put price (dollars)	Delta	Gamma	Theta	Vega
109	116	1,796.875	–0.4745	0.2605	–0.5988	14.6019
108	67	1,359.375	–0.3917	0.2514	–0.5786	14.0972
107	63	984.375	–0.3129	0.2319	–0.5339	13.0052
106	44	687.500	–0.2412	0.2041	–0.4700	11.4501
105	30	486.750	–0.1790	0.1712	–0.3941	9.6078

spreads require the buying of an at- or near-the-money put and the selling of a put that is farther from the money.

Assume that as you contemplated this spread in early May 2004, you would have seen that:

- September CBOT 10-year Treasury note futures were trading at 109-06.
- There were 101 days to September option expiration.
- The implied volatility for all strike prices was 8.3percent.

Given all this, the option prices and risk parameters for the 109 through 105 put strike prices would have been those shown in Exhibit 19.4.

Because of the long time to expiration and the relatively high implied volatility, these options may seem on the expensive side. The real issue is what kind of returns any of a variety of spreads can generate. Consider four possible bear put spreads using the five puts of Exhibit 19.4:

A: Buy the 109 put; sell the 108 put.

B: Buy the 109 put; sell the 107 put.

C: Buy the 109 put; sell the 106 put.

D: Buy the 109 put; sell the 105 put.

Assume further that after the passage of 14 days (so there are 87 days left to option expiration), the futures prices have fallen and the implied volatilities have risen as specified in Exhibits 19.5, 19.6, and 19.7.

EXHIBIT 19.5

Ending I

	Initial	Ending I
Futures price	109-06	108-12
Implied volatility	8.3%	8.8%
Days to expiration	101	87

Spread A

	Initial put price (64ths)	Put price (dollars)	Ending put price (64ths)	Put price (dollars)	Result (64ths)	Result (dollars)	ROI (%)
Buy 109 put	–115	–1,796.875	137	2,140.625	22	343.750	
Sell 108 put	87	1,359.375	–104	–1,625.000	–17	–265.625	
Spread	–28	–437.500	33	515.625	5	78.125	17.86

Spread B

	Initial put price (64ths)	Put price (dollars)	Ending put price (64ths)	Put price (dollars)	Result (64ths)	Result (dollars)	ROI (%)
Buy 109 put	–115	–1796.875	137	2,140.625	22	343.750	
Sell 108 put	63	984.375	–77	–1,203.125	–14	–218.750	
Spread	–52	–812.500	60	937.500	8	125.000	15.38

Spread C

	Initial put price (64ths)	Put price (dollars)	Ending put price (64ths)	Put price (dollars)	Result (64ths)	Result (dollars)	ROI (%)
Buy 109 put	–115	–1,796.875	137	2,140.625	22	343.750	
Sell 108 put	44	687.500	[illegible]	[illegible]	–10	[illegible]	
Spread	–71	–1,109.375	83	1,296.875	12	187.500	16.90

Continued

EXHIBIT 19.5

Ending I (*Continued*)

Spread D

	Initial put price (64ths)	Put price (dollars)	Ending put price (64ths)	Put price (dollars)	Result (64ths)	Result (dollars)	ROI (%)
Buy 109 put	–115	–1,796.875	137	2,140.625	22	343.750	
Sell 108 put	30	468.750	–37	–578.125	–7	–109.375	
Spread	–85	–1,328.125	100	1,562.500	15	234.375	17.65

These exhibits show how the four spreads can be expected to perform given each of three endings.

Ending I shows a 26/32 drop in the futures price and a 0.5 percentage point increase in implied volatility. In dollar terms, while selling the 108 put certainly paid down more of the 109 put price than selling any of the other strike prices did, this spread generated only a $78.125 net gain. Granted, the other spreads cost more initially, but they also generated larger dollar gains. In terms of return on investment (ROI), notice that spread A and the far more expensive spread D generate essentially the same bang for the buck. (Note that ROI is the result divided by the initial cost of the spread and multiplied by 100 to arrive at a percentage: 78.125 ÷ 437.50 = 0.1786, which multiplied by 100 is 17.86%.)

In dollar terms, the wider spreads are clearly preferable to the narrower, even though the ROIs don't make a convincing case for that conclusion.

Ending II shows both a larger drop in the futures price and a larger implied volatility increase. The results here begin to illustrate the wisdom of selling a strike price that is farther from the money, regardless of how much that increases the initial cost of the spread. The initial positions are exactly the same as those for Ending I, but the results are nothing like them.

Notice that again the wider the spread, the greater the dollar gain. Spread A earned back the initial cost plus 75 percent more, but Spread D earned back the initial cost plus 95 percent more. Note also that while Spreads B and C underperformed Spread A in ROI terms given Ending I, they outperform it on this basis given Ending II. Spread C outperforms Spread A by a great deal.

Ending III assumes a yet larger 5-14 futures price drop and a 1.1 percentage point implied volatility increase. Once again, the wider spreads outperform the narrower in both dollar and ROI terms, as Exhibit 19.7 shows.

EXHIBIT 19.6

Ending II

	Initial	Ending II
Futures price	109-06	105-08
Implied volatility	8.3%	9.0%
Days to expiration	101	87

Spread A

	Initial put price (64ths)	Put price (dollars)	Ending put price (64ths)	Put price (dollars)	Result (64ths)	Result (dollars)	ROI (%)
Buy 109 put	–115	–1,796.88	276	4,312.50	161	2,515.62	
Sell 108 put	87	1,359.38	–227	–3,546.88	–140	–2,187.50	
Spread	–28	–437.50	49	765.63	21	328.13	75.00

Spread B

	Initial put price (64ths)	Put price (dollars)	Ending put price (64ths)	Put price (dollars)	Result (64ths)	Result (dollars)	ROI (%)
Buy 109 put	–115	–1,796.88	276	4,312.50	161	2,515.62	
Sell 108 put	63	984.38	–183	–2,859.38	–120	–1,875.00	
Spread	–52	–812.50	93	1,453.13	41	640.63	78.85

Spread C

	Initial put price (64ths)	Put price (dollars)	Ending put price (64ths)	Put price (dollars)	Result (64ths)	Result (dollars)	ROI (%)
Buy 109 put	–115	–1,796.88	276	4,312.50	161	2,515.62	
Sell 108 put	44	687.50	–144	–2,250.00	–100	–1,562.50	
Spread	–71	–1,109.38	132	2,062.50	61	953.12	85.92

Continued

EXHIBIT 19.6

Ending II (*Continued*)

Spread D

	Initial put price (64ths)	Put price (dollars)	Ending put price (64ths)	Put price (dollars)	Result (64ths)	Result (dollars)	ROI (%)
Buy 109 put	–115	–1,796.88	276	4,312.50	161	2,515.62	
Sell 108 put	30	468.75	–110	–1,718.75	–80	–1,250.00	
Spread	–85	–1,328.13	166	2,593.75	81	1,265.62	95.29

EXHIBIT 19.7

Ending III

	Initial	Ending III
Futures price	109-06	103-24
Implied volatility	8.3%	9.4%
Days to expiration	101	87

Spread A

	Initial put price (64ths)	Put price (dollars)	Ending put price (64ths)	Put price (dollars)	Result (64ths)	Result (dollars)	ROI (%)
Buy 109 put	–115	–1,796.88	358	5593.75	243	3,796.88	
Sell 108 put	87	1,359.38	–304	–4,750.00	–140	–2,390.63	
Spread	–28	–437.50	54	843.75	21	406.26	92.86

EXHIBIT 19.7

Ending III (*Continued*)

Spread B

	Initial put price (64ths)	Put price (dollars)	Ending put price (64ths)	Put price (dollars)	Result (64ths)	Result (dollars)	ROI (%)
Buy 109 put	–115	–1,796.88	358	5,593.75	243	3,796.88	
Sell 108 put	63	984.38	–254	–3,968.75	–191	–2,984.38	
Spread	–52	–812.50	104	1,625.00	52	812.50	100.00

Spread C

	Initial put price (64ths)	Put price (dollars)	Ending put price (64ths)	Put price (dollars)	Result (64ths)	Result (dollars)	ROI (%)
Buy 109 put	–115	–1,796.88	358	5,593.75	243	3,796.88	
Sell 108 put	44	687.50	–208	–3,250.00	–164	–2,562.50	
Spread	–71	–1,109.38	150	2,343.75	79	12,34.38	111.27

Spread D

	Initial put price (64ths)	Put price (dollars)	Ending put price (64ths)	Put price (dollars)	Result (64ths)	Result (dollars)	ROI (%)
Buy 109 put	–115	–1,796.88	358	5,593.75	243	3,796.88	
Sell 108 put	30	468.75	–166	–2,593.75	–136	–2,125.00	
Spread	–85	–1,328.13	192	3,000.00	107	1,671.88	125.88

A WORD OF CAUTION

Options with more time to expiration cost more than options with less time to expiration, all else the same. Further, the wider the spread, the greater the initial cost. These examples illustrate that these extra costs aren't necessarily a bad thing. Both the corn and 10-year Treasury note option trades show that trade potential, for this kind of spread, seems to vary directly with initial cost.

This claim has limitations. If you sell an option that is too far out of the money, you will reach a point of diminishing returns. The sold option will accomplish so little, both in the way of reducing the initial cost and in terms of somewhat lessening exposure to time decay, that you might as well have traded an outright put or call.

CHAPTER 20

More on Bear Put Spreads

Expressing a Bearish Opinion but with Reservations

One aspect of options that people often seem to overlook is that they can be combined in spreads that allow the expression of various degrees of market sentiment—or, perhaps, various degrees of confidence in your market outlook. Futures admit only two sentiments—bullish or bearish. The trouble with this is that you aren't always that sure. When you find the arguments for a downtrending market largely persuasive but still have reservations, you may want to consider trading a bear put spread.

The mirror image of a bull call spread, a bear put spread involves the buying of a put that is at or near the money and the selling of a put that is far enough out of the money to have a delta in the 0.20 to 0.30 range. (Of course, put deltas are negative when you buy the put and positive when you sell the put.)

HORSES FOR COURSES–LOCATING THE RIGHT SITUATION

You might see CBOT mini-sized Dow futures trading at 10,461 with implied volatility trading at 16 percent. While this level may be the result of a nice rally, the recent economic news might suggest a slowing economy and weaker corporate earnings. All in all, this might seem like a good time to sell the market, which you can do in several ways:

- When you have more than ordinary confidence in your market forecast, the best way to sell the market is probably to sell CBOT mini-sized Dow futures.

- When you have fairly strong confidence in your market forecast but still have small residual doubt, you can buy a put option on CBOT mini-sized Dow futures.
- When you are guardedly bearish—are leaning in a bearish direction but have serious reservations that a surprise development could push prices up rather than down—you can trade a bear put spread using these options.

Take the first possibility in which you sell a futures contract. Suppose that after 21 days the Dow reaches one of four levels—10,063, 9,665, 10,859, or 11,257. At 16 percent implied volatility and with a 21-day trade horizon, these index levels are one and two standard deviations below and above 10,461.

When you sell futures, the trade will generate positive results when the market goes down but negative results when the market goes up. Further, the futures gains or losses are symmetrical. When the market drops by 300 points, you will gain that much. When the market rallies by 300 points, you will lose that much.

When you buy a put—e.g., the 10,400 strike price put—you gain when the market goes down but lose when it rallies. However, the gains will be smaller and the losses will be much smaller. In fact, they will never exceed the price paid for the option. Assume you paid 240 index points for the 10,400 put with 60 days to option expiration and unwound the position 21 days later. Exhibit 20.1 enumerates the gains and losses to such a short futures position and to the put position at each of the four index levels mentioned. Note that all prices are given in index points, not dollars. To translate these into dollars, multiply index values by the $5 contract multiplier.

EXHIBIT 20.1

Contrasting Sold Futures and Bought Put Results

Sell Futures			Buy 10,400 Put			
Ending Futures Prices	Initial Futures Price	Futures Results	Ending Put Prices	Initial Put Price	Put Result	Put-Futures Difference
9,665	10,461	796	753	240	513	–283
10,063	10,461	398	422	240	182	–216
10,859	10,461	–398	64	240	–176	222
11,257	10,461	–796	16	240	–224	572

The minus signs in the Results columns are losses. The minus signs in the Put-Futures Difference column are indications of when the put underperforms or outperforms the futures position. If the index falls to 9,665, the put will earn 283 points less than the futures, hence the –283. If the index rallies to 11,257, the put will lose 572 points less than the futures, and to lose less is to outperform the futures. When traders have less than total faith in their forecasts, or limited ability to weather losses, it often seems worthwhile to accept a limited upside in exchange for a greatly reduced downside.

The 10,400–9,900 bear put spread reduces your upside participation rather severely, to be sure, but it also reduces the downside potential to a small fraction of the downside potential of the futures trade. The downside part of the picture is the primary motivation for trading these spreads. When you simply cannot tolerate large losses, however unlikely you think they may be, the put spread can be a useful trading tool.

STRUCTURING THE TRADE

This trade structure is exactly like the structure of the trades discussed in Chapter 19. Typically you will buy a put that is close to the money. With the stock index futures contract trading at 10,461, the 10,400 put is the closest to the money and so the logical choice.

Because there is no free lunch (as is illustrated in the discussion of bull call and bear put spreads in Chapter 19), you must be careful about the choice of the strike price to sell. When you place it too close to the strike price of the option you buy, you will lower the cost of the spread, but you will also lower its earning potential. A good rule of thumb is the 0.20 to 0.30 delta rule. The option you sell should have a delta in that range. That is probably the best cost-performance trade-off.

Some books on options suggest counting strike prices. They advise selling an option that is three strike prices lower—or two, or four. At different times to expiration, these strike prices can have very different deltas in some markets. You may be limiting your trade in a way you won't like. The delta rule is a better idea.

To illustrate, consider how two trade structures might perform in the case where you put on the trade with 60 days to option expiration and unwind it 21 days later with futures trading at 10,063. First, assume that you bought the 10,400 put on CBOT mini-sized Dow futures and sold the 10,000 put. Exhibit 20.2 shows the details of this trade.

The minus signs in the two Price columns indicate payouts for bought options. Minus signs in the Result column indicate losses. The

EXHIBIT 20.2

Bear Put Spread Details and Results

CBOT minisized Dow Futures	10,461		10,063		
Days to expiration	60		39		
Implied volatility	16%		16%		
Put strike price	**Price**	**Delta**	**Price**	**Result**	**ROI**
December 10,400 put	–240	–0.45	422	182	
December 10,000 put	95	0.23	–179	-84	
Bear put spread net	–145		243	98	
Bear put spread $ net	–725.00		1,215.00	490.00	67.59%

EXHIBIT 20.3

A Wider Spread Generates Larger Returns

CBOT minisized Dow Futures	10,461		10,063		
Days to expiration	60		39		
Implied volatility	16%		16%		
Put strike price	**Price**	**Delta**	**Price**	**Result**	**ROI**
December 10,400 put	–240	–0.45	422	182	
December 9,900 put	72	0.23	–136	–64	
Bear put spread net	–168		286	118	
Bear put spread $ net	–840.00		1,430.00	590.00	70.24%

values in the Bear put spread net row are the sums of the values in each column, and the Bear put spread $ net row translates these net amounts into dollar values by multiplying index points by $5.

Notice that the sold 10,000 put exerts considerable drag on the earnings of the spread. Despite this, the $490 gain seems solid enough, and so does the 67.59 percent return on investment (ROI). Remember, the ROI is the dollar result divided by the dollar price paid for the spread (490 ÷ 725).

Second, consider what the result of selling the 9,900 strike price would be. Exhibit 20.3 makes the same assumptions as Exhibit 20.2 except for the use of this 9,900 put.

You can see that this spread cost slightly more to put on, but it made more in both dollar and ROI terms. This is a significant difference in per-

EXHIBIT 20.4

The Futures, Put, Put Spread Contrast

Ending Futures Prices	Futures Results	Put Results	Spread Results	Spread-Futures Difference
9,665	796	513	243	–553
10,063	398	182	118	–280
10,859	–398	–176	–112	286
11,257	–796	–224	–153	643

formance, and these are both appropriate structures in terms of initial delta levels. You can imagine that, say, a 10,400–10,200 spread would cost very little and earn even less.

This diminished result might have a different aspect when you consider how this spread might perform when the stock market rallies rather than drops. Exhibit 20.4 reprises the futures and options results of Exhibit 20.1 and adds the results that you can expect from a 10,400–9,900 bear put spread given the four ending stock index futures prices used in the earlier exhibit and the assumptions that shape these option spread trades.

The bear put spread earns considerably less than either the futures or the put when the market drops. Two aspects of this prompt people to use these spreads despite these reduced earnings. The most obvious reason for using this kind of spread involves what happens if the market rallies against any of these positions. The spread trader loses 643 index points less than the futures trader. Less obvious, but important to consider, is the fact that the spread trader can trade two spreads for 96 index points more than the cost of one put. A stock index futures move to 9,665 would earn two spreads 486 index points which is only 27 points less than one put would earn. This may be worth thinking about when you evaluate the question of whether to spread or not to spread.

THE PRICE-TIME INTERACTION (AN ADVANCED IDEA)

Your market outlook is not the only factor to consider when you trade option spreads. You may have a bearish outlook but with serious reservations, and this may lead you to the brink of choosing to trade a bear put spread. Fine. But check the time factor before you go past the brink. Depending on where you are on the days to option expiration timeline, these spreads can generate somewhat different results, even if the market behaves in the same way each time. You don't want this to surprise you, so it will be worthwhile to consider why this may be the case.

Time decay and the mechanics of option price change interact in an interesting way and in slightly different ways depending on where you are on the time to expiration timeline and on which strike prices you use. Also, options that are near the money react to these factors very differently from options that are deeply in or out of the money. A somewhat contrived set of circumstances and trades using options on 10-year Treasury note futures will be helpful in isolating the relevant phenomena.

Assume that 10-year Treasury note futures are trading at 112-10 at the start of each trade and at 108-10 when the trades are unwound after the passage of 21 days. Assume, also, that the implied volatilities for all the puts involved are 7.5 percent throughout (this is unlikely ever to be the case, but making this assumption helps to isolate the interaction of price change and time decay). This 108-10 price is approximately two standard deviations below the starting price, given the 21-day time horizon and the 7.5 percent implied volatility.

One further assumption is that one of these trades was put on with 90 days to option expiration and unwound with 69 days to expiration. The second was put on with 60 days to expiration and unwound with 39 days to expiration. The third was put on with 30 days to expiration and unwound with 9 days to expiration. Exhibit 20.5 shows how you can expect each of these three trades to perform given these assumptions.

As elsewhere, these Treasury option prices are given in 64ths. On a quote screen, the 97/64 price of the 112 put in Exhibit 20.5a would be shown as 1-33 (or, sometimes, 1'33). The dollar values in the Bear put spread $ net row are the result of dividing the Bear put spread net value by 64 and multiplying the result by 1,000 (e.g., 46 ÷ 64 = 0.71875, 0.71875 × 1,000 = 718.75).

Notice that the shorter the time to option expiration when the trade is put on, the better the result of the bear put spread.

The first option pricing factor to consider is delta. The delta of an option indicates the ratio of option price change to futures price change. When you see an option with a –0.46 delta, you know that the option price will move roughly 4.5/32 for every 10/32 futures price move. The price of an option with a –0.20 delta will move roughly 2/32 for every 10/32 futures price move. Also, as an option moves more deeply into the money, the delta will approach 1.00. This tells you that the option is trading more and more like a futures contract. That is, when an option has a 0.998 delta, its price will move essentially one-for-one with the futures price.

EXHIBIT 20.5

Bear Put Spreads Ranging across Time

a

10-Year Treasury Note Futures Price	112-10		108-10		
Days to option expiration	90		69		
Implied volatility	7.5%		7.5%		
Put strike price	**Price (64ths)**	**Delta**	**Price (64ths)**	**Result (64ths)**	**ROI**
Buy 1 112 put	–97	–0.4618	254	157	
Sell 1 109 put	31	0.2049	–114	–83	
Bear put spread net	–66	–0.2569	140	74	
Bear put spread $ net	–1,031.25		2,187.50	1,156.25	1.12%

b

10-Year Treasury Note Futures Price	112-10		108-10		
Days to option expiration	60		39		
Implied volatility	7.5%		7.5%		
Put strike price	**Price (64ths)**	**Delta**	**Price (64ths)**	**Result (64ths)**	**ROI**
Buy 1 112 put	–77	–0.4568	243	166	
Sell 1 109 put	18	0.1585	–92	–74	
Bear put spread net	–59	–0.2983	151	92	
Bear put spread $ net	921.875		2,359.375	1,437.50	1.56%

c

10-Year Treasury Note Futures Price	112-10		108-10		
Days to option expiration	30		9		
Implied volatility	7.5%		7.5%		
Put strike price	**Price (64ths)**	**Delta**	**Price (64ths)**	**Result (64ths)**	**ROI**
Buy 1 112 put	–52	–0.4439	236	184	
Sell 1 109 put	6	0.0802	–59	–53	
Bear put spread net	–46	–0.3637	177	131	
Bear put spread $ net	–718.75		2,765.625	2,046.875	2.85%

EXHIBIT 20.6

Tracking Changing Deltas

	Initial	Ending	Initial	Ending	Initial	Ending
Futures price	112-10	108-10	112-10	108-10	112-10	108-10
Days to expiration	90	69	60	39	30	9
112 Put	–0.4618	–0.8428	–0.4568	–0.9115	–0.4439	–0.9980
109 Put	–0.2049	–0.5696	–0.1585	–0.5965	–0.0802	–0.7023

When you buy an option, an increasing delta is to your advantage. When you sell an option, an increasing delta is a disadvantage. Exhibit 20.6 displays the deltas of the 112 and 109 puts on 10-year Treasury note futures as they would have been at the beginning and end of each of these three trades.

Notice that the initial deltas of the 112 put are close to the same at 90, 60, and 30 days. The deltas of the 109 put are a different story. As the time shortens, so do these deltas, drastically. Further, this two standard deviation price change causes a remarkable change in all the deltas. At 69 days, the delta of the 112 put is slightly over –0.84. At 39 days, the delta of the 112 put is over –0.91. This option is now very close to indistinguishable from a futures contract in terms of how it will trade. And at nine days, the delta of this put is essentially 1.00. Keep in mind that these delta pairs represent states at the ends of a process. These changes in deltas will have been gradual. What matters is that as the futures price dropped, the 112 put traded more and more like a futures contract. These delta changes served to maximize the price changes of the 112 put which, to a buyer of this option, is helpful.

The deltas of the 109 put for each time pair increased as well. Yet the deltas at 69 and 39 days are only slightly different and only slightly greater than the –0.50 delta of an at-the-money put. Even at nine days, the delta of the 109 put remains far from as large as the 112 put delta. This indicates that the prices of the 109 put at the various times to expiration are increasing but not as fast as the prices of the 112 put. An option seller wants as little price change as possible, so these smaller delta changes are also helpful.

Of course, time decay works against option price increases. This is why option buyers think of time decay as an unfriendly force and option sellers think of it as a friendly force. A bear put spread trader is both a buyer and a seller. You might think you can't have it both ways on this

EXHIBIT 20.7

Tracking Changing Thetas

	Initial	Ending	Initial	Ending	Initial	Ending
Futures price	112-10	108-10	112-10	108-10	112-10	108-10
Days to expiration	90	69	60	39	30	9
112 Put	–0.5888	–0.3857	–0.7226	–0.3399	–1.0240	–0.0187
109 Put	–0.4218	–0.6418	–0.4398	–0.8454	–0.3805	–1.6015

matter of time decay, but you can. Exhibit 20.7 lays out the thetas of these puts at the two futures prices and various times to expiration. Theta, remember, is the option risk parameter that indicates how sensitive the price of an option is to time decay. A larger theta indicates that this option will be affected more by a specified time change than will an option with a smaller theta.

Notice that during each trade, the theta of the 112 put decreases. In fact, at a 108-10 futures price and with nine days to expiration, the theta of the 112 put all but evaporates. This option is so deeply in the money that time decay cannot harm it much at all. This is another aspect of what it means to say that at this point on the option timeline and at this futures price, this option is trading like a futures contract. Futures prices are insensitive to time as long as the contract is trading, and this option price is largely insensitive to futures price change as well.

In contrast, the theta of the 109 put increases during each trade. Notice that between 30 and 9 days, the theta of the 109 put quadrupled. Between 60 and 39 days, the theta of the 109 put almost doubled. These large increases in theta tell you that time decay is becoming more and more of a factor for the 109 puts, as opposed to the 112 puts where it becomes less and less of a factor. This increasing time decay will overcome more and more of the effect of the increasing deltas of the 109 put. For an option seller, this is more good news.

In sum, the 109 deltas increase but to lower levels than those reached by the 112 put deltas. Combined with that, sellers of 109 puts can expect time decay to beat back a large part of the effect of the increasing deltas. Clearly, the dynamics of price change and time decay interact in ways that seem to help both legs of these option spreads, but they seem to help more when the spread is put on with 60 days or less to option expiration.

A FABRIC OF TRADE-OFFS.

The world of options is no more perfect than any other world you may encounter. The options world is a fabric of trade-offs, and it often seems that you can find as many ideas about what constitutes the optimal trade-off as you can find people willing to offer advice about trading.

This consideration of how deltas and thetas interact might seem to suggest that bear put spreads are appropriate only close to option expiration. That isn't the intention. Rather, this discussion is meant to suggest a good way to think about the time factor in these trades and to illustrate the importance of this interaction of option pricing factors.

Traders must consider what the market may do in the next period of time, decide how much trading capital they are willing to risk on any one trade, and formulate a trading goal. As long as this is done with an awareness of the delta-theta interaction, among other things, any time horizon may be appropriate. This is up to each trader. This discussion calls this factor to your attention and provides a framework for thinking about it that may be helpful. Once you see this, you can very possibly do the necessary thinking in a very informal way.

A WORD OF CAUTION

Bear put spreads can be useful trading tools. They limit your exposure to loss, they allow you to express degrees of confidence in your outlook, and they allow you to capitalize on certain option phenomena apart from what the underlying market may do.

When considering this kind of trade, in any market, you must be aware that placing strike prices too close together can seriously limit your earnings potential. At best, these trades will generate only modest results, and you don't want them to be too modest. However, shrewdly managed, bear put spreads can produce a steady stream of modest returns for low risk.

CHAPTER 21

A Fed Funds Synthetic Binary Option

Expressing a Contrary Opinion

Fed watching has become a major pastime in recent years. The Fed (technically, the Federal Open Market Committee, or FOMC, but in popular usage, the Fed) only directly influences the overnight rate at which bank members of the U.S. Federal Reserve System borrow and lend excess reserves. Still, what the Fed does sends ripples throughout U.S. interest rate markets. U.S. Treasury yields will react to a Fed move, and so will mortgage rates. As a result, Fed policy has become a matter of interest to more than just investment professionals. In the weeks and days before a Fed meeting, a common topic of conversation concerns what the Fed might do and what the implications of the expected move might be.

One useful way to express your opinion about what the Fed may or may not do is to use CBOT Fed funds options to structure a synthetic binary option. Typically traded in the over-the-counter derivatives markets, binary options offer only two outcomes. If an anticipated event occurs, the options generate a payout. If the event does not occur, the option does nothing. This is perfect for the Fed meeting situation. The Fed either will shift its Fed funds target rate or will not—no in between.

A binary option is really nothing more than a call or put spread with a very narrow strike price interval. Because of this narrowness, the spread has the potential for only a modest payout, but it doesn't cost much to put on. This runs contrary to the earlier advice to beware of choosing strike prices that are too close together. Granted, this limits the potential of the trade, but in the face of uncertainty, it may be worthwhile to give a little in that regard in exchange for having so little trading capital at risk.

One thing to be cautious about in considering a trade based on what the Fed may do is whether the anticipated change has already been priced into the market. If it has, there is no point in making the trade. Fortunately, the Fed funds futures market can help you assess the market situation.

WHAT THE MARKET SAYS

Listening to a market report in the days or weeks prior to a fed meeting, you may hear the commentator say that the Fed funds futures market is pricing in a 78 percent probability that the Fed will boost its fund funds target rate 25 bps, or whatever the case may be. These people are using probability math, and you can do the same thing.

Consider the situation on April 28, 2004, roughly a week before the May 4 Fed meeting. The 98.99 May Fed funds futures price implied a 1.01 percent Fed funds rate for May (100 minus the price gives the implied fed funds rate). The target rate was then 1.00 percent. The Fed had been inactive for many months, and the market expected the Fed to leave the 1.00 percent target rate unchanged at the May meeting.

To see what the futures market implies about the probability of a move, you can use a formula that isn't as tricky as it may look:

$$1.00\% \times 4/31 + [1.25\%p + 1.00\%(1 - p)] \times 27/31 = 1.01\%$$

In this formulation, p is the probability that the Fed will raise the target rate to 1.25 percent and $(1 - p)$ is the probability that it will leave the target unchanged. The 4/31 notation is the number of premeeting days in May when the target rate is known, and the 27/31 notation indicates the number of days for which the target rate is not yet known. It is possible, but unnecessary, to make this look more algebraic.

Solving for p, you can discover that p equals 0.0459. That is, there is a 4.59 percent probability that the Fed will raise the target rate 25 bps at the May meeting and a 95.41 percent probability that the Fed will not change the target rate at that meeting.

In case your algebra is a bit rusty, here is the step-by-step process for solving for p. First, convert 4/31 and 27/31 into decimal form by dividing 4 by 31 to get 0.129 and by dividing 27 by 31 to get 0.871. Next, rearrange the term $1.00\%(1 - p)$ into $-1.00\%p + 1.00\%$. These two steps result in this array:

$$1.00\% \times 0.129 + [1.25\%p - 1.00\%p + 1.00\%] \times 0.871 = 1.01\%$$

Now multiply 1.00 percent by 0.129 and the three terms inside the brackets by 0.871 to produce this array:

$$0.129 + 1.0888p - 0.871p + 0.871 = 1.01$$

Move the 0.129 and the 0.871 to the other side of the equals sign by changing their signs to produce:

$$1.0888p - 0.871p = 1.01 - 0.129 - 0.871$$

Do the subtraction to produce:

$$0.2178p = 0.01$$

Divide both sides by 0.2178 to produce:

$$p = 0.0459$$

That accounts for the 4.59 percent probability claim. The probability that the Fed will take no action is the result of subtracting 4.59 from 100, or 95.41 percent.

Take another situation that promises to be more interesting. In late July 2004, the August Fed funds futures were trading at 98.59, which implied a 1.41 percent August Fed funds rate. At its June 30, 2004, meeting, the Fed had boosted the target rate to 1.25 percent, and the market expected another 25 bp boost at the August 10 Fed meeting. To assign a probability to that move, you can solve for p given this version of the formula:

$$1.25\% \times 10/31 + [1.50\%p + 1.25\%(1 - p)] - 21/31 = 1.41\%$$

Following the same steps as before, this becomes:

$$1.25 - 0.3226 + [1.50p - 1.25p + 1.25] \times 0.6774 = 1.41\%$$
$$0.4033 + 1.0161p - 0.8468p + 0.8468 = 1.41\%$$
$$1.0161p - 0.8468p = 1.41 - 0.4033 - 0.8468$$
$$0.1693p = 0.1599$$
$$\mathrm{p} = 0.1599/0.1693 = 0.9445$$

At this point, the Fed funds futures market assigned a 94.45 percent probability that the Fed would raise its target rate 25 bps at the August 10 meeting. The limitation of this calculation is that it assumes that the Fed has two choices—to move the rate as specified or do nothing. In fact, the Fed can work from a richer menu. It can boost the target rate 25 bps, 50 bps, or even 75 bps. And it can do nothing or lower the target rate. Still, this calculation can help you read the market.

A QUICK AND DIRTY MARKET READ

The Fed funds futures spreads can help you arrive at more or less the same point as the probability calculation. The task is to look at the month-to-month spreads between the fed funds rates that the futures prices imply.

To find a futures implied rate, remember, simply subtract the futures price from 100. The 98.74 August futures price in Exhibit 21.1 implies a 1.26 percent Fed funds rate (100 – 98.74). To find the spreads, subtract the April implied rate from the May implied rate, the May from the June, and so on down. A spread between 1 and 10 bps (0.01 to 0.10) is the result of normal compounding and yield curve effect and indicates that the market expects no action. Spreads greater than 10 bps indicate that the market expects a move. It is not so much the futures price or the implied Fed funds rate that tells the story as it is the dislocation in the spreads. If the futures prices in Exhibit 21.1 were 99.00, 98.92, 98.84, 98.76, for instance, this would indicate that the market expects no move. These spreads are all 8 bps and well within the normal range. What would be interesting would be a series of 8 bp spreads and then a skip to 16 bps.

Also, it matters where in the month the Fed meeting is. In 2004, there were meetings on May 6, June 30, August 10, and September 21. Because the June and September meetings were late in the month, the result of a Fed move would not affect that month's Fed funds price enough to matter, so the relevant spread for the June meeting is the June–July. The August meeting is early enough that the relevant spread is the July–August.

Exhibit 21.1 shows the range of Fed funds prices, implied Fed funds rates, and month-to-month spreads that were in the market on April 28, 2004.

The 16 bp July–August spread indicates that even at this early date the market was expecting the Fed to raise its Fed funds target rate at the August 10, 2004, meeting. The 8 bp June–July spread suggests that the market expected no move at the June 30 meeting.

The market consensus began to shift shortly after the May 4 meeting, as Exhibit 21.2 shows. The May 4 fed statement, though hardly a model of clarity, suggested that concerns about the employment situation were

EXHIBIT 21.1

The Fed Funds Futures Market–4/28/04

Futures Month	Futures Price	Fed Funds Implied Rate	Spread
April	99.00	1.00	
May	98.99	1.01	0.01
June	98.98	1.02	0.01
July	98.90	1.10	0.08
August	98.74	1.26	0.16

abating and concerns about inflation buildup were on the rise, so the Fed could see its way to a measured approach to heading off inflation. Exactly what that meant, nobody was sure, but it seemed to be a call for a tightening of monetary policy during the summer months.

The 15 bp July–August spread of Exhibit 21.2 indicates that the expectation of a Fed move at the August meeting was still in the market, but the 12 bp June–July spread suggests that the market was beginning to see economic indicators that foretold faster than expected inflation buildup and that it now was leaning toward a Fed move in June and another in August.

A very few days later, the signs of inflation buildup looked stronger and motivated a stronger reaction from the market. Notice the June–July and July–August spreads in Exhibit 21.3.

The fact that the June–July spread had ballooned to 19 bps indicates that the market was now all but certain that the Fed would feel compelled to raise the Fed funds target rate at the June 30 meeting. Further, the 98.78 July

EXHIBIT 21.2

The Fed Funds Futures Market–5/6/04

Futures Month	Futures Price	Fed Funds Implied Rate	Spread
May	98.99	1.01	
June	98.98	1.02	0.01
July	98.86	1.14	0.12
August	98.71	1.29	0.15
September	98.59	1.41	0.12

EXHIBIT 21.3

The Fed Funds Futures Market–5/11/04

Futures Month	Futures Price	Fed Funds Implied Rate	Spread
May	98.99	1.01	
June	98.97	1.03	0.02
July	98.78	1.22	0.19
August	98.57	1.43	0.21
September	98.40	1.60	0.17

EXHIBIT 21.4

The Fed Funds Futures Market

Futures Month	Futures Price	Fed Funds Implied Rate	Spread
May	99.00	1.00	
June	98.99	1.01	0.01
July	98.77	1.23	0.22
August	98.56	1.44	0.21
September	98.41	1.59	0.15

futures price indicates that the June move is already in the market. At this point, May 11, making a trade to try to take advantage of the 99.00 to 98.75 (or a 1 to 1.25 percent shift in the Fed funds target rate) ceased to make sense.

Going forward, the June–July spread ranged between 0.19 and 0.22 bps. Exhibit 21.4 shows the situation on May 21, 2004.

Yet this doesn't mean that no trade makes sense. Given a steady stream of economic reports calling attention to troubling Consumer Price Index (CPI) data, rapidly rising industrial commodities prices, or rampaging gasoline prices, you might have begun to wonder whether a 25 bp move would be enough. You might have begun to wonder whether the flow of economic data during the rest of May and into June would force the Fed to make a 50 bp move at the June meeting, and perhaps another 25 bp move in August.

STRUCTURING A SYNTHETIC BINARY OPTION

A 50 bp fed move at the June meeting would drive the July futures price down toward 98.50. Because this was definitely not in the market as of May 21, a July Fed funds put spread becomes a possible trade.

The CBOT Fed funds options trade in quarter basis point ticks (a quarter basis point is 0.0025 in decimals), and the dollar value of one-quarter basis point in this market is $10.4175. Further, these options trade in 6.25 bp strike price intervals. That is, between the 98.75 and 98.50 strike prices, there are three more strike prices: 98.6875, 98.6250, and 98.5625. (Some quote services round these to three decimal places: e.g., 98.688 or 98.623.) These narrower strike price intervals lend themselves to the structuring of synthetic binary options.

Given that the move to 98.75 is already mostly in the market and that you see at least some chance of a 50 bp move, you might buy the July 98.75 Fed funds put and sell the July 98.6875 put. Exhibit 21.5 shows the initial market conditions as of May 21, 2004.

Consider two possible outcomes. At the June meeting, the Fed may raise the target rate to 1.25 percent. This would result in almost no change in the July futures price. On the other hand, the Fed might raise its target rate 50 bps, to 1.50 percent. In this case, the July futures price will immediately drop toward 98.50. Exhibits 21.6a and 21.6b show what kinds of results you should see on July 1, the day after the Fed meeting.

Exhibit 21.6a shows that the initial cost of this spread would have been three-fourths of a bp on May 21 (0.0075 in decimals). At $10.4175

EXHIBIT 21.5

Initial Market Conditions–Fed Funds Puts

Futures Price	98.765		
Days to Expiration	70		
Put Strike Price	**Put Price**	**Delta**	**Implied Volatility**
98.7500	0.0350	0.46	19.42%
98.6875	0.0275	0.32	26.84%
98.6250	0.0175	0.22	28.94%
98.5625	0.0075	0.11	27.49%

EXHIBIT 21.6a

Ending I, Given a 25 bp Fed Move

	Initial	**Ending I**	**Result I**
Futures Price	98.765	98.765	
Implied volatility	(see Exhibit 21.5, col. 4)	No change	
Days to expiration	70	29	
Strike price	**Put price**	**Put price**	
Buy 98.75 put	–0.0350	0.0200	–0.0150
Sell 98.6875 put	0.0275	–0.0125	0.0150
Spread	–0.0075	0.0075	0.0000

EXHIBIT 21.6b

Ending II, Given a 50 bp Fed Move

	Initial	Ending II	Result II
Futures price	98.765	98.50	
Implied volatility	(see Exhibit 21.5, col. 4)	No change	
Days to expiration	70	29	
Strike price	**Put price**	**Put price**	
Buy 98.75 put	–0.0350	0.2500	0.2150
Sell 98.6875 put	0.0275	–0.1900	–0.1625
Spread	–0.0075	0.0600	0.0525

a quarter bp, this amounts to \$31.2525. Notice that if the Fed does only what is already in the market, this spread will do nothing—as indicated by the zero in the result column. However, if the Fed surprises the market with a 50 bp move, Exhibit 21.6b shows that the spread can earn 5.25 bps (0.0525). This translates into \$218.7675 (21 quarter bps times \$10.4175).

A WORD OF CAUTION

The assumptions of this discussion do not describe all the possible outcomes. For instance, if the Fed were to make the expected 25 bp move, the July price could move to exactly 98.75 or even overshoot the mark slightly—say, to 98.745 or 98.74. This would affect the result of the Ending I situation slightly, and the spread could generate a small loss. Remember, though, that the maximum possible loss for spreads of this kind is the initial price paid—in this case \$31.2525 for a one-lot spread.

Also this discussion makes no mention of implied volatility changes. A repricing of the options with a range of implied volatility increases showed almost no difference in the results. Because of that, it seemed permissible to ignore that factor.

IN SUM

While \$218.77 is not a large amount of money, the 700 percent ROI of Exhibit 21.6b indicates that this trade delivers a lot of bang for not many

EXHIBIT 21.7

Accounting for Size

Position Size	Amount at Risk	Potential Gain
1-lot	$31.2525	$218.7675
10-lot	$312.5250	$2,187.6750
100-lot	$3,125.2500	$21,876.7500
1,000-lot	$31,252.5000	$218,767.5000

bucks. Further, the small cost of initiating this spread makes it possible to trade spreads of this kind in size. Exhibit 21.7 takes the cost and the potential result up in multiples of 10.

The arithmetic of Exhibit 21.7 is trivial, but the potential results assuredly are not.

CHAPTER 22

A Flock of Option Butterflies

A Safer Way to Sell Volatility

Several option spreads have rather fanciful names. *Butterfly, condor, iron butterfly,* and *alligator* spread are a few that you may see mentioned. All these are multilegged spreads and, to some market users, seem designed primarily to generate fees for brokers. This isn't entirely fair (or entirely unfair). Yet there are times when, say, a butterfly spread can be a useful trading tool.

THE BASIC IDEA

You can structure a butterfly entirely of puts, entirely of calls, or with puts and calls mixed. This discussion focuses on either-or butterflies. The structure is the same in either the put or the call case. You choose three strike prices at equal intervals and buy one each of the highest and lowest strike price options and sell two of the middle strike price options. The thicker, two-option part of the spread is the body of the butterfly, and the outlying bought options are the wings. Apparently, early options traders thought the expiration analysis payout diagram looked like a butterfly coming toward them. This takes about the same amount of imagination as looking at the constellations of the night sky. You may remember, as a child, saying, "That's a bear? Come on."

The basic idea is that you think futures will be at or close to the middle strike price at option expiration. You also expect the options you sell to expire valueless, or very nearly so. This will enable you to keep most of the price you collect when you initially sell them. Because this is a key part of the strategy, you want to trade butterflies during the period of maximum time decay—the last three or four weeks before expiration—and to hold these spreads in place until option expiration.

Importantly, butterflies are primarily volatility trades. The body of the trade is the pair of sold options, and, always, severe time decay is the option seller's friend. Also, you sell options when implied volatilities are trading above the long-term median historical volatility and you have reason to believe that the volatility in question will revert to this median level, or even below it. All this leads to a key notion for butterfly traders: You should trade butterflies only when you are comfortable with the idea of being at short volatility.

When you sell options, you can expect large losses if the market moves at all far from the strike price that you sell. This is why you buy the wings of the butterfly. These two options limit the loss potential of these spreads to the net price paid. When the futures trade above the highest strike price or below the lowest strike price, the bought options earn enough to offset the losses the sold options are making. So a butterfly is a sold option (two, actually) with a kind of safety net around the edges.

A YELLOW BUTTERFLY FOR WHEN CORN MIGHT TRADE LOWER

Consider the corn futures market as it might have appeared to you during the summer of 2004. Corn futures prices had been rather high earlier in the year, well over $3 per bushel. Suppose that with 21 days to the expiration of the July options, July futures were trading at $2.31 per bushel and that implied volatility was trading at 24 percent at every option strike price.

This 24 percent implied volatility is close to the historical median for this time of year, but declining prices tend to reduce implied volatility in the grain markets. Because of this, you may well have decided that this was not a bad time to be at short volatility.

Suppose, further, that your sense of the corn market was that the futures price would meet strong support at $2.20 per bushel and that it would be unlikely to stray very far from that level by the expiration of these options. This is a situation tailor-made for a put butterfly.

Given these data and suppositions, you might have bought one July 240 corn put, sold two July 220 corn puts, and bought one July 200 put. This spread will generate optimal results if futures trade to exactly $2.20 per bushel at option expiration. It will earn slightly less if the futures trade to a point slightly below $2.20. And it will make a loss if futures trade far

EXHIBIT 22.1a

Futures Settle at Middle Strike Price at Option Expiration

	Initial		Ending I		
July corn futures price	2.31000		2.20000		
Days to option expiration	21		0		
Implied volatility	24%		NA		
Put Strike Prices	**Price**	**Delta**	**Price**	**Result**	**ROI**
Buy one July 240 corn put	–0.11000	–0.740	0.20000	0.09000	
Sell two July 220 corn puts	0.02750	0.380	0.00000	0.02750	
Buy one July 200 corn put	–0.00125	–0.005	0.00000	–0.00125	
Butterfly net price	–0.08375	–0.365	0.20000	0.11625	
Butterfly $ net price	–418.75		1000.00	581.25	139%

below $2.00 per bushel or far above $2.40 per bushel. The three parts of Exhibit 22.1 show how this corn put butterfly will perform if the options expire with futures at $2.20 per bushel (Ending I), $2.18 per bushel (Ending II), or $1.90 per bushel (Ending III).

Grain futures and option on these futures are often quoted in cents per bushel. This discussion converts all these prices into dollars per bushel and uses decimal fractions. Thus, the 0.11 initial price for the July 240 corn put indicates 11 cents per bushel. The 0.0275 initial price for the two July 220 puts indicates a 2.75 cent per bushel price or, in some quote systems, a 2 ¾ cents per bushel price.

The minus signs in the Price columns indicate prices paid for bought options. Prices without minus signs are prices collected from selling options. The minus signs in the Result columns indicate losses. The prices in the Butterfly net price row are the sums of the prices or results in the individual leg rows—e.g., the initial –0.08375 Butterfly net price is the sum of –0.11, 0.0275, and –0.00125. Finally, the amounts in the Butterfly $ net price row result from multiplying the Butterfly net price by 5,000 bushels, the size of the corn futures contract—e.g., the final 0.11625 result times 5,000 comes to the $581.25 net gain for this situation.

EXHIBIT 22.1b

Futures Settle at $2.18 per Bushel at Option Expiration

	Initial		Ending II		
July corn futures price	2.31000		2.18000		
Days to option expiration	21		0		
Implied volatility	24%		NA		
Put Strike Prices	**Price**	**Delta**	**Price**	**Result**	**ROI**
Buy one July 240 corn put	–0.11000	–0.740	0.22000	0.11000	
Sell two July 220 corn puts	0.02750	0.380	–0.04000	–0.01250	
Buy one July 200 corn put	–0.00125	–0.005	0.00000	–0.00125	
Butterfly net price	–0.08375	–0.365	0.18000	0.09625	
Butterfly $ net price	–418.75		900.00	481.25	115%

Volatility is irrelevant at expiration, hence the NA. The value of the 240 put is the strike price minus the ending futures price. The values of the other two puts are zero because the strike prices minus the ending futures price result in either a zero or a negative number which, by convention, becomes zero. In the case of Ending I, the 240 strike price minus the 220-cents futures price results in a 20-cents option price. The 220 and 200 puts expire valueless. This ending situation results in the maximum possible return for this butterfly under these market conditions.

The situation in which the futures price traded to $2.18 per bushel shows a slightly smaller gain than the gain for Ending I, but $481.25 is still more than the initial price paid for this butterfly. This amounts to a 115 percent return on investment (481.25 ÷ 418.75 = 1.1493).

The situation in which the futures trade down to $1.90 per bushel generates a loss, but notice that it is still smaller than the price paid for the butterfly. This illustrates the advantage of the butterfly structure. The two sold puts would have lost $0.5725 per bushel by themselves, or a total of $2,862.50 for one butterfly. The two bought calls reduce the net loss to $0.07375 per bushel, or $368.75 per butterfly. This $368.75 loss may be unpleasant, but it will be far less damaging to a trading account than a $2,862.50 loss.

EXHIBIT 22.1c

Futures Settle Below Lowest Strike Price at Option Expiration

	Initial		Ending III		
July corn futures price	2.31000		1.90000		
Days to option expiration	21		0		
Implied volatility	24%		NA		
Put Strike Prices	**Price**	**Delta**	**Price**	**Result**	**ROI**
Buy one July 240 corn put	–0.11000	–0.740	0.50000	0.39000	
Sell two July 220 corn puts	0.02750	0.380	–0.60000	–0.57250	
Buy one July 200 corn put	–0.00125	–0.005	0.11000	0.10875	
Butterfly net price	–0.08375	–0.365	0.01000	–0.07375	
Butterfly $ net price	–418.75		50.00	–368.75	–88%

A GREEN BUTTERFLY FOR WHEN FIVE-YEAR TREASURY NOTE FUTURES TRADE IN A RANGE

A difficult market for many futures traders is one that seems stuck in a relatively narrow trading range. Even with reduced transaction costs, this kind of market can be expensive to trade in, and the rewards are seldom great enough to compensate for the cost. One way to approach this kind of market is to use butterfly spreads.

Suppose that you had noticed that December five-year Treasury note futures were trading at 110-07 and had been trading in a relatively narrow range for some weeks. The current 110-07 was near the bottom of the range, and a futures price between 111-00 and 111-20 was near the upper boundary of this range.

Your market analysis may have suggested that the nature of the economic news that had been issuing forth was a big part of what accounted for this range. The indicators for and against growth and for and against a buildup of inflation might have been so evenly balanced that the market could not find reasons to make a large move in either direction. Further, you may have seen no reason to believe that this situation would resolve itself in the next month or so.

Apart from the price situation, you might have taken a look at the volatility situation and found that implied volatility was trading at 5.1 percent. With 21 days to option expiration, five-year Treasury note futures median volatility is 4.7 percent. A 5.5 percent volatility is at the 75th percentile (see the five-year Treasury note volatility cone on page 260). So this might have seemed a good time to be at short volatility.

Further, the price and volatility situations might have suggested that a call butterfly using December calls on December five-year Treasury note futures might have been a good way to trade this market.

The structuring of this spread requires care. You often hear people say that they like to have the options they sell pay for the options they buy. You can go overboard with this notion.

You might think it attractive to buy one December 110.5 call, sell two December 111 calls, and buy one December 111.5 call. This version of the butterfly spread would have cost only 4/64, or $62.50. A butterfly spread achieves its maximum earnings potential when the futures price settles exactly at the middle strike price at option expiration. Exhibit 22.2 illustrates this situation, assuming that the futures contract settles exactly at 111-00 at option expiration.

An important point that is made in the discussion of bull call spreads (see Chapter 19) is that when you choose strike prices that are too close

EXHIBIT 22.2

The Highest This Butterfly Can Fly

	Initial		Ending		
December five-year Treasury note futures price	110-07		111-00		
Days to December option expiration	21		0		
Implied volatility	5.1%		NA		
Call Strike Price	**Price (64ths)**	**Delta**	**Price (64ths)**	**Result (64ths)**	**ROI**
Buy one December 110.5 call	–26	–0.42	32	6	
Sell two December 111 calls	30	0.56	0	30	
Buy one December 111.5 call	–8	–0.17	0	–8	
Butterfly net price	–4	–0.03	32	28	
Butterfly $ net price	–62.50		500.00	437.50	700%

together, you lower the price but limit the earning potential of the option spread. The same is true of butterflies. The most you can earn with the butterfly structure of Exhibit 22.2 is $437.50. That is a huge result in ROI terms, but 700 percent of not much is still not much.

With this cautionary note as background, consider a butterfly in which you would have bought the December 110.5 call as before, but this time you would have sold two December 111.5 calls and bought one December 112.5 call. This butterfly would have cost three times as much, given the assumptions at work here, but it may have been worth it.

Exhibit 22.3 shows how this December five-year Treasury note call butterfly might have performed given four endings. Ending I shows that the best possible result occurs when the futures price settles exactly on the middle strike price at option expiration. Endings II and III show that if the futures price misses the target by a little in either direction, this butterfly will still perform well but not quite as well as it will given Ending I. Finally, Ending IV shows that if the futures prices settles well above the 112.5 strike price, the gains of the two bought calls will offset the losses of the two sold calls and hold the loss to the initial price paid. This is the safety net at work.

You can see the advantage of choosing strike prices that are at least slightly farther apart in the case of Ending I. The butterfly of Exhibit 22.3

EXHIBIT 22.3a

Futures Settle Exactly on the Middle Strike Price at Option Expiration

	Initial		Ending I		
December five-year Treasury note futures price	110-07		111-16		
Days to December option expiration	21		0		
Implied volatility	5.1%		NA		
Call Strike Price	**Price (64ths)**	**Delta**	**Price (64ths)**	**Result (64ths)**	**ROI**
Buy one December 110.5 call	–26	–0.42	64	38	
Sell two December 111.5 calls	16	0.34	0	16	
Buy one December 112.5 call	–2	–0.05	0	0	
Butterfly net price	–12	–0.13	64	52	
Butterfly $ net price	–187.50		1,000.00	812.50	433%

costs three times more than the one of Exhibit 22.2, but the earnings potential of this butterfly, given Ending I, is far greater in dollar terms.

Exhibits 22.3b and 22.3c illustrate another strong reason for preferring the Exhibit 22.3 version of the five-year Treasury note call butterfly—namely that it is far more forgiving of results that are fairly wide of the forecast mark. Indeed, this trade will outperform the Exhibit 22.2 trade, in dollar terms, even if the futures price settles as much as 12/32 away from the 111-16 futures price target at option expiration. At a 111-28 futures price, the Exhibit 22.3 butterfly would gain $468.85. At a 111-04 futures price, it would gain the same $468.85. It follows that it will still show positive results if the futures settle even farther away from the middle strike price. Clearly, using the wider strike price intervals not only increases the earnings potential of this spread, in the case where the futures price is exactly on target, but it also significantly increases the amount of price room in which you can earn a significant return.

Notice, in Exhibit 22.3d, that the 304/64 loss of the December 111.5 calls that were sold is 4-48 (or, sometimes, 4'48) in conventional fixed-income price notation. This would amount to a $4,750 loss if you had simply sold two December 111.5 calls. The wings of the butterfly hold that to the initial price paid—$187.50.

EXHIBIT 22.3b

Futures Settle Slightly Below the Middle Strike Price at Option Expiration

	Initial		Ending II		
December five-year Treasury note futures price	110-07		111-14		
Days to December option expiration	21		0		
Implied volatility	5.1%		NA		
Call Strike Price	**Price (64ths)**	**Delta**	**Price (64ths)**	**Result (64ths)**	**ROI**
Buy one December 110.5 call	–26	–0.42	60	34	
Sell two December 111.5 calls	16	0.34	0	16	
Buy one December 112.5 call	–2	–0.05	0	–2	
Butterfly net price	–12	–0.13	60	48	
Butterfly $ net price	–187.50		937.50	750.00	400%

EXHIBIT 22.3c

Futures Settle Slightly Above the Middle Strike Price at Option Expiration

	Initial		Ending III		
December five-year Treasury note futures price	110-07		111-18		
Days to December option expiration	21		0		
Implied volatility	5.1%		NA		
Call Strike Price	**Price (64ths)**	**Delta**	**Price (64ths)**	**Result (64ths)**	**ROI**
Buy one December 110.5 call	–26	–0.42	68	42	
Sell two December 111.5 calls	16	0.34	–8	8	
Buy one December 112.5 call	–2	–0.05	0	–2	
Butterfly net price	–12	–0.13	60	48	
Butterfly $ net price	–187.50		937.50	750.00	400%

EXHIBIT 22.3d

Futures Settle Well Above the Highest Strike Price at Option Expiration

	Initial		Ending IV		
December five-year Treasury note futures price	110-07		114-00		
Days to December option expiration	21		0		
Implied volatility	5.1%		NA		
Call Strike Price	**Price (64ths)**	**Delta**	**Price (64ths)**	**Result (64ths)**	**ROI**
Buy one December 110.5 call	–26	–0.42	224	198	
Sell two December 111.5 calls	16	0.34	–320	–304	
Buy one December 112.5 call	–2	–0.05	96	94	
Butterfly net price	–12	–0.13	0	–12	
Butterfly $ net price	–187.50		0.00	–187.50	0

A WHITE BUTTERFLY FOR WHEN COTTON IS TRADING EVER LOWER

Different markets have different pricing and volatility characteristics that can lead to rather different results for butterfly structures that look similar on the surface. The supply-demand situation of the cotton market was roughly similar to the supply-demand situation of the corn market during the summer of 2004. Report after report showed world supplies to be growing faster than world demand for cotton. As the story developed, cotton prices dropped farther and farther.

Suppose that three weeks before expiration of the July cotton options, July cotton futures were trading at 69.12 cents per pound and implied volatility was trading at 29.8 percent. You might have had reason to think that futures would trade down to 66 cents per pound at option expiration but not much lower. If your strategy of choice was a cotton put butterfly, you might have bought one July 69 cotton put, sold two July 66 cotton puts, and bought one July 63 cotton put. Exhibit 22.4 shows what kinds of results you could have expected if the futures had landed right on the 66-cents mark (Ending I), had traded slightly below that (Ending II), and had traded all the way down to 60 cents per pound at option expiration (Ending III).

Notice that the initial price of this cotton put butterfly is 0.616 cents per pound. The cotton futures contract contains 50,000 pounds, so the dollar value is cents per pound multiplied by 50,000 pounds with that result divided by

EXHIBIT 22.4a

Futures Settle at Middle Strike Price at Option Expiration

	Initial		Ending I		
July cotton futures	69.12		66.00		
Days to expiration	21		0		
Implied volatility	29.8%		NA		
Put Strike Prices	**Price**	**Delta**	**Price**	**Result**	**ROI**
Buy one July 69 cotton put	–1.908	–0.48	3.000	1.092	
Sell two July 66 cotton puts	1.508	0.50	0.000	1.508	
Buy one July 63 cotton put	–0.216	–0.09	0.000	–0.216	
Butterfly net price	–0.616	–0.07	3.000	2.384	
Butterfly $ net price	–308.00		1,500.00	1192.00	387%

EXHIBIT 22.4b

Futures Settle at 65.55 Cents per Pound at Option Expiration

	Initial		Ending II		
July cotton futures	69.12		65.55		
Days to expiration	21		0		
Implied volatility	29.8%		NA		
Put Strike Prices	**Price**	**Delta**	**Price**	**Result**	**ROI**
Buy one July 69 cotton put	–1.908	–0.48	3.450	1.542	
Sell two July 66 cotton puts	1.508	0.50	–9.000	0.608	
Buy one July 63 cotton put	–0.216	–0.09	0.000	–0.216	
Butterfly net price	–0.616	–0.07	2.550	1.934	
Butterfly $ net price	–308.00		1,275.00	967.00	315%

EXHIBIT 22.4c

Futures Settle Below Lowest Strike Price at Option Expiration

	Initial		Ending III		
July cotton futures	69.12		60.00		
Days to expiration	21		0		
Implied volatility	29.8%		NA		
Put Strike Prices	**Price**	**Delta**	**Price**	**Result**	**ROI**
Buy one July 69 cotton put	–1.908	–0.48	9.000	7.092	
Sell two July 66 cotton puts	1.508	0.50	–12.000	–10.492	
Buy one July 63 cotton put	–0.216	–0.09	3.000	2.784	
Butterfly net price	–0.616	–0.07	0.000	–0.616	
Butterfly $ net price	–308.00		0.00	–308.00	0

100 cents. To save a step, you can just multiply cents per pound times 500. In this case, the 0.616 net price paid comes to $308 (0.616 × 500).

You can see that Ending I produced the best result and that missing the 66 cents per bushel mark by only 0.45 cents (Ending II) presents a result that is $225 lower (1,192 – 967).

Finally, the wings of this butterfly held the loss in Ending III to the initial price paid. The two sold options on their own would have lost \$5,246 (–10.492 × 500). This is an even larger difference than the one in the case of the corn butterfly. This seems an especially strong motive for using the butterfly structure—given the assumed market outlook.

A WORD OF CAUTION

Never confuse *can't lose much* with *can't lose*. Option butterflies will not lose more than the initial price paid, but there are situations, only two of which are illustrated, in which these losses will occur.

It is important to remember that these are essentially volatility trades. You should trade butterflies only when you are comfortable with the idea of being at short volatility. Also, because the key element of these trades is the body of sold options, you want as much time decay as possible. This makes butterflies appropriate during the last three or four weeks before option expiration. Butterflies put on with, say, 75 days to option expiration and held in place for two or three weeks will prove to be disappointing trades.

Sharply rising implied volatilities can harm these fragile creatures. This is why, contrary to the advice contained in the discussion of other option spreads, you should hold butterflies in place until option expiration. This adds another wrinkle to these trades. Most of the exchanges automatically exercise any options that expire in the money unless the option holder gives directions to the contrary. If you do not want to assume the long or short futures positions that these options imply, you must be certain that your broker knows this and passes the word to the clearinghouse.

However, when you observe these precautions, you can find that option butterflies make it possible to trade markets that might otherwise prove difficult to trade successfully. Further, while the spread structure strictly limits the earnings potential, butterfly trades can generate healthy returns under the right circumstances. At the same time, the loss potential is modest enough that even the worst case will not be ruinous. In sum, butterflies are well worth having in your spread trading repertoire.

CHAPTER 23

Buying Straddles and Strangles

Spread Strategies for When You Just Don't Know

Situations arise in trading life in which it is impossible to know what will happen next in whatever market is under discussion. In a closely contested election race for the U.S. presidency, you simply cannot know how the stock market will react, no matter which side wins. You have to wonder whether the winner will push for policies that promise to boost the economy or for policies that will drag down economic growth. If the perception is that this will be a time of robust growth, the stock market will rally. Otherwise, it may well falter.

In the grain markets at the beginning of harvest, you simply cannot know, for certain, whether this is a large crop that will depress prices or a short crop that will send prices soaring. The fields can look lush, yet the yields can be disappointing. Until the grain is actually in the bins, the size of the crop cannot be known—for certain.

Either of these cases presents stock and futures traders with a dilemma. You must either decide to sit out this dance or choose a partner. And if you choose wrong, you will take a loss.

Even in situations such as the ones described, options spread traders can earn solid, if unspectacular, gains by buying straddles or strangles. These option spreads are often referred to as *volatility trades*. You make these trades when you believe the market is poised to make a strong move but have no idea in which direction the market will go.

THE BASIC IDEA

The basic idea of either straddles or strangles is that you buy both a put and a call. If the futures shoot up, the call will generate a gain greater than the loss from the put. If the futures price drops sharply, the put will generate the gain.

The difference between these two option spreads lies in your choice of strike prices. Suppose CBOT mini-sized Dow futures are trading at 10,000 with 58 days to option expiration and 8.8 percent implied volatility. Exhibit 23.1 shows the prices and deltas for a range of put and call strike prices. Options on CBOT mini-sized Dow futures are quoted in index points, and their dollar value is the product of the index point quotation and the $5 multiplier that applies to the underlying futures. It is important to remember that the put deltas have negative value. Most quote screen displays assume that and do not insert the minus signs.

To buy a straddle, you typically buy the at-the-money, or nearest-the-money, put and call. In this example, this is the 10,000 puts and calls. To buy a strangle, you buy more or less equally out-of-the-money puts and calls. Given the data of Exhibit 23.1, you might choose to buy the 9,700 put and the 10,300 call, each with a delta close to 0.20. Both spreads will generate gains when the futures price moves sharply in either direction and, especially, when implied volatilities increase. Both will generate losses when the prices and the implied volatilities remain stable.

As a general rule, strangles seem the wiser choice for option buyers. They cost less, to begin with, and they generate gains that are not vastly different from those of a straddle. As a result, they generate more bang for the buck.

EXHIBIT 23.1

Put and Call Prices and Deltas

Strike Price	Calls	Deltas	Puts	Deltas
9,700			37	0.19
9,800			61	0.28
9,900			95	0.42
10,000	140	0.51	140	0.49
10,100	96	0.39		
10,200	63	0.29		
10,300	40	0.20		

A PREELECTION DILEMMA FOR STOCK INDEX TRADERS

During the run-up to the 2004 U.S. Presidential election, there were periods when the U.S. stock market seemed to be treading water, just waiting to see what would happen on November 2. During the last half of October, CBOT mini-sized Dow futures traded in a relatively narrow range between 9,988 and 9,740. This kind of trading range tends to pull the volatility out of the market, and on October 21, 2004, the implied volatility on the at-the-money call option on CBOT mini-sized Dow futures was trading at 8.3 percent with the futures trading at 9,863. This might well have seemed a good time to buy a straddle or strangle. The question remains concerning which kind of option spread to choose. The proof is in the performance of the two option spreads, of course.

STRUCTURING THE OPTION SPREAD POSITIONS

The straddle strike price choice seems obvious. The December 9,900 call and put are close to the money, so that is probably the place to put a straddle in this situation.

A good rule of thumb for choosing strangle strike prices is to use options with deltas in the 0.20 to 0.30 range. On October 21, 2004, the December 10,100 call had a 0.24 delta, and the December 9,700 put had a –0.30 delta, so those seem appropriate choices.

Exhibit 23.2 illustrates the straddle-strangle difference. The assumption is that both trades were put on on October 21 with CBOT mini-sized Dow futures trading at 9,863, at 57 days to option expiration, and 8.3 percent implied volatility. A further assumption is that these trades were unwound on November 3, the day after the election, at a 10,141 futures price, with 44 days to option expiration, and 12.9 percent implied volatility.

A word about the volatility assumption is also in order. Implied volatilities typically exhibit a skew. That is, farther out-of-the-money options trade at higher or lower volatilities than at-the-money options. The trades in Exhibit 23.2 assume flat volatilities. That is, on October 21, the assumption runs that all strike prices traded at 8.3 percent implied volatility and that they all traded at 12.9 percent implied volatility on November 3.

The minus signs in the October 21 option price column indicate that these are bought options, and buying options involves a cash outflow. You collect the price of sold options, hence the positive numbers in the November 3 Price column. Notice that both put legs of these spreads lost. When the futures price drops, of course, the put legs of these spreads generate the

EXHIBIT 23.2

Deciding Which Is Better—Straddle or Strangle Performance

	10/21/04		11/3/04		
Futures price	9,863		10,141	278	
Days to expiration	57		44	13	
Implied volatility	8.3		12.9	4.6	
Options	**Price**	**Delta**	**Price**	**Result**	**ROI**
December 9,900 call	–111	0.46	324	213	
+ December 9,900 put	–148	–0.54	84	–64	
= December 9,900 straddle	–259	–0.08	408	149	
Straddle $ value	–1,295		2,040	745	57.53%
December 10,100 call	–45	0.24	202	157	
+ December 9,700 put	–62	–0.30	37	–25	
= December 10,100-9,700 strangle	–107	–0.06	239	132	
Strangle $ value	–535		1,195	660	123.36%

gains, and the calls will show the losses. The straddle and strangle rows sum the put and call prices and results, but these prices and results are given in index points. The Straddle $ value and Strangle $ value rows multiply those sums by the $5 multiplier that generates the dollar equivalent value of CBOT mini-sized Dow futures and options positions.

ASSESSING THE STRADDLE AND STRANGLE RESULTS

You can look at these results in a variety of ways. In raw dollar terms, the straddle earned slightly more—$745 to $660.

The maximum possible loss for either of these spreads is the initial price paid. This gives rise to another way to look at the straddle-strangle trade-off. Ask yourself whether you would rather risk $1,295 for the chance to earn $735 or risk $535 for the chance to earn $660. The straddle costs very much more and earns very little more. This balancing of risk and reward makes the choice seem fairly obvious. The strangle, at least given these assumptions, looks like the better deal.

You can somewhat formalize this risk-reward trade-off in terms of a return on investment (ROI) calculation. The exhibit shows the straddle to have a 57.53 percent ROI, while the strangle has a vastly better 123.36% ROI. To calculate the ROI for either trade, divide the result (dollar or index point) by the initial price of the spread (e.g., $745 straddle result divided by the $1,295 straddle price equals 0.5753, or 57.53%).

A PREHARVEST CORN DILEMMA

Toward the end of August 2004, traders contemplating the corn futures market faced a dilemma similar to the one facing stock index futures and options traders. The corn crop that was on the verge of being ready for harvest had the look of a bumper crop. It had gone into the ground under nearly ideal conditions, the growing weather all summer had been almost perfect, and farmers had switched acres from soybeans to corn. All of that led to the expectation that this would be a huge crop, and a huge crop drives prices lower.

Still, appearances can be deceiving. Grain trade veterans can remember times when all the signs were good but the crop was disappointing. One mildly alarming fact in late summer 2004 was that December corn futures had traded from $2.2775 per bushel on August 2 to $2.4275 per bushel on September 1. If this suggested that somebody out there knew something, maybe this crop would disappoint the market and prices would soar higher. On the other hand, if this did prove to be a bumper crop, prices could trade sharply lower.

For a futures trader, this might have seemed perplexing. For an options trader, this had the look of a situation tailor-made for buying a straddle or a strangle.

STRUCTURING THE TRADE

On September 1, 2004, December corn futures were trading at $2.4275 per bushel, and the December options had 86 days to expiration and were trading at 30 percent implied volatility. The December 240 call and put were close to the money, making that a good straddle strike price. The December 270 call and December 220 put had deltas in the 0.20 to 0.30 range, so they were good strike prices for strangle purposes. December corn had traded all the way down to $2.06 per bushel by October 1. This was a market response to a growing body of information that this was a bumper corn crop. Implied volatilities tend to fall off a bit after harvest regardless of how the crop turns out. In this case, the huge crop did much to calm fears about supply adequacy, and the implied volatilities traded down to 25 percent or thereabouts. Exhibit 23.3 shows how the straddle and strangle would have performed assuming that both trades were put on on September 1 and unwound on October 1.

In contrast to the stock index example where both puts lost money when the futures market rallied, both corn calls made losses when the market

EXHIBIT 23.3

Evaluating Corn Staddle and Strangle Performance

	9/1/04		10/1/04		
December corn futures price	2.4275		2.06	–0.3675	
Days to expiration	86		56	30	
Implied volatility	30		25	-5	
Options	**Price**	**Delta**	**Price**	**Result**	**ROI**
December 240 call	–0.15375	0.56	0.00500	–0.14875	
+ December 240 put	–0.12625	–0.44	0.34500	0.21875	
= December 240 straddle	–0.28000	0.12	0.35000	0.07000	
Straddle $ value	–1,400.00		1,750.00	350.00	25.00%
December 270 call	–0.05000	0.26	0.00000	–0.05000	
+ December 220 put	–0.05000	–0.23	0.17125	0.12125	
= December 270-220 strangle	–0.10000	0.03	0.17125	0.07125	
Strangle $ value	–500.00		856.25	356.25	71.25%

traded sharply lower. In this case, of course, both puts more than overcome those losses, and both option spreads show positive results. Interestingly, the strangle outperforms the straddle in both dollar and ROI terms. Granted, $6.25 isn't much of an advantage, but it does go on the plus side of the ledger.

Both the stock index example and the corn example demonstrate that, even when it is impossible to guess how the market will respond to economic and political events, you can find trades that will enable you to benefit from whatever the market does. The gains are unlikely to be of the blockbuster variety, but option straddles or strangles provide means to keep on trading and with limited risk.

A NOTE ON STRADDLE AND STRANGLE FOLKLORE

The search for reasons to prefer straddles uncovered some interesting market folklore. Some traders apparently have the intuitive sense that strangles do well when the underlying futures make a very large move but do less well when the move is a gentler one. These people also believe that while strangles may outperform straddles when there is a long time until expiration, straddles will perform better when the time to expiration is shorter—five weeks or less.

Veteran traders often say these things with such assurance that it is difficult to doubt them. It is probably always a good idea to put notions such as these to the test in at least a few market situations.

The corn market in late spring 2004 provided interesting examples for such testing. Suppose your market research had led you to decide to buy either a corn straddle or a corn strangle on May 17, 2004, and to unwind either spread 14 days later on June 1. Further, you could have chosen either July options, which had 39 days to expiration, or December options, which had 193 days to expiration.

Consider, first, the trades using the July options. On May 17, July corn futures were trading at $2.9525 per bushel, and July option implied volatility was trading at 32.8 percent. On June 1, the July futures price was $3.25 per bushel, and, assuming no volatility skew, July implied volatility was trading at 36 percent.

The July 300 call and put strike prices seem the obvious choices for the straddle. As for the strangle, the July 320 call and 280 put have deltas in the 0.20 to 0.30 range, so they seem likely candidates for the strangle. Exhibit 23.4 illustrates how the July 300 straddle and July 320-280 strangle would have performed, given these data and assumptions.

Alternatively, on May 17, you could have traded straddles or strangles using December options. December corn futures on that day were

EXHIBIT 23.4

Corn Straddle and Strangle Performance with Short Time to Expiration

	5/17/04		6/1/04		
July corn futures price	2.9525		3.24	0.2875	
Days to expiration	39		24	14	
Implied volatility	32.8		36	3.2	
Options	**Price**	**Delta**	**Price**	**Result**	**ROI**
July 300 call	−0.10625	0.47	0.27375	0.1675	
+ July 300 put	−0.15125	−0.53	0.03375	−0.1175	
= July 300 straddle	−0.25750	−0.06	0.30750	0.0500	
Straddle $ value	−1,287.50		1,537.50	250.00	19.42%
July 320 call	−0.04375	0.25	0.14250	0.09875	
+ July 280 put	−0.06125	−0.29	0.00750	−0.05375	
= July 320-280 strangle	−0.10500	−0.04	0.15000	0.04500	
Strangle $ value	−525.00		750.00	225.00	42.86%

trading at $2.88 per bushel with 193 days to expiration, and implied volatility was trading at 30 percent.

At this futures price, the 290 strike price seems the appropriate one for the December straddle. Because of the longer time to expiration, the strangle strike prices must be much wider apart to meet the rule of thumb

EXHIBIT 23.5

Corn Straddle and Strangle Performance with Long Time to Expiration

	5/17/04		6/1/04		
December corn futures price	2.88		3.1925	0.3125	
Days to expiration	193		179	14	
Implied volatility	30		35	5	
Options	**Price**	**Delta**	**Price**	**Result**	**ROI**
December 290 corn call	–0.24	0.53	0.46375	0.22375	
+ December 290 corn put	–0.26	–0.47	0.17250	–0.08750	
= December 290 corn straddle	–0.50	0.06	0.63625	0.13625	
Straddle $ value	–2,500.00		3,181.25	681.25	27.25%
December 310 corn call	–0.16375	0.41	0.35375	0.19000	
+ December 270 corn put	–0.16250	–0.34	0.10500	–0.05750	
= December 310-270 corn strangle	–0.32625	0.07	0.45875	0.13250	
Strangle $ result	–1,631.25		2,293.75	662.50	40.61%
December 320 corn call	–0.13375	0.35	0.30625	0.17250	
+ December 260 corn put	–0.12250	–0.28	0.07875	–0.04375	
= December 320-260 corn strangle	–0.25625	0.07	0.38500	0.12875	
Strangle $ result	–1,261,25		1,925.00	643.75	50.24%
December 330 corn call	–0.10875	0.30	0.26500	0.15625	
+ December 250 corn put	–0.09000	–0.22	0.05750	–0.03250	
= December 330-250 corn strangle	–0.19875	0.08	0.32250	0.12375	
Strangle $ result	–993.75		1,612.50	618.75	62.26%

concerning deltas. Exhibit 23.5 explores three strangle possibilities—the December 310-270, 320-260, and 330-250 strangles. Again, these examples assume the absence of a volatility skew.

Exhibit 23.5, in conjunction with Exhibit 23.4, makes several things clear. First, these longer-dated December options cost a great deal more than the shorter-dated July options. Many options traders find paying this much for options anathema. Second, the option spreads of Exhibit 23.5 earn far more than the spreads of Exhibit 23.4. This is true in both dollar and ROI terms. Third, the longer-dated straddle earns more than the shorter-dated straddle either way you consider these results. Finally, the July 320-280 strangle and the December 330-250 strangle both earn more than twice as much as the July and December straddles, respectively, in ROI terms.

Granted, this is only one situation, but based on this evidence, the market folklore seems not to hold up.

WHEN THE MARKET DOES NOTHING, OR ALMOST NOTHING

An important consideration in formulating any trading plan is what will happen if everything goes wrong that can go wrong. For option buyers, the maximum possible loss is the price paid. The worst thing that can happen to a straddle or strangle buyer is for the market to do nothing, or almost nothing, and for implied volatility to dwindle. Suppose that the U.S. stock market had collectively yawned after the November 2 U.S. election and decided there was nothing in these results to get excited about either way.

In the face of that kind of reaction, December CBOT mini-sized Dow futures might have inched up or down a few points, and implied volatility might have sagged off slightly from its already low 8.3 percent of October 21. Say the futures were trading at 9,943 on the day after the election and that the implied volatility on the options had edged down to 8.0 percent. Exhibit 23.6 uses the same initial data as Exhibit 23.2 but assumes this more muted reaction to the election news.

You can see that both the straddle and strangle would have made losses in this situation. More specifically, the puts in both spreads would have lost far more than the calls would have gained. Yet both losses are far smaller than the price paid for these option spreads, and those prices define the worst-case losses. Also, notice that the strangle loss is slightly less than the straddle loss, yet the strangle ROI looks worse, as will always be the case. Despite this ROI artifact, strangles seem preferable, even in situations that lead to losses.

An important advantage of keeping these trades well away from option expiration involves the time value of the options. Because the options in Exhibits 23.2 and 23.6 were almost a month and a half away

EXHIBIT 23.6

Straddles and Strangles Can Lose When the Market Doesn't Cooperate

	10/21/04		11/3/04		
Futures price	9,863		9,943	80	
Days to expiration	57		44	13	
Implied volatility	8.3		8.0	–0.3	
Options	**Price**	**Delta**	**Price**	**Result**	**ROI**
December 9,900 call	–111	0.46	132	21	
December 9,900 put	–148	–0.54	89	–59	
= December 9,900 straddle	–259	–0.08	221	–38	
Straddle $ value	–1,295		1,105	–190	–14.67%
December 10,100 call	–45	0.24	50	5	
+ December 9,700 put	–62	–0.30	28	–34	
= December 10,100–9,700 strangle	–107	–0.06	78	–29	
Strangle $ value	–535		390	–145	–27.10%

from expiration, they still had a good bit of time value, and that cushioned the loss in the case of the Exhibit 23.6 situation.

A WORD OF CAUTION

The example of Exhibit 23.6 serves as a reminder that both straddles and strangles can suffer losses when futures prices remain relatively stable and the implied volatility stays the same or declines. These losses can be minimized by buying options with a relatively long time to expiration, which subjects them to relatively less time decay than options that are within the last month to expiration and by selling the options back to the market well in advance of option expiration while they still have significant time value. Nevertheless, it is good to keep the potential dangers of this, or any, trade in mind and to have a plan ready for dealing with them. This can be as simple as deciding in advance that you will unwind the trade and take the loss if it goes against you a specified amount. No one likes to take losses, but the worst trading horror stories all seem to involve people who either ignored the loss in the blind hope that the market would come back their way or behaved like the little boy who, having a stomach ache from overeating, ate more.

CHAPTER 24

A Corn and Soybeans Volatility Spread

The crucial role of implied volatility in options trading is well known. So important is this option pricing factor that experienced options traders often say that unless you have an opinion about volatility, you should stay away from options.

Perhaps less well known is the fact that different but related markets can follow diverging implied volatility paths. This, in turn, can create intriguing trading opportunities because you can structure options trades based on your expectations concerning relative differences in volatility movement—much as you can structure futures trades based on your expectations concerning relative differences in price movement. Take the case of the 2003 corn and soybean markets for example.

The common wisdom is that the soybean market is more volatile than the corn market. Certainly, from the vantage point of early September 2003, this seemed to be the case. The two markets seemed poised to head down divergent paths. The corn crop that was about to be harvested seemed large. The soybean crop was harder to get a handle on. One market commentator said that she expected a very large price move in soybeans but couldn't figure out whether it would be up or down. This kind of wild card status boosts volatility.

This volatility situation seems tailor-made for a relative value volatility trade using straddles or strangles, because straddles and strangles are volatility spreads.

A straddle involves trading both a call and a put at the same strike price, usually at the money. A strangle involves trading both a call and a put at out-of-the-money strike prices, usually the same distance from the money. In this situation, expecting a huge soybean move and increasing volatility and little corn price movement along with stable or declining volatility, you might consider buying a soybean straddle and selling a corn strangle.

MARKET BACKGROUND

Consider that on September 15, 2003, November soybean futures were trading at 619 cents per bushel. November options on soybeans were trading at close to 20 percent implied volatility with 40 days to option expiration. Based on these market data, the at-the-money 620 November soybean call was trading at 16 cents per bushel, and the November 620 soybean put was trading at 17 cents per bushel. Given that you expect a huge price move, in some direction, and a sharp increase in volatility, buying the 620 straddle might have seemed a good way to trade this soybean situation.

On the same day, December corn futures were trading at 227 cents per bushel. Options on these futures had 68 days to expiration and were trading at 19.5 percent implied volatility. Based on these market data, the out-of-the-money 240 December corn call was trading at 3 cents per bushel, and the 220 December put was trading at 4 1/2 cents per bushel. Because you are selling the corn options and expect corn volatility to remain stable or drop, this corn strangle seems the better choice because it will give you more room to make at least some money.

Because your expectation would have been that soybean volatility would be the active one, you might wonder why you should have even bothered with the corn strangle. For one thing, the spreading of the two markets allows you to more nearly isolate the volatility factor. For another, the presence of the short corn strangle reduces the exposure of the aggregate position to time decay. Thus, adding the corn strangle to the mix gives you more margin for error in predicting when the soybean volatility change will occur. Finally, as with any good spread trade, this straddle-strangle spread gives you more ways to be right. There are more situations that can generate at least some profit.

STRUCTURING THE TRADE

In structuring such a trade, you can balance the soybean and corn option positions so that both have roughly equal exposure to volatility change. You can also neutralize any residual directional exposure in these two option spreads.

To isolate the volatility factor, you need to ratio the trade so that the soybean straddle and the corn strangle will respond equally to equal

EXHIBIT 24.1

Initial Market Conditions and Selected Option Greeks (September 15, 2003)

November Soybean Futures			
Futures Price	619		
Days to Option Expiration	40		
ATM Implied Volatility	20.16%		
November 620 Soybean Straddle	**Option Price (¢/bu)**	**Delta**	**Vega**
620 call	16	0.503	0.875
+620 put	17	–0.496	0.875
= 620 straddle	33	0.007	1.750
December Corn Futures			
Futures Price	227		
Days to Expiration	68		
Implied Volatility	19.48%		
December 240-220 Corn Strangle	**Option Price (¢/bu)**	**Delta**	**Vega**
240 call	3	0.267	0.375
+220 put	4.5	−0.339	0.375
= Strangle	7.5	−0.072	0.750

changes in implied volatility. Exhibit 24.1 displays the relevant option risk parameters (the greeks).

Vega is the option risk parameter that relates option price change to changes in volatility. The 1.75 vega of the November 620 soybean straddle in Exhibit 24.1 predicts that a one percentage point increase in implied volatility will increase the straddle price by 1 3/4 cents per bushel. In contrast, the 0.75 vega of the December corn strangle predicts that a one percentage point implied volatility change will move the corn strangle price by 3/4 of a cent per bushel. To neutralize this difference in responsiveness to volatility change, you can divide the soybean straddle vega by the corn strangle vega.

$$1.75 \div 0.75 = 2.33$$

This tells you that you need to sell 233 of these corn strangles for every 100 soybean straddles that you buy. Such an aggregate position will be close to vega neutral—initially. If both implied volatilities change the same amount, the trade should generate essentially no result.

To satisfy yourself that these two positions will be vega neutral, you can multiply the soybean straddle vega by the number of straddles bought and the corn strangle vega by the number of strangles sold, as in Exhibit 24.2.The slight mismatch is the result of rounding in the ratio calculation, and it is trivial. This indicates that if both implied volatilities change by the same amount, then these two option positions will generate similar results.

A further refinement concerns directionality. Notice that the soybean straddle, with its 0.007 delta, has only very slight directional exposure. Indeed, a 100-straddle position will have a delta of 0.7 ($0.007 \times 100 = 0.7$). Because futures contracts have a delta of 1.0, by definition, you can eliminate most of this directionality by selling one November soybean futures contract for every 100 of the November 620 option straddles that you buy.

The 0.072 delta of the corn strangle indicates that this position has more directional exposure than the soybean straddle. What this means is that buyers of this option spread will find that it does slightly better in a rising market than in a falling market. Exhibit 24.3 creates a hypothetical

EXHIBIT 24.2

Establishing Straddle Vega Neutrality

	Vega	Number of Straddles	Position Vega
Soybean straddle	1.75	100	175.00
Corn strangle	0.75	–233	–174.75
Net vega			0.25

EXHIBIT 24.3

Demonstrating Directionality in a Corn Strangle

	Initial	Delta	Ending I	Ending II
Corn futures price	230		245	215
Days to expiration	60		53	53
Implied volatility	20%		25%	25%
240 corn call	3.375	0.314	11.875	1.375
220 corn put	3.375	–0.278	1.375	11.0
Corn strangle	7	0.036	13.25	12.375

situation in which the initial futures price is centered between the call and put strike prices.

The two endings occur seven days later. Both endings involve a five-point increase in implied volatility. The only difference is that Ending I takes the futures price up 15 cents per bushel while Ending II takes the futures price down 15 cents per bushel. You can see that the call gained more when the futures price rose than the put gained when the futures price fell. The call and put deltas tell you this should be the case. The actual 0.072 strangle delta is twice that of the hypothetical 0.036 delta, so the performance difference will be even more pronounced.

Because you are selling this strangle, you must change the sign of its delta to 0.072. To neutralize this directional exposure, you can buy seven December corn futures contracts for every 100 strangles you sell. Here, you are selling 233 strangles to achieve vega neutrality. That means that it will take 17 corn futures to neutralize this directional exposure (0.072 × 233 = 16.78).

This aggregate position—long 100 November 620 soybean straddles, short 1 November soybean futures, short 233 December 240-220 corn strangles, and long 17 December corn futures—should respond only if the soybean volatility increases relative to the corn volatility.

ASSESSING POSSIBLE RESULTS

This trade can produce a variety of results. Changes in the prices of the underlying futures contracts should have almost no effect, because of the use of futures to establish initial delta neutrality. Also, because of the vega weighting, parallel volatility shifts should produce essentially no result. However, if corn volatility increases relative to soybean volatility, this trade can generate a loss.

For the purpose of illustrating the positive potential of a trade such as this, consider the market situation right after the October 10, 2003, crop report when the rumors of a disappointing soybean crop became established fact. In the face of disappointing yields, the November soybean futures price soared into the low \$7.30s per bushel, and the implied volatility for the November 620 options shot up to 35.5 percent. At the same time, corn yield predictions proved to be on target, and the December futures price dropped only slightly while the implied volatility came down 5 percentage points. Suppose you caught the wave with soybean futures trading at 729 1/2 cents per bushel. Exhibit 24.4 shows the before and after details given these assumptions.

This exhibit translates the futures and options prices into dollars per bushel. Further, the fractions are converted into decimal form. Thus the

EXHIBIT 24.4

One Possible Outcome

	9/15/03	10/10/03	Result ($/bu)	Result ($/Contract)	Position Size	Gain or Loss (nearest $)
November soybean futures price	6.19	7.295	1.105	5,525	−1	−5,525
Days to expiration	40	15				
Implied volatility	20.16%	35.47%				
November 620 call	0.16	1.10125	0.94125			
November 620 put	0.17	0	−0.17			
620 straddle	0.33	1.10125	0.77126	3,855	100	385,500
December corn futures price	2.27	2.24	−0.03	−150	17	−2,550
Days to expiration	68	43				
Implied volatility	19.48%	15.00%				
December 240 call	0.03	0.005	−0.025			
December 220 put	0.045	0.02875	−0.01625			
240-220 strangle	0.075	0.03375	−0.04125	206.25	−233	48,056
Spread net result						425,481

619 cents per bushel of many quote services becomes $6.19 per bushel. In the exhibit, the dollar sign is understood. The Result ($/bu) column shows soybean futures to have gained $1.105 per bushel. The Result ($/Contract) column multiplies that by 5,000 bushels to show that one contract gained $5,525. The –1 in the Position Size column indicates that you sold one contract, so this part of the trade generates a loss.

Skipping down to the December 240-220 strangle row, the value of the corn strangle dropped $0.04125 per bushel, or $206.25 per contract.

However, you initially sold these 233 strangles, as indicated by the –233 in the Position Size column, so that becomes a positive in the Gain or Loss column. The rest of this exhibit should be straightforward.

You can see that, given these assumptions, both the long soybean straddle and the short corn strangle generated gains while both futures positions suffered losses. What matters most is that the aggregate result is a $425,606 gain.

A WORD OF CAUTION

It is important to remember that this is a view-driven trade that is based on opinions about both price movements and volatility developments in these markets. If your opinion turns out to be wrong, this trade can generate losses. However, when your assessments are on the money, trades like this one can be gratifyingly in the money.

A STRATEGIC EXTENSION

At times, it makes sense to put on a trade and unwind the whole thing when you see it reach a certain goal. At other times, you may have reason to unwind a fraction of the trade and let the rest ride. In mid-September 2003, you might have bought 200 of the soybean straddles and sold 466 of the corn strangles based on an opinion that:

- There would be a major soybean implied volatility surge immediately following the October 10 crop report.
- If the soybean crop turned out to be even worse than feared, there might be another surge in the next week or so after the report.

Based on this, your trading plan might have been to unwind half your position on October 10 and to wait and see what would happen in the next few days.

The first half of the trade would have produced the results of Exhibit 24.4. By October 14, the badness of the crop yield news and the scramble to buy scarce supplies had driven the November soybean futures price up to $7.38 per bushel. Soybean implied volatility had sagged off to 30 percent, but that was still well higher than the initial 20.16 percent. The December corn futures and implied volatility had drifted slightly lower. If you had decided to unwind the rest of this trade on October 14, the results would have been similar to those shown in Exhibit 24.5.

This second part of the trade earned $37,375 more than the first part did, an almost 9 percent improvement. It is tempting to think that you should have let the entire position ride the extra four days. What allows

EXHIBIT 24.5

Extending the Trade

	9/15/03	10/14/03	Result ($/bu)	Result ($/Contract)	Position Size	Gain or Loss (nearest $)
November soybean futures price	6.19	7.38	1.19	5,950.00	–1	–5,950
Days to expiration	40	11				
Implied volatility	20.16%	30.00%				
November 620 call	0.16	1.18	1.02			
November 620 put	0.17	0	–0.17			
620 straddle	0.33	1.18	0.85	4,250.00	100	425,000
December corn futures price	2.27	2.22	–0.05	–250.00	17	–4,250
Days to expiration	68	43				
Implied volatility	19.48%	14.00%				
December 240 call	0.03	0.0025	–0.0275			
December 220 put	0.045	0.03125	–0.01375			
240-220 strangle	0.075	0.03375	–0.04125	206.25	–233	48,056
Spread net result						462,856

you to resist this temptation is the awareness that, after the crop report, market participants could have taken another look at the situation and, instead of concluding that it was worse than they first thought, concluded that it wasn't so bad after all.

If this second thought had reduced concerns, the soybean futures price and the implied volatility could have fallen back considerably. Had that happened, the decision to unwind the first half of the trade would have seemed a shrewd one.

A FURTHER WORD OF CAUTION

The highest volatility levels in the agricultural markets occur during the period before harvest when yields are in doubt. The more uncertain people are about yields, the greater the volatility. Once people achieve a measure of certainty about the nature of the crop, for better or for worse, volatility tends to fall off.

Based on this, the August–September period, just before the U.S. harvest, seems to offer good opportunities for volatility trades. Another time when such a trade is likely to seem attractive is during the January–February period when the South American soybean crop is almost ready for harvest. Other volatility opportunities may emerge from time to time as well. But the August–September and January–February periods seem to offer the most opportunity to make volatility trades in the agricultural markets.

Another trade that might be attractive would spread Kansas City wheat against Chicago corn or soybeans. The key here is that the winter wheat crop is harvested starting in May and ending in July. The corn and soybean crops are harvested later. Because of this, it might be possible to catch wheat volatility on the decline and corn or soybean volatility on the rise.

What might seem attractive in the abstract, relative to these volatility trades, might seem less so once you look at the actual numbers. These are not trades you can put on automatically just because it is that time of year again. Rather, before you venture into such a trade, you'd better know something about market expectations, and you'd better have confidence in your sources.

This soybean-corn volatility spread would have produced excellent results in 2003, as the exhibits show. The story was different in 2004. Both harvests produced large crops, and the prices fell, as did volatilities. This is definitely a story-driven trade, and the story wasn't there in 2004.

CHAPTER 25

Options on 5-Year and 10-Year Treasury Note Futures

Volatility against Volatility

One set of spread trades that can, at the right times, produce gratifying results involves the spreading of one option spread against another. The idea is to capture not the relative price change but the relative implied volatility change.

To amplify that, a yield curve spread trader operates on the basis of a rationale along these lines:

- The Fed is likely to raise its target rate at the next meeting.
- The market thinks the projected increase won't be enough to head off inflation buildup.
- Because of that, 10-year Treasury note yields may rise more than 2-year or 5-year yields and widen the spread.
- Therefore, it is time to buy a yield curve spread using futures to capture this relative difference in price changes

Futures spreads allow you to express just such a market opinion based on what you expect the price of one futures contract to do relative to another.

Options allow you to add a volatility dimension to your thinking. In fact, options professionals often say that if you don't have an opinion about volatility, in addition to an opinion about price, you have no business going anywhere near options. As an options spread trader, you might operate on the basis of a rationale along these lines, with the first three bullets being the same as the futures spread trader's rationale. What is new is this:

- The implied volatility for options on 10-year Treasury note futures seems high, while the implied volatility for options on 5-year Treasury note futures seems more fairly valued.

- If the market concerns about inflation potential don't prove true, the 10-year implied volatility is likely to settle back to more normal levels while 5-year volatility is likely to stay close to where it is now.
- Therefore, it is time to structure an options trade to capture this difference in volatility reactions.

FORMULATING A VOLATILITY OPINION

Fortunately, volatility opinions are not hard to formulate. Suppose you had been looking at the markets in options on Treasury note futures in early summer 2004. You might have noticed that September 5-year Treasury note futures were trading at around 107-16. Also, with 66 days to the expiration of the September options, the implied volatilities of these options were trading at around 5.2 percent. At the same time, September 10-year Treasury note futures were trading at 107-18, but the implied volatilities were trading at around 8.5 percent.

A look at the relevant volatility cones (see Exhibits 18.11 and 18.12 in Chapter 18) suggests that the five-year implied volatility is trading close to its long-term median of approximately 5 percent, given this amount of time to option expiration. But the 10-year implied volatility, at 8.5 percent, seems very high. The long-term median for this time to expiration is closer to 7 percent. Indeed, this 8.5 percent reading is approximately 0.75 of a percentage point higher than the 7.75 percent 75th percentile level.

A large part of the motivation for this high 10-year implied volatility came from market participants' memories of what had happened during the summer of 2003. Because of the way the U.S. economy was stumbling during the spring of 2003, the market consensus was that the Fed should lower its fed funds target rate 50 bps at its June 2003 meeting. When the Fed lowered the target rate only 25 bps, the market reacted violently.

Normally, when the Fed lowers its target rate 25 bps, you expect to see two-year and five-year Treasury note yields drop almost that much but ten-year Treasury note yields drop only 5 or 10 bps. In this case, 10-year yields soared. Consider that on June 13, roughly a week and a half before the June 2003 fed meeting, the 10-year constant maturity Treasury note yield was 3.20 percent. On July 11, it was 3.72 percent, and by August 15, it was 4.49 percent. This sharp increase in 10-year yields had a devastating effect on holders of mortgage-related portfolios, and the way to defend against such devastation is to buy options.

In the late spring of 2004, the Fed had signaled its intention to start raising its fed funds target rate, and a potentially dangerous inflation buildup seemed underway even though the Fed was saying that inflation wasn't a threat. A large number of market participants weren't so sure, and the wounds from a year earlier were still fresh.

Normally, if the Fed raises the target rate 25 bps, you can expect to see two-year Treasury note yields rise close to that amount and ten-year Treasury note yields rise less—perhaps 5 or 10 bps. However, if inflation proved to be a bigger problem than the Fed was letting on and if the market perception was that the Fed wasn't taking strong enough action to head off inflation, then longer-term yields might rise sharply. You might see two-year yields rise 20 or 25 bps and ten-year yields rise 40 or 50 bps, or even more.

This could batter all kinds of mortgage-related holdings, and the portfolio managers who held these kinds of assets weren't going to be caught two years in a row. They flocked to the options markets in order to prepare for the worst. This precautionary action on their part probably accounts for most of the run-up in the 10-year implied volatilities.

If that is why the 10-year implied volatility is so high and if the Fed's inflation view proves to be more nearly correct than the other view that is in the market, then you might have expected the 10-year implied volatility to drop sharply in the month or so following the June 2004 fed meeting. Meanwhile, the five-year implied volatility would be likely to change little or not at all.

STRUCTURING A TRADE

One way to trade such a volatility opinion as this is with option straddles or strangles on 5-year and 10-year Treasury note futures.

Straddles and strangles are volatility strategies. You buy a straddle or a strangle when you don't know whether the next move will be up or down but you expect either an increase in volatility or a large move in either direction—that is, when you do not have a view on direction, but you do have a view on volatility. You sell a straddle or a strangle when you expect volatility to decline or for there to be relatively little price action.

To buy or sell a straddle, you buy or sell a call and a put with the same expiration and the same strike price, usually at or close to the money. With September five-year Treasury note futures trading at 107-16, the September 107.5 call and put are the logical straddle choices. They are right at the money. With September 10-year Treasury note futures trading at 107-18, you can trade either the September 108 call and put or the September 107 call and put. These are not at the money, which is 107-18, but they are close.

A strangle is the same idea except that you use strike prices that are approximately equally out of the money. That is, with September futures at 107-16, you might choose to trade the September 109 call and the September 106 put. A good rule of thumb is that these options should have deltas in the 0.20 to 0.30 range.

Given the opinion that the inflation fears currently in the market are indeed largely illusory and that the 10-year implied volatility will fall sharply while the 5-year implied volatility does little or nothing and Treasury futures prices move only slightly during the next month or so, you might trade this opinion by buying a September straddle or strangle on 5-year Treasury note futures and selling a September straddle or strangle on 10-year Treasury note futures.

Exhibit 25.1 summarizes the components of the transaction and their option "greeks." The values called greeks are available from numerous quote sources and options pricing programs. They look more complicated than they are, at least for present purposes.

By way of brief review, delta indicates how much an option price will change for a given futures price change (see Chapter 18 for a more detailed discussion). Gamma indicates how much the delta of the option will change for a given futures price change. Theta relates to time decay, hence the negative values. Basically, it indicates how much a given time change will cost the option. It is enough here to realize, for example, that the passage of time will cost the 10-year straddle, with its –1.4962 theta, a lot more than it will cost the 5-year straddle, with its –0.9188 theta. Vega indicates how much the option price will change for a given change in implied volatility. The 23.3052 vega of the five-year straddle indicates that a one percentage point implied volatility change will move the price of this straddle 23.3 64ths. Of course, all these factors interact, so for option buyers, time decay is working at cross-purposes with volatility increases.

The choice of the 107.5 strike price puts the 5-year straddle squarely on the money, and the choice of the 108 strike price puts the 10-year straddle slightly away from the money. The general trading goal is that if the five-year volatility does essentially nothing and that the five-year futures price changes only slightly, this straddle will lose only a slight amount or, perhaps, gain a small amount. If the 10-year volatility falls to a level close to its long-term median, as you predict, the short 10-year straddle will generate a gain in the sense that you will keep most of the proceeds gathered from selling the straddle. However, to isolate the volatility factor, you need to ratio the trade so that both straddle positions will respond equally to equal changes in implied volatility across the yield curve.

EXHIBIT 25.1

Initial Market Conditions and Relevant Option Greeks

5-Year Treasury Note	FVU4				
Futures price	107-16				
Days to expiration	66				
Implied volatility	5.20%				
Strike Price	**Option Price (64ths)**	**Delta**	**Gamma**	**Theta**	**Vega**
107.5 call	61	0.5036	0.2619	−0.4594	11.6526
+107.5 put	61	−0.4948	0.2619	−0.4594	11.6526
= Straddle	122	0.0088	0.5238	−0.9188	23.3052
109 call	25	0.2688	0.2166	−0.3801	9.6453
+106 put	24	−0.2586	0.2124	−0.3728	9.4590
= Strangle	49	0.0100	0.4290	−0.7529	19.1043

10-year Treasury note	TYU4				
Futures price	107-18				
Days to expiration	66				
Implied volatility	8.50%				
Strike Price	**Option Price (64ths)**	**Delta**	**Gamma**	**Theta**	**Vega**
108 call	86	0.4617	0.3188	−0.7484	11.6085
+108 put	114	−0.5367	0.3188	−0.7478	11.6085
= Straddle	200	−0.0750	0.6376	−1.4962	23.2170
110 call	41	0.2732	0.2671	−0.6270	9.7304
+106 put	56	−0.3557	0.2928	−0.6875	10.6635
= Strangle	97	−0.0825	0.5599	−1.3145	20.3939

The straddle lines on the initial market conditions table show the vegas for the two straddles to be 23.3052 for the 5-year straddle and 23.2170 for the 10-year straddle. This means that the price of the 5-year straddle will respond slightly more to a given volatility increase or decrease than the price of the 10-year straddle will.

To neutralize this difference in responsiveness to volatility change, you can divide the 5-year straddle vega by the 10-year straddle vega.

$$23.3052 \div 23.2170 = 1.003799$$

EXHIBIT 25.2

Establishing Straddle Vega Neutrality

	Vega	Number of Straddles	Position Vega
5-year straddle	23.3052	1,000	23,305.2
10-year straddle	23.2170	–1,004	–23,309.9
Net vega			–4.7

This tells you that if you sell 1,004 10-year straddles for every 1,000 5-year straddles that you buy, your total position will be close to vega neutral. If both implied volatilities change the same amount, the trade should generate essentially no result.

To satisfy yourself that these two positions will be vega neutral, you can multiply each straddle vega by the number of straddles bought and sold, as in Exhibit 25.2.

The slight mismatch is the result of rounding in the ratio calculation and is trivial. This indicates that these two options positions will do essentially nothing if both implied volatilities change the same amount.

A further refinement concerns directionality. Notice that the 107.5 five-year straddle delta is 0.0088. This is the sum of the put and call deltas.

Call delta (0.5036) + Put delta (–0.4948) = Straddle delta (0.0088).

This means that the five-year straddle has slight directional exposure. It will perform slightly better if the futures price rises than it will if the futures price falls. Indeed, a 1000-straddle position will have a delta of 8.8 ($0.0088 \times 1000 = 8.8$). Because futures contracts have a delta of 1.0, by definition, you can eliminate most of this directionality by selling 9 five-year Treasury note futures contracts for every 1,000 of the 107.5 option straddles that you buy.

The –0.0750 delta of the 10-year straddle indicates that this position has significantly more directional exposure than the 5-year straddle. To eliminate most of the directionality, you can sell 75 ten-year Treasury note futures for every 1,004 of the 108 option straddles that you sell. Note that because you are selling this straddle, the negative sign changes to positive. Thus, to neutralize this positive directionality, you must sell futures. If you were buying this straddle, you would buy futures to offset the negative value.

This aggregate position—long 1,000 107.5 five-year straddles, short 1,004 108 ten-year straddles, short 9 five-year Treasury note futures, and short 75 ten-year Treasury note futures—should respond only if the ten-year

EXHIBIT 25.3

Establishing Strangle Vega Neutrality

	Vega	Number of Straddles	Position Vega
5-year strangle	19.1043	1,000	19,104.3
10-year strangle	20.3939	–937	–19,109.1
Net vega			–4.8

Treasury note implied volatility decreases relative to the five-year Treasury note implied volatility.

The structuring of the strangles version of this trade works the same way, but the final position looks rather different.

First, notice that the five-year strangle vega is 19.1043, while the ten-year strangle vega is 20.3939. When you divide the five-year strangle vega by the ten-year strangle vega, you will discover that the ratio for this trade is 0.936765.

$$19.1043 \div 20.3939 = 0.936765$$

This tells you that to achieve vega neutrality with these two strangles, you will need to sell 937 ten-year strangles for every 1,000 five-year strangles that you buy.

Again, you can verify the vega neutrality of a position long 1,000 five-year strangles and short 937 ten-year strangles by multiplying the strangle vegas by the number of strangles, as in Exhibit 25.3.

Second, the strangle deltas are also somewhat different. The 0.01 five-year strangle delta indicates a need to sell 10 five-year Treasury note futures for every 1,000 five-year strangles that you buy (0.01 × 1,000 = 10). The –0.0825 ten-year strangle delta indicates a need to sell 73 ten-year Treasury note futures for every 937 ten-year strangles that you sell (0.0825 × 937 = 77.3). Note again the need to change the sign of the ten-year delta because of the selling of the strangle.

ASSESSING POSSIBLE RESULTS

Straddles and strangle spreads such as these can produce a variety of results, depending on what happens in these markets. Changes in the prices of the underlying Treasury note futures should have almost no effect, because of the use of the futures contracts to establish initial delta neutrality. Given the vega weighting, parallel volatility moves should also produce essentially no result. If the 5-year Treasury note implied volatility decreases relative to the 10-year Treasury note implied volatility, this trade can generate a loss. But, in any situation where the 10-year volatility decreases relative to the 5-year volatility, this trade should generate gains.

To see how both the straddle spread and the strangle spread trades might play out, assume that 14 days after putting on either trade (that is, with 52 days to option expiration), five-year Treasury note futures were trading at 107-12, down 0-04, and five-year implied volatility had dropped from 5.20 to 5.10 percent. Also on this day, assume that 10-year Treasury note futures were trading at 107-16, down 0-02, and 10-year implied volatility had dropped 1.5 points to 7.00 percent.

One more assumption requires mention. These exhibits embody the assumption that implied volatilities are the same at every strike price. In order to simplify the examples the volatility skew that is typically found in these markets is ignored.

Given these assumptions, the straddle spread would have performed as shown in Exhibit 25.4.

To make the arithmetic easier, the option prices are given in 64ths, so the 122 five-year straddle price would be 1-58 (1 and 58/64 percentage points of par). The minus signs in the Initial Price and Ending Price columns denote bought positions, while the positive values indicate sold positions. The values in the Result column are for one straddle or one futures contract. Finally, to derive the Dollar Result, multiply the futures results by the number of contracts (e.g., \$125 × 9 contracts = \$1,125). To derive the straddle results, divide the result by 64, multiply by 1,000 to arrive at the dollar value of one straddle, and multiply by the number of

EXHIBIT 25.4

A Possible Straddle Spread Result

	Initial Price	Ending Price	Result	Dollar Result
Buy 1,000 five-year 107.5 straddles	–122	106	–16	–250,000.00
Sell 9 FVU4 futures	107,500.00	–107,375.00	125	1,125.00
Sell 1,004 ten-year 108 straddles	200	–148	52	815,750.00
Sell 75 TYU4 futures	107,562.50	107,500.00	62.50	4,687.50
Net result				571,562.50

EXHIBIT 25.5

A Possible Strangle Spread Result

	Initial Price	Ending Price	Result	Dollar Result
Buy 1,000 five-year 109-106 strangles	–49	37	–12	–187,500.00
Sell 10 FVU4 futures	107,500.00	–107,375.00	125	1,250.00
Sell 937 ten-year 110-106 strangles	97	–53	44	644,187.50
Sell 77 TYU4 futures	107,562.50	–107,500.00	62.50	4,812.50
Net result				462,750.00

straddles bought or sold (e.g., in the case of the 10-year straddle, 52 ÷ 64 = 0.8125 × 1,000 = 812.50 × 1,004 = 815,750).

Given the same assumptions about futures prices and implied volatilities, the strangle would have performed as shown in Exhibit 25.5.

As always, you face the question of whether to use straddles or strangles to express your volatility outlook. The trade-off is the same as when you must choose between straddle and strangle in a single market. If your forecast is completely accurate, the straddle will generate a larger gain as Exhibits 25.4 and 25.5 suggest. The strangle version puts less of your trading capital at risk. Further, while the strangle dollar gains are smaller, the return on investment is likely to be greater.

A WORD OF CAUTION

It is important to keep in mind that these are view-driven trades. Here your opinion involves implied volatility changes rather than price changes. This is still a speculative trade, and you won't always call the volatility market correctly, any more than you always will call the price market correctly. Strangles typically give you a little more wiggle room. You trade some earnings potential for that extra flexibility.

Remember, too, that any options trade is subject to time decay, and there can be slippage because of rounding in the vega ratios and the delta calculations. Awareness of these aspects of these trades and careful monitoring of your trades should allow you to forestall any adverse developments before they get out of hand.

That said, situations arise from time to time when it makes sense to use straddles or strangles to express your market opinion concerning implied volatility levels and how they may change in the coming weeks.

CHAPTER 26

Sell a Straddle or Sell a Strangle

Two Option Spreads for Going-Nowhere Markets

When a market is moving in a fairly narrow range, futures trades tend not to work well, but times like these provide opportunities to sell straddles or strangles.

You buy straddles and strangles when you expect a big market move but aren't sure whether the market will shoot up or down. That's another way of saying that bought straddles and strangles are volatility spreads. When you sell these spreads, you do so because you expect the market to do essentially nothing during the term of the trade. It may bounce around in a narrow trading range, but it won't do much. Normally, if a market stays in such a range for any length of time at all, implied volatilities fall. Thus both time decay and decreasing implied volatility benefit straddle and strangle sellers.

FOCUS ON CRUDE OIL

Options on crude oil futures might have seemed a likely market for straddle and strangle selling during the early fall of 2004. Crude oil futures prices reached historic highs in late September, but they tended to hit a peak and fall back, test the peak again and fall back again. Also, implied volatilities seemed rather high. Looking forward, you might well have thought that the futures would trade in a range between $48 and $52 dollars per barrel for some time and that implied volatilities would have to abate somewhat.

Near the beginning of October 2004 you might have seen the market data depicted in Exhibit 26.1.

EXHIBIT 26.1

Options on Crude Oil Futures–Prices and Deltas

Futures Price	49.91			
Days to Expiration	21			
Implied Volatility	38%			
Strike Prices	**Call Price**	**Call Delta**	**Put Price**	**Put Delta**
47.0			0.68	0.24
47.5			0.82	0.28
48.0			0.98	0.32
48.5			1.17	0.36
49.0			1.38	0.40
49.5	2.02	0.55	1.61	0.45
50.0	1.77	0.51	1.86	0.49
50.5	1.54	0.47	2.13	0.53
51.0	1.34	0.42		
51.5	1.16	0.38		
52.0	0.99	0.34		
52.5	0.85	0.31		
53.0	0.72	0.27		

To sell a straddle, you sell a call and a put with the same expiration and the same strike price. Typically, you choose the at-the-money strike price—in this example, the 50 call and put. At the prices shown in Exhibit 26.1, you would have collected \$3.63, or \$3,630 per straddle (3.63 × 1,000 barrels in one crude oil contract).

To sell a strangle, you sell a call and a put with the same expiration but different strike prices. These should be approximately equidistant from the money, and a good rule of thumb is that they should have deltas in the 0.20 to 0.30 range. Given the data in Exhibit 26.1, a likely choice would have been the 53 call and the 47 put. Both are approximately \$3 away from the money, and both have mid-20s deltas. Given that you would collect \$0.72 per barrel in selling the call and \$0.68 per barrel in selling the put, this strangle would bring in \$1.40, or \$1,400 for the 1,000 barrel contracts.

This seems like a huge difference in money collected, and a common knee-jerk reaction is that it is better to sell straddles because you collect so much more money from selling at-the-money options than you do from selling out-of-the-money options. If you work through a few examples, you will see that it isn't obvious that straddles are the way to go.

DEVELOPING AN OUTLOOK AND A TRADING PLAN

One thing about which you must have an opinion when you contemplate trades such as these is where the futures price might go during the term of the trade. It is seldom a good idea to hold option positions inside of 10 days to expiration, so assume that you plan to sell one or the other of these spreads with 21 days to expiration and plan to unwind the trade with 10 days to expiration. So what you want to know is roughly what is possible in the way of a futures price move in that time.

Implied volatility readings can help you figure out what the market thinks. The 38 percent implied volatility of Exhibit 26.1 indicates a 68 percent probability that a year from now the crude oil futures price will fall in a range plus or minus 38 percent of the current price. That is plus or minus one standard deviation. That may seem interesting but useless. However, a simple arithmetic sequence allows you to break that down into something relevant to any time span you choose—here, 11 days. Exhibit 26.2 displays the steps for the values of Exhibit 26.1.

This result indicates a 68 percent probability that 11 days forward, the crude oil futures price will fall somewhere between $53.20 and $46.62 per barrel, these values being plus or minus one standard deviation. This does not assign any probability to either boundary but only claims that the price will fall somewhere in that range.

By way of exploring sold straddle and strangle potential, consider eight possible endings. Assume that:

- You will unwind the spreads with 10 days to expiration in all eight cases.
- Implied volatility drops to 35 percent in the first four cases.

EXHIBIT 26.2

Estimating Futures Price Potential with Implied Volatilities

	Calculation	Result
Find the number of 11-day periods in a year	365 ÷ 11	33.2
Find the square root of that number	v33.2	5.76
Divide the implied volatility by the square root	0.38 ÷ 5.76	0.066
Multiply the futures price by that factor	49.91 × 0.066	3.29
Add the result to the futures price	49.91 + 3.29	53.20
Subtract the result from the futures price	49.91 – 3.29	46.62

- Implied volatility drops to 32 percent in the second four cases.
- The ending prices are the four shown in Exhibit 26.3a and repeated in Exhibit 26.3b.

Notice that the futures prices for endings I and V are the same as the initial futures price. Also, the futures prices for endings III and VII represent the one standard deviation drop calculated in Exhibit 26.2. The ending II and VI futures prices are midway between the initial price and the ending III and VII prices, and the ending IV and VIII prices are again that far below the ending III and VII prices. These choices are purely arbitrary for the sake of showing how these spreads might perform. This is only one side of the coin, of course. The prices could just as well have gone up by these amounts, but these falling prices serve to make the point.

Notice that if the futures price remains the same or falls to only \$48.26 per barrel and the implied volatility falls three percentage points to 35 percent at 10 days to option expiration, as shown in Exhibit 26.3a, the 50 strike price straddle will earn \$1.32 per barrel or \$0.95 per barrel. These values translate into \$1,320 (1.32 × 1,000) or \$950 for each one-lot straddle. Given the same assumptions, the 53-47 strangle will earn \$0.95 or \$0.75 per barrel. However, at a \$46.62 per barrel futures price, still with 35 percent implied volatility and 10 days to expiration, the straddle will lose \$0.05 per barrel while the strangle still earns \$0.11 per barrel. At futures prices much below that level, both spreads will show losses.

A larger drop in the implied volatility will ease the loss situation somewhat, as Exhibit 26.3b illustrates.

This extra three-percentage-point drop in the implied volatility allows both straddle and strangle sellers to keep more of the money collected at the outset. Notice also that at a futures price of \$46.62, the straddle shows a \$0.03 per barrel gain. That isn't much, but it isn't negative. However, the strangle earns \$0.20 per barrel at that futures price and implied volatility.

THE STRADDLE-STRANGLE TRADE-OFF

These examples show clearly that straddles generate more initial income than strangles, and they earn more than strangles as long as the underlying futures market stays at or close to the price at which the straddle was sold. When you buy either of these option spreads, it makes sense to look at return on investment (ROI). When you sell these option spreads, you collect the price of the sold options at the outset. What is interesting in this case is to look at what percentage of that you keep. Exhibit 26.4 shows these values.

EXHIBIT 26.3a

Comparing Sold Straddle and Strangle Performance

	Initial	Ending I		Ending II		Ending III		Ending IV	
Futures price	49.91	49.91		48.26		46.62		44.97	
Days to expiration	21	10		10		10		10	
Implied volatility	38%	35%		35%		35%		35%	
Strike Price	**Option Prices**	**Option Prices**	**Result**	**Option Prices**	**Result**	**Option Prices**	**Result**	**Option Prices**	**Result**
50 call	1.77	–1.11	**0.66**	–0.47	**1.30**	–0.15	**1.62**	–0.04	**1.73**
50 put	1.86	–1.20	**0.66**	–2.21	**–0.35**	–3.53	**–1.67**	–5.06	**–3.20**
	3.63	–2.31	**1.32**	–2.68	**0.95**	–3.68	**-0.05**	–5.10	**–1.47**
53 call	0.72	–0.23	**0.49**	–0.07	**0.65**	–0.01	**0.71**	0.00	**0.72**
47 put	0.68	–0.22	**0.46**	–0.58	**0.10**	–1.28	**–0.60**	–2.37	**–1.69**
	1.40	–0.45	**0.95**	–0.65	**0.75**	–1.29	**0.11**	–2.37	**–0.97**

EXHIBIT 26.3b

Comparing Sold Straddle and Strangle Performance

	Initial	Ending I		Ending II		Ending III		Ending IV	
Futures price	49.91	49.91		48.26		46.62		44.97	
Days to expiration	21	10		10		10		10	
Implied volatility	38%	32%		32%		32%		32%	
Strike Price	**Option Prices**	**Option Prices**	**Result**	**Option Prices**	**Result**	**Option Prices**	**Result**	**Option Prices**	**Result**
50 call	1.77	–1.01	**0.76**	–0.39	**1.38**	–0.11	**1.66**	–0.02	**1.75**
50 put	1.86	–1.10	**0.76**	–2.13	**–0.27**	–3.49	**–1.63**	–5.05	**–3.19**
	3.63	–2.11	**1.52**	–2.52	**1.11**	–3.60	**0.03**	–5.07	**–1.44**
53 call	0.72	–0.18	**0.54**	–0.04	**0.68**	–0.01	**0.71**	0.00	**0.72**
47 put	0.68	–0.16	**0.52**	–0.50	**0.18**	–1.19	**–0.51**	–2.31	**–1.63**
	1.40	–0.45	**1.06**	–0.54	**0.86**	–1.20	**0.20**	–2.31	**–0.91**

EXHIBIT 26.4

Percentage of Initial Income Retained by Crude Oil Straddle and Strangle Sellers

Futures Price	49.91	48.26	46.62	44.97
50 straddle at 35% implied volatility	36.36%	28.17%	–1.37%	–40.50%
53-47 strangle at 35% implied volatility	67.86%	53.57%	7.86%	–69.29%
50 straddle at 32% implied volatility	41.87%	30.58%	0.83%	–39.67%
53-47 strangle at 32% implied volatility	75.71%	61.43%	14.29%	–65.00%

The arithmetic is the same as for the ROI calculations in other chapters. For example the 36.36 percent results from dividing the 1.32 result in Exhibit 26.3a by the 3.63 initial income. Obviously, when the losses begin, the percentages are worse for the strangle sellers even though the dollar amounts are less.

Perhaps the ultimate trade-off between selling one or the other of these option spreads is the one between absolute dollars earned and room to maneuver if the market becomes more active than you had anticipated.

Put another way, it is probably fair to say that you should sell straddles only when you are very confident that the underlying futures market will move, at most, only a small amount during the term of the trade. If you have this kind of confidence, the straddle will make you more money. Given less than absolute confidence, strangles may seem the better idea, for they give you more time and room to unwind the trade with at least a small gain, should the market become active.

DIFFERENT MARKETS, DIFFERENT RESULTS

Straddles and strangles may not react in exactly the same way in every market. Different volatility levels and price structures can make some markets seem to allow more leeway in terms of how static the underlying futures market must be for option spreads to generate worthwhile returns. In some cases, the strangles make money across a wider range of futures prices. In other cases, the strangles begin to lose money at the same futures price levels as the straddles, but the strangles will lose less.

For a quick look at five other markets that cover a range of kinds of underlying futures, consider how straddles and strangles might perform given essentially the same assumptions as those behind the crude oil examples. Options on S&P 500 futures trade at the Chicago Mercantile Exchange (CME). Options on five-year Treasury note futures and corn futures trade at the Chicago Board of Trade (CBOT). Options on gold futures trade at the COMEX division of the New York Mercantile Exchange. And options on coffee futures trade at the New York Board of Trade (NYBOT).

Exhibits 26.5–26.9 show the relevant details. The prices were determined by the same implied volatility-based exercise as the one shown in Exhibit 26.2. The sequence of days to expiration is the same in every case. And the volatility drop is proportional. Again, the rising price half of the picture has been left out. The results would be approximately mirror images. In these examples, with futures prices falling, the prices of buying back the sold calls decrease while the prices of buying back the sold puts increase. In the mirror image rising price examples, the call prices would increase while the put prices would decrease. The ultimate results would be more or less similar.

To find the dollar values of any of the S&P 500 results, multiply the index points given in Exhibit 26.5 by \$250. The 10.68 point result for the 1,125 straddle translates into a \$2,670 gain.

All the option prices in Exhibit 26.6 are given in 64ths. To translate these results into dollars, divide by 64 and multiply by 1,000. The 20/64 result for the 111 straddle becomes \$312.50 ($20 \div 64 = 0.3125$, $0.3125 \times 1{,}000 = 312.50$).

The COMEX gold contract prices are in dollars per troy ounce, and one contract contains 100 troy ounces. The results in Exhibit 26.7 translate easily into one-lot dollar value if you simply move the decimal two places to the right—e.g., the 4.04 result from selling the 420 straddle becomes \$404.

NYBOT coffee futures prices are in cents per pound for a 37,500-pound contract. That is, the initial 74.20 futures price in Exhibit 26.8 is seventy-four point two cents per pound. Similarly, the 1.64 result of selling the 75 straddle is one point sixty-four cents per pound. Multiplied by 37,500, this becomes a \$61,500 gain.

Corn futures are priced in cents per bushel, and each contract contains 5,000 bushels. The 206 initial futures price is two hundred six cents per bushel, although some quote sources show this as \$2.06. The 1.875 result of selling the 220-200 strangle amounts to one and seven-eighths cents per bushel or \$9,375 for a one-lot strangle ($1.875 \times 5{,}000$).

EXHIBIT 26.5

Comparing Sold Straddle and Strangle Performance of Options on S&P 500 Futures

	Initial	Ending I		Ending II		Ending III		Ending IV	
Futures price	1,126.00	1,126		1,122		1,098		1,084	
Days to expiration	21	10		10		10		10	
Implied volatility	38%	35%		35%		35%		35%	
Strike Price	**Option Prices**	**Option Prices**	**Result**	**Option Prices**	**Result**	**Option Prices**	**Result**	**Option Prices**	**Result**
1,125 C	15.14	–9.80	**5.34**	–4.15	**10.99**	–1.36	**13.78**	–0.33	**14.81**
1,125 P	14.14	–8.80	**5.34**	–17.14	**–3.00**	–28.35	**–14.21**	–41.31	**–27.17**
	29.28	–18.60	**10.68**	–21.29	**7.99**	–29.71	**–0.43**	–41.64	**–12.36**
1,150 C	5.80	–1.89	**3.91**	–0.51	**5.29**	–0.10	**5.70**	–0.01	**5.79**
1,100 P	5.04	–1.49	**3.55**	–4.35	**0.69**	–10.10	**–5.06**	–19.18	**–14.14**
	10.84	–0.45	**7.46**	–4,86	**5.98**	–10.20	**0.64**	–19.19	**–8.35**

EXHIBIT 26.6

Comparing Sold Straddle and Strangle Performance of Options on Five-Year Treasury Note Futures

	Initial	Ending I		Ending II		Ending III		Ending IV	
Futures price	111-00	111-00		110-20		110-08		109-28	
Days to expiration	21	10		10		10		10	
Implied volatility	4.1%	3.8%		3.8%		3.8%		3.8%	
Strike Price	**Option Prices**	**Option Prices**	**Result**	**Option Prices**	**Result**	**Option Prices**	**Result**	**Option Prices**	**Result**
111 C	28	–18	**10**	–8	**20**	–3	**25**	–1	**27**
111 P	28	–18	**10**	–32	**-4**	–51	**–23**	–73	**–45**
	56	–36	**20**	–40	**16**	–54	**2**	–74	**–18**
112.5 C	10	0	**10**	0	**10**	0	**10**	0	**10**
109.5 P	10	0	**10**	–1	**9**	–3	**7**	–8	**2**
	20	0	**20**	–1	**19**	–3	**17**	–8	**12**

EXHIBIT 26.7

Comparing Sold Straddle and Strangle Performance of Options on COMEX Gold Futures

	Initial	Ending I		Ending II		Ending III		Ending IV	
Futures price	417.30	417.30		412.23		407.16		402.09	
Days to expiration	21	10		10		10		10	
Implied volatility	14.1%	12.9%		12.9%		12.9%		12.9%	
Strike Price	**Option Prices**	**Option Prices**	**Result**	**Option Prices**	**Result**	**Option Prices**	**Result**	**Option Prices**	**Result**
420 C	4.40	–2.38	**2.02**	–0.94	**3.46**	–0.29	**4.11**	–0.07	**4.33**
420 P	7.09	–5.07	**2.02**	–8.70	**–1.61**	–13.12	**–6.03**	–17.97	**–10.88**
	11.49	–7.45	**4.04**	–9.64	**1.84**	–13.41	**–1.92**	–18.04	**–6.55**
435 C	0.76	–0.09	**0.67**	–0.02	**0.74**	0.00	**0.76**	0.00	**0.76**
405 P	1.44	–0.32	**1.12**	–0.98	**0.46**	–2.84	**–1.40**	–5.08	**–3.64**
	2.20	–0.41	**1.79**	–1.00	**1.20**	–2.84	**–0.64**	–5.08	**–2.88**

EXHIBIT 26.8

Comparing Sold Straddle and Strangle Performance of Options on Coffee Futures

	Initial	Ending I		Ending II		Ending III		Ending IV	
Futures price	74.20	74.20		72.13		70.06		68.00	
Days to expiration	21	10		10		10		10	
Implied volatility	32%	29.4%		29.4%		29.4%		29.4%	
Strike Price	**Option Prices**	**Option Prices**	**Result**	**Option Prices**	**Result**	**Option Prices**	**Result**	**Option Prices**	**Result**
75 C	1.90	–1.08	**0.82**	–0.43	**1.47**	–0.13	**1.77**	–0.03	**1.87**
75 P	2.70	–1.88	**0.82**	–3.30	**–0.60**	–5.07	**–2.37**	–7.03	**4.33**
	4.60	–2.96	**1.64**	–3.73	**0.87**	–5.20	**–0.60**	–7.06	**–2.46**
80 C	0.51	0.10	**0.41**	–0.02	**0.49**	0.00	**0.51**	0.00	**0.51**
70 P	0.71	–0.20	**0.51**	–0.57	**0.14**	–1.33	**–0.62**	–2.57	**–1.86**
	1.22	–0.30	**0.92**	–0.59	**0.63**	–1.33	**–0.011**	–2.57	**–1.35**

EXHIBIT 26.9

Comparing Sold Straddle and Strangle Performance on CBOT Corn Futures

	Initial	Ending I		Ending II		Ending III		Ending IV	
Futures price	206	206		202		198		194	
Days to expiration	21	10		10		10		10	
Implied volatility	23.4%	21.5%		21.5%		21.5%		21.5%	
Strike Price	**Option Prices**	**Option Prices**	**Result**	**Option Prices**	**Result**	**Option Prices**	**Result**	**Option Prices**	**Result**
21[illegible] C	2.875	–1.375	**1.50**	–0.50	**2.375**	–0.125	**2.75**	0.00	**2.875**
21[illegible] P	6.875	–5.375	**1.50**	–8.50	**–1.625**	–12.125	**–5.25**	–16.00	**–9.125**
	9.75	–6.75	**3.00**	–9.00	**0.75**	–12.25	**–2.50**	–16.00	**–6.25**
22[illegible] C	0.75	–0.125	**0.625**	0.00	**0.75**	0.00	**0.75**	0.00	**0.75**
20[illegible] P	2.125	–0.875	**1.25**	–2.00	**0.125**	–3.875	**–1.75**	–6.75	**4.625**
	2.875	–1.00	**1.875**	–2.00	**0.875**	–3.875	**–1.00**	–6.75	**–3.875**

While these examples vary considerably in detail, you should be able to see that the basic trade-off between absolute dollars gained and maneuvering room remains essentially the same in all these cases. Again, it probably comes down to how convinced you are that your forecast of a static market is correct.

A WORD OF CAUTION

Straddle and strangle sellers must remember that selling options exposes them to the possibility of large losses. If you sell a call and the market rallies, you can lose—seemingly without limit. If you sell a put and the market plunges, you can lose all the way to zero. In the case of straddles and strangles, you are selling both a put and a call. This exposes you to losses in either direction.

For this reason, you need to have an exit plan ready, and you need to pay careful attention to what your market is doing—both in price and implied volatility terms—because a large increase in implied volatility can be almost as damaging to these positions as a strong price move.

That said, these option spreads can be useful trading tools in dead markets—as long as you're sure the market will stay dead for the term of your trade.

CHAPTER 27

Call Calendar and Diagonal Spreads

Trading in a Quiet Market

Markets can go dead in the water at times, a situation that can frustrate stock and futures traders. In the fixed-income markets, for example, there can be days and even weeks that journalists might call slow news days. The Fed may be in an inactive phase. The economic data that are coming out may promise neither much in the way of economic growth nor much in the way of inflation buildup. In the markets, these periods often seem more like no news days than slow news days.

During such a time, anyone hanging around the Chicago or New York markets is likely to hear traders say that they are going home, or on vacation, because whatever markets they trade are dead.

This situation need not afflict option spread traders. Even when the futures market is doing nothing, or very little, the options on that futures market are undergoing time decay. To option buyers, of course, this is a bad thing. But option spread traders can trade call calendar spreads in which they sell a shorter-dated call and buy a longer-dated call in a given market—say options on 10-year Treasury note futures. This kind of spread allows you to capitalize on just this time decay aspect of options—on the mechanics of option pricing, if you will. These spreads enable you to generate at least small gains when many another trading strategy cannot.

CHOOSING THE MOST EFFECTIVE STRIKE PRICES

As a general rule, options traders like to use out-of-the-money options. If 10-year Treasury note futures are trading at 110-00, the 110 call is at the money. The 111 call, 112 call, and on up are out of the money because the futures price hasn't reached that level. People prefer the out-of-the-monies because these deliver more bang for the buck on a percent return basis. Typically, you want to use options that, initially, have a delta in the 0.20 to 0.30 range. That seems to be the sweet spot in most situations.

FOCUS ON TIME DECAY

A curious aspect of option pricing is time decay. An option is a wasting asset. This makes sense if you think about the 112 call when futures are trading at 110-00, as mentioned earlier. This option requires a large price move to be worth anything at expiration. The greater the time to expiration, the more chances for the big price move to happen.

If the futures price and the volatility just sit there, the option price will decay steadily. Exhibit 27.1 illustrates.

In this exhibit, as elsewhere, Treasury option prices are given in 64ths. On a quote screen, the September 112 call price at 105 days to expiration will be 1-03 (or in some cases 1'03). This translates to one and 3/64 percentage points of par. The arithmetic is easier to take in at a glance if the typical 1-03 becomes 67. The dollar prices for these and other Treasury options used divide

EXHIBIT 27.1

An Illustration of Time Decay—September and July 112 Calls on 10-Year Treasury Note Futures

September 10-Year Treasury Note Futures Price	109-24
Short-Term Interest Rate	1%
September Implied Volatility	8.3%
July Implied Volatility	8.5%

September 112 Call				July 112 Call			
Days to Expiration	Option Price (64ths)	Option Price ($)	Delta	Days to Expiration	Option Price (64ths)	Option Price ($)	Delta
105	67	1,046.88	0.33	40	27	421.88	0.24
100	64	1,000.00		35	24	375.00	
95	61	953.13		30	20	312.50	
90	58	906.25		25	15	234.38	
85	55	859.38		20	11	171.88	
80	53	828.13		15	7	109.38	
75	50	781.25		10	3	46.88	
Decay	17			Decay	24		

the 64ths price by 64 and multiply by 1,000 to take the price up to the appropriate dollar equivalent value for one contract (e.g., 67 ÷ 64 = 1.046875, 1.046875 × 1,000 = 1,046.875, rounded to 1,046.88).

You can see that the September 112 call loses roughly 3/64 (or $46.88) every five days, for a total of 17/64 [or $265.63 = 1,000 × (17/64), or 1,046.88 – 781.25]. The example holds everything steady except time to expiration, so this price decay is due only to time.

Time decay accelerates during the last 40 or 50 days to expiration as the July 112 call prices illustrate. Notice that where the September call lost 17/64 (67-50), the July call lost 24/64 (27-3).

Large futures price changes, large implied volatility changes, or both can overcome time decay, but it's still there. By way of experiment, suppose four situations involving the September 112 call:

1. Hold the futures price constant, increase implied volatility from 8.3 to 9.3 percent, move the time from 105 days to 75 days.
2. Increase the futures price from 109-24 to 110-24, hold implied volatility constant at 8.3 percent, move the time from 105 days to 75 days.
3. Increase the futures price as in Situation 2, increase the implied volatility as in Situation 1, and move the time to 75 days.
4. Increase the futures price as in Situation 2, increase the implied volatility as in Situation 1, but move the time only 1 day to 104 days.

Exhibit 27.2 shows the option price changes you could expect.

Note especially the contrast between the Situation 3 and 4 prices. All that's different between these two situations is the passage of 29 more days in Situation 3. Even in the face of major price and implied volatility moves, time decay erodes value.

EXHIBIT 27.2

The Influence of Futures Price and Implied Volatility Changes on Option Prices

Situation	Days to Expiration	Call Price (64ths)
1. Implied volatility up	75	61
2. Price up	75	72
3. Price and implied volatility up	75	84
4. Price and implied volatility up	104	104

STRUCTURING A CALL CALENDAR SPREAD

A call calendar spread allows traders to take advantage of the different ways time decay affects longer-dated and shorter-dated options. When you buy (or go long) a spread, you do so in the expectation that the spread will widen. Here the relatively slower time decay of the longer-dated September option and the relatively faster time decay of the shorter-dated July option widen the spread 5/64 even though the underlying futures price remains stable at 109-24 and the implied volatility of the September call remains at 8.3 percent while the implied volatility of the July call remains at 8.5 percent. Because of this variation in time decay, a call calendar spread can make a little money even in a dead market.

To put on a call calendar spread, a trader initially sells the shorter-dated call and buys the longer-dated call, both at the same strike price. Experienced traders say this trade should be unwound when the price of the shorter-dated option approaches zero or when the shorter-dated option has approximately 10 days left to expiration.

Exhibit 27.3 shows the essential details of a trade based on the July and September 112 call prices from Exhibit 27.1.

A trader selling the July 112 call collects 27/64, or $421.88, hence the positive numbers in the exhibit. A trader buying the September 112

EXHIBIT 27.3

Call Calendar Spread–Assuming a Stable Market

		Initial	Ending
Futures Price (September 10-year Treasury Note)		109-24	109-24
Days to Expiration	July Options	40	10
	September Options	105	75
Implied Volatility	July Options	8.5%	8.5%
	September Options	8.3%	8.3%

Options	Price (64ths)	Price ($)	Price (64ths)	Price ($)	Result (64ths)	Result ($)
Sell July 112 Call	27	421.875	–3	–46.875	24	375.000
Buy September 112 Call	–67	–1,046.875	50	781.25	–17	265.625
Spread Net	–40	–625.000	47	734.375	7	109.375

call pays 67/64, or $1,046.88, hence the negative numbers in the exhibit. In sum, it will cost $625.00 to put on a 1-lot trade. It will cost $62,500 to put on a 100-lot trade.

Assuming no change in the futures price or the implied volatility and the passage of 30 days, the July 112 call price will have decayed to 3/64. This leg of the trade thus earns 24/64, or $375. The September 112 call price decays to 50/64, so this leg of the trade loses 17/64, or $265.63. The net position is 7/64, or $109.37, to the good. This is a 17.5 percent return on investment (109.375 ÷ 625), which is pretty good in a market that is doing absolutely nothing.

Actually, this trade has a slight bullish bias built into it. It will do better if the futures price rises slightly. Volatility changes can affect it as well, but this discussion ignores that aspect of this trade. The call calendar spread will generate losses if the futures price drops. To see why this is so, notice the deltas in Exhibit 27.1. The September 112 call has a 0.33 delta. This indicates that the price of this option will increase a third of a point for every one-point increase in the futures price. The July 112 call has a 0.24 delta, but the fact of selling this option changes the sign to negative. This means the net delta, initially, is 0.09. A one-point futures price move will cause the price of this spread to increase about a tenth of a point.

To see the significance of this bias, assume the futures price rises a half point from 109-24 to 110-08 or a full point to 110-24 as illustrated in Exhibit 27.4.

The half-point futures increase bumps the spread gain up to 13/64, or $202.87. The full-point futures increase bumps the spread gain up to 20/64, or $312.50.

However, mirror image downward futures price moves will generate losses as Exhibit 27.5 shows.

That slight upward bias is appealing if it is reasonable to expect a slight increase in futures prices during the term of the trade. However, if futures prices rise beyond the 112 strike price, the spread will widen for a time and then begin to narrow. At a 113-00 futures price, all else being the same, the net gain will be 21/64. At a 114-00 futures price, the spread will have withdrawn to 10/64.

CALL DIAGONAL SPREADS

In the spring of 2004, with the Fed apparently poised to start raising its fed funds target rate, a rallying fixed-income market didn't seem like a real possibility. Indeed, some commentators opined that a fed move could drive 10-year yields up by as much as 60 basis points.

EXHIBIT 27.4

Call Calendar Spread–Assuming Futures Rally but Stable Volatility and the Passage of 30 Days

a: Futures to 110-08

		Initial	Ending
Futures Price (September 10-year Treasury Note)		109-24	110-08
Days to Expiration	July Options	40	10
	September Options	105	75
Implied Volatility	July Options	8.5%	8.5%
	September Options	8.3%	8.3%

Options	**Price (64ths)**	**Price ($)**	**Price (64ths)**	**Price ($)**	**Result (64ths)**	**Result ($)**
Sell July 112 Call	27	421.875	–7	–109.375	20	312.250
Buy September 112 Call	–67	–1,046.875	60	937.500	–7	–109.375
Spread Net	–40	–625.000	53	828.125	13	202.875

b: Futures to 110-24

		Initial	Ending
Futures Price (September 10-year Treasury Note)		109-24	110-24
Days to Expiration	July Options	40	10
	September Options	105	75
Implied Volatility	July Options	8.5%	8.5%
	September Options	8.3%	8.3%

Options	**Price (64ths)**	**Price ($)**	**Price (64ths)**	**Price ($)**	**Result (64ths)**	**Result ($)**
Sell July 112 Call	–27	421.875	–12	–187.500	15	234.375
Buy September 112 Call	67	–1,046.875	72	1,125.000	5	78.125
Spread Net	–40	–625.000	60	937.500	20	312.500

EXHIBIT 27.5

Call Calendar Spread–Assuming Futures Fall but Stable Volatility

a: Futures to 109-08

		Initial	Ending
Futures Price (September 10-year Treasury Note)		109-24	109-08
Days to Expiration	July Options	40	10
	September Options	105	75
Implied Volatility	July Options	8.5%	8.5%
	September Options	8.3%	8.3%

Options	**Price (64ths)**	**Price ($)**	**Price (64ths)**	**Price ($)**	**Result (64ths)**	**Result ($)**
Sell July 112 Call	27	421.875	–2	–31.250	25	390.625
Buy September 112 Call	–67	–1,046.875	41	640.625	–26	–406.250
Spread Net	–40	–625.000	39	609.375	–1	–15.625

b: Futures to 108-24

		Initial	Ending
Futures Price (September 10-year Treasury Note)		109.24	108-24
Days to Expiration	July Options	40	10
	September Options	105	75
Implied Volatility	July Options	8.5%	8.5%
	September Options	8.3%	8.3%

Options	**Price (64ths)**	**Price ($)**	**Price (64ths)**	**Price ($)**	**Result (64ths)**	**Result ($)**
Sell July 112 Call	27	421.875	–1	–15.625	26	404.250
Buy September 112 Call	–67	–1,046.875	33	515.625	–34	–531.250
Spread Net	–40	–625.000	32	500.000	–8	–125.000

Still, the futures prices seemed to be trading in a narrow range. One way to trade an essentially stable market where the downside fear is greater than the upside expectation involves a call diagonal spread, which is a variation of the call calendar spread. The difference is that where the calendar spread involves options with different times to expiration but the same strike price, the diagonal spread uses different times to expiration and different strike prices.

Exhibit 27.6 uses the prices of the September 112 call from Exhibit 27.1 but uses the prices of the July 111 call rather than those of the July 112 call.

Notice that this July 111 call experiences more severe time decay than the July 112 call, and, assuming no futures price or implied volatility change, this widens the spread 17/64 rather than the 7/64 of the calendar spread. Exhibit 27.7 shows how this spread can be expected to perform when neither the futures price nor the implied volatility changes during the term of the trade. The 17/64 spread widening results in a $265.62 net gain.

EXHIBIT 27.6

An Illustration of Time Decay–September 112 Call and July 111 Call on 10-Year Treasury Note Futures

September 10-Year Treasury Note Futures Price	109-24
Short-Term Interest Rate	1%
September Implied Volatility	8.3%
July Implied Volatility	8.5%

September 112 Call				**July 111 Call**			
Days to Expiration	**Option Price (64ths)**	**Option Price ($)**	**Delta**	**Days to Expiration**	**Option Price (64ths)**	**Option Price ($)**	**Delta**
105	67	1,046.88	0.33	40	46	718.75	0.35
100	64	1,000.00		35	41	640.63	
95	61	953.13		30	36	562.50	
90	58	906.25		25	31	484.38	
85	55	859.38		20	25	390.63	
80	53	828.13		15	19	296.88	
75	50	781.25		10	12	187.50	
Decay	17				34		

EXHIBIT 27.7

Call Diagonal Spread–Assuming a Stable Market

		Initial	Ending
Futures Price (September 10-year Treasury Note)		109.24	109-24
Days to Expiration	July Options	40	10
	September Options	105	75
Implied Volatility	July Options	8.5%	8.5%
	September Options	8.3%	8.3%

Options	Price (64ths)	Price ($)	Price (64ths)	Price ($)	Result (64ths)	Result ($)
Sell July 111 Call	46	718.750	–12	–187.500	34	531.250
Buy September 112 Call	–67	–1,046.875	50	781.250	–17	–265.625
Spread Net	–21	–625.000	38	593.750	17	265.625

Note also that the initial delta of the July 111 call is 0.35. Again, this will be a negative value because the July 111 call is sold. What matters is that this removes most of the directional bias from the trade. As a result the trade will perform only slightly better when futures prices rise, but it will do far better than the calendar spread when futures prices decrease. Exhibit 27.8 illustrates this using the same assumptions that shaped Exhibits 27.4 and 27.5.

Notice that the diagonal spread costs less to put on than does the calendar spread. This and the greater spread widening when futures do nothing make for an 81 percent return on investment. Even when the futures price drops a full point, the ROI will still be almost 43 percent. This diagonal spread makes money in all the situations described because this spread is closer to delta neutral and because of the time decay differential.

A WORD OF CAUTION

These examples assume that the implied volatility is the same across all the strike prices and that implied volatility remains unchanged as futures prices

EXHIBIT 27.8

Call Diagonal Spread–Assuming Futures Rally or Fall but Stable Volatility

a: Futures to 110-08

		Initial	Ending
Futures Price (September 10-year Treasury Note)		109-24	110-08
Days to Expiration	July Options	40	10
	September Options	105	75
Implied Volatility	July Options	8.5%	8.5%
	September Options	8.3%	8.3%

Options	Price (64ths)	Price ($)	Price (64ths)	Price ($)	Result (64ths)	Result ($)
Sell July 111 Call	46	718.750	–20	–312.500	26	406.250
Buy September 112 Call	–67	–1,046.875	60	937.500	–7	–109.375
Spread Net	–21	–328.125	40	625.000	19	296.875

b: Futures to 110-24

		Initial	Ending
Futures Price (September 10-year Treasury Note)		109-24	110-24
Days to Expiration	July Options	40	10
	September Options	105	75
Implied Volatility	July Options	8.5%	8.5%
	September Options	8.3%	8.3%

Options	Price (64ths)	Price ($)	Price (64ths)	Price ($)	Result (64ths)	Result ($)
Sell July 111 Call	46	718.750	–32	–500.000	14	234.375
Buy September 112 Call	–67	–1,046.875	72	1,125.000	5	78.125
Spread Net	–21	–328.13	40	625.00	19	296.87

EXHIBIT 27.8

Call Diagonal Spread–Assuming Futures Rally or Fall but Stable Volatility (*Continued*)

c: Futures to 109-08

		Initial	Ending
Futures Price (September 10-year Treasury Note)		109-24	109-08
Days to Expiration	July Options	40	10
	September Options	105	75
Implied Volatility	July Options	8.5%	8.5%
	September Options	8.3%	8.3%

Options	**Price (64ths)**	**Price ($)**	**Price (64ths)**	**Price ($)**	**Result (64ths)**	**Result ($)**
Sell July 111 Call	46	718.75	–6	–93.75	40	625.00
Buy September 112 Call	–67	–1,046.875	41	640.625	–26	–406.250
Spread Net	–21	–328.13	35	546.88	14	218.75

d: Futures to 108-24

		Initial	Ending
Futures Price (September 10-year Treasury Note)		109-24	108-24
Days to Expiration	July Options	40	10
	September Options	105	75
Implied Volatility	July Options	8.5%	8.5%
	September Options	8.3%	8.3%

Options	**Price (64ths)**	**Price ($)**	**Price (64ths)**	**Price ($)**	**Result (64ths)**	**Result ($)**
Sell July 111 Call	46	718.750	–3	–46.875	43	671.875
Buy September 112 Call	–67	–1,046.875	33	515.625	–34	–531.250
Spread Net	–21	–328.125	30	469.000	9	140.625

change. Neither assumption is likely to hold true. Typically, fixed-income call implied volatility decreases the farther from the money the strike price is. Perhaps more importantly, a rising futures market is likely to dampen implied volatility while a plunging futures market (rising yields) is likely to increase it.

These 8+ percent implied volatilities seem rather high relative to the long-term mean of historical volatility. Suppose that during the term of the calendar spread, the futures price rises to 110-08 and the implied volatilities fall a half point to 8 percent (for the July 112 call) and 7.8 percent (for the September 112 call). Exhibit 27.9 shows that the trade will do less well—earning 9/64 rather than 13/64 (compare with Exhibit 27.4).

Suppose, however, that yields increase enough to drive the futures price down to 109-08, and the implied volatilities increase a half point to 9 percent and 8.8 percent. Then the calendar spread will earn 4/64, even with the assumed volatility increase, as Exhibit 27.10 shows.

EXHIBIT 27.9

Call Calendar Spread–Assuming Futures Rally and Implied Volatilities Fall

Futures to 110-08
July Implied Volatility to 8%
September Implied Volatility to 7.8%

		Initial	Ending
Futures Price (September 10-year Treasury Note)		109-24	110-08
Days to Expiration	July Options	40	10
	September Options	105	75
Implied Volatility	July Options	8.5%	8.0%
	September Options	8.3%	7.8%

Options	**Price (64ths)**	**Price ($)**	**Price (64ths)**	**Price ($)**	**Result (64ths)**	**Result ($)**
Sell July 112 Call	27	421.875	–5	–78.125	22	343.750
Buy September 112 Call	–67	–1,046.875	54	843.750	–13	–203.125
Spread Net	–40	–625.000	49	765.625	9	140.625

EXHIBIT 27.10

Call Calendar Spread–Assuming Futures Fall and Implied Volatilities Rise

Futures to 109-08
July Implied Volatility to 9%
September Implied Volatility to 8.8%

		Initial	Ending
Futures Price (September 10-year Treasury Note)		109-24	109-08
Days to Expiration	July Options	40	10
	September Options	105	75
Implied Volatility	July Options	8.5%	9.0%
	September Options	8.3%	8.8%

Options	**Price (64ths)**	**Price ($)**	**Price (64ths)**	**Price ($)**	**Result (64ths)**	**Result ($)**
Sell July 112 Call	27	421.88	–2	–31.250	25	390.625
Buy September 112 Call	–67	–1,046.875	46	718.750	–21	–328.125
Spread Net	–40	–625.00	44	687.500	4	62.500

In sum, these are trades that use the mechanics of option pricing to generate small gains in markets where most strategies cannot. While it is useful to focus on time decay alone to illustrate what these trades primarily depend on, it is important to remember that options are never one-factor trades. All the pricing factors and risk parameters must be taken into account for the final result.

An Afterword

The intention of this book is not to discuss every spread that has ever been traded. Rather, the plan has been to discuss a representative selection that covers the main kinds of spreads. The thought is that if you can see what kind of thinking goes into the structuring of a new crop-old crop spread in one market that is essentially a U.S. market and in another that is a world market, then you will be able to apply this knowledge to any crop market that you may want to trade. Similar generalization should be possible from all the kinds of spreads discussed.

By now, you have noticed that all the examples used have been drawn from markets traded on U.S. exchanges. This is a matter of familiarity and access. It doesn't mean that spreads are not available in other markets. Indeed, some very interesting ones are. The discussions included here should enable you to adapt this thinking about spreads to any of these other markets.

The real skeleton of this book, and the source of its completeness, lies in its discussion of why so many professionals trade spread strategies, its emphasis on how to structure trades and analyze results, its tying of spread structure and trading strategy to basic market economics, and its attempt to establish a consistent spread logic.

This discussion draws upon many years of conversation with, and reporting on the trading practices of some of, the best professionals in the futures and options business. People in several fields make much of the idea of conforming to best practice. This book attempts to report on what seems to be best practice in the trading of spreads in all sorts of markets and in all kinds of economic situations.

Be warned, this book offers no magic formula. Spread trades, being speculative, will bring a mixture of successes and failures—winners and losers. Professional traders know that some fraction of their trades will be winners, another fraction of their trades will break even, and a third fraction will be losers. That's just trading life. The key to long-term success is to find a way to maximize the proportion of winners and to minimize the other kinds of results.

The professional traders trade spreads because spreads give them more ways to be right and so shift the odds of success in the traders' favor. The assumption of the professionals seems to be that a relatively steady stream of modest gains is preferable to the occasional blockbuster.

To return to the baseball analogy of Chapter 1, the professional spread traders seem to believe that a trading approach that leads to the hitting of a whole lot of singles and to very few strikeouts is preferable to an approach that produces the occasional towering home run—however exciting and attention grabbing that may be—interspersed among a blizzard of strikeouts. Over the long term, slow and steady can win a lot of races.

People trade futures and options for a variety of reasons. For some, trading is a kind of entertainment. The reason to trade is to experience the thrill of the spectacular result, however rare it may be. People who trade for this kind of satisfaction are unlikely to find spreads appealing.

However, if you trade because you want to generate a steady stream of positive results—that is, if you're in it for the money—you might want to think about adding both futures and option spread strategies to your trading repertoire. This book will have succeeded if it helps you get off to a good start in this quest.

Appendix

Sources of Helpful Information

The amount of helpful literature on spread trading is surprisingly small, given that this is how the professionals tend to trade. However, if you mine back issues of *Futures* magazine, you will find a number of helpful articles.

Perhaps the richest sources of potential help are the major brokerage houses. Most of the larger firms have staff members who devote their working hours to studying these markets and thinking about how various spread trades may work in the coming weeks and months. An excellent place to turn when you want to learn about the current situation in any of the spread markets is your broker. Any broker should be able to connect you, directly or indirectly, with the people in that firm who do this kind of work.

The U.S. futures exchanges cited throughout the text all have Web sites on which you can find the data you need about the various contracts, historical prices, and exchange literature that can be helpful. These Web sites are all set up a little differently, and each exchange approaches the idea of user education differently. Because of this, generalizations are difficult, but it is well worth the time to explore the sites of any exchange on which you trade or plan to trade. The relevant Web sites are:

Chicago Board of Trade: www.cbot.com

Chicago Mercantile Exchange: www.cme.com

One Chicago: www.onechicago.com

New York Mercantile Exchange: www.nymex.com

New York Board of Trade: www.nybot.com

Kansas City Board of Trade: www.kcbot.com

For interest rate data and information about the monetary policy of the Federal Reserve, the Board of Governors of the Federal Reserve System Web site is unmatched: www.federalreserve.gov. On the home page, near the bottom, you will see a heading: "Recent Statistical Releases." Under this, the link "All Statistical Releases" will get you to the pages that include the H.15 reports of all the relevant interest rates. Also on the home page, there is a menu on the left that includes the heading "Monetary Policy." This will get you to the meeting calendar, the statements that the Fed issues, and a variety of other interesting items.

For all the agricultural markets, the Economic Research Service of the U.S. Department of Agriculture can be extremely helpful. In attempting to understand the supply-demand situation in any of these markets, a good place to start is at: www.ers.usda.gov/Publications/Outlook/

Finally, for general background on the futures markets, two books are absolute classics. For a general understanding of how Treasury futures work and of the factors that drive these prices such as carry and cheapest to deliver status, you cannot do better than to study:

> Galen D. Burghardt, Terrence M. Belton, et. al., *The Treasury Bond Basis*, revised edition (McGraw-Hill: New York. 1994).

For a solid understanding of the agricultural markets, the classic study is:

> Thomas Hieronymous, *Economics of Futures Trading for Personal and Commercial Profit*, second edition (Commodity Research Bureau, Chicago, 1977).

INDEX

CPSIA information can be obtained
at www.ICGtesting.com
Printed in the USA
JSHW061828031222
33632JS00001B/46

9 780071 448444